Complete Catalogue of Collection of Specimens of Japanese Art

Complete Catalogue of Collection of Specimens of Japanese Art

including Notes and Commentaries and Reference to the Other Note Books belonging to the Collector

by Ernest Francisco Fenollosa

Facsimile edition

with transcription, annotation and translation in Japanese

by

Seiichi Yamaguchi

Professor Emeritus, Saitama University

Series: Series: Collected Works of Japanologists

Eureka Press

Complete Catalogue of Collection of Specimens of Japanese Art,
including Notes and Commentaries and Reference to the Other Note Books
belonging to the Collector, by Ernest Francisco Fenollosa
Edited by Seiichi Yamaguchi
Series: Collected Works of Japanologists

フェノロサ手稿「日本絵画蒐集作品解説付総目録」復刻・翻刻・邦訳集成
山口静一 編・訳

First published in 2020
by Edition Synapse for Eureka Press
2-17-5-201 Nagata-cho, Chiyoda-ku
Tokyo 100-0014, Japan

© 2020 Seiichi Yamaguchi

Photograph © 2020 Museum of Fine Arts, Boston

ISBN: 978-4-86166-212-6 (Eureka Press)

Acknowledgement.

Publisher would like to thank Aizu Museum, Waseda University for the permission to reproduce the original notebook in their collection

&

Museum of Fine Arts, Boston for the permission to use the images of their art objects.

All rights reserved. No part of this book may be reprinted or reproduced or utilized in any form or by any electronic, mechanical, or other means, now known or hereafter invented, including photocopying and recording, or in any information storage or retrieval system, without permission in wiring from the publishers.

Printed and bound in Japan by Hirakawa Kogyosha Co. Ltd.

Selected Paintings from Fenollosa-Weld Collection, Museum of Fine Arts, Boston

^{S}17 Copy of Jurojin
Kano Shunsen Tomonobu

^{S} 59 Dragon
Mori Sosen

42 Deer and Bamboo / Cherry Tree
Kano Tan'yû

S43 Tartars Hunting
Kano Motonobu

S79 White Fox
Formerly attributed to Maruyama Ôkyo

S80 Tiger
Ganku

S139 Hunter Taking Aim at a Deer
Katsushika Hokusai

S151 Dragons
Nakabayashi Chikutô

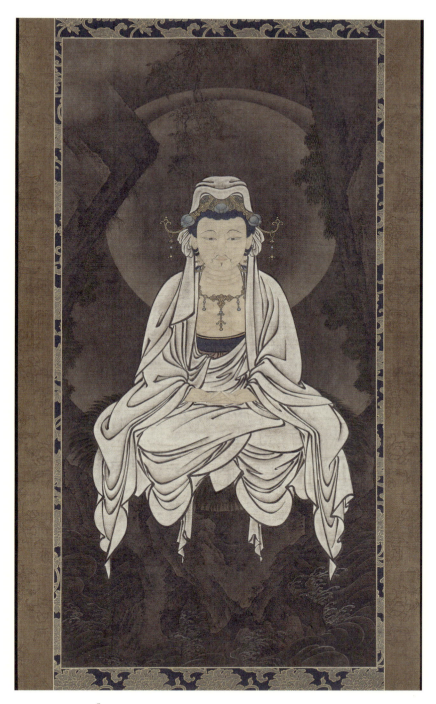

S152 White-robed Bodhisattva of Compassion
Kano Motonobu

S164 Deer
Ganku

Contents

Plates ··· v

Introduction by Seiichi Yamaguchi ·· xiv

Part 1: Facsimile Reprint of Complete Catalogue of Collection of Specimens of Japanese Art including Notes and Commentaries and Reference to the Other Note Books belonging to the Collector Ernest Francisco Fenollosa ··········· 1

Part 2-1: Transcription of the 'Catalogue' including Index by Ernest Francisco Fenollosa ·· 201

Part 2-2: Editor's Notes & Glossary ··· 257

Part 3-1: Introduction in Japanese by Seiichi Yamaguchi / 訳者序文 ········ 275

Part 3-2: Translation of the 'Catalogue' in Japanese /
邦訳 日本絵画解説付総目録 ··· 287

Part 3-3: Editor's Notes in Japanese / 作者および引用人物等註解 ······ 347

Part 3-4: Editor's Commentaries on the Plates in the Frontispiece in Japanese /
口絵について ·· 367

Part 3-4: List of Access Number of Museum of Fine Arts, Boston /
MFA 収蔵番号対照表 ··· 371

INTRODUCTION

This publication of the notebook of Ernest Francisco Fenollosa (1857-1908) will make available for the first time the catalogue of his collection of Japanese paintings described by the collector himself by reproducing the entire pages in facsimile format with the transcription, the Japanese translation and new annotations.

The most remarkable point of this notebook is that Fenollosa mentions his opinions on Japanese art in his own voice, while his many other writings both in English and Japanese are more or less modified by editors or translators as many of them were posthumously published.

The notebook consists of four parts; the title page, the preface (2 pp.), the catalogue (190 pp.) and the index (5 pp.). Though the title says "Complete" Catalogue of specimens, this notebook was in fact the catalogue of *kakemono* (hanging scroll) and includes item nos. 1-263 only. Writing in the Preface, Fenollosa divided the collected paintings (he called them "specimens" as a Spencerian sociologist) into some divisions, like Division A "*Kakemono,*" Division B *Byōbu* (folding screen), etc. He also made notebooks on "Biography of Japanese and Chinese artists" and on "Signatures and seals of artists".

In each entry of the catalogue, after remarking the artist names and the title of painting, as the title page of the notebook says, he included "commentaries and notes" which shows very interesting and suggestive views on each painting. In some cases, he criticized its composition, coloring, brush touches and other points. Then he introduced other opinions of noted contemporary Japanese artists and antiquarians whom he consulted or employed as advisors. Sometimes his criticism was even directed at those advisors unreservedly, as 'Mr. Kano is speaking from the narrow point of view which regards all "bunjin" element as evil' (s.76). Lastly he gave his own estimation. In this regard, too, he did not hesitate to retract his former criticism when he met with a better specimen of the same artist (s.101).

In the lower part of the title page Fenollosa included the collector's address and the date. "Kaga Yashiki" was the official residences for foreign teachers of Tokio University built at the site where a villa of the Kaga clan previously stood. The place is now in the Hongo campus of University of Tokyo. (He was a professor of political philosophy, political economy and history of philosophy during the age of Tokio University.) The date "December 1880" shows the time when he began to write this catalogue. An additional writing of the date 1889 (s.17), four years after he ceased his collecting activity can also be found.

The index must have been privately prepared for his future study of Japanese art history. The artist names and the number of their specimens are alphabetically arranged. For this volume in addition to the original index in English transcription, a new index is included with more detailed information; not only artist names but other persons and proper nouns are quoted, with their short profiles and annotations in "*aiueo*" (Japanese alphabetical) order for the sake of Japanese readers in the Japanese translation.

It was in 1920, more than 11 years after Fenollosa's death, that the existence of a continuation (hereafter "Notebook No.2) to the Catalogue of *kakemono* ("Notebook No.1") became known. In January of that year the Walpole Galleries, New York, offered at auction the books and manuscripts from the library of Fenollosa, which included the following part of the *Kakemono* Catalogue. The Auction Catalogue comments as follows: "Manuscript in pencil. Notes on his own collection of Japanese paintings. Written on about 69 pp. in a 4to volume, the items are numbered from No.264 to No.517. A few are described in detail; others have nothing but the titles. A few signatures and seals have been copied."

Many of the manuscripts exhibited in the auction were purchased by Dr. Ernest G. Stillman and later contributed to the Harvard College Library (now in the collection of the Houghton Library, Harvard University). But the Notebook No.2 is not included in the Houghton collection. It is still missing. Notebook No.1 (here reproduced) was not in the auction catalogue of the Walpole Galleries, which means that it was already missing at that point in 1920.

Between December 1929 and June 1931, an art historian Akiyama Teruo (1888-1977) was studying Japanese art in America and Europe as an inspector of the Tokyo Imperial Museum (now Tokyo National Museum). While he was in Boston, he found an old autographed notebook at a bookstore and bought it, which proved to be the Notebook No.1.

The first news of this Notebook was released by Matsuoka Yuzuru, a friend of Akiyamama, in the literary magazine *Serupan* (May, 1933) published by *Daiichi-shobō*. He introduced the details of the Notebook and hoped its Japanese translation would be published as soon as possible, which did not unfortunately happen at the time.

The Notebook No,1 was donated by Akiyama Terufumi, Professor Emeritus of Ochanomizu Women's University and Teruo's grandson, to Aizu Museum, Waseda University and now in their collection. I am grateful to the Museum and Professor Akiyama Terufumi for allowing this publication.

Towards the end of 1884 when Fenolla was appointed a member of art education committee by the Japanese government he ceased collecting paintings. In the next year eagerly persuaded by William Sturgis Bigelow (1850-1926), who had already collected tens of thousands of Japanese art-works for sufficiency of the Museum of Fine Arts, Boston, he sold his collection of about one thousand pieces of Japanese arts to Dr. Charles Goddard Weld (1867-1911), another Bostonian collector, with the understanding that it was to remain permanently in the Museum of Fine Arts (MFA), Boson as the Fenollosa-Weld collection.

Though some items Fenollosa collected and catalogued in this notebook are no longer in the collection, the majority of the masterpieces in the catalogue are still held by the MFA, Boston, and we can appreciate their images in the museum's website with the new commentaries based on today's studies, which are quite different from the ones in this notebook by Fenollosa, a leading Japanese art collector in the 1880's.

In the transcribed entry of each item in this volume, the accession numbers to the MFA's database are added based on the researches through past-day's materials and various pictorial records published by MFA, but it must be pointed out that the whereabouts of some items in the volume are not clear and thus the numbers for them are missing.

Seiichi Yamaguchi

Emeritus Professor, *Saitama University*

April, 2020

E. F. F.

Catalogue and
descriptions of
Ernest's own collection
begun in 1880

Oct 1909

Complete Catalogue
of
Collection of specimens of
Japanese
Pictorial Art,
including
notes and commentaries
and references
to the other note books belonging to
the collector.

Ernest Francisco Fenollosa
No. 1. Kaga Yashiki
Hongo.
Tokio
Japan
December 1880.

Catalogue.

Division A.

Kakemonos.

Note. The numbers are attached to separate works, whether of one or more than one picture. In the latter case the secondary numbers mark the parts of the work, which are numbered in the order in which they should be hung and from right to left. In most cases nothing is here said concerning the signature on the Kakemono, though sometimes there is given the translation of the writing on the box. For the signature, the note-book on signatures must be regularly referred to. For the biography of the artists named, the note-book on that subject must be consulted, although an occasional point of interest will here be given. Special criticisms of leading Tokio artists and critics are appended. The pictures are described so much in detail only as is necessary for their identification, and the understanding of their subject, and the most striking of their peculiar excellencies. For the subjects generally the note-book on Art Motives must be referred to. Dates, if at all, are given here only approximately. In some cases an attempt is here made to describe the excellent qualities of pictures both from a Japanese point of view and from a foreign. In general only enough is given here, to make the other note-books of service in explaining the collection.

1. A small figure-painting of the Buddhist God, Jiso.

This is in the finest style of very old Japanese Buddhist painting. It is said to be by Kose no Kanaoka, about 1000 years old. But Mr. Ninagawa, Kano Yeitoku, and Setsuan say it is not Kanaoka himself, for it has not quite his boldness of touch, but is by his son or grandson, say about 900 yrs. old. The secret of applying gold so as to be permanent was lost soon after this period. On the other hand Mr. Shimoda and Mr. _____ declare it to be a genuine Kanaoka. All testimony about such old paintings is doubtful. The beauty of line and color far surpasses that of later Buddhist works. But in boldness of line and grandeur of color it is inferior to some of the pictures said to be by Kanaoka now kept in Kioto. It has been finally determined by the present Sumiyoshi of Tokio, to be the work of Kose no Genkei. Bought from Akamatsu.

sent fall of 1880. from him

S. 2. 1—6. Bird and flower pieces painted by Wankin in 1877 or 78. These may be considered as one work, or as four different works, namely, 1, 2, 3-4, 5-6. For convenience they are classed as one.

   1. Two wild ducks flying up from the reeds. This is delicate in feeling and color, but not strong in any respect.

   2. Two peacocks on the trunk of a bending pine. This is fine chiefly in composition.

   3. A pheasant among the peach blossoms. This is very rich in color, but not so pure in feeling.

   4. Quail and bush with yellow flowers. This is in the true noble Japanese feeling, and from the native point of view, as in truth, the best of the six pictures.

   5. Two herons on a rock and pine tree. The purity of the grey tones is excellent. This is the next to the best of the six.

   6. Two herons on the branch of a red plum tree. This is the realization of a dream Wankin had on a New Year's eve. It has three of the emblems of happiness. It is not a strong picture.

"3. A picture of hen, cock, and chickens with rocks. and purple flowers above. This is a copy by an artist named Toho, from a fine picture of the Chinese artist O-jiakusui of Gen. Mr. Kano says it is a rather poor copy, in that the artist has not succeeded in execution to produce the effect he wished. On the other hand Mr. Hasegawa says it is a very fine copy. I am inclined to agree with the latter, that the tenderest, most tasteful Chinese effect is reached with considerable skill. In feeling it is far superior to Nanping. The peculiar ribbed Chinese silk adds to the effect. This is a pure mirror of Chinese feeling. The lines of the rock, the delicacy of color, and lightness of tone are the conspicuous elements. Bought from Yamanaka.

"4. A small landscape in grey by Buncho. This is a winter scene with rocks, frozen river, bare trees, and towering cliffs. Snow is in the air. The cold misty effect is rendered in the manner peculiar to this artist. It is an ordinary, not remarkable specimen.

5. 5. A small picture of two snowy herons on a branch of red plum blossoms partially covered with snow. By Onishi Keisai, the pupil of Soshiseki and teacher of Shiuki. This is a pretty good specimen of this artist. He is notorious for painting the heads of his birds too large, as here. The feeling is very pure, especially in color, and is rather Japanese than Chinese. The execution is peculiar; not at all in the manner of Nanping and the ordinary work in his school, but apparently modeled after the Ganku branch of it. The touch of the brush in the stem and branches of the plum tree is much like Ganku. Upon the box is written "Sagi Kobai" literally "White herons, red plum blossoms." Upon the back of the Kakemono is written "Onishi Keisai." Upon the face "Keisai" alone appears. The simple pure color and the confused masses of the boughs so spiritedly drawn are the beautiful features.

§ 6. A small picture of rooster, hen, and chicks, with lilies above. by Ko-ōki. This name is not known among the list of artists. Upon the box is written "Nishino toyen Niudo." This Mr. Kano thinks is the name of a nobleman of Kioto. The style is interesting as being out of the influence of any one school. The coloring is strong and coarse. There is no purity of feeling. But there is a strength of effect which few later Japanese pictures of birds and flowers have. I saw several pictures by this artist in Osaka, and they all had the same qualities. Perhaps he was not a professional.

§ 7. A hawk upon a rock, with part of a pine tree. by Buncho. This is mostly in ink, but there are brownish tones about it, which make it look like Sepia. Setsuan questioned the genuineness of this picture, saying the signature is that of the early days of Buncho, but the style is of his later days. On the contrary Mr. Kano says the style is that of his youth, that it is genuine, and in the second class in excellence of Buncho. I am inclined to agree with the latter opinion, except that I think it should be ranked as third class, or ordinary. There is no doubt in my mind as to its genuineness. It is the manner of Buncho in its immaturity.

(Note. When hereafter the terms, first, second, and third class specimens or styles of any artist are used, the following will always be meant. In the first class are put only those rare pictures of their author in which his own style has attained the maximum of its freedom and strength, roughly judging, from two to five per cent of the works of an artist. By the second class is meant all those pictures in which the artist has attained striking excellence without reaching the utmost limit of his power, comprising perhaps fifteen or twenty per cent of an art-its works, or at least fifteen or twenty per cent of those original works which remain to be seen. No true estimate of proportion beyond this can be made. By the third class or ordinary style is meant all the rest of an artist's work, including the larger bulk, and the more commonly seen specimens. This distinction and these proportions are given as practically convenient and in the rough correct by Mr. Kano Yeitoku.)

5. 8. A small picture of Benten with her biwa. by Tsunenobu. This has the real Tsunenobu touch, but must be ranked with the ordinary run of his productions. Of these it is a good typical specimen. On the box is written "Benzaiten" "Tsunenobu."

5. 9. A fine painting of Kanzan and Jittoku, the Chinese Buddhists, by Mochizuki Gyokusen, the best pupil of Ganku. This is considered by Mr. Kano Yeitoku one of the best productions of modern Japanese Art. It is a very original picture both in conception

and execution. The artist inherits the spirit of Gauku, but it has clothed its work in an entirely new form. The drawing, from a foreign point of view, is about the best to be found in Japan. The hands and feet especially the former are very truthfully rendered. The faces are most expressive, and the masses of hair finely rendered in a manner adapted from Gauku. The flow of lines in the postures, limbs, and drapery is wonderful. The unity of line is only the formal side of the unity of the feeling which lies in the soul of the figures, the expression of their eager intent in some unseen object beyond the picture. This shows the artist's genius, not to distract the attention from the idea of the faces by introducing the interesting object into the picture. The lines have a different touch from Gauku's, less massive and more sinuous. The color is meagre and amounts to nothing, but the composition is great. This picture shows some influence of the Okio style. Bought from Yamanaka.

S. 10. One of the best representations of Benten in existence, by Tosa Mitsuoki, one of the greatest artists of the Tosa school. Mr. Kano says it is the best specimen of this artist, having the very highest dignity and purity. It is not in ordinary Tosa style, but in that highest model of the old Yamato style which the later schools debased and rendered grotesque. The rock is in the style of Kanaoka, and is derived from the Chinese style in the To dynasty. The figure is nearly in the pure Kanaoka style. Mr. K. says the genius of Mitsuoki is shown in placing the biwa horizontally, instead of inclined as universally represented. This gives the figure great peaceful dignity. Mr. Ninagawa who is not an artist but an antiquarian says it is a poor picture because it has no nobleness and dignity! Mr. Hasegawa says it is one of the finest specimens of Mitsuoki. Setsuan says it is very noble and pure. I think the color is distinctive of Mitsuoki, though Mr. Kano does not. The coloring has that same quality of delicious delicate satiny tones which I have marked in all of his good works. In delicacy of drawing he also excels. The details of his quail and grasses are microscopic. (See No. 60) But he has no power to treat great forcible subjects. In this picture his lines and conception are the grandest and most forceful I have seen. In technique he is unsurpassed in his own school. This Benten shows to perfection his handling of the brush in drawing and coloring. The water is somewhat weak. Presented by Mr. Wakai of Kosho Kuaicha. I say the picture has no relation to Kanaoka, rather to Chinese of Sen as seen through the mediumship of Tanyu. 1st class.

5-11. A waterfall among the mountains by Buncho. This is a very remarkable piece of work for a Japanese. I have seen no other like it, and no Japanese critic to whom I have showed it has ever seen another like it. Its most noticeable peculiarity is its attempt at Chiar'oscuro. I have seen such an attempt in the pictures of no other artist at all, and in those of Buncho only to a limited extent. In the second place the force of execution and carelessness of touch are remarkable even for Buncho. In the third place, the coloring is peculiarly Buncho's in the pieces executed after his own taste. Buncho however, insisted that a great artist must paint in all styles; and his practice was in accordance with his precept. Thus, Letsuan says he studied oil-painting, when a youth under the instruction of Shiba Kokan, who had learned from a Dutchman in Nagasaki; but early in life abandoned the practice. If this be true, it explains the peculiar coloring and shading of some of his later pictures. Especially is this true in the present case. This picture is viewed to best effect from a distance of 20 or 30 feet, as if it were an oil painting. The only other work of this artist having similar coloring that I have seen, is the makimonos of scenes on the

Tokaido exhibited by the Daimio Matsudaira at Uyeno, May 1880. This mine is considered one of the finest works in the first class of Buncho, by everyone who has seen it, including Mr. Kano. The latter and Setsuan agree that the artist must have been about forty years of age, when it was painted. Upon the box is written, "Taki, sansui", "Tani Buncho". The force of the water flow in this picture is almost equalled by that in the two screens of Okio owned by Nishimura of Kioto, and by these alone. As is evident, the touch follows no rule. Bought from King.

S. 12. Tiger seated beneath a tree on whose branches rests a bird. by Gankn. This is a fair specimen of Gankn's ordinary style, such as are still offered for sale, and seen in Kioto collections. It cannot be compared with his great works. Mr. Kano Y. was inclined to think it not genuine. Lt. Suan assures me it is genuine. For my part I am certain of its genuineness, it being much better than several I saw in Kioto, vouched for by all the Kioto critics. It has the touch of Gankn, but not his highest power of idea. He studied tigers from life. It is better than Okio's ordinary work. The signature is undoubtedly genuine. Painted in his later years.

S. 13. A family of monkeys sporting on a tree growing from the sides of a chasm. Sosen. This is the very best of Sosen's second class, according to general agreement. For miniature monkeys it is his best. The composition is much finer than is usual with this artist. His landscape however is meagre in invention and his execution of it is not strong. There is no other artist who has portrayed monkeys so truthfully, though many more nobly. This artist knows little about coloring. from K.K.K.

" 14. Pictures of Jiorojin with his deer. Shingetsu. A fine specimen of this artist whose pictures are rare. This is the best of his second class according to Kano Yeitoku. A common specimen says Ninagawa, who always disparages my pictures, and exalts his own. A very fine specimen says Hasegawa Settei, the present representative of the school of Sesshiu. Very fine say Setsnan and Mr. Kanda. It is the best original Shingetsu I have yet seen (1180.) Some of his screens must have been greater. This Jiorojin is in the true Shingetsu style, although a subject treated with similar arrangements by all the artists of his time, and by some

for centuries later. The simplicity of it recalls the noble feeling of the artists of those times. The stamp is genuine. The manner is much like Sesshu, but not so forceful or facile. On the box is written "Jioroqin" "Shiugetsu".
Bought from Tazawa.

S. 15. Two wild horses in the snow amid wild mountain scenery. Motonobu. This rare specimen is in the second class of Motonobu. Such things are rarely seen. The stamp upon it gives the name of Shoyei, Motonobu's son; and several critics, Ninagawa, Kanda, and others had agreed that it was Shoyei. Messrs. Matsuwo and Wakai, Directors of the Kosho Kuaisha, thought it a very remarkable work to see. But Mr. Kano Yeitoku, has in his inherited collection of copies and originals from the old masters, copies of six panels of a screen by Motonobu, of which he recognizes this as the original of one panel. This identifies it as Motonobu himself, and that it was taken from an old screen, perhaps partly destroyed, and mounted as a Kakemono. Afterward some artist, Kano probably, who held a seal of Shioyei, stamped it such according to his erroneous opinion. It certainly has the treatment of black of Motonobu. The touch is more mysterious and nervous than that of his ordinary style. I do not know whether the falling water is intended to be encased in ice. The excellence of the whole to the Japanese mind of taste lies in the exalted feeling of wildness and majestic dreariness of life in such a landscape. The very look of the horses seems to show their appreciation of the forlorn grandeur of their own position. Unless one can forget scientific pedantry and open his soul to the deep mysterious feeling of their pictures, one can never appreciate the great things of Chinese and Japanese art. On the box is written "Setsu ten ma kiba" literally "Snow inside, wild horse." "Kano Shioyei Hogen." Bought in Tokio.

S. 16. Fishing village. Copy from Sesshu. This simple but attractive little picture shows finely the common ground between Modern European landscape feeling, and the best old Japanese. It might well be Marblehead or any other New England coast town. The manner is distinctly of Sesshu, and the signature of Sesshu is given. Mr. Kano Yeitoku and Hasegawa Settei are quite certain that it is not an original. They think the signature manifestly a forgery, and the touches, especially in the houses, too stiff and lacking picturesqueness and vigor. On the other hand Mr. Ninagawa says it is undoubtedly genuine; and Mr. Setsuan will not hear for a moment of its being other than genuine. The signature even he thinks is genuine. As a mere matter of testimony the former opinion ought to have most weight, considering the familiarity of the two artists with the best work of Sesshu. Again my own opinion would incline me to that side, the signature looking to me false, and the touch evidently weaker than Sesshiu's ordinary landscapes. Nevertheless it is a fine work. All agree that if it is not Sesshiu, it is a copy from him of very early date, perhaps made during his lifetime. It is also done by a good artist. The weak points are such as a foreigner would not easily recognize unless instructed; and the impression one gets of the picture from a little distance is exactly that of a landscape by Sesshiu. Evidently the chief excellence in this case lies in the purity of its landscape feeling.

51 17. Jiorojin. A copy from Sesshiu's picture by Kano Tomonobu 1880. Of the copy as such we need merely say that it is faithfully executed. The original is one of the most important pictures in Japan. It is considered by critics to be the finest work of Sesshiu now known. It has a curious history. Undoubtedly painted by Sesshiu during his sojourn in China, it had made its way

to the palace of the King of Corea in Seoul the capital of that country. When Kato Kiyomasa entered the capital in the name of Taiko, the Japanese tyrant, at the head of the conquering invaders, he secured this treasure among others after the sack of the palace, and brought it back with him to Japan. It (was lately) is now in the family treasury of Prince Hachisuka of Tokio, and is regarded as one of the greatest pictorial gems in the country. Mr. Kano has a fine copy of it. The excellence of the picture lies in its extraordinary mysterious effect upon the soul of the beholder. This is acheived first by the extraordinary face and figure of Jiorojin. The face is that of a God, not a man, and with its strong features peers out weirdly from the paper. The figure is very original, bent as it is, with strange unsymmetrical almost hesitating lines. The color too on the face and figure is equally extraordinary and adds to the weirdness. But how can one fittingly describe the other elements in the picture. The deer is the double of the man-god. The great pine trunk on the left runs into the halo back of the head, and is there transmuted into a dream of itself. The branches which it throws off intermingle in glorious mystery with the trunk and branches of a white plum tree in blossom, and this witch network of boughs runs through the halo, and around and across the head. Their execution is stupendous. The silvery quality of the lights and dark outlines has seldom been equalled in any work, and never in combination with such lines. What rule was followed in drawing these branches? None, the composition is stupendous, unexpected, a revelation of power, mystery, and supernatural charm. The sprays of white plum curve across the picture like snaky living fingers. The staff of the old man, a glorious knotty stick, rises in deeper massy curves into the melee of lines and shades. It is an individual creation so great, so perfect, that it is its own law. Nothing but itself can judge it.

In the field of ideal art this must certainly be reckoned one of the most extraordinary creations the world has seen. Subject, line, and masses are fused together into a single idea, so deep, metaphysical, supernatural, that it seems to require a superhuman mind for its conception. Unfortunately the mass of Japanese at the present day can see little more in this than an interesting antiquity. The Kanos alone appreciate the deeper meaning. Even Hasegawa does not, I am sure, by the poor copy he has made for himself. Not a thing must be changed, not a line or shade.

Probably the original of this is the one which Prof. Wheeler of Sapporo bought in Osaka, and had burned up in his house in 1880. In 1889 I hear from Mr. Brooks that Prof. Wheeler's picture was quite a different one. Also the original came out in an exhibition in 1888.

5. 18. Yoshitsune and Benkei on the bridge. Ikkei, one of the best Kioto artists of the last generation. A pupil of Totsugen. The manner of this is mostly in that of the Okio school. There is some Kano and a bit of Tosa element in it. The coloring is rather original. This is appreciated by a good deal of modern taste. The gradations are very pure. The interest of the picture does not lie in the faces and the expression of emotion, but in the color, touch, and gradations. The drawing of Benkei is rather spirited. It is a good picture for a modern.

5. 19. Chinese mountain landscape. Taniu. This is roughly drawn, and is a fair specimen of Taniu's second class of landscapes, says Mr. Kano. It was formerly one of a set of three; as is known by the fact that Taniu painted the same or a similar subject many times over as one of a set of three. I have not yet been able to find the name of the Chinese scene from which these innumerable modifications are taken. The

good landscape effect reached through such very careless touches is most characteristic of Tanin. I say third class.

S. 20. "A cluster of botans beaten by wind and rain, Sorin. This artist was formerly painter to the daimio of Awari. It is very finely conceived and executed. The grace of the curves of resistance is noticeable; the relief given to the petals of the flowers, as distinguished from the ordinary flatness of Japanese flower painting, and the variety of form and color in the leaves, all these qualities mark this as quite an original work. Its unity of line and subject is perfect. Pictures of this artist are rare in Tokio.

S. 21. Colored painting of Sumidagawa at Mukojima in old times by Kano Yusen, or Kano Sukenobu, the great grand father of Kano Tomonobu. This is painted in that one of the Kano styles, which is nearest to Tosa in feeling, though the touch is different. Mr. Kano says this is the very best work of this artist, who was not especially celebrated. Tsukubayama looks natural rising at the North.

"22. A large picture of two carps leaping among the spray and waves at the foot of a large waterfall. Ranko. This artist is one of the greatest of modern times (This is an exaggerated opinion) next to Ganku. This picture is much disliked both by foreigners and most Japanese critics, by the former, because it is too unnatural, by the latter, because it does not follow their narrow canons. They admit its strength however, and power over the beholder. It has no gracefulness says Kano Yeitoku. True, but it has the higher quality of power. The artist knew what he was doing. He has deliberately sacrificed the actual lines of nature, and all graceful feeling, to an extraordinary composition of lines expressing his feeling in a most powerful manner, to one who will throw away his prejudices sufficiently to receive the impression, thus realizing most boldly the true artistic end. Everything I have seen of this artist is remarkably fine. Bought from Yamanaka —

"23. Landscape with dog and pups. Nanping. This is not so striking and beautiful as some of Nanping's work. But it has the merit of being genuine, according to universal consent at a time when thousands of imitations abound. Mr. Kano calls it a good specimen of the second class. Its subdued style is highly appreciated by Japanese. The painting of the dog has the best mild expression of animal painting from Nanping's brush, for which he is celebrated. The signature

is undoubtedly genuine. The tree, flowers and grasses are characteristic of Nanping's best delicacy of execution. The picture as a whole is weak in composition, and has no effect, like too many of the productions of this artist. It is painted on thick Chinese silk manufactured for the purpose. On the box is written "Nanping ga."
Presented by Mr. Lyman —

"24. Large Buddhist picture", with many divinities in circles, red, blue, yellow, green &c. The artist is unknown, probably not more than a hundred years old. It has been retouched within a few years. Its execution has no value from a native point of view. Its general design shows something of the better qualities in recent Buddhist painting. The color is rich without being very good. On the whole it is better than the ordinary run of later Buddhist paintings which foreigners buy up with eagerness. The porcelain ends are very fine, in old Japanese blue, and much appreciated by natives. On the box is written "Kinjo Kawon" meaning "many Kinjo's".

S. 25. Large landscape of Mt. Yorozan in Mino. Sugawara Rankei. This was painted only 20 years ago by a descendant of an ancient noble house, though not greatly celebrated as an artist. It is rather in the manner of the Okio school. The perspective is faulty. It is contradictory in that it represents all seasons at once. This is purposely done. The painting is excellent though not great. The distant mountain is the finest part of it. On the box is written "Yorozan Shinkei" "Sugawara Rankei". Kiosai says this artist attained the highest local celebrity in the province of Echizen. He afterwards come to Kioto and lived in Sanjo. Very celebrated.

$26. A set of 3 by Taniu. His second quality of Excellence, says Mr. Kano. Painted when he was 69 years old. Their excellence consists in their freedom and poetic Expression. These served as models for the rapid work of later generations.

1. Onagadori with Kaido flower.

2. Rihaku looking at the waterfall. Rihaku was a noted poet of the To dynasty, who describes in one of the most famous of his poems in the heart of the mountains he discovered a great waterfall. In later Japanese art, any picture of a Chinese looking at a waterfall is said to be Rihaku. It was a favorite subject of old Chinese painters.

3. Plum branch and moon. A common subject at this period. Painted in Taniu's most rapid yet fascinating manner. The touch is in the Gyo manner. Mr. Kano says this is a fine subject and shows good feeling.

Bought from King — Collection of

^{s}27. Chinese in villa gazing at mountain scenery. Kano Tanshin Morimichi, the grandfather of Kano Tambi Moriki. This is a direct copy from a famous picture by Ōki, a celebrated Chinese artist of the So dynasty. In Japan the works of this artist are exceedingly rare. This is charming in conception and treatment. The poets in the house are finely drawn, and the erratic trees have been a model for many good things of the Japanese. This artist was a little later than Bayen. A magnificent landscape of Eastern art. Highest ideality. Finest copy in existence probably, much better than retined in museum.

^{s}28. A set of 3 fine pictures by the same artist, the later Tanshin. For modern pictures these have very refined taste and execution. Among the best works of this artist, though not strictly original.

1. Chinese mountain scenery, with hut in the foreground. Although this is not a direct copy from Motonobu, yet all the parts of it are adapted from landscapes of Motonobu, and here combined

anew into an original picture. The delicacy of finish is essentially from Motonobu in one of his landscape styles.

2. A picture of Jukurokujin, Keikaboku, and Saisho the servant. The design of this is directly copied from a famous picture of Motonobu, except that the original is in black alone, whereas this has Tanshin's color, and a certain weak delicacy of feeling added. Its execution is perfect in its way.

3. Ideal Chinese landscape, ricefields &c. This like No. 1. is an adaptation from Motonobu, but not a direct copy. Its peculiarity of soft quiet brownish color is Tanshin's. Altogether these three form a charming work.

Bought from Kosho Kuaisha who got them from Daigen

"29. A set of 3 pieces by Tanin. These are good specimens of Tanin's third or ordinary style. They were painted at the age of 69. Their execution is careless, and lacks the inimitable technique of touch for which Tanin was so celebrated and which characterizes

No. 32 in the highest degree. They have power, but not noble, and deep feeling.

1. dragon and waves. The dragon of the typhoon has risen into the air, and the frenzied water from which he has emerged leaps after in tumultuous heaps. The pillar is here strongly drawn.

2. Kanzan and Jittoku. These are not Sennin, but the servants of Bukkanzenji, an ancient Chinese priest, who became his disciples. They studied the Zen sect of Buddhism, and were noted among the Chinese for their learning. They are much honored by the Zen sect in Japan. They have been a favorite subject of the artists in all times. They communicated great thoughts to one another by secret gestures of hand and feature. For further facts about them, the books on such subjects must be consulted. These are executed in Taniu's coarsest style.

3. The storm dragon returning to the water. This one Mr. Kano says is the best of the three.

S'30. A set of three by Kano Tsen. These are said by his son Kano Yeitoku to be the finest specimens he has ever seen of this master. They were painted when he was from 48 to 50 years old. The style of the various parts of these most delicate landscape paintings is taken piecemeal from Motonobu and the old Chinese artists of the So and Gen dynasties, notably the architecture from Konkuntaku. The original Tsen element is the composition of the parts into a peculiar feeling of colored beauty. The feeling is essentially Tenish. The coloring is so tender as to leave nothing to be desired. The structures represented are ideal or actual old Chinese palaces. There is a soft atmospheric effect about them, which establishes their excellence among the works of this period. The box in which they are kept is of the finest Kiri wood, and must have belonged to a prince. The writing upon it is in the handwriting of his son Kano Seisen. On the outside is written "Sambukutsui" Tsussi

Rokaku" i.e. Landscape of mountain palaces. "Iken in Hojin." On the inside is written "Yoshin (Seisen) wrote this."

1. Shows a palace by a lake with a long distance lost amid gold clouds.

2. Shows in the foreground the terrace and part of the garden of a palace, a beautiful middle distance of shore, and fine overhanging peaks. The tree trunks are especially fine, and the finish is perfection.

3. Shows a winter scene, a villa in snow near a bamboo grove, with a shore of yellow grasses in the middle distance. There is no great strength in any of these pictures.

Bought from Kosho Kuaisha, who got them from Daizen.

S. 31. A set of three by Kano Tsunenobu. These are said by Yeitoku and Tomonobu to be the very finest work of Tsunenobu. The subjects are the most common among all artists, and Tsunenobu frequently painted them. But these specimens have far better line and color than ordinary, so that they present to a Japanese great nobleness of feeling. The delicacy of the suggested color is noticeable. The lines are very strongly drawn. Such large specimens of these gods are rare. The mounting is old. On the box is written Fukuroku jin, Yebisu, Daikoku, Sambuku, Hogen Kosen's painting.

1. Daikoku astride of his bag of wealth, pounding with a hammer. Several of his jewels have escaped on the ground. The combinations of black and green in the drapery, has almost the texture of velvet.

2. Fukurokujin, deer, and Stork. A very noble composition, well composed in line, with its grand pine tree

3. Yebisu catching a red fish. Mr. Ninagawa says this is the best of the three, and with respect to the purity of the tones and gradations of the ink he is right. The rock on which the figure stands is unequaled in tone by any of this style. There is the same refined atmospheric tone which characterizes all good Kano pictures

from Taniu downward in all three pictures. Bought from Kosho Kuaisha, 1st class.

s 32. A set of three in black of Taniu. This is one of the most notable sets of Taniu in Japan. Mr. Kano says they are the best of his pictures. Executed with the _So_ touch of the brush. The clouds are inimitable in their transparent black, rapid but perfect gradation, enormous sweeps, with broken bits of light scattered through them, where the impetuous sweep of the wet brush was checked by the firm hand. This effect has never been imitated or successfully copied by any other Kano artist. Indeed the method of execution is well nigh inconceivable. The soulful quality of the pictures is however their greatest excellence. The spectator bows before their mysterious suggestions, their poetical rendering of the destructive power of nature.

1. The storm dragon descending through the whirls of sulphurous cloud. This shows the

peculiar excellence of the technique in the highest degree. The light spots in the midst of the black are wonderful. The identification of the mysterious and hideous dragon with the unearthly cloud is fine. The whirl of the lighter cloud below is full of power and mystery. The spectator stands awe struck at the exquisiteness of the thought which grasps the full grandeur and intensity of the subject in its colorless crystal vision.

2. The storm rolls far over the middle distance in the great gulf of Suruga Bay, as seen by the spectator on the heights of Idzu. In the midst of the forbidding clouds, the Kaminari, or thunder god Raiden, leaps with his circlet of rattling drums, while forks of red lightning radiate into the seething abyss below. Far above the troubled region of storm, calm Fuji lifts her reverend white head into the clear sky in magnificent contrast to the confusion of unequilibrated power below. The sweep of the brush in the lower clouds is stupendous. The Japanese usually like this the best of the three

3. The storm dragon ascending from the abyss, high in air amid similar whirls and depths of lowering typhoon cloud. The feeling and touch are similar to No. 1, but not so intense or wonderful.   Bought from Kosho Kuaisha, owned formerly by Daizen.

5. 33. A small set of three in black by Tanin. This is agreed by all to be the very finest specimen of Tanin's first class. Mr. Kano Yeitoku says there is nothing else of Tanin's to be compared with these; they are even better than the preceding. They cannot be copied. They were painted at the age of from 30 to 40, when Tanin was possessed of his greatest vigor. Their excellence consists, according to Mr. Kano, in the harmony of the relations of every line to the others, the rich beauty of the black, the purity and tenderness of tone and effect. In style of touch they are between Gyo and Shin.

   1. Branch of a plum tree with the Kakessu bird. This illustrates most strongly the beauty

of the black. When we remember that the effect is reached at a single dash, its transparency and richness is astonishing. The beauty of the simple lines too in their steady deliberate vital unsteadiness is most striking. This is a common subject, but has never been more finely treated.

2. Portrait of Yuima, a Hindoo philosopher, older than Daruma, who finally submitted to the Buddhist religion in his old age. He had been an independent thinker in the time of Shaka, with a system not greatly differing from the latter's. It was Monju, the pupil of Shaka, who discussed with Yuima and converted him to the doctrines of Shaka, of whom he became a personal disciple. Mr. Kano says, and I think it true, that this portrait may be called the finest in the whole range of Japanese art. The exquisite drawing of the features has been equalled in no other. The melancholy calm resigned features of the handsome old face, are wonderful in their power. The eye, though fixed in thought, is pregnant with

life and soul. This is the highest point to which portrait painting can attain without the introduction of shadow. He holds in his hand the hossu, a wand used and waved by Buddhist chief priests in funeral and other high ceremonies. In the Zen sect every priest has one.

3. Anagadori and Kaido flower. This is very beautiful in arrangement and execution, having softer qualities than No. 1. If these tender qualities do not touch the soul of the beholder, then there is no method of communicating appreciative feeling for them.

Bought from Kosho Kuaisha; formerly owned by Daijen.

34. A set of three landscapes in black by Kano Seisen. These are in his second best style, according to his brother Geitoku. They were painted when he was very young, perhaps only 20. He had been a great student of Sesshu, and this his early work reflects the style of the master, although there is an original element in it. Indeed the middle one is said

to be adapted directly from a well-known design by Sesshiu. They are ideal landscapes. Their excellence consists in the beauty of their black contrasting with gold in the clouds, the grand drawing of the trees and rocks, which recalls the best period of the Kanos. The touch of the brush is not like that of Sesshiu. The mounting is old, especially fine, and suited to the dark refined tones of the pictures.

1. Ideal mountain landscape. The rock and trees in the foreground are especially fine; the rocks of the mountain are very strong, and the effect of the picture is sharp and clear like that of an etching.

2. Ideal landscape with rustic bower in which are resting Fukurokujin, and Keikaboku. Saisho the boy feeds the sacred deer. A strange tree rises above. The effect of the whole is powerful, beautiful, and full of the mystery of the ways of the Gods.

3. Ideal winter mountain landscape. The tender tones of the ~~color~~ black contrasting with the white of the snow are fine.

Bought from Kosho Kuaisha; onnedby Daizen.
I say they are 1st class of Seisen.

S. 35. A marriage or New Year's set of three by
Seisen. Mr. Kano calls them only second class;
but they seem to me to be of a very great degree
of excellence. They were probably painted to
order by some prince at the time of his marriage.
They contain all the lucky emblems. The artist was 30 yrs. old when they were painted.
Mr. Kano says that the fault of these pictures
lies in their coloring, which is not harmonious
and lacks dignity. The lines are tolerable.
My own impression is that the drawing is poorer
than the color, which is quite rich and
fascinating. The mounting is princely, and
they are finished in the best of styles; being
types of those kakemonos prized by princes
in later times.
 1. This comprises the elements of the stork
and pine.
 2. Jiu-jin, the god of longevity and
talents. The drawing of this is in the style
of the older masters, but the coloring

is Sesien's own, and very rich and striking. The figure seems to lie against a soft back ground of sweet atmosphere.

3. Red plum tree and sacred turtle. From the mouth of the latter, in spiral form ascends the sacred fortunate breath, or "good air" bearing its inspiration.
Bought from Yamanaka. 2nd class.

S. 36. A set of three large ones by Buncho. Mr. Kano says these are the best ones of the 2nd grade of Buncho. Mr. Letsnan agrees with him. In the execution of these Buncho has been in some sort the follower of Sesshu; but they are so individual, that the Sesshu quality is lost in the good or bad genius of Buncho.

1. Ideal landscape. The cliff on head is strangely beetling, and the touch careless in the extreme. Below amidst masses of rock, and in the shadow of lowering clouds a palace is seen with its foundations in the water. This is the poorest of the three. Whatever excellencies it has, are possened

in a much higher degree by No. 3.

2. Jiurojin. This is an original figure of Bunchō's in his own style, which here approaches that of the Kanos. Mr. Setsuan and Mr. Nakai think it is a fine figure. To me it possesses great coldness and lack of feeling. I cannot call it great. It possesses no genius.

3. An ideal landscape, by far the finest of the three, and in some respects one of the most striking in the whole range of Japanese art. The body of the picture is occupied by an enormous outlandish doublehorned cliff, which falling away toward the foreground ends in great heaps of sloping boulders from which mass of rubbish a long line of trees has sprung which stretch far up the sides of the cliff. Below nestled amid the boulders a mountain hut and a cleared space are seen, whence on the right a river stretches back around the base of the cliff till lost in the distance behind it. A wreath of cloud shrouding the bosom of the hill, half conceals the topmost pines, and, unusual thing, casts a shadowy gloom on all below it. The most extraordinary feature of the

picture is its attempt to produce an effect of light, which plays with delicious gleam on the boulders and tree trunks in the foreground, and upon the sides of the double cliff, whose masses cast real shadows upon one another and the river below. The gradations are everywhere delicate and silvery, and the black touches exceedingly strong. This almost reaches the freedom of Kakei, without passing through the medium of Kano. 1st class Isdomei? Bought from a man to whom pawned.

37. A set of 2 by Tsunenobu. These are very large and handsomely mounted. They are in Tsunenobu's second grade of excellence. They are both representations of a sacred lion, a bush of botans, and a cliff above. Monju rode on a lion, which was therefore considered a noble subject among Buddhists. Botans are always represented with lions, because these flowers grew and lions abounded on sacred Tendaiyama in China where Monju lived. The washes of ink are very crisp and beautiful, and the lions are better drawn than is usual with his school. What color there is in pleasant

contrasting with the greys. On the box is written "Nipuku tsui, botan shishi, Hogen Yoboku.
Bought from King - collection of some Kuwazoku

S. 38. A set of three remarkably large ones by Taka-nobu Yeitoku, the father of Kano Yeitoku's adopted father. He was not a very celebrated artist, but these are his best specimens. Probably painted to order for some prince.
   1. Waterfall and white flowers. Mysterious and rather powerful.
   2. Mr. Kano says this is adapted from old Chinese. A life size picture of a Sennin of Kuwan dynasty, who, first, as a common man stole a magic peach from his friend Tobosaku a sennin, which he ate, thus becoming a sennin himself. It is rare to find such a large figure in later Kano painting.
   3. Waterfall with red flowers.
     Bought from King - Collection of the same Kuwazoku

S. 39. A copy of a famous large mountain landscape of Bagenkin of Gen by Gentaro an as yet unknown Japanese artist. I have seen another copy of this same picture at Hasegawa's. The composition is very fine and bold. The touch and style of coloring show well the transition from the noble style of So, to the weaker feeling of Min. This copy probably has not the harmony of color and softness of atmosphere of the original. The coloring is not so pure. The character of the touch, the composition, and the general conception of the color, are all that this picture can be said to illustrate. It is striking however, and such a large one is rarely found.

S. 40. A very curious picture of 10 Rakan. No name is attached, and the painter is unknown. It is clear by the touch that the artist belonged to no known school of painter. As Mr. Kano says, "it was not an artist who painted it." But that depends upon what we mean by artist. It was probably a priest, perhaps of Kioto, at first an amateur, but who developed a style of his own in his love for the art. Surely the sweep of the brush in the ink lines is like that of no other artist. This settles that it is not a copy, though the lines of the brush above in their great strength might have been from the brush of Cho Densu. The figures too utterly lack that grace which is common to the "professional Buddhist painter." The design is indeed earnest but not graceful, the features are distorted, and there were many things the artist did not know. But he was filled with his conceptions, and was blessed with a love and knowledge of color vouchsafed to but few Japanese artists. In this the color lies the greatness of the picture. I have seen but few things which equal its dazzling tones. It needs only to place it beside any other thing we have praised for brilliancy to see its extraordinary excellence. From the fact of there being 10 Rakan only, it seems probable that this was one of a set of 50 pictures of 500 Rakans. The simplicity of the whole is primitive and touching. One must forget the distortion in contemplation of the excellencies. Bought from King.

41. Large picture of peacock, white plum tree, and flowers. Nimkin: This gorgeous picture was painted for the National Exhibition at Uyeno in 1878. The paralyzed artist was occupied 3 months upon it. He considered it his masterpiece. It was his last important work. The drawing is not strong, but this we can excuse the unfortunate artist. The composition too is a little confused toward the foreground. But the execution of details is masterly, and the color of the whole and of the parts is very beautiful. The artist and his friends considered it his masterpiece from the care and accuracy with which each detail of flower and

leaf is rendered. Indeed Munkin considered the lower part of it to be the best. There is no one left in Tokio who can equal it, and no one in Japan with such a feeling for color. My appreciation of this picture made bright Munkin's last year. The thing must be considered as a refined symphony in beautiful color. I cannot consider it Munkin's best work, or equal in quality of imagination and force to his earlier sketches. See No. 45. Remounted to my order.

S. 42. A set of 2 large pictures of deer, by Tanin. These are reckoned by every Japanese critic who sees them as the best of Tanin's first class, or at least just closely following No. 33 in excellence. They were painted when the artist was 66 yrs. old. The distortions of the drawing displeases foreigners, and it is at first difficult to appreciate the ground of the raptures of native beholders. Mr. Kano says one Excellence consists in the overcoming of the difficulties of Execution. The color of the deer is exactly right. The red one is slightly better than the white. The chief Excellence lies in the "dignity" of the picture, the soft yet strong, delicate yet simple, touch, pose, color, and general atmosphere. "This quality no artist can copy says Mr Kano. We admire these pictures because they give us the noblest ideal impression of a deer." This appreciation undoubtedly depends upon the possession of a "classic" taste; just as our cultivated feelings at once gravitate to that which bears the stamp of ancient Greece, whatever be its peculiarities or deformities. The whole picture is filled with what Japanese or Chinese would at once recognize as peaceful nobleness. The study of Chinese poetry may enable us to appreciate this Eastern classical feeling.

 1. White deer and green bamboo.
 2. Red deer and white cherry tree. This deer is much the better of the two; and the drawing of the cherry tree is magnificent—

The branches and blossoms also are most feelingly rendered in the highest classical style. The touches on the tree trunk every true artist will recognize as marvellous. Even the weeds in the foreground are full of spiritual excellence to the Japanese aesthetic souls.

Mr. Kano Yeitoku knew these pictures by reputation, having in his own collection copies made by his ancestors, on which is written "In possession of the Tokugawa family." They may have been lost in the ruin of the Shoguns fortunes. There are no other Tanius of their stamp known to be in existence.

543. A set of two landscapes, by Kano Motonobu. These are large and in every way a most extraordinary works. No critic to whom I have shown them has ever seen anything equal to them before, or even of their kind. They represent a hunting scene in the mountains of China by the Royal or Mandarin's huntsmen. They probably were painted originally upon a ten panelled screen, which explains the fact that they are but two halves of one picture. The conception is grand in the extreme, almost equal to old Chinese in feeling. The drawing is in Motonobu's strongest. The stratification and other formation of rocks is most impressively given. The drawing of figures and horses is most spirited, the action intense. The drawing of the trees is unique and powerful. Mr. Hasegawa had never seen trees drawn in such a manner. The color is glorious what there is of it, deep violet and golden and gray. The contrast of the yellow hues and the lingering traces of gold, throws into a soft charming violet the manes and limbs of

the neutral ink. These may be called the finest landscapes of Motonobu, and they certainly have qualities which the work of no other artist possesses. Their last excellence of course lies in their spiritual power over the beholder, who gazes in amazement at their impression panorama filled with unearthly beauty, knowledge, and life. I have since discovered that these were formerly on the sliding doors of Daitokuji, Kioto. See Note book of Biography. Sold about 40 years ago. In highest decorative style of Motonobu.

5. 44. Three large monkeys on a tree. Sosen. This is in the ~~middle~~ style of Sosen. The color is richer than is usual, and the drawing more accurate. There is as usual a lack of the divine fire and imagination. But this realizes the highest perfection to which the noted style of this painter could attain. Butsu No. 59 — The faces of the monkeys are the central point.

5. 45. Branches of plum trees, and blue bird. Munkin. This is perhaps the finest of this artist's work, and yet it is only a sketch. The composition of the several branches in radiating lines with the bird at their focus is great. The touch also is very powerful, and in some respects original. The beauty of the grey and black is considerable. But the color is the point where the artist has impressed his originality — The red, grayish, and greenish plum blossoms make an extraordinary passage of subdued and varied color, which culminates in the perfect colors of the bird. Imagination and strong feeling rule this picture, and it was struck off according to the artist's own fancy, not to fulfil an order, in the heat of inspiration. It was painted when Munkin was a rising young artist, 20 yrs. old or so, and had not been seized with the fatal paralysis which so early put

an end to his wonderful growth. The feeling in this may be compared with the fine things of the old masters, being altogether beyond the conventionalities of the later Nanping school. It is a fresh addition to Japanese conceptions.

"46. Red plum blossoms and moon; Hoitsu, the prince and painter, who renounced his rank and fortune, and traversed the country on foot sketching. He followed in the style of Korin, as being striking, and easily conveying impressions. This is a fair specimen of this artist. The stems and blossoms are painted in the Korin manner, though with a more modern, appreciative, and less hard and grotesque feeling. The moon is original being outlined only with a circular sweep of gold cloud. It is the type of Hoitsu's feeling at its pleasantest. He is far inferior in greatness of soul and strength to Korin. But see Nos.

S. 47. Small simple mountain landscape. Tanin. This is in his commonest or poorest manner, and yet is not bad. After seeing his better works it may be compared, but need not here be dwelt upon. The scene seems to be similar to that of many others of his landscapes.

S. 48. White eagle on a rock. A copy from Kiso Kotei, the Chinese Emperor of So. This is old, painted on Chinese silk, and according to Ninagawa the antiquarian, and also Mr. Kano, must have been executed in China 350 or 400 years ago. Very few genuine works of Kiso Kotei are in existence. This copy probably lacks the great strength and vigor of the original. It is beautiful however in its simplicity, and should be compared with the similar subject by Tanin. Bought from Tazawa.

s. 49. A single branch of ~~Lotoos~~ Fuyo. Tsunenobu. This simple work shows well the ordinary style of flower painting of the Kano school at this period. It has a delicacy and artistic meaning, without ever appreciating the side of flower beauty realized by the Nan king school. It is directly derived from old Chinese flower painting, as may be seen from a copy by Tanin in my album.

s. 50. Eagle on a pine branch covered with snow. Wankin. This was about the last painting from his brush, being executed the month before he died. It has no special qualities, but is a common specimen of Wankin's later style.

from here sent april 1881.

51. A large picture of Shoki about to kill a green devil which he has under his foot. Bunrin of the Shijo or Okio school. In fierceness, force, and grotesqueness this outranks all other Shoki's. The weight and pose of the massive figure is well rendered. The flying folds of drapery are conceived with an unintelligent brutal strength. Bunrin aimed evidently to render the powerful and horrible as such, and to make a sensation. The foreshortened drawing of the foot is rather unique, and the strength of the left arm and hand are praiseworthy. As a piece of painting the face with its masses of hair must be considered quite wonderful. The devil however is not so executed and conceived as to add to the picture. What color there is is poor and after the manner of Buncho. The style in general is of the Okio school, but modified to imitate the grosser features of Ganku and Buncho. It probably succeeds well in rendering the impression the artist desired. Mr. Kano says it is good, but not very great, since it is only strong. It is coarse

and has no refined artistic feeling. Mr Hasegawa says this picture is not interesting, and shows the corruption of the Ganku style. Mr. Kano says this reminds him of Hokusai. Whenever the Okio style degenerates, he thinks, it always tends toward Hokusai. To the foreign eye it is certainly an interesting, if not an admirable picture. Bought from Yamanaka.

s. 52. The female Sennin, Seiyobo, with her two female attendants, one carrying a dish of sacred peaches, the other the long fan-screen. They are floating through the clouds, with gleams of light breaking here and there through the suggested mists. By Korin, of the Okio school. The figures are graceful in their drawing, and dignified in pose. The drapery, decidedly Okioish, is very finely managed, especially the long mantles which float on the wind in yielding twisted broken curves. The touch in every part is firm and clear. But the chief beauty of the picture lies in its color, which, while quiet and less obtrusive than that of the great colorists of the Kano, Tosa, and Buddhist schools, is perhaps more charming and subtle. The brilliant key is reached only once in the handle of the wing shaped fan which the principal figure carries. The execution of the beam of light which falls across the figure on the left is striking in the technical knowledge it displays. The weakest thing in the picture is the faces, which are all alike, and though dignified, possessing no great character. This however may have been the intention of the artist, to represent the unaffected calmness of such exalted minds. As a whole, though not strong, it is among the most beautiful of its school, which generally is quite lacking in color. Mr. Hasegawa says of it that it is very good, and the artist must be put in the same rank with the great Keibun. As a picture this is as good as the large Ippo No. 84, described later on, he thinks. Mr. H. met this artist in Kioto 53 years ago. He was then about 40 years old. Mention of the composition should

not be omitted, achieved by the position of the
large fan-banner nearly over the head of the
chief figure. Bought from Yamanaka—

53. Small picture of a badger sitting on
the snow with a few sprays of grass. Ippo.
This is one of the best things of the Okio school,
although one of the simplest. The badger
is erect on his hind legs with his fore-
paws in the act of beating his chest, while
his cunning suspicious head looks off through
the cold misty air, as though his attention
had been attracted by some noise. The whole
pose of the animal is the perfection of naturalness. The execution however is that which most
astonishes. The drawing with no outlines in
the first place is perfect. In the second the execution of the hair all over the body is microscopic, every individual hair white, gray, black
and brown being represented with skilful fidelity.
The spirit however is not lost in this detail.
From a distance the figure stands out with almost the clearness of an etching, the black of the

paws and face giving character and force to all the gradations. According to Japanese mythology the badger possesses a soul, and, like the fox is able to bewitch the unwary among men. This picture therefore must be considered as more than the mere representation of an animal, since it attempts to render the spiritual power and ~~and~~ realistic weirdness which the native sees underneath its animal nature. Mr. Kano says of this picture that its excellence shows that Ippo is next to Okio in the Shijo school. The sprays of grass are very fine in execution and feeling. Mr. Hasegawa says it is better than Okio's for No. 79. In this he is clearly wrong, and is regarding only what is mechanical in the picture. When the badger strikes his chest or his belly, it gives out a sound like a drum. Bought from Yamanaka

54. Landscape in black. Renzan, best pupil of Ganku. This is good in conception, fine in composition, and unique and picturesque in execution. Two men stand in the foreground on the bank of a river, calling for the ferry boat

which lies half concealed among the sedge and rocks. The ferryman's house lies behind a pine clump of trees in the middle distance. A cliff rises behind with the new moon at its edge. The tones in this are original and tender, masses taking the place of lines. There is an original element added to that of Ganku, somewhat influenced perhaps by bunjinpa. So soft and pure are the gradations that they almost represent color. Renjan is perhaps the finest landscape painter of modern times. Mr. Kano and Mr. Hasegawa had never seen his work before, but thought it fine. He is not known outside of the Kioto district.

S. 55. Bust of Monju in black. Cho Densu. The face is kinder and more spiritual than is usual in old Buddhist paintings. The touches in the drapery are very strong and characteristic of this artist. The hair is finely painted for the old style and with a fine effect of black. Clouds obscure the bust below; thus probably the

figure is meant to be flying through the air. This picture has been much reduced in size, but originally had no other figure beside this. Mr. Hasegawa says that, although the picture bears no signature, yet it so well bears the stamp of the master that there is little doubt of its genuineness. Mr. Kano said it was a very fine picture and probably a genuine Cho Densu. Its fineness consists in its mild, kind, nobleness of expression, and well befits the supposed bearer of glad tidings from India to China.
Bought from Yamanaka —

56. Blue Quagadori on a branch of a tree
Kaidzyu kind of cherry —
with red flowers. Minenobu, younger brother of Chikanobu. This represents the later form of the Tanin period. It is very pure and pretty, but has no element of greatness in it. The coloring is good, and the picture well unified in the darker mass of the bird. Mr. Kano Tomonobu says that Minenobu is the ancestor of his branch of the Kano house, i.e. the one into which he is adopted. And Mr. Yeitoku says it is a very good specimen of this artist, who was not greatly celebrated.

S. 57. A red fox dozing beside a spray of purple asters. Sketch by Letsuzan, one of the great pupils of Okio. The method of coloring the fox is fine, as is the whole expression of rest and muscular relaxation. The tail which sweeps into the foreground is a mere blur of color, while the head, upon which the attention is to fall is clearly cut against the light background, thus displaying the artist's knowledge of the optical law of the focus. The sketch of the asters behind is pleasant. This shows finely the union of the naturalistic and picturesque qualities of the Okio school, which is not always so successfully achieved. Mr. Hasegawa says it is as good as Ippo's badger. Mr. Kano, while he thinks it good, calls it inferior to the Shioki of the same artist, see No. 88. A most artistic sketch.

S. 58. Shioki and tiger in black. Kingiokusen. This artist is one of the early ones who painted in the black style in Japan. His pictures are very rare, Mr. Kano & Mr. Hasegawa never having seen one before. This is the only one I have seen. The figure is quite grotesque, but powerful in its drawing. It is cold and material, in this respect resembling the common work of Sesshiu. The difference between this and Sesshiu to the foreign eye would be slight, since it appears to be mostly technical. Mr. Hasegawa says that "it probably shows this artist at his best. He lived about the time of Masanobu." He says further that "below the waist the form is rather poor; but then", he says, "in old pictures the form was generally not good. He cannot be called one of the finer Japanese painters." Mr. Kano says it is like the style of Doan the pupil of Sesshiu, but not so good. It must be genuine, for, the artist being unknown, and not being a very great picture, no one would copy it. It is a pretty good picture, however. Bought from Yamanaka. He was a very famous pupil of Motonobu.

"S. 59. A black dragon in whirling descent through the cloud masses of a typhoon. By Sosen, the famous painter of monkeys. This is one of the notable pictures of modern times, for several reasons. First, no one in Tokio or in Osaka so far as I can learn, had ever seen or heard before of a dragon painted by Sosen. It is therefore perhaps a unique work of this artist. Second, in comparison with the many other works of Sosen I have seen, it is by far the finest. In his monkey and deer pictures realism seemed to be his chief object, and his composition and drawing of accessories was generally weak. Thus I had placed him in the modern schools as quite inferior to Okio and Ganku. But this picture exhibits a height of ideality, a possession by the spirit of beauty, a magnificent composition, and a strong sure drawing, such that he becomes at once lifted up to the level of the greatest reformers of the last century. Third, it is quite original in conception and manner. It owes nothing to Taniu, the great painter of dragons in storm. Its method of gradation is quite different from that of the Kano school. It is not rough and picturesque like the Ganku style; and while its touch approaches somewhat to the Okio manner, its feeling is quite peculiarly its own. Moreover it is what no dragon before has been, positively realistic in its drawing. The great scaly serpentine body actually curves and looks solid, now projecting forward into the light of its attendant flame, now retreating back into the shadowy mass of the cloud. One is prompted to ask from what natural model this was studied; and the answer is suggested, from some enormous serpent which must have reached Japan as a curiosity during Sosen's life. The fourth remarkable thing about the picture is the fact that it is one of the finest dragons ever painted by any artist, ancient or Modern, Chinese or native. This is shown first in the conception which is exceedingly grand and powerful, next in the gradations of black which are as exquisite in their beauty as they must have been difficult of execution, but chiefly, as is seen at first glance, in the magnificent composition of curving lines, in which respect this picture almost stands alone in all Eastern art. The dragon himself forms a system of complicated spirals, against which the terrific strength of the clawed limbs breaks in straighter masses of harmonious divergence, while the shifting lines of the curling flame play like luminous bands of wind-lifted shroud, before, around, and behind the rolling form of the glorious monster, the mantle of its unearthly majesty. If we add to this the whirling masses of the cloud itself, and picture these several elements as fused into the transcendent unity of the artist-poet's conception, until line and spirit are one in significance and actuality, we may then realize the exalted character of this work. If Ganku with all his power had been so true to himself, as Sosen in this picture, he might have attained the height of the great artists of the climactic period of old Chinese painting.

Bought from Yamanaka

Sosen is a very great artist in other subjects than monkeys. In his great works he rivals any artist of modern times.

5/ 60. Three quail and grasses. Tosa Mitsuoki. This is the subject for painting which this artist for 250 years has had the highest reputation. It is thought very much of by Japanese even of the present day. This is in his fine simple style of painting this subject. The excellencies and weaknesses are apparent, first among the former the microscopic fidelity in the painting of the quails' plumage, and second the soft melting poetic satiny tone which characterizes the whole picture, seeming to be at one with the style of drawing and the character of the composition, thus realizing a certain unity and delicate feminine refinement of feeling. Its weaknesses, are, of course, this very femininity which seems almost unworthy of a man, rather clumsy and woodeny outlines, and the lack of all significant masses. Nevertheless I can appreciate what the Japanese mean when they speak of the superior artistic beauty of Mitsuoki. This is far weaker than the Benten No. 10. before mentioned, this being his more common style, and that his uncommon.

From Yamanaka

S. 61. A small picture of Shioki on a mule. Sesshin. It is surprising how much is suggested by this meagre sketch. The two trees on the right and the lines of the ground are a mere scratch. The mule is done with a few vigorous touches of deeper tone; but Shioki is sketched with great power in firm angular black lines, his whole fly-away attitude and fierce expression well exhibiting the eagerness of his search. The use of black is masterly. Mr. Hasegawa says that 40 yrs ago this picture was brought to his house for criticism, and after considerable discussion by the artists of the day, it was decided to be genuine, and bought by one of the Tokugawa cabinet officers for 21 Rio, a sum now equal to 140 yen. Still it is of course not one of the great things of Sesshin.
From Yamanaka. Miniature copy by Tanyu exists in collection of Mr. Kuki.

S. 62. A small picture of Quannon on a rock in black. Kano. This is so darkened by age as to give no effect at a distance. Quannon is drawn simply with graceful outline. The drawing of the rock and water is in very strong Chinese style.

The expression of the face is not very noble. The feeling on the whole is something like that of Mokkei. Mr. H. says this is surely genuine, and a good specimen. He considers this artist as great as Sanki, and greater than Motonobu. Motonobu may be more original, but not so great he thinks in execution. He became very celebrated after his death. His pictures now very rare. Mr. Kano says of it that while he does not feel absolutely sure of it, yet it is what would be usually accepted by artists as Kano.
From Yamanaka

5' 63. The seven gods of happiness. Tanshin, the son of Tanin. This is an ordinary representation of this subject. Fukurokujin is dancing with a child. Tanshin was not a great artist, simply copying his father's style. Four of the Gods are acting the part of musicians. Bisjamon sits haughtily alone, while Hotei sits watching with a childish grin. The arrangement is very good for this subject. Mr. Kano says it is a common specimen of Tanshin. Mr. H. thinks it a good picture for Tanshin. My own opinion is that it is rather a superior specimen.

S. 64. Dragon ascending on a storm cloud. Nikka of Shijo school. This is very simple, but mysterious. Its peculiarity is that while other dragons have been painted with strongly outlined form, this has no outline, but is melted into the mass of the cloud in such a manner that one must use his imagination to see it, as in Nature. The upward sweeping motion is fine, while a jet of lightning-like flame sweeps downward. This shows the Okio style of sketching in some degeneracy of execution, though still retaining power in conception. The artist has no great celebrity. Mr. Kano thinks it approaches to Hokusai. The artist is one of the good pupils of Toyohiko.

S. 65. Portrait of Yuima, Tsunenobu. This is one of the best portraits of the Kano school, next to Taniu's Yuima. The simplicity of it is remarkable. The lines are not hard, but executed with a broad yielding touch of the pen, such that they represent the curves rather than the boundaries of surfaces. Thus there is a tender, melting sympathetic treatment which is in complete unity with the pathetic face of the old man. To my mind there is more artistic feeling and power than in Tsunenobu's later and harder, even if grander, mannered style. An effect is realized something like that which Gankū consciously sought after and attained. Mr. Kano says that the artist was not perhaps much over 20 when it was painted. He considers it very good for his pictures at that age, but not equal to his later ones.   1st class.

" 66. A small heron on a rock. Sketch by Sesson. This is simple and rough. It is what the Japanese of taste greatly admire. The tones of the ink and the execution are considered perfect. It has not so much feeling to the foreign eye. The bits of bamboo are peculiarly striking and Sessonish. Of course it does not exhibit Sesson's great style. Mr. H. says, certainly genuine, at first glance, but a common specimen. Mr. K. says, good, and belongs to Sesson's middle class.
    From Yamanaka.

S. 67. Chinese philosopher or Sennin, among the rocks of a mountain. by Goshosen (early part), a Chinese artist of the middle of Min Dynasty. He was a very noted artist, Mr. Kano says; and this, he assures me, is a fine specimen. It is a picture which Japanese artists would always consider great, and worthy to rank with the great productions of earlier days. It has none of the sickly weakness of most of Min work. The execution of the rocks is regarded as especially fine, their masses and mild strong touch reminding one strongly of Shohaku. The figure is drawn with great knowledge of the use of the brush. The simplicity, directness, and force of the whole feeling are grand. Still to my mind it is colder and less deep in feeling than the great works of To and So. Very good indeed for Min.
From Yamanaka.

S. 68. ~~Birds of Paradise~~ Chinese pheasants on a rock, with bamboo, roses and a large peach tree. Chinnanpin. A characteristic specimen of this artist, whose pictures are much sought after at the present day. Its chief beauty is its delicacy of drawing and coloring.

That of coloring is hardly surpassed by any artist.
It is not perfectly harmonious however. Nanpin's
coloring was a revelation to the Japanese at Nagasaki. The rose blossoms and leaves are in the
perfection of his delicate style. The peaches
also are carefully painted. The execution of the
principal bird is remarkable. This picture also
shows Nanpin's faults, his over finish, his lack
of composition, strength of drawing, and of harmony
in tone. Mr. Kano is inclined to doubt its genuineness, but he does the same of every noted Nanpin
in Tokio. Mr. Hasegawa is certain it is genuine,
although he is inclined to think the signature was
afterward put in when the old had been cut off.
He says it is a fine specimen, uncommonly so,
the coloring being Nanpin's best, but the strength
of drawing not his greatest. My own opinion is
that there is little doubt of its genuineness. Mr.
Miyatsuka is certain it is genuine. All other critics
whom I have consulted say likewise.
  From Yamanaka.

S. 69. Lotus flower and leaves. Wunkei, a pupil of Sesshiu. This is certainly simple and beautiful in its drawing, although meagre in masses and in color. Far weaker than anything of Sesshiu. For this reason it is especially liked by "bunjin". It is finely preserved, and its cloth mounting is splendid and old. Mr. H. says that it is a very good specimen of Wunkei, who was the direct student of Sesshiu, and whose paintings are now very rare. Mr. K. says it is good, but does not consider the artist as anything remarkable. It shows the more feminine developement of the Sesshiu influence, as Sesson and Shinsetsu represent the masculine. From Yamanaka

S. 70. Small mountain landscape. Okio. This is a notable work, chiefly because genuine landscapes by this epochal artist are very rare. In the second place it merits attention from its own peculiar excellencies, and signs of originality. Its most notable excellence is its beautiful soft atmospheric effect, showing the mist as shining through the crystal ether of genuine mountain air. This is a new quality. Again there is an attempt at perspective, even among such difficult altitudes. There is an absence of the throwing up of the horizon line, so that the distant hills give their true feeling of altitude above us. Third the rocks are drawn with that realistic touch which Okio had discovered, showing their solidity, hardness, planes of cleavage, and ragged edges. Similar qualities are developed to a less degree in the pine tree. The cloud effects and distant hills are also finely rendered. It is discernable at once however that Okio had studied from the Ming artists. The composition and arrangement is more or less theirs, and the tree suggests them. In fact, if we compare the Ming landscapes with those of the later Okio school, we shall see that this distinctly exhibits the transition from the former to the latter. We may see moreover in this the distinctive weakness of Okio's pictures as pictures, namely their lack of any distinctive and significant masses of dark and light. The secret of this quality, Okio, with all his scientific observation of nature, never learned, and in this essential element fell far below the level of the old masters. Mr Kano says this is undoubtedly genuine, and a very rare subject, so rare indeed that no one would have a motive to forge it. Mr. Hasegawa says that this was painted perhaps after seeing Bayen or Baki, but he is mistaken, for, as said, it is more like Miy work. He says further that it is a very fine specimen of Okio's landscape, its purity being very prominent.

5.
71. View in the celebrated bay of Wakanoura in Kii, by Ippo. This is a simple like by our reckoning, but is remarkable for a Japanese. Perspectives, aerial and linear, are well rendered. The gleam of the water on the beach is a bit of naturalism new to Eastern art. The bending pine trees with risecurv sand-bound root are common on every Japanese low shore. The blue is regarded rather as a quality of gray than as a positive color. The poem above says, "Who would not come to the Bay of Wakanoura to

behold the gem of his soul." This is a place renowned in Japan for its scenery. This was painted in the period of Tenmei, when Ōkyo was about   years old.

72. Tokei - sketch of crows and moon
72. Group of flowers, plum tree, and 28 birds of different species - Shiuki. This painting although too crowded and too little unified as a picture, is especially valuable as a specimen of bird drawing. The small birds chiefly in the upper part of the picture are very finely and picturesquely drawn and colored. The branches and blossoms of the plum tree as also the bits of bamboo are a fine specimen of the painting of the later Nanping school. There is a fresh deliciousness about the coloring which appears again in Mnukin, and is the only distinctive excellence of the artists of this century. This must be regarded as a group of studies, rather than as a picture. Mr. K. says this is much like Nanping, especially in the flowers, but far less, nobly, than the picture of the Sanji No. Mr. Hasegawa said this was painted in the

finest style of Nanping, this being even better than the Sangi in many respects, which latter is more in the style of Rioki.

S. 73. Riotobin the Sennin teaching his magic arts to Shoriken another Sennin, the one who frequently is represented as floating on a fan. Design of Ganki copied by Taniu. First as a copy I judge this to be pretty good, since it is better than Taniu himself could paint in his own design. It probably is inferior to the original in gradation, and in the drawing of parts especially the feet. But it retains the deep intense expression of the great period of Chinese painting, and well illustrates Ganki's conception and composition, if not his execution. The chief excellence of this, as of the old Chinese school as distinguished from the Japanese in general, is that the drapery, though skillfully executed, is not so done as to draw attention to its manner from the central motive of the subject,

in this case the attitude and countenances of the two figures. On the contrary the execution, strong without being exaggerated, is rather a pure mirror through which the artist's thought is seen. It is not necessary to describe what is so patent, the power of the faces and the nobleness of the attitudes. Mr. Kano says this is one of the very fine designs of Sanki. It has nothing of the peculiarities of Tanin in it.
From Yamanaka

S. 74. Large Quannon as fisherman's daughter. Tozan of the Shijo school. This isolated figure has some merits, but is not so interesting as many works of this school. There is a cold unsympathetic manner and tone about the whole which repels. The face is the weakest part, being quite Japanese in type rather than fine old-time Chinese. The lower part of the drapery is however quite fine both in its flowing folds and in its color, while the basket and fish is really a good piece of painting. This, of course, is the degenerating of the Okio school, but it still retains elements

of greatness. Mr. K. calls it ordinary, of not
sufficient nobleness, and inferior to the work
of Korrin No. 52. Mr. H. thinks it noble
enough for Quannon in this capacity. Its color
he considers pretty good, but its drawing of
lines not great. Its proportions are those of
an ordinary Japanese woman. Togan is pupil
of Tetsuzan

" 75. Group of people sheltered from a sudden
shower under a gateway. Icho, son of the first
Icho. This subject gives grand opportunity for
displaying the genre painting peculiar to the Icho
school. Here ladies, and servants, artisans and
carpenters, pilgrims and farmers, climbing boys,
cake sellers, and nursemaids with babies have
huddled together to escape a wetting. A group of
blind musicians are hurrying along the street on
the right, and in the foreground two boys are
hurrying on a packhorse. It is one of the finest
and most comprehensive specimens to be found
of this style. Mr. Kano at first thought that it
might be by the first Icho, but if so, he said it
was not a good specimen of Icho's execution,

being too weak. If it be a copy, he said it must be from one of Itcho's finest designs. Mr. H. however, said at once that it was by the second Itcho, a very fine picture, though not so strong as his father. The son painted under the same name and signature; so many have thought his designs to be merely copies, when they were really independent works. This shows the popular painting of Japan 100 years before Hokusai was born. The three kinds of cloth in the mounting are magnificent.

5'76. Botans, bamboo, and queer water worn rock. Bayitsu. This is the style admired at the present day, something between the Nanping style and Bunjinga. The artist is considered very expert in the use of his brush; but, while his bamboo is well drawn, there is no very great artistic feeling in the picture. It is at best, clever. Mr. Hasegawa however, says of it, "the height of power is in this picture, and it is to be classed with Ippo's best work."

He considers him one of the best of the recent artists. Says he died something more than 10 years ago. Mr. Kano says this artist was the teacher of Katei, now living in Tokio, and is not so good as Shuiki. Mr. Kano is speaking from the narrower point of view which regards all "bunjin" element as evil.

77. White falcon on a rock by the ocean. Tanin. This is rather better than the ordinary specimens of Tanin. Its chief excellence is the majesty of the bird's attitude, and noble independence of expression as it gazes off over the mist-hidden sea. The rock is also very strongly painted, and the water has a power of whirl and shock peculiar to the drawing of Tanin. The contrast also of the white of the bird with the dark of the rock adds purity and further grandeur to the whole. The fault lies in the hasty execution, and careless reliance upon a mannerism, which in Tanin's old age too often served him as an infallible receipt for

inspiration. The red orb of the sun, rolling through clouds above hardly gives the suggestion of light, and is never intended to do so in Eastern painting. The mounting is very old. The subject of this was undoubtedly suggested by Kiso Kotei. The bird is inferior to Sanraku or Chokuan. Bought from King.

51 78. Fujiyama seen from one of the mountain passes. Tanzan, pupil of Taniu. Mr. Kano says this is genuine and a common specimen. Mr. H. says it is rather poor, and that Tanzan's pictures are so rare, because nobody cared to order from such a common artist. On the other hand Mr. Setsuan said he considered Tanzan one of the best pupils of Tanin. This is the only one I have ever seen, and since it was painted at the age of 67, it undoubtedly exhibits a mature but hasty mannerism in which the best genius of the artist is far from appearing. The low natural slope of the mountain is far more impressive than the common exaggerations of its angle. It is degenerate Tanin.

5. 79. White fox sitting out in the night mist. Okio. This is in the first class of Okio. It is not the drawing of the animal alone which renders this great, masterly and accurate though it is. It is not the foreshortening of the head which seems to project from the background. Neither is it the technique which casts semi transparent mists across the figure. But it is the spiritual and supernatural meaning of the whole thing, which is a step beyond the mere naturalness which was too often the sole aim of Okio. The mysterious white fox, the most knowing and dangerous in his bewitching powers of all animals, sits in the weird moonlight like a ghost half hidden behind a ghostly shrubby screen, casting his cold piercing glance into the very heart of the startled beholder, until the fascination of his gaze enables one to understand the superstitious fears and legends of a simple unscientific people. This is great art, to render a nation's belief or fear, in its strongest essential imaginative power, in a

concrete force which renders unnecessary abstract descriptions or story. This was painted in the period of Aingei. The sprays of grass, mysterious, almost without beginning or end, add form and give tone to the picture. Mr Hasegawa says, strangely enough, that this reminds him of Tanin. He is referring evidently to the studies from Nature, such as Kano Monki possesses. Mr. Kano says it is undoubtedly genuine, and very impressive; still it does not show Okio's greatest power of drawing. Mr. Miyatsuka said it was the finest Okio he had ever seen. It is certainly the greatest I have yet seen with the exception of Mr. Nishimura's screens at Kioto. From Yamanaka

5' 80. Tiger peering over the edge of a cliff. Ganku. This is the next best of Ganku's Tigers, so far as I have seen, to the one on my pair of screens. Its excellencies are many and great. Its conception, powerful, solid, intense. Its unity and composition of line simple, unconscious, and great. Its execution in Ganku's greatest, picturesque, powerful style. The striped fur is well rendered, but all force is concentrated in the tiger's eager, cruel, face, and in the half curved, projecting, supporting leg and claw. The body as a whole seems to be thrown forward out of a mysterious misty background. The bit of bamboo on the left is perfect, and reminds one somewhat of Lesson. In all great qualities this must be compared with the old masters of Japan and China, with the additional merit of being original in style. One of Ganku's most vigorous productions. From Yamanaka.

5. 81. 1.42. Birds & flowers. Mosen. This is almost the best flower painting of the Kano school. The gradations in the flowers are so pure

and the color in the greens is such that they seem almost like tinted ivory. The rocks also are very strongly drawn. Only secondary to the masses of flowers are the birds which enter into the composition of each. No 1. has botans and golden pheasants. The composition and coloring is less pleasing than in No. 2, which shows sort of a white pheasant, and flowers like hollyhocks. Mr. Kano says that these are the very best specimens of Yosen's work. In many respects they are like the pictures of Ojiakusai, though some of the flowers are like Shunkio. He says artists of this period took their subjects from the great Chinese painters of So and Gen, especially in flowers, although they had a style of their own. They are not direct copies, but adaptations. Their color is the richest ever used by Kanos, and probably shows us what the great old Chinese flower pieces looked like when they were nearly new. If I remember correctly, they are almost exact copies of designs by Shunkio in Shoma Kioku. From Yamanaka—

"82. Great waterfall in Mino. Ricks of the Shijo school. This is one of the fine things which shows the power in the new style. The old Kano waterfalls had fallen in gentle sliding curves as if in a lazy tumble. This curves on the brink, and then falls at once in almost straight lines with tremendous force and weight, the impression of which is heightened by the splash and scattering of the foaming mass as it strikes on the projecting rocks near the bottom, where the seething spray has been rendered in attempt by a thoroughly new method. The side sprays of the fall leaping in tiny streams from crag to crag, like exquisite lace-work, add to the beauty and break the monotony of the great central mass. All the lines of white water are well brought out against the masses of rock and dark foliage. We may say that this artist has not been content to copy, but has been studious in receiving new fresh impressions from nature. Mr. H. says this is a good specimen, but its execution is not equal to Toyohiko's. Mr. K. says it is very fine, Mr. Yamanaka admiring it as much as I do. From Yamanaka — Probably a pupil of Toyohiko. A great picture.

S. 83. Pine tree and two peacocks in black. Ōkio. This, though not so good as the fox, is a fine specimen of Ōkio. The pine tree is in Ōkio's original strong peculiar style. The peacocks however are the best in drawing. The noble pose and unity of mass of the one on the tree being especially impressive, while the mere execution of the female below is even finer. Thus the head of the latter, half turned on one side, is drawn with such knowledge, that it projects from the picture with solidity, although it is relieved by no shading. The execution of all the feathers, especially the smaller ones about the neck, is very fine, and exhibits Ōkio's peculiar masterly technique. As a whole the picture impresses by its simple lines, and as a Japanese suggested, its greys and gradations are so managed as to give the impression of positive color. This is the only attempt I have ever heard of, of painting a peacock in ink alone. Mr. Kano says there is no doubt that this is genuine, and must be ranked in the second class of Okio, the composition being especially fine. Its fault is a certain stiffness which is always visible in Okio's work. Mr. Hasegawa said it was genuine, as also Setsuan who greatly admired it. Bought in Tokio. Remounted by myself.

84. Group of large pine trees in snow landscape. Ippo. One of the finest landscapes of the Okio school. The conception is admirable, but the execution, in full harmony with it, is even greater, realizing winter to the full. The glorious masses of the ancient trees covered heavily with snow stand out in relief from the background of snow hills, as if seen through a stereoscope. The black edges of the trunks under the snow are so given as to help to produce this lively effect. Perhaps the greatest wonder is the execution of the snow lying on the pine foliage, which is mostly the white

ground of the silk, yet seeming to lie upon the outspread branches. Altogether the execution of this is so wonderful that one may fairly doubt if a European artist could begin to reproduce such an effect in water colors at all. Certainly it could not be done with any such simple direct means. This picture cannot be praised too highly, and with the badger No. 53. it proves the greatness of Ippo, as almost the rival of Okio. Mr. K. thought it very fine. He said Ippo was far greater than Seisen and almost equal to Okio. Mr. H. called it in the best style of the Okio school, far greater than the Richo waterfall. From Yamanaka

85. Quannon seated on a rock. Black drawing by Yasunobu. A very good specimen for this artist. The lines of the drapery are quite beautiful, and the expression of the face is really sweet and feminine. The masses of the rock are subdued and refined, the only deep black in the picture being in the head

and shoulders. Altogether there is a unity and a refined feeling in this picture and a style of finish, which I have nowhere else seen equalled by this artist. Mr. Kano calls it a very good one of the 2nd class. From King.

5. 86. Mountain landscape with rain. Hosen. This is hardly more than a sketch, and needs no description. The mountain dome above is noble with light on its edge. Mr. Kano said it was painted when the artist was young, that it is a common specimen, and more in the style of his father. 3d class.

5. 87. Female tiger and young. Ganku. Not so good as the preceding, No 80. This is much milder in expression and in drawing, less distinct, and less well composed. The rocks above are not strong either. The artist was less in earnest when he painted it. Still it is not a bad specimen for his common ones.

5, 88. Sketch of Shioki in red. Tetsuzan. In outlines merely, yet strongly put together and finely executed in lines of varying thickness. The expression of the face is very strong and peculiar, and the management of the drapery is original. Mr. Kano considered this to be a very good work of the Okio school, and a good typical specimen of this artist.

5, 89. Tiger coming down between two rocks to drink. Ganku. Very curious picture. Drawing distorted, face of tiger poor, stripes not blended, rocks bold but tremblingly executed. This is the poorest of my Ganku tigers, and it shows well the weakness of the old man in his last years. The manner of painting still however, retains much of its former glory, the giant inside of the artist refusing to die.

^{S} 90–1, & 2. Portraits of the two famous Yamat Tekkai Sennin. Chikanobu. These are painted in a rough shapeless style, hard and without inspiration. Yet Mr. Kano says that they are remarkably good specimens of this artist, being in his 2nd class. If this be so, it shows that Chikanobu had degenerated to a level far below his father. No. 2, the left one, is the best in every respect. To show the poorness of these, they should be compared with Ganki. No. 2 has some individuality worth noticing. Bought from King — Collection of same Kwazoku as before

^{S} 91. Mt. landscape in bunjinga style. Buncho. This exhibits well what attractive qualities bunjinga possesses. Soft grays make a background for a few black queerly shaped touches and some trees of darker mark. This is meant to be hardly more than symbolical painting, still it contains a picturesqueness and free artistic execution recognizable by the unprejudiced eye. Mr. Kano called it a good one of the 2nd class of Buncho, and in the style of Taigado. All bunjin greatly admire it. Bought from Shimoda —

S. 92. Sauji and Karassu on a branch of a tree covered with snow. Hanabusa Itcho. A very odd picture in Itcho's clever unexpected style of composition. The two birds one pure white and the other pure black stand one above another but facing in opposite directions. A vine with red berries winds round the branches and falls from above, these spots of blood red, giving the only color in the picture. The picture is striking and bold, and full of genius. Mr. Kano says it is undoubtedly genuine, although its execution is not very masterly for Itcho.

S. 93. Portrait of the Sennin, Oshikio. By Gido of the Shijo school. This is a hasty sketch, but has the excellencies of the Okio rapid manner. The man sits leaning against a rock, an axe in his hand, and with a rapt upward gazing face. This somewhat approaches bunjinga in manner. Mr. Kano called it good; and it is such as Japanese of modern taste admire.

S. 94. Tobosaku. Ranko. This picture, though small is excellent in all respects, drawing, shading, artistic touch, and expression. Especially well is the avaricious delight of the robber shown, as he lifts to his lips the coveted form of the magic peach. Mr. Karu thought it fine.

S. 95. Birds & flowers. Banzan. A little better than this artist's ordinary work. In his 2nd class perhaps. Shows the increasing weakness of the Nanping school. The color is rather good.

S. 96. Branch of cherry tree and water. Mochi-zuki Giokusen, the son of Gankei's pupil. This is a sketch made for me at Kioto in 1882. The artist seems to have left the Gankei style, and to have been absorbed into the commonplace of the degenerate Okio.

S. 97. Plum tree and roses. Korrun, the young daughter of Nmkin. Childish, but interesting on that account.

S. 98. Eagle on a rock with water below. Munkiu. This is strong for Munkiu, but shows that strength is not Munkiu's strong point. The color is harsh, and the waves are thin and splashy. Still it is original among modern productions.

S. 99. Narrow mountain landscape in black. Tame Hoichi. This is common, but good and honest in effect. Shows the "Commoner" sort of good painting. (?) Since found that this is Hokusai.

100. Eagle on pine tree by Kano Utanosuke. This is one of the most celebrated paintings of Utanosuke, and perhaps the best of the few now remaining. Kano Moritaka has in his collection a copy of this made by Tanin. It was celebrated through this copy for years in the Kano family; but they never knew what had become of the original. I bought it in the summer of 1881, at Yamanaka's, Osaka. Utanosuke rarely painted such large pictures, Mr. Kano says. The bird is the finest eagle I have seen in Japanese art.

It seems to have the nobleness and keenness of a supernatural being. The pine tree is very powerful, and somewhat in the style of his father. The spikes of the leaves however have been retouched by a later hand, according to Kano Yeitoku, who took the greatest interest in examining it. The rest of the work is finely preserved. This picture almost reaches the simplicity and unconscious grandeur of the "great works" of So. Indeed it is not impossible that it may be a copy of a great Chinese work, but this is unfounded conjecture. The seal is genuine. Facsimiles of the two seals are to found in Honcho Gashi. It is considered by all the Tokio critics one of the finest of old Japanese paintings. It is believed to have come from the Konoke collection, Osaka. The grandeur of it consists. Possibly it belonged to the Hachisuka collection. One of the finest Kakemonos in existence. All Japanese are carried away by it.

Gone here on Sept. March 1883

S. 101. Monkeys on a cherry tree swinging in the wind and rain. Sosen. Of all the finely i.e. minutely executed pictures of monkeys by this artist, this is on the whole the best I have ever seen. The criticisms made on Nos. 13 & 44 must in this case be taken back. Sosen here reaches great artistic heights. The cherry tree is considered by Jap. artists to be a splendid piece of painting. The composition with its lines of repetition is perfect. As for the rest the picture describes itself. Bought in Kioto Summer of 1881. All Japanese to whom I have shown it consider it to be of the best of Sosen's first class. Formerly belonged to the collection of a Kioto gentleman.

102. Small Chinese landscape. Shubun. In his characteristic style, with his strange scratchy etching like touches. Its goodness lies in an elevation of poetic sentiment approaching the Chinese. A copy of this picture by one of the descendants of Tanin is in the collection

of Kano Moritaka. All the Tokio artists agree that this is a genuine Shubun. To me it is certain that this is the genuine work of this artist. No other touch is just like it in the history of Eastern art. In comparing Moritaka's copy with this, it was clear the former was copied from this identical picture. Obtained from an Osaka dealer who bought it from the collection of the Konoke family. Mr. Kanda had never seen such a fine specimen of Shubun. Some critics think that the seal was put on afterward.

Sc. 103. Chinese landscape and palace. By Bun-o, Son of Buncho. This is one of the finest specimens of Bun-o's original style, which is more regular if weaker than his father's. This landscape is very impressive, and gives one a pure Chinese impression. This is remarkable for a style which is not itself derived from the Chinese as the Kano is. But indeed Mr. Kano Tettoku says that the foreground including the trees and man are almost copied from a design by Kakei; the touch of the brush however is somewhat different and more stiff. Its magnificence of composition is undoubtedly from Kakei. As for the palace, the style of it is derived from Kuntaku & Kameiyen. The upper rocks however are much in the Buncho manner, rather artificial, and lacking the freedom and blending of the great Chinese masters. The gradations throughout the whole picture are extremely beautiful, and though not managed at all like the Chinese, yet are so fine as to make up for some lack of strength in the drawing. Indeed then the work is notable, since it is an original conception of the very Chineseness of Chinese, recalling the very masters themselves, yet not like them. It is like perfect moonlight after the sun. This artist has not been so celebrated in Japan as he deserves. He is one of the best of modern times. Bought from King.

5. 104. Mountains and mist in moonlight. Bunsin. Remarkably poetic. Style of Giok-Ran with Bunninish modifications. The writing on the picture says "this is the night before the full moon — the nearest approach

the effect of moonlight breaking through clouds in Jap. art. The Kanos admire it. Fr. Yamanaka.

5. 105. Hotei. by Keishoki. This though small is most characteristic of Keishoki's touch, and can be put in his second class. He is tickling his nose to make himself sneeze. On the box is written "Picture of Hotei about to sneeze". The cloth mounting is very old. Bought in Tokio. Criticized as genuine by Kano Yeitoku & Kano Tomonobu. All Tokio gentlemen consider fine. Kawasaki thinks first class. Sumiyoshi thinks cloth remarkably fine.

× ? 106. Small landscape in rain. Toyohiko. Simple and characteristic of this artist's style. The silvery tones on the foreground water as of sun shining through the shower, were intended for this, and are simply beautiful. This is Toyohiko's ordinary style. 106. Tosa Mitsushige — Rakan.

S. 107. Kaido flower and Shijukara bird. Matsumura Keibun. The most beautiful painting by Keibun I have ever seen.

Bought in Osaka. This shows the greatest height reached by flower painting of the pure Okio school. Lightness of touch, grace of form, and beauty of color are very notable. In the first class of Keibun. Bought from Uyemura, who in former years bought many first class things from good families, that had been pawned. All the Tokio artists consider it 1st class of Keibun.

On the box is preserved a letter signed by Keibun acknowledging to the owner the receipt of the price of this picture which had just been painted for him, 5 bus (at that time).

S. 108. Bamboo in Snow and Sparrows. Keibun. Mostly in grey. Almost as beautiful as the preceding. The box is not

the true one belonging to this picture, therefore the writing on it has no significance.
This is perhaps the finest black flower and bird painting of the Okio school. From Osaka.
Considered by artists to be 1st class of Keibun.
It was one of a set of 3, belonging to Nishio Bankichi which he broke.

109. Keishoki. Small colored landscape. A beautiful little bit of Chinese scenery in the more angular style used by Geiami in his colored pictures, and partly borrowed from Shubun. Mr. Kano considered this genuine, and a very interesting fine and rare landscape. It recalls the landscape feeling of the Sentopind in China. The color is thin & harmonious. The very roughness of stroke is the sign of its freedom & feeling.

110. Buddhist painting of Monju on a lion. Kose Toshihisa. The lines of the figure are very delicate, though the lion is too stiff. The coloring however is very rich, and still shows the influence of Kanaoka. It says on the back of this that it is by Bunkan Shonin.

Kano himself considers the picture 900 yp. old.
This writing however is of a much later date,
~~Kawasaki Mitsuo~~ says time of Tametaka.
and by no means to be trusted. The present
Sumiyoshi of Tokio, the most able critic of
such pictures in Japan, assures me it is by Kose
Yoshihisa, and his opinion is probably correct.
I can see myself that it shows all the char-
acteristics of the later Kose school, somewhat
weakened by an admixture of Tosa element.
 On the outside it says that this picture
was dedicated (to some temple) on Dec.
25th, 9th year of Anyei. The box does not
belong to the picture. Bought in Osaka.
A very fine specimen of middle age Buddhist
painting. Mr. Kano considers this better than Fiso. No. 1.
He thinks inside cloth as old as the picture.
 III. Choso sitting on a pine tree.
 Ganki. This is declared by him one to be genuine.
I saw it in Kodaiji Kioto in Summer of 1880, where it was the
property of the priest. We could not then agree about
the price. In the summer of 1881 I saw it again, and
finally bought it for 50 yen, the priest considering that
he presented it to me as a favor. The certificate accompanying is a genuine one by Tanin, his handwriting being at once identified by the Kanos.

Mr. Kano Tomonobu criticized it as genuine before my buying it. Kano Yeitoku confirmed it. No one dissents.

The perfection of powerful simple stroke is in it. But the great point is the face with its intense expression, and magnificent drawing. The very soul of this second St. Simon Stylites, with his magical Sennin power, gleams through his eyes. He sits on a nest in a pine tree, which can just be descerned below. A cloud obscures part of the picture on the right. It has probably been reduced a little in size, though not greatly Mr. Kano thinks.

112. Fine Shaka on a Throne. Takuma Tamehisa. The lines of this are considered very fine. Kano Tomonobu criticized it to be by Tamehisa. Yeitoku is sure it is Tamehisa. Matsuura, Ninagawa, & Kiosai agreed it was Tamehisa. Sumiyoshi, on the other hand, at first sight, said it was not very good, not Japanese at all, probably some unknown Chinese. In Dec. 1882, about a year after, he saw

it again, and at once pronounced it to be Japanese & by Kose Arihisa, considering it quite fine. This contradiction takes away much of the weight his criticism would otherwise have had. To me it appears clear, that the strokes are not at all in Kose style, but decidedly in that of Takuma. It was bought from the magnificent collection of the priest of Daiyoji, Tokio, and has always been considered to be by Tamehisa. Its ends are rock crystal. Sumiyoshi said the cloth was very fine, though of course comparatively new. Kawasaki says silk not older than 600 yrs. Yamana says Chinese.

S. 113. picture of the banks of Sumidagawa Sukoku. Very characteristic. Temple of Ushi no Gozen in the distance. It is Spring. Mists are over the rice fields. Cherry trees are in blossom. Farm houses peep from under clusters of trees. Ferry boats and fishing boats are plying in the river. This is perhaps the finest of Japanese landscapes in Kano style, the main Kano school chiefly painting Chinese landscapes or in a Chinese manner. This gives almost the exact appearance of the scene, but with high artistic generalizations. The pleasure parties in the boats and the scenes on the banks are interesting. Crows fly away over the fields. This is in the first class of Sukoku. The box has nothing to do with this picture. This well shows Yedo suburbs 200 years ago. Mr. Kano, and all artists say this is the finest small work of Sukoku.

5/114. 1-2 A set of 2 snow landscapes. by Genki, by some considered the best pupil of Okio.

No. 1. Shows a small farming hamlet high on the mountain side and half buried in snow. The tone and execution of this are most tender and pure. All is most beautifully and finely rendered. The effect is less bold than in Oppo's landscapes, but more poetical and refined. Indeed this realizes in the Okio manner landscape feeling of the best Chinese period.

No. 2. Shows a ravine in the side of a mountain. This is more clever than deep feeling. Snow and ice are in the ravine, but a stream falls out below.

On the pictures it says Genki copied this, wh. undoubtedly means that it was copied from nature. It also says it was done in the autumn. The snow falls early on the heights around Kioto. The pure tone of the mounting cloth harmonizes with the soft delicacy of the picture. Mr. Kano considers this better than Ippo, indeed one of finest things of Shijo school. First class of Genki.

S. 115.$^{1-2}$ A set of 2 small landscapes. Buncho. These are characteristic of the artist, with their high rocks, half shadows, mild mists, and vigorous foregrounds. These have true atmospheric tones. There is some element of Kakei in them, and a little of Okio.

No. 1. has a palace built over a brook in the immediate foreground, a Chinese scene.

No. 2. has a man crossing a bridge in the immediate foreground. These have more freedom than any Japanese modern painting, except the best of Ganku. Both are autumn scenes. Kiosai doubted if they were genuine. Kano says they are fine for his youth, 30 yrs. old. The idea much like Sesson. He says it is a good specimen of his ordinary work. Matsuwra considered them genuine.

116. Kano   Kanzan + Jittoku

S. 117.¹⁻² A set of 2, dragon & tiger, by Goshun. These are queer specimens, especially the tiger. The dragon is in Goshun's ordinary manner, when he is painting after Okio style. This dragon is No.1. The upward whirl of cloud with its black opening is Okioishi. The dragon himself has original power, and his soft group look as if he were clothed in an armor of steel. The plum branch is in his own rapid manner. No. 2, the tiger, is probably an experiment of his with a very soft hair brush such as is used in some kinds of bunjinga. I have never seen any other picture of any artist painted in the same touch. The Japanese artists do not like it, for it does not fall into any of their categories. Foreigners do not like it, because it looks unnatural. I alone see the artist's intent, and his high degree of success. The tiger is half sleeping in the sun. The touches of bamboo are masterly. The beauty of black and white is high. Kano considered the touch in tiger very original. I have since found that this use of "soft brush" was one of Goshun's regular methods. Undoubtedly genuine & good specimens. Bought in Kioto, at Sagakichi's.

S. 118. A small painting of a group of monkeys. Sosen. This is in his middling rough style. The hair is mostly in broad washes. The faces are most artistically painted. The composition is not striking, but the monkeys themselves are interesting in action. The box does not belong to the picture. All critics consider them genuine. remounted by me.

S. 119. Three wild ducks standing on the edge of a frozen pond. By Manju. There is no composition here, and the picture is extraordinarily simple. But the interest centres in the ducks themselves which are most beautifully painted with soft grays. The legs are a little weak. Mr. Kano and others say this is so fine in execution, it might almost be mistaken for Okio's. Indeed there is hardly any difference between these and Okio's ducks. The tones of grey in their plumage are almost unsurpassed. The box tells the subject on the outside. & Bap says "Two wild ducks on a Snowy Shore. design". Manju must be one of the pupils of Okio.

120. Kano Motonobu. large black pine & birds.

S. 121. Rough landscape. Ganku. This is in the rugged picturesque manner of Ganku's later years. This probably represents the summer house of rustic build belonging to some man who loves tea ceremonies, by the side of a lake. Two men are starting off for an aesthetic picnic with their lunch baskets. The faces are dots and blurs like Turner's. The box does not belong to the picture. Kano considers it in Ganku's ordinary style. This is Chinese scene & Kano confirms it is picnic, box differents

122. Small landscape. Oguri Sotan. The works of this artist are extremely rare, and this is an especially fine one. The crystalline rocks, and the pine trees are painted in a style of his own, though somewhat reminding of Bayen. The distance reminds quite strongly of Shubun. The bit of clouded sky beyond the mountains is a touch of naturalism not often found in old pictures. The effect of distance is finely rendered. Indeed the whole work is superior

to that of Shubun No. 102.). The cloth is very old. The following poem is written above the picture."

* The mountains are blue and the water green. How old is that temple?! The mist is hanging from the top of the pagoda." On the inside of the box is written a certificate of genuineness, by some one whose name cannot be easily read. It says the poem was written by Made no Ocho, and his seal is on the picture. The outside of the box mentions Made Koji as the writer of the comment. Madeno Koji or Manoi no Koji was priest of Sokokuji, where Sotan lived; also called Shitsuto Ocho, and also Baigan. Common name Dzuikin. Lived in the era Onin. Both Kano Seitoku & Tomonobu, criticize it to be a fine specimen of Sotan. His works very rare. Formerly in Konoike collection in Osaka. Nomura and Kashiwagi consider it fine.

S. 123. 1—2. Landscapes by Bunrin. No. 1 is a winter or rather early spring landscape. The snow is melting away from the foreground under the genial sun. The fresh green of bushes and young verdure is appearing beneath the late snow. A plum tree is just breaking into blossom. Others are not yet ready for it. A fisherman is spreading his net on the river in the foreground. Beyond rises the as yet unbroken dome of snow. The atmosphere is filled with damp which for the moment half obscures the sun. This is the most delicate and delicious painting of Bunsen I have seen; without any unnatural straining after effect, and yet showing his original genius in its purest phases. No. 2. is far less successful. The artist failed to realize fully what he aimed at, having broken up the unity of the whole. Yet parts are interesting. He intended to represent the sun shining through the clouds of a breaking storm; the rain still falling; the mountain stream falling like a cataract, trees & rocks wet; the whole scene lying on the side of a mountain, and some foresters just about to cross the swollen stream on a dangerous bridge. The sun shows the upper mountain white against a fragment of dark storm-cloud. When looked at in the light of this original attempt the picture becomes interesting. He failed chiefly through attempting to introduce color. This represents a fall scene.

S. 124. 1–3. As set by Tanin. No. 1. is a landscape of powerful composition. No. 2. a Fukusuken jiu. No. 3. a landscape still more powerful. The letters on the black box are written in silver. This is a very powerful set, bought fr. Yamanaka. When the two Kano's saw it, they at once called it very bad, an imitation by some ignorant fellow, much to my surprise. Of course great weight is due to their testimony. On the other hand Matsuura the Antiquarian went into raptures over them, and said that they were the finest set he had ever seen, such hardly ever to be found again. Hasegawa Settei also, after careful inspection pronounced them to be in the 1st class of Tanin. Kiosai thought them fine, tho' not quite up to 1st class. My own impression is that they are genuine & fine. The roughnesses about them are frequent on other Tanin's declared genuine by the Kano's, and in many qualities they are better than some they endorse. Tamiyoshi in presence of the two Kanos, could not help contradicting them, and calling them quite fine. Fumiyoshi thinks signatures good.

125. Yoshinobu, Yoshitsune on horseback. This is one of a former set of three, of which two were sold to Mr. George Emery. It is a "good 2nd class" specimen of the artist, and is almost a copy from a famous design of Tanyu. The coloring is well done.

126. Sosen Akinobu - Chinese pheasants.

127. Seiko. Bridge at Tofukuji in Fall. This is quite beautiful. Good for recent Shijo. The subject is interesting on account of association with Cho Densu's life.

128. Tsurugawa Tansen. Stork Sun & waves.

129. Tansetsu, storks and plum

This is a common specimen. Already is far toward the uninspired degeneration of the Tanyu style.

S. 130. 1-3. Large paintings by Seisen. These are very handsomely mounted, and were undoubtedly painted to the order of some prominent Daimio man. The leaves on the bottom are probably the crest of some Daimio. They are in Seisen's finest style of execution, and almost recall the strong days of Chinese painting. Altogether they make one of the handsomest sets of Kakemonos in existence, though their subjects are not especially interesting.

No. 1 is a group of botans and a rock. This is apure Chinese style, and if not copied directly, is in close imitation of some painting by Ojiakusai or Chosho. The rock is finely painted, showing the best work of later Kano style, and the small botan shrub, the bamboo and dandelion at the bottom are nearly perfect in their way. The upper leaves are almost exactly copied from Ojiakusai.

No. 2. The Buddhist lion, sitting with Rakan-like contemplation at the entrance of his den. A Corean friend said he looked like Daruma.

This is quite in the style of Isen, but the color is more muddy. It is one of the strongest paintings of the latest Kano. The finest points are the leaves and grasses hanging from the rocks, and the broken foreground under the signature. These points remind one of Chinese So + Gen painting. Indeed it is possible that this design is taken wholly from a Chinese original, now lost.

No. 3. This is another botan picture, but less well composed than the other, and fewer interesting points. It is copied either in whole or part from some Chinese flower picture, and shows just what Chosho must have looked like, when he was new. There is a decided nobleness about these pictures in spite of their defects.

These three represent subjects symbolical of Monju.

Kano considers them 1st class of Seisen Yeitoku Says about 30 years old, when painted

131. Kionobu — 4 sleepers.

132. Josen Yukinobu, Tobosaku.
Not a celebrated artist. His works are rare. Ancestor of Tomonobu, who says this is a very fine specimen of him. It is indeed better than most post-Tsunenobu work, being nearly up to that master. Indeed Josen is already full of the new excellence which was lighting up Chisen, and founding the fourth movement in the Kano school.

133. Yukinobu, figures.

134. Jorin Yoshinobu - mellow & Sangi.

135. Shubun 2 small landscapes in circle.

136. Kano Yusen   netsu. Kiku.
The mounting of Kiku cloth is in harmony
with the picture. Formerly one of a set of
3 owned by Yamanaka. Tomonobu praised
it as very good for this artist. It is tender
and the coloring is soft. A representative
specimen of the work of the subordinate
Kanos of the day —

137. Yusei – Squirrel & chestnuts

138. Ganki – Sennin

139. Hunter seeking deer. Hokusai. This is a rare specimen, H.'s painted work being extremely scarce. The strange color, like oil, and the peculiar method of drawing are easily recognizable. (Many bad forgeries of Hokusai are now being made for foreigners.) His true touch is firm though grotesque. Every critic says this is genuine. Not so good as Kōmei picture, signed "Hokusai"

very characteristic of Hokusai's later manner.

H. 140. Scene on Lake Seiko. By Wankoku Togan, the socalled 6th from Sesshu (including S. as No. 1.) Sumiyoshi says subject is Seiko, Sugrahiro says 6th from Sesshu. Boye says Wankoku Hogen. Sumiyoshi says good picture.

S. 141. Quiet winter scene. Kiho. This although executed in rough style, and therefore not so well appreciated by Japanese; is really a fine work of genius; since what degree of dark and light and what color there is, is so managed, as to give at the distance of 25 feet a strong realistic impression. This is a simple farm among the mountains. The plum blossoms are almost coming out under the snow. The half frozen brook feels its way along its bed. This is a Chinese landscape

S. 142. Group of growing flowers. Hoitsu. This is one of the most splendid specimens of the Korin style. The grace of form and richness of color speak for themselves. The method of grading leaves is quite like Korin. Sumiyoshi says genuine, tho' not great Specimen. Kano thinks fine —

S. 143. Large picture of a Rakan. Kawo. This is very powerful, the expression of face intense. The hand is too small. Mr Kano says this is surely not Nen Kawo, the touch being different; and thinks perhaps it may be by another Kawo at the time of San-setsu. On the other hand Matsuura says it is genuine Kawo, made with soft brush; Hasegawa said it was Kao after taking it home to criticize; Kucien guessed it was Kao from a distance, without seeing bag or seal. It is a question hard to determine.

Kano says it is nothing very good. Everybody else thinks it a very fine thing, whether it be by Kao or not. The seal appears to be a genuine old one. It is true, that it appears to me to be unlike Kao's ordinary works, although very fine. Kiosai said that the rocks are drawn like Kao, and no one else would do such a Daruma. This he says, is the Rambioshi, style of touch like oar leaves. This is Kao's usual style, and this is finest specimen of Kao, he says. Kashiwagi said that seal looks genuine, and that only reason for not calling it Kao was be its unusual style. He considered it a fine work. So also Nomura. Sumiyoshi thinks not older than 300 yrs. I think really Kao —

S. 144. Peach blossoms, willow, and yellow birds. Baiyten. Fine scratchy drawing. Coloring delicate and striking. Fine composition. Everybody admires this, Matsuura calling it the finest specimen of Baitōn. Birds are Ocho — Kano thinks fine — teacher of Katei of Tokio

S. 145 — 1 — 2. by Raisho. No 1. is pheasants and cherry blossoms. The color on the neck of the bird is good.

No. 2 is deer and flowers. This is soft and tender, but not great. These are the finest specimens of Raisho I have ever seen, and came from Kioto. All critics consider these to be in the first class of Raishi. They were originally exhibited at a government loan collection made for me in Kioto.

S. 146. Fujiyama, clouds, & landscape. Tangei. This was presented to me by Mr. Kodera's uncle, of Himeji, to whom I sent an oil painting of the Franconia Old Man on his 70th birthday. He was the teacher of Hōtei. A rare thing, & characteristic, though not very great. — Subject, Fuji, Seikenji Okitsu temple, Miwo Coast. Boxcar "Spring Fuji", Un gala Belair. Kiomigaseki on Tokaido, famous poem made there by courtiers.

S. 147. 1-3. Hōtei & 2 flower pieces. No. 1 is plum. No. 3 bamboo. Tanin. No. 2 Hōtei. Kano Eitoku called them common specimens of Tanin, painted at about the age of 50. This is correct. They are not great, but they are simple and pure, and well represent the type of those sweet

fine things, wh. spread throughout Japan, gave
Taniu his hold of the common appreciation, and
dominated the practice of artists. Genuine, but
only 3d class. No. 3 is Miyama hojiro bird (whitecheek)
Tomonobu says very likely painted at a dinner.

S. 148. 1–3.   Taniu. 2 storm dragons,
   & Shoki on a tiger.
The Kanos say of these that they are 1st class of
Tanui. Should say on general grounds that they are next
best to my Yuima set (No. 33); but the Fujiyama set
is in rarer style. Hasegawa thought them first class.
Kiosai called them first class. Matsumura thought
them fine, but not equal to Fukurokou set (No. 124). The
transparency of the ink, and purity, and high tone
is what the Kanos admire in them. Inside
of box certified by Kohitsu, professional
judge of handwriting.

S. 149. 1-3. Chokuan the 2nd.

This is a very fine set of a very fine artist. 1 is the hawk on willow branch; 2 the hawk grasping heron, 3 the hawk pouncing on duck. Greatest hawk painter of Japan. Ink & strokes tremendous & artistic. Matsuura said he had never seen a painting of willow so fine as No. 1. Hasegawa said they were so fine, that they seemed to be by his father the 1st Chokuan. No. 1 indeed has elements of the 1st Chokuan. Kiosai never saw so fine a specimen before. The drawing + ink on no 1. is stupendous. Both this artist and his father were as celebrated for hawks and eagles, as Sosen is for monkeys. Kano Y. says a very fine specimen. Artist famous at his time. Afterwards forgotten for more careful school. He is decidedly inferior in power to his father. Mr. Nomura says very black touches are characteristic of Soga school. (?) No. 2 is reproduced in Gonse from a printed copy. Famous design. Bought from Yamanaka.

150. 1 – 3. Kimura Nagamitsu.

Lei toku says works of this artist are very rare. This is a very fine specimen. His style is peculiar to himself. All Japanese of pure literary taste admire it. Kashiwagi, & Nomura considers it among the most striking of my collection. In the homely unadorned design the free pure depths of feeling comes forth. The very carelessness of the execution is in harmony with its special ideality.

No. 1. Sennin lying in boat. poorest of the three. Sipo on tree above man sleeping.

No. 2. Kinzanji temple on Lake Sei ko. Meagre strange, and great. Touch has greatest power in a style afterward much used by Sanraku.

明石掃部頭

No. 3. Kantoshi in banishment. Noblest original expression of figures, equal to Motonobu. Horse is also splendidly conceived and executed. These are a good test as to whether one really perceives the high excellence of Japanese.

No other such striking work of this artist is known to exist. from Yamanaka.

S. 151. 1-2. Chikudō. (Chikutō). both of dragons and water. The outlines of dragons are taken from designs by Shoō, Seid says on pictures. But the forms are quite different from Shoō's, and the whole touch and style are original. Particularly the waves of No. 2 are noticeable as rendering frothy mass and not outline of splashes. Cloudy is pure and grand. The touch of brush is half bunjingwish, & half Okioish, specially in washes. Very grand, pure, pictures, high, original feeling, approaching great Chinese. Mr. Kano says that this method of painting foam is not entirely original since Tanin sometimes did it. Matsuura says much better than ordinary bunjinga landscapes of Chikutō. Can be considered as among his best works. He is a Kioto artist half of Shijō school. Bought in Kioto.

152. Quannon — Motonobu.
Mr. Kano said that Motonobu's portrait of Buddha sold by Shosen to Okurasho has been considered the best of Motonobu; but this can now be said to be better, therefore the greatest Motonobu in existence. It is not a copy from Godoshi as some supposed. An original work, M's best in both color and drawing. The Kanos in Tokio have a copy of this by Tanin; and they have been studying and copying this design

for ages, without ever having seen the original, or knowing when it was. A greater work than the colossal Nehanzo of Mot. at Miokakuji Kioto. For so old a picture on silk, this is well preserved. Has noblest feelings. Kano calls it the finest picture in my collection! The execution of the rocks is considered by Kano to be unsurpassed. The whole effect nearly rises to the simple grandeur of Godoshi. The starry effect of the white would not have been noticeable when new. The double halo is effective & original. Lines in drapery most powerful. The calm unearthly grandeur grows on one. Matsuura offered me 150 yen for it. It formerly belonged to the collection of the daimio Hachisuka of Awa. The touch in the rocks of this is absolutely uncopiable. In this Motonobu's style is merely the clearest form of expressing his idea of rock. instantaneous, inspired, not a manner. Of Motonobu middle period. Kashiwagi said it was finest picture in my collection. Yamanaka sold me this cheap, thinking it or calling it Cho Densu. Tanyu's copy of this afterward (1883) sold in Tokio for 350 yen. Has now become a celebrated work in Tokio, having been several times exhibited.

153. Shaka. Yeiken.
Mr. Kano says this is very fine and well painted. Done he thinks about the period of Tanin. The coloring is the best part of it. He says it is quite possible that the design is taken from old Chinese.

S. 154. Large tiger. Ganku.
Kiosai says this is equal to Ganku's peacock. Matsuura says good, but others as good can be found. Kashinagi considers almost equal to deer (No.) The fur is wet, & thus the usually blurred stripes are stippled. Also the wet gleam is well brought out on the top of the head. The air is full of driving mist. Some Japanese consider the bamboo especially fine, as Kano said, it is almost like Sesson. Probably in Ganku's later years. About best tiger of Ganku. Bought in Kioto.

Such large powerful tigers of Ganku are now very rare.

155. Yojo. Kwazan.

This represents Shin no Yojo, in the famous historical scene in which he attempts the life of the Chinese Emperor. It is a very large and remarkable specimen of figure painting. Its style is between that of Okio, and that of Ganku. The power of the picture is unmistakeable, and Japanese immediately exclaim at it. Coloring is also well done. Yokoyama Kwazan, who must be distinguished from Watanabe Kwazan, must be considered as one of the greatest artists of modern Kioto. The Mtg. is old and splendid, and harmonizes with the picture.

156. 1-3. Kano Yasunobu, set of 3, 2 landscapes and Fukurokuju.

Kano Yeitoku and all agree that these are absolutely 1st class of Yasunobu — drawing firm and clear, and color beautiful. Only equalled by the Kuanon of Yasunobu in Chishakuin, Kioto.

1. Best landscape. Clear pure atmosphere, delicious foreground. Total feeling very much like Sesshiu. Yet touch characteristic.

2. Fukuroku, deer, and stork, made into a circular design. This is done with the utmost cleverness, no circular outline being given. The lines in drapery here are the best of Yasunobu, the face also is most characteristic of his best work; also the color with its ivory softness is unsurpassed.

3. Snow landscape; this is poorer, and seems more like the degenerate works of the immediate descendants of Yasunobu.

The whole set is very noble and beautiful, and illustrates well the essential differences between this artist and his two brothers.

S. 157. Peacocks. Hoyen.
 Kiosai says this is very fine, but not equal to Gankei's peacock. Matsuura says very fine. Kanos also admire it. The drawing of the flower petals, and the delicate gradations of the leaves are noticeable. Whatever stiffness there may be in the birds, is derived from Okio. Composition fine. Such a carefully deep colored large bird piece of Hoyen is very rare. —Yamanaka—

S. 158. Rough monkeys. Sosen.
 Kiosai says this is the finest picture of the Shijo school he has ever seen. Matsuura says this style of Sosen is very rare. This is finer, he thinks than 101. I have never seen any other one in such a rough style. Kanos call it first class. All admire its amazing artistic power of execution. The fur is represented by coarse grading melty touches with a wide soft hair

brush. What knowledge is contained in such a head that can bring out such a thing by such means. This has a deep tone like the old masters, quite unlike Sosen's ordinary work. Really to be ranked with old masters. Bought in Kioto. All critics admire it. The best of Ronse's illustrations of Sosen are in this style. It is among his most powerful and artistic works. 1st class.

S 159. Peacock. Gankei. This is one of the most extraordinary of Japanese paintings. In it the wild genius of Gankei reaches high point. The bird with spread wing perched on the edge of the cliff, is like a demon bird. The leaves are finely painted, the two bits of red coming in with effect. This is unlike any other Eastern painting. The composition, subject and drawing spring from original vigor and ideas. The Kanos considered it very great. Gankei's style is unlike any Chinese. Such a picture of peacock is unique they say. It impresses one with great feelings. Hasegawa says that this is better than Nanping, although usually Nanping is better than both Gankei & Okio. Kiōsai thought it magnificent. It is in Gankei's sketchy style on paper. Greater I think, than Gankei's celebrated careful peacock in Kioto. Yamanaka. Probably toward the end of Gankei's middle period.

S. 160. 8 Gods of happiness. Kwazan the 8th one on the left is Otafuku, not the name of any particular person; any ugly woman is called Otafuku. This is a most clever picture, and well sustains the reputation of Kwazan. The Gods are slightly hilarious with saké. Benten pours more, with smiling face. Bisgamon is already overcome. It is very comical. The execution in the faces, and in the well flowing drapery is beyond all praise. It is not exaggerating to say that this is one of the best drawn pictures Japan ever produced.

161. Flowers and birds. Rioki?

Feitoku says this is poorer than Koyoshin. Not Rioki, or a copy. But a genuine unknown Min. Few know the genuine Rioki. Most called so are false. Hasegawa calls this a good genuine specimen of Rioki. My own opinion is that it is not genuine Rioki. All Tokio Riokis are false. Only 1 or 2 in Kioto are genuine. This is a good specimen of "Tokio Rioki". Since writing the above Mr. Nomura has critiqued this to be surely of Gen. The method of shading the rock shows it. There is an old seal on the side, not yet deciphered. I also think it to be of Gen, and quite fine.

162. Donohue. Wild Mountain landscape
This is inferior to Donohue's greater works, still it retains a measure of the artist's strange unearthly genius. It is half like Buson and the Makaroni school; but strange silvery lights play through it, and it has true landscape power.

163. Fukurokuju — Ganku

Kano Yeitoku says this may be called next best to Ganku's peacock. As to the subject, he says that children are considered a fortune. Fukuroku then with child is God of Fortune. I think this is doubtful. It is perhaps some forgotten legend of a child being carried off to the Sennin heaven to have long life conferred upon him. It was probably to hang up at a birth. Some think it may have been tried in imitation of a Christian painting. If not a legend, it is the genial expression of a hope or well-wishing to a child. Kashiwagi thinks this theory is correct. Kashiwagi says surely genuine. It is in Ganku's later style, and somewhat affected in drapery by Okio influence. Such foreshortening of a child's leg is a unique thing in Japanese art. Even a naked child is unique. Yamanaka

164. 2 deer, Ganku.

Yeitoku calls this very greatest of Ganku, far greater than Okio. Haryama says finest of Ganku. Okio more mild & noble, but not so strong. Matsuura says there is no other such Ganku in existence. Painted probably when about 40.

The mountain is the finest part. Every body is struck at the sight of this; and all say "we never knew Gankū could paint like that". Mr. Nakai admired it so much, that he carried it to Kioto to be copied by process on silk, but it could not be done. Bought in Tokio from Kin. Kashiwagi, Mr. Nomura, Mr. Saw all called it Gankū's finest work. The greatness lies first in natural conception of deer, in management of hair and spots, so as to bring out form in relief without shadows; the hair itself executed neither too fine nor too coarse; the Mt. behind, which may be considered equal to Sesshu in force & simplicity; the soft warm swimming atmosphere behind the deer in which the Mt. side seems to quiver. Japanese say this is equal to Okio, but it is far ahead of Okio. It is the greatest painting of modern times in Japan probably, Gankū being the only modern artist who in knowledge, vigor, + ideal feeling approaches Sesshū. Some Japanese consider the mountain the finest part of it. It is undoubtedly a work of Gankū's middle age, say about 40. [35?] Austin Robertson raved over it as the finest Kakemono he had ever seen, and far ahead of Landseer. It is one of the greatest animal paintings in the world.

165. Tree, flowers, & bird — Koyoshin. Mr. Kano Yeitoku says this is in the regular style of the famous bird painter at the beginning of Min. Hasegawa says the idea is better than Rioki, the execution not so good. All artists admire its grandeur of conception. The birds are the hahacho. I consider it one of the very finest of the Min bird pictures, equal to the finest genuine Rioki's. Its grandeur is almost unsurpassed in bird pieces. Its execution is not the greatest, but simple, vigorous, direct. Bought from Yamanaka. The strong dominating dark branch of the tree is grandly painted.

166.¹⁻² Toyohiko. Set of 2 landscapes.
      These are in the middle class. They are good and clear in execution.

167.¹⁻² Tsukioka Sessai – set of 2, figure pieces.
      These are not so strong as the works of his father Settei; but they are of much the same character. The coloring is careful and good.

S/68. 1-3, Naonobu set of 3. Daruma, heron and lotus.
300 yrs-old. First class Kano Yeitoku

S/69. 1-3. Tanshin Morimasa, set of 3, Rihaku, birds and flowers. 1st class of Tanshin, according to everybody.

S. 170. 1-3. Tanyu- copy from Masanobu set of 3. Confucius and 2 disciples.

S.171. Sueyori – black flowers and bird.
First class. In fine~ Kano Yeitoku

172. Motonobu. painted fan — figures.
 box says Kohogen - really Suyeyori in all probability - no seal. good average picture of Motonobu School, and interesting as showing the prevalent style of gilt fans.

S(173. Morikage— rough landscape, river scene
 Ueno[?] thinks signature is not genuine, and as to painting very risky. Tomonobu thought it one of finest landscapes ever seen, almost up to Sesshu. My own opinion is that it is surely genuine, clever and good; but too grotesque and meagre to be considered of high rank. It is typical however of a great deal that Morikage did, and was admired for in his day.

S. 174. Kano Yeino, small landscape "Scenery a poem in early Spring in Royri" on box. Yeitoku says fine. Works of this artist very rare. This retains traces of the proto Yu style of Kano painting. Tomonobu thought it very interesting and good.

S. 175. Kano Yosen Shuko, portrait, Shukotan — middle class, 50 yrs. old. says Yeitoku. A good typical specimen of Yosen's style in painting faces, and of later Kano work. Its excellence goes beyond mere form, and even reaches the sphere of high soulful expression.

S. 176. Shoyei - Spray of botans, colored.
Genuine Certificate by Yeishin & Otherwise Yeitoku would hardly think it genuine, lonesty middle
class he says. He thinks cloth paper repaired & Sumiyoshi thought fine. I say, one of the most splendid
flower paintings of early Kano. Tomonobu admired.
Color peculiar, rich and surprising, of a most
original and decorative tone. Most artistic.
Bought in Nagoya 1882.

S. 177. Chinese boys at palace gate, Hoyen.
This is one of the most delicate, pure, and
carefully thought-out and finished works of this
master.

S. 178. Kaihoku Yusetsu - Jurojin.
Very rare says Yeitoku. Roap says "Jurojin"
but both Kanos say surely Ninnas. A very
striking picture; having something of the
power of Sesshu in it.

S. 179. Geiami; small landscape.

S. 180. Soga Shotei. 2 horsemen. Small. Another name for Shohaku undoubtedly. Say Kano. "Jasokkers" on picture. Very fine. This is one of the most delicate works of Shohaku. Ink magnificent. Drawing of horses fine. A great work worthy of a great European artist. Every one admires.

S. 181. Kano Ko-Yeitoku - bird and flowers. colored. genuine, in gold, says Yeitoku picture only a little large in beginning Camellia flower. bird probably pigeon. Middle class, about 30 gm. so says Yeitoku. A good sample specimen, I think. It does not have the greater qualities of Yeitoku 3d clan

S. 182. Chorinsai. 2 young hawks. Small.

S. 183. 1-2. Tanyu — set of 2. Carp & waterfalls. Yeitoku Tanyu first class of Tanyus.

S. 184. Hoyen — Fine landscape with waterfall.

S. 185. 1-3. Tanyu. set of 3. Yokihi; birds & flowers. Small.
1. "Hakukanbird" & botan "on back." They (the Kanos) say Sanko bird
2. Yokihi, usually subject connected with botan.
3. Sanko bird & botan.

Yeitoku says these are first class of Tanyu. Suchfine timed ones of Tanyu are very rare indeed. Designs are his own, not Chinese. Done as early as 30 years old. Sumiyoshi says "worth 150 yen". Kanos say these and Unima set are best of Tanyu.

S. 186. Tsunenobu – branch of tree.
Fine Kclass of his youth say Kanos. Subject
parasitic cherry – signature genuine, 20 yrs old

S. 187. Yofu – small black landscape
Kanos & Sumiyoshi think fine

S. 188. Giokuraku – bird & branch, colored.
  Shijukara bird, Yeitoku says genuine
middle class – Flower is Mokugei, certificate
by Yeishuken genuine

*189. Yokoyama Kuazan. Colored landscape. Chinese scene. boy says "Good harvest". Men are drunk in congratulation of good times.

S.190. Hokusai. Colored landscape.

S. 191. Sukoku Copy of flowers & bird for Naturo.
Kawarahiwa bird — upper flower Mokugei.
All say a very medzurashi thing.

S. 192. Cho Densu. Seated Rakan colored.
"12th Rakan, Kadaka Daisa Sonja",
on top, writing on box by Tanyu, Yeitoku says
middle class, Sumiyoshi says genuine

193. Kano Sansetsu, dragon.
   gordai Tsunogoro Sama? Uiitokin Sama 1st rank
   of middle class.

S. 194. Kano Tohaku Hotei.
   name Tohaku Chikanobu, Kano Think

S. 195. Buzen— night landscape, small.

S. 196. Goshun— landscape,

S. 197. Kaihoku Yusho, Kinko Sennin,
Yeitoku says middle class, Sumiyoshi says good

S. 198. Tosa Mitsuoki, Figure piece, male, one of the 6 brooks famous in poetry, Tamagawa of Yamashiro, Manhoseibachi Shunjei, the Court poet who made the poem about this river. The poem itself is written on the picture, "I will stop my horse, and make it drink of the Tamagawa, whose clean water gives dews to this yamabuki". (Yellow flower)
Very different.

S. 199. Seiki — landscape.
Subject is Togen scenni of peach valley.
Not different.

S. 200. Kano Chikanobu. 3 happy gods. Middle class says Ukitoku — formerly one of set of 3 — 40 yr. old says Kano. Sitzel Hotei Yebisu & Daikoku.

S. 201. Gido. Daikoku

S. 202. Gido. 8 Sennin — Kano don't know what the Sennin are doing — but the small circles above are stars

S. 203. Oguri Sōtetsu, birds and flowers

S. 204. Yamada Dōan - bird on branch bird is Jutaichō. Kano & Sumiyoshi say gwd. His pictures rare. Jutaicho means "longevity-carrying bird."

S. 205. Tosa Mitsunari - female figure. 1st class of Mitsunari says Sumiyoshi - Boy says "Court Lady under a Cherry. 4th Comment by an imperial relation."

S: 206. Kano Atsunobu. Yuseki. The 3 Founders pictures of Sosen's ancestors are very rare. This is good & interesting. Sumiyoshi says (said) poem says "Dries when touched by the lips. There is no taste to this sweet dew." Kanos never saw before.

S: 207. Ikkin, sketch of tree and bird.

S. 208. Nikka - Charcoal burning.

S. 209. Tanyu. Portrait of Chinese Emperor
Yeitoku says middle class. So Sumiyoshi -
Emperor in Bureau of Shin - Signature Sword
Hogen - about 50 years 0)

S. 210. Yosai. Kuanon.
Yosai when old. Kano & Sumiyoshi say
genuine.

211. Nagaku — monkey on rock.

212. Tsukioka Settei, Group of women — He says "Prostitutes of 3 cities". Yeitoku thinks made figure Tokio, Sumiyoshi thinks life in Kioto, age 67. Sumiyoshi says intensely fine thing.

213. Toyokuni — figures & screens. Subject "Upper classed Genji" etc. This is 2nd Toyokuni whose first name was Kunisada. He was artist who illustrated the novel of Genji. Intensely fine thing, all say.

S.214. Unkinobu. Figures and boat. Subject Hanrei + seishi. Yeitoku says middle class. Sumiyoshi says better than Kenjo box says Yokihi — is wrong.

S.215. Tosa Mitsutada. Horai. Sumiyoshi says genuine, painted about Kempo.

S.216. Ganrei. Landscape with canal.

S. 217, Kano Takanobu, Rihaku.
Yeitoku thinks that style not so modified by time
of Takanobu - perhaps by Koi's son.

S. 218, Bunrin, Large snow landscape.

S. 219. Josui, Great waterfall

S. 220. Soshiseki - rooster and flowers

S. 221, 1-2. Tanshin, Morimasa. set of 2, Chinese landscapes.
Subject four seasons. Kano Say genuine

S. 222, 1-2. Nishikawa Tsukenobu. set of 2, female figures.
Sumiyoshi thinks later and false. Yeitoku thinks fine. Tomano surely genuine & fine. Sumiyoshi is mistaken about his age. Unkoku was pupil of Matahei. Much later I say. The girls are portraits of those who wrote the annexed poems.

223. Shokado – portrait of Yamabe no Akahito (one of poets)
genuine says Yeitoku — Sumiyoshi.

224. Ashikaga Yoshimochi. Toba
some say subject is Yoshimi – probably Toba
says Yeitoku. Yeitoku says genuine. Formerly
had Jiun certificate says he; Certificate by
Kohitsu Riohan.

S. 225. Jowun. heron and lotus.
1st class say both Kano & Sumiyoshi. something
equal to Tanyu. Chajin would like it, the
most chajin thing

226. Morikage — Toba.
Middle class say Sumiyoshi & Kaitoku
genuine. Kaitoku has copy. Cloth fine
This is a tea man's picture say Sumiyoshi

S. 227. Shohaku. horses.
Sumiyoshi thinks interesting

S. 228. 1-2. Kano Mitsunobu – Set of 2.
landscapes

S. 229. Tosa Mitsubumi. 7 gods
Good for him says Sumiyoshi, but not much of an
artist. Name to be pronounced 'Mitsunaya'

S¹ 230, Donshu Tengu and birds,
"Made in Kayei" subject King of Tengus and the birds are attendant Tengus,

S¹ 231, Morikage Botans,
all say first class. rarest thing he ever. made.
known "Mugeisai" is names.

S¹ 232, Kwakei - Burning of Eastern Hongwanji
"Higashi Hongwanji fire" - autry

S. 233. Copy of Chinese landscapes falsely said to be by Isen.

S. 234. Maruyama Oshin, wide landscape Ambos says "Green trees & spring rain Arashiyama".

S. 235. Kano Kiuyen — heron and lotus. Sumiyaki things rather interesting — good for Kiuyen, a rare thing. Kano says genuine. This Kiuyen he thinks is about Genroku period.

S. 236, 1-3. Kano Yosen — set of 3, Jurojin and dragons.
Upper class of middle rank, very good, says Yeitoku Sumiyoshi that very fine, middle subject. Jero taken fr Sesshu's design with modifications.

S. 237. Hiakkoku, lotus and bird, finely painted, by Tomonobu & Sumiyoshi. Both is different, tho' name is same.

S,238. 1-3. Kano Yeishuku. set of 3.
Jurojin, and landscapes.
1. Spring + summer. 2 Jurojin 3. autumn
+ winter; waterfall is sign of summer, because then
liked best. First class of Yeishuku says Yei Tokio

S,239. Seisen. Copy of Chinese landscape by Sonkuntakio.
original owned by Tokugawa Mayji Hitotsubashi.
good copy

S. 240, Kano Chikanobu. Willow & Swallows.
First class say all painted at same time as
Chikanobu 242, about 30 yrs old. Swallows
migrate hither when willow are green.

S. 241, Kano Tsunenobu Fukurokuju.
Ueitoku thinks painted when young. 30 yrs. or so.
3d class

S. 242, Kano Minenobu. bamboo snow & sparrows,
very good says Ueitoku & middle class say Tomonobu
sparrow is an honest bird, eats only little worms that
grow on bamboo.

S. 243¹⁻² Genya - set of 2. Small landscapes
very fine say Yeitoku & Sumiyoshi probably
2 of an original hakkei.

S. 244¹⁻² Kawo - set of 2. Kanzan & Jittoku
Yeitoku thinks false - that is, very old copies.
Sumiyoshi thinks genuine & fine.

S. 245.¹⁻² Hasegawa Tohaku. set of 2. Landscapes
very fine copies of Choshun Motonobu + one
middle class of Tohaku.

S. 246, 1-2. Toshun set of 2, figures. Subject is the preservation of health by Seninshin by sneezing no 1. & shampooing No. 2, Ueitoku thinks surely older than Motonobu & by the original Doki Toshun, pupil of Chukwan Sumyoshi says fine & rare.

S. 247, 1-3. Kano Toshun set of 3. plums &c. Ueitoku says surely by old Toshun Sumiyoshi says cloth very fine & rare — pine & plum arranged in style of flower arranging art. good pictural artist set used for congratulations. pine is young pine. Surely a New Year set. No. 3 is the best one says Ueitoku.

S. 248. 1-3. Kano Yusei ~~Tsunobu~~ Tara-. set of 3.
Sun & waterfalls.
Yeitoku says middle class of him
1. of Kegon waterfall at Nikko.
2. middle sun & water. Sumiyoshi says finely done
3. Jakko waterfall. Nikko. —
Sumiyoshi says fine set

S. 249. 1-2. Kano Samboku, Set of 2, Storks,
Man who painted very little? Said to have
spent his life in playing go. Sumiyoshi thinks
a fine set good monkey

S. 250,¹·² Kano Gsen. Set of 2, botans.
Was 20 years old — says Yeitoku. First class
for his young years. Used on congratulatory
occasions, my fine + his own designs, not
copied from Chinese says Yeitoku

S. 251, 1-2. Kano   , Set of 2, flowers
in ink. He (Yeitoku & Sumiyoshi) think seal
on 2 is genuine, on 1 is false — perhaps from screen
Sumiyoshi says by some pupil using Yeitoku's seal

S. 252, 1-3. Tosa Mitsuyoshi, Set of 3, storks and quail. Very good set for him, but not very good in itself. Except quail, the subjects signify happiness & good wishes. 1. Kiku & quails 2. storks & pine 3. corn & quail.

S. 253. Kano Naonobu — Toemmei. Painted when about 20 says Tomotada, good rough not tea picture. But this rough picture ordinary loved because he was a great tea man himself, and for simplicity.

S. 254. Hoyen Landscape of Biodoin, boxes different.

S. 255. Icho, piper and toys. seller of cake + midzname toys. Sumiyoshi boy has cake, + barrel arm — umbrellas large fan is his sign. Man has dress of foreigner with false beard, blow pipe to attract children. Yei-toku thinks a copy. Sumiyoshi thinks fine. Kano M— Morch thinks fine

S. 256. Yogetsu Hotei.
Yeitoku says signature is very fine & very good
Signature "Shakushu Yogetsu". Yeitoku says
first class.

257. Kano _____ . hawk and bird.

S. 258. Minenobu — Sparrow & rice field.
Yeitoku & Tomonobu say first class.

S. 259. Tangen — pine branches,
Mounting very fine; Kano says picture genuine,
pretty good. Name Morihiro. Certificate
by Akura Kosai, a Kioto critic who lately died

S. 260, 1-2. Toyeki. Set of 2. landscapes.
Chinese landscapes in style of Sesshu —
genuine, says Kano, but not first class.
Cannot identify the landscapes

261. Yukinobu. female in house
One of subjects in Genji Monogatari. box says
"Ishiyama scene" of author. Potash is not so says
Sumiyoshi - Potash, one the 2 seaside chapters.

262. Kano Shosen. group of Storks.
a common specimen says Kano. Hogen, between
30 + 40 years old.

263. Sukoku and son. Fukuroku & children
Son's name Sukei — this a seal. Kano Tomonobu says very fine & interesting. Perhaps
almost first class of Sukoku, box different.

Atsunobu 3 founders	206	Chikanobu willow	240
Bagenkin copy Gantan	39	Chikuto 2 dragons	151
Baiitsu botans	76	Chinese sennin Gen?	138
Baiitsu, peach & bird	144	Chinese flowers	161
Banzan Kwacho	95	Chinese tree & birds	165
Buddhist	24	Cho Densu Monju	53
Buddhist Rakan	40	Cho Densu Rakan	192
Buddhist Monju	110	Chokuan 2 – 3 hawks	149
Buddhist Shaka	112	Chorinsai – hawk	182
Buddhist Shaka Yuken	153	Donshu landscape	162
Buncho landscape	4	Donshu Tengu 230	170
Buncho hawk	7	Gankei Choso	115
Buncho waterfall	11	Ganku – tiger & tree	12
Buncho 3 Jurojin	36	Ganku tiger & cliff	80
Buncho - Bunjin sansui	91	Ganku tiger & young	87
Buncho 2 landscape	115	Ganku – rough tiger	89
Bun o landscape	103	Ganku – landscape	121
Bunrin Shoki	51	Ganku Tiger & bamboo	154
Bunrin moon sansui	104	Ganku Fukuroku	163
Bunrin 2 landscape	123	Ganku – deer	164
Bunrin Snow landscape	218	Ganku – peacock	157
Buzen landscape	195	Ganrei landscape	216
Chikanobu 2 Sennin	90	Geiami landscape	179
Chikanobu 3 Gods	200	Genki 2 landscape	114

Genya 2. landscape	243	Ippo landscape	71
Gido Oshitsu	93	Ippo — snow pine	84
Gido Daikoku	201	Isen 3. landscapes	30
Gido 8 sennin	202	Isen copy Chinese (false)	233
Giokusaku flowers	188	Isen 2. botans	250
Giokusen, Kanzan+J.	9	Josen — Tobosaku	132
Giokusen 2nd cherry	96	Kaisen botans	237
Goshosen figure	67	Kano Kanzan+J.	116
Goshun 2. tigers & dragon	117	Kano pine + birds	120
Goshun landscape	196	Kano squirrel	137
Hoitsu plums	46	Kano fan	172
Hoitsu flowers	142	Kano 2 bl. flowers	257
Hokusai hunter	139	Kano hawk	207
Hokusai landscape	190	Kano Kuanon	62
Hokusai landscape	99	Kano Rakan	143
Hoyen peacocks	157	Kano 2. Kanzan+J.	244
Hoyen Karako	171	Keibun kaido	107
Hoyen waterfall	184	Keibun snow bamboo	108
Hoyen Biodoin	259	Keisai herons	5
Icho, heron+crow	92	Keishoki landscape	109
Icho piper	255	Keishoki Hotei	105
Icho 2nd — people in rain	75	Kiho landscape	144
Ikkei Ushiwaka	18	Kingyokusen, shoki	58
Ikkium tree & bird	207	Kionobu 4 sleepers	131
Ippo badger	53	Kiso Kotei, copy eagle	48

Kiuyen heron	235	Motonobu 2 sansui	43
Koin Seiobo	52	Motonobu horses	15
Koki - rooster	6	Nagaku monkey	211
Kose Jizo	1	Nagamitsu 3	150
Korwen plum	97	Nanping dogs	23
Kuazan Jojo	155	Nanping pheasant	68
Kuazan 8 gods	160	Naonobu 3, Daruma	168
Kuazan, landscape	189	Naonobu, Tosemmei	255
Kwakei - fire	232	Nikka, charcoal burning	208
Manju ducks	119	Nikka - dragon	64
Minenobu bamboo	242	Nishikwa Tsukenobu 2	222
Minenobu sparrow	258	Okio, landscape	70
Minenobu bird	56	Okio, white fox	79
Mitsubumi 7 gods	229	Okio - peacock	83
Mitsunari female	205	Oshin landscape	234
Mitsunobu (Kano) 2. sansui	228	Raisho 2 deer &c.	145
Mitsuoki Benten	10	Rankei - landscape	25
Mitsuoki quail	60	Ranko - carp & water	22
Mitsuoki figures	198	Ranko, Tobosaku	94
Mitsutada Horai	215	Richo waterfall	82
Mitsuyoshi 3 storks	252	Renzan landscape	54
Morikage botans	231	Sansetsu - dragon	193
Morikage Toba	220	Seiki landscape	199
Morikage landscape	173	Seiko Tofukuju	127
Motonobu Kwanon	152	Seisen 3, landscape	34

Tanyu, white hawk	77	Tozan, Kuanon	74
Tanyu 3. Fukurokin	124	Tsukioka Sessai, 2 figures	167
Tanyu 3 Hotei	147	Tsukioka Settei, woman	212
Tanyu 3 Shoki	148	Tsunenobu Benten	8
Tanyu 3. copy Masanobu	170	Tsunenobu. 3. Gods	31
Tanyu 2. waterfall	183	Tsunenobu 2. lions	37
Tanyu 3. Yokihi	185	Tsunenobu, Fuyo	49
Tanyu Emperor	209	Tsunenobu, Yuima	65
		Tsunenobu, Yuima	186
Tanzan Fujiyama	78	Tsunenobu, Fukurokin	241
Tetsuzan Shoki	88	Tsuruzawa Tansen	128
Tetsuzan, Fox	57	Utanosuke, eagle	100
Tohaku (Has.) 2. Sansui	245	Unkei, Lotus etc.	69
Tohaku (Kano) Hotei	194	Unkin - peacock	41
Tobun 2. figures	246	Unkin - plum	45
Toho, copy Ojakusui	3	Unkin - eagle	50
Tokei, Crow at moon	72	Unkin - eagle	98
Torin Yoshinobu Sangi	134	Unkin 6. Flowers etc	2
Tosa Rakan	106	Unkoku Seiko	140
Toshun. 1st. 3 Sun	247	Yamada Doan, bird	204
Tosui, waterfall	219	Yasunobu 3. Fukurokin	156
Towun, heron	225	Yasunobu Kuanon	85
Toyeki 2. landscapes	260	Yeino landscape	174
Toyohiko 2. Sansui	166	Yeitoku 1st. Bird	181
Toyokuni - figures	213	Yeitoku 2d. 3. Tobosaku	38

Yeishuku 3. Jurojin	238
Yofu - Landscape	187
Yogetsu Hotei	256
Yosai Kwanon	210
Yosen 2. Kwacho	81
Yosen Landscape	86
Yosen Shuko	175
Yosen 3 Jurojin	236
Yoshimochi Toba	224
Yoshimochi Yoshitsune	125
Yukinobu female	261
Yukinobu Seishi	214
Yukinobu female	133
Yusei Terminchi 3	248
Yuzetsu (Kashoki) Jurojin	178
Yusen 1st Kiken	136
Yusen 2d Sumidagawa	21
Yushof Kinko	197

Complete Catalogue
of
Collection of specimens of
Japanese
Pictorial Art
including
notes and commentaries
And references
to the other note books belonging to
the collector

Ernest Francisco Fenollosa
No. 1 Kaga Yashiki
Hongo,
Tokio
Japan
December 1880

Catalogue

Division A

Kakemonos

Note. The numbers are attached to separate works, whether of one or more than one picture. In the latter case, the secondary numbers mark the parts of the work, which are numbered in the order in which they should be hung and from right to left. In most cases, nothing is here said concerning the signature on the kakemono, though sometimes there is given the translation of the writing on the box. For the signature, the note-book on signatures must be regularly referred to. For the biography of the artists named, the note-book on that subject must be consulted, although an occasional point of interest will here be given. Special criticisms of leading Tokio artists and critics are appended. The pictures are described so much in detail only as is necessary for their identification, and the understanding of their subject and the most striking of their peculiar excellencies. For the subjects generally the note-book on Art Motives must be referred to. Dates, if at all, are given here only approximately. In some cases an attempt is here made to describe the excellent qualities of pictures both from a Japanese point of view and from a foreign. In general, only enough is given here, to make the other note-books of service in explaining the collection.

S1. A small figure-painting of the Buddhist Gods, Jiso.
This is in the finest style of very old Japanese Buddhist painting. It is said to be by Kose no Kanawoka, about 1000 years old. But Mr. Ninagawa, Kano Yeitoku, and Setsuan say it is not Kanawoka himself, for it has not quite his boldness of touch, but is by his son or grandson, say about 900 years old. The secret of applying gold so as to be permanent was lost soon after this period. On the other hand Mr. Shimoda and Mr. __ declare it to be a genuine Kanawoka. All testimony about such old paintings is doubtful. The beauty of line and color far surpasses that of later Buddhist works. But in boldness of line and grandeur of color it is inferior to some of the pictures said to be by Kanawoka now kept in Kioto. It has been finally determined by the present Sumiyoshi of Tokio, to be the work of Kose no Genkei. Bought from Akamatsu. (MFA:11.4080)

Sent fall of 1880, from here.

S2. 1-6. Bird and flower pieces painted by Wunkin in 1877 or 78. These may be considered as one work, or as four different works, namely, 1, 2, 3-4, 5-6. For convenience they are classed as one.
   1. Two wild ducks flying up from the reeds. This is delicate in feeling and color, but not strong in any respect.
   2. The peacocks on the trunk of bending pine. This is fine chiefly in composition.
   3. A pheasant among the peach blossoms. This is very rich in color, but not so pure in feeling.
   4. Quail and bush with yellow flowers. This is in the true noble Japanese feeling, and from the native point of view, as in truth, the best of the six pictures.
   5. Two herons on a rock and pine tree. The purity of the grey tones is excellent. This is the next to the best of the six.
   6. Two herons on the branch of a red plum tree. This is the realization of a dream Wunkin had on a New Year's eve. It has three of the emblems of happiness. It is not a strong picture.

S3. A picture of hen, cock, and chickens with rocks. And purple flowers above. This is a copy by an artist named Toho, from a fine picture of the Chinese artist Ojiakusui of Gen. Mr. Kano says it is a rather poor copy, in that the artist has not succeeded in execution to produce the effect he wished. On the other hand Mr. Hasegawa says it is a very fine copy. I am inclined to agree with the latter, that the tenderest, more tasteful Chinese effect is reached with considerable skill. In feeling it is far superior to Nanping. The peculiar ribbed Chinese silk adds to the effect. This is a pure mirror of Chinese feeling. The lines of the rock, the delicacy of color and lightness of tone are the conspicuous elements. Bought from Yamanaka. (MFA:11.4664)

S4. A small landscape in grey by Buncho. This is a winter scene with rocks, frozen river, bare trees, and towering cliffs. Snow is in the air. The cold misty effect is rendered in the manner peculiar to this artist. It is an ordinary, not remarkable specimen.

S5. A small picture of two snowy herons on a branch of red plum blossoms partially covered with snow, by Ônishi Keisai, the pupil of Soshiseki and teacher of Shiuki. This is a pretty good specimen of this artist. He is notorious for painting the heads of his birds too large, as here. The feeling is very pure, especially in color, and is rather Japanese than Chinese. The execution is peculiar; not at all in the manner of Nanping and the ordinary work in his school, but apparently modeled after the Ganku branch of it. The touch of the brush in the stem and branches of the plum tree is much like Ganku. Upon the box is written "Sagi Kobai", literally "White herons, red plum blossoms." Upon the back of the kakemono is written "Ônishi Keisai." Upon the face "Keisai" above appears. The simple pure color and the compressed masses of the boughs so spiritually drawn are the beautiful features.   (MFA:11.4793)

S6. A small picture of rooster hen, and chicks, with lilies above, by Ko-Ôki. This name is not known among the list of artists. Upon the box is written "Nishino-toyen Niudo." This Mr. Kano thinks is the name of a noble man of Kioto. The style is interesting as being out of the influence of any art school. The coloring is strong and coarse. There is no purity of feeling. But there is a strength of effect which few later Japanese pictures of birds and flowers have. I saw several pictures by this artist in Osaka, and they all had the same qualities. Perhaps he was not a professional.   (MFA:11.4741)

S7. A hawk upon a rock with part of a pine tree, by Buncho. This is mostly in ink, but there are brownish tones about it, which make it look like sepia. Setsuan questioned the genuineness of the picture. saying the signature is that of the early days of Buncho, but the style is of his later days. On the contrary Mr. Kano says the style is that of his youth, that it is genuine, and in the second class in excellence of Buncho. I am inclined to agree with the latter opinion, except that I think it should be ranked as third class or ordinary. There is no doubt in my mind as to its genuineness. It is the manner of Buncho in its immaturity.

(Note. When hereafter the terms, first, second, and third class specimens or styles, of any artist are used, the following will always be meant. In the first class are put only those rare pictures of their author, in which his own style has attained the maximum of its freedom and strength, roughly judging, from two to five per cent of the works of an artist. By the second class is meant all those pictures in which the artist has attained striking excellence without reaching the utmost limit of his power, comprising perhaps fifteen or twenty per cent of an artist's works, or at least fifteen or twenty per cent of those original works which remain to be seen. No true estimate of proportion beyond this can be made. By the third class or ordinary style is meant all the rest of an artist's work, including the larger bulk, and the more commonly seen specimens. This distinction and these proportions are given as practically convenient and in the rough correct by Mr. Kano Yeitoku.)

S8. A small picture of Benten with her biwa by Tsunenobu. This has the real Tsunenobu touch, but must be ranked with the ordinary run of his productions. Of these it is a good typical specimen. On the box is written "Benzaiten" "Tsunenobu."

S9. A fine painting of Kanzan and Jittoku, the Chinese Buddhists, by Mochizuki Giyokusen, the best pupil of Ganku. This is considered by Mr. Kano Yeitoku one of the best productions of modern Japanese Art. It is a very original picture both in conception and execution. The artist inherits the spirit of Ganku, but it has clothed its work in an entirely new form. The drawing, from a foreign point of view, is about the best to be found in Japan. The hands and feet, especially the former are very truthfully rendered. The faces are most expressive, and the masses of hair finely rendered in a manner adapted from Ganku. The flow of lines in the postures, limbs, and drapery is wonderful. The unity of line is only the formal side of the unity of the feeling which lies in the soul of the figures, the expression of their eager interest in some unseen object beyond the picture. This shows the artist's genius, not to distract the attention from the idea of the faces by introducing the interesting object into the picture. The lines have a different touch from Ganku's, less massive and more sinuous. The color is meagre and amounts to nothing, but the composition is great. This picture shows some influences of the Okio styles. Bought from Yamanaka. (MFA:11.4712)

$10. One of the best representations of Benten in existence, by Tosa Mitsuoki, one of the greatest artists of the Tosa school. Mr. Kano says it is the best specimen of this artist, having the very highest dignity and purity. It is not in ordinary Tosa style, but in that highest model of the old Yamato style which the later schools debased and rendered grotesque. The rock is in the style of Kanawoka, and is derived from the Chinese style in the To dynasty. The figure is nearly in the pure Kanawoka style. Mr. K. says the genius of Mitsuoki is shown in placing the biwa horizontally, instead of inclined as universally represented. This gives the figure great peaceful dignity. Mr. Ninagawa who is not an artist but an antiquarian says it is a poor picture because it has no nobleness and dignity! Mr. Hasegawa says it is one of the finest specimens of Mitsuoki. Setsuan says it is very noble and pure. I think the color is distinctive of Mitsuoki, though Mr. Kano does not. The coloring has that same quality of delicious delicate satiny tones which I have marked in all of his good works. In delicacy of drawing he also excells. The details of his quail and grasses are microscopic. See No. 60. But he has no power to treat great forcible subjects. In this picture his lines and conception are the grandest and most forceful I have seen. In technique he is unsurpassed in his own school. This Benten shows to perfection his handling of the brush in drawing and coloring. The water is somewhat weak, Presented by Mr. Wakai of Kosho Kwaisha. I say the picture has no relation to Kanawoka, rather to Chinese of Gen as seen through the mediumship of Tanyu. 1st. class. (MFA:11.4565)

$11. A waterfall among the mountains by Buncho. This is a very remarkable piece of work for a Japanese. I have seen no other like it, and no Japanese critic to whom I have showed it has ever seen another like it. Its most noticeable peculiarity is its attempt at chiaroscuro. I have seen such an attempt in the pictures of no other artist at all, and in the others of Buncho only to a limited extent. In the second place the force of execution and carelessness of touch are remarkable even for Buncho. In the third place, the coloring is peculiarly Buncho's in the pieces executed after his own taste. Buncho however, insisted that a great artist must paint in all styles: and his practice was in accordance with his precept. Thus Setsuan says he studied oil- painting when a youth under the instruction of Shiba Kokan who had learned from a Dutch-man in Nagasaki; but early in life abandoned the practice. If this be true, it explains the peculiar coloring and shading of some of his later pictures. Especially is this true in the present case. This picture is viewed to best effect from a distance of 20 or 30 feet, as if it were an oil painting. The only other work of this artist having similar coloring that I have seen, is the makimonos of scenes on the Tokaido exhibited by the Daimio Matsudaira at Uyeno, May 1880. This of mine is considered one of the finest works in the first class of Buncho, by everyone who has seen it, including Mr. Kano. This latter and Setsuan agree that the artist must have been about forty years of age, when it was painted. Upon the box is written "Taki" "Sansui" 'Tani Buncho." The force of the water-flow in the picture is almost equalled by that in the two screens of Okio owned by Nishimura of Kioto, and by these alone. As is evident, the touch follows no rule. Bought from King.

S12. Tiger seated beneath a tree on whose branches rests a bird, by Ganku. This is a fair specimen of Ganku's ordinary style, such as are still offered for sale, and seen in Kioto collections. It cannot be compared with his great works. Mr. Kano Y. was inclined to think it not genuine. Setsuan assures me it is genuine. For my part, I am certain of its genuineness, it being much better than several I saw in Kioto, vouched for by all the Kioto critics. It has the touch of Ganku, but not his highest power of idea. He studied tigers from life. It is better than Okio's ordinary work. The signature is undoubtedly genuine. Painted in his later years. (MFA:11.4698)

S13. A family of monkeys sporting on a tree growing from the sides of a chasm, Sosen. This is the very best of Sosen's second class, according to general agreement. For miniature monkeys it is his best. The composition is much finer than is usual with this artist. His landscape however is meagre in intention and his execution of it is not strong. There is no other artist who has portrayed monkeys so truthfully, though many more nobly. This artist knows little about coloring. From K.K.K.

S14. Picture of Jiorojin (*sic*) with his deer. Shugetsu. A fine specimen of this artist whose pictures are rare. This is the best of his second class according to Kano Yeitoku. A common specimen says Ninagawa, who always disparages my pictures, and exalts his own. A very fine specimen says Hasegawa Settei, the present representative of the school of Sesshiu. Very fine say Setsuanand Mr. Kanda. It is the best original Shugetsu I have yet seen (1880). Some of his screen must have been greater. This Jiorojin is in the true Shiugetsu (*sic*) style, although a subject treated with similar arrangements by all the artist of his time, and by some for centuries later. The simplicity of it recalls the noble feeling of the artists of those times. The stamp is genuine. The manner is much like Sesshu, but not so forceful or facile. On the box is written "Jiurojin" "Shiugetsu." Bought from Tazawa.

S15. Two wild horses in the snow amid wild mountain scenery. Motonobu. This rare specimen is in the second class of Motonobu. Such things are rarely seen. The stamp upon it gives the name of Shoyei, Motonobu's son; and several critics, Ninagawa, Kanda and others had agreed that it was Shoyei. Messrs. Matsuwo and Wakai, Directors of the Kosho Kwaisha, thought it a very remarkable work to see. But Mr. Kano Yeitoku has in his inherited collection of copies and originals from the old masters, copies of six panels of a screen by Motonobu, of which he recognizes this as the original of one panel. This identifies it as Motonobu himself, and that it was taken from an old screen, perhaps partly destroyed, and mounted as a kakemono. Afterward some artist, Kano probably, who held a seal of Shoyei, stamped it such according to his erroneous opinion. It certainly has the treatment of black of Motonobu. The touch is more mysterious and nervous than that of his ordinary style. I do not know whether the falling water is intended to be encased in ice. This excellence of the whole to the Japanese mind of taste lies in the exalted feeling of wildness and majestic dreaminess of life in such a landscape. This very look of the horses seems to show the appreciation of the forlorn grandeur of their own position. Unless one can forget scientific pedantry, and open his soul to the deep mysterious feeling of their pictures, one can never appreciate the great things of Chinese and Japanese art. On the box is written "Setsuten Makiba" literally "Snow inside, wild horse." "Kano Shoyei Hogen." Bought in Tokio.

^{S}16. Fishing village. Copy from Sesshiu. This simple but attractive little picture shows finely the common ground between modern European landscape feeling, and the best old Japanese. It might well be Marblehead or any other New England coast town. The manner is distinctly of Sesshiu, and the signature of Sesshiu is given. Mr. Kano Yeitoku and Hasegawa Settei are quite certain that it is not an original. They think the signature manifestly a forgery, and the touches, especially in the houses, too stuff and lacking picturesqueness and vigor. On the other hand Mr. Ninagawa says it is undoubtedly genuine; and Mr. Setsuan will not hear for a minute of its being other than genuine. The signature even he thinks is genuine. As a mere matter of testimony the former opinion ought to have more weight, considering the familiarity of the two artists with the best work of Sesshiu. Again, my own opinion would incline me to that side, the signature looking to me false, and the touch evidently weaker than Sesshiu's ordinary landscapes. Nevertheless it is a fine work. All agree that if it is not Sesshiu, it is a copy from him of very early date, perhaps made during his lifetime. It is also done by a good artist. The weak points are such as a foreigner would not easily recognize unless instructed; and the impression one gets of the picture from a little distance is exactly that of a landscape by Sesshiu. Evidently the chief excellence in this case lies in the purity of its landscape feeling.   (MFA:11.4139)

^{S}17. Jiorojin (*sic*). A copy from Sesshiu's picture by Kano Tomonobu 1880. Of the copy as such we need merely say that it is faithfully executed. The original is one of the most important pictures in Japan. It is considered by critics to be the finest work of Sesshiu now known. It has a curious history. Undoubtedly painted by Sesshiu during his stay in China, it had made its way to the palace of the King of Corea in Seoul the capital of that country. When Kato Kiyomasa entered the capital in the name of Taiko, the Japanese tyrant, at the head of the conquering invaders, he secured this treasure among others after the sack of the palace, and brought it back with him to Japan. It is now (was lately) in the family treasury of Prince Hachisuka of Tokio, and is regarded as one of the greatest pictorial gems in the country. Mr. Kano has a fine copy of it. The excellence of the picture lies in its extraordinary mysterious effect upon the soul of the beholder. This is achieved, first by the extraordinary face and figure of Jiurojin. The face is that of a God, not a man, and with its strong features peers out weirdly from the paper. The figure is very original, bent as it is, with strange unsymmetrical almost hesitating lines.

The color too on the face and figure is equally extraordinary and adds to the weirdness. But how can one fittingly describe the other elements in the picture. The deer is the double of the man-god. The great pine trunk on the left runs into the halo back of the head, and is there transmuted into a dream of itself. The branches which it throws off intermingle in glorious mystery with the trunk and branches of a white plum tree in blossom, and this witch network of boughs runs through the halo, and around and across the head. Their execution is stupendous. The silvery quality of the light and dark outlines has seldom been equaled, in any work, and never in combination with such lines. What rule was followed in drawing these branches? None, the composition is stupendous, unexpected, a revelation of power, mystery, and supernatural charm. The sprays of white plum curve across the picture like snaky living fingers. The staff of the old man, a glorious, knotty stick, rises in deeper massy curves into the melee of lines and shades. It is an individual creation so great, so perfect, that it is its own law. Nothing but itself can judge it. In the field of ideal art this must certainly be reckoned one of the most extraordinary creations the world has seen. Subject, line, and masses are pressed together into a single idea, so deep, metaphysical, supernatural, that it seems to require a superhuman mind for its conception. Unfortunately the mass of Japanese at the present day can see little more in this than an interesting antiquity. The Kanos alone appreciate the deeper meaning. Even Hasegawa does not, I am sure, by the poor copy he has made for himself. Not a thing must be changed, not a line or shade. Probably the original of this is the one which Prof. Wheeler of Sapporo bought in Osaka, and had burned up in his house in 1880. In 1889 I hear from Mr. Brooks that Prf. Wheeler's picture was quite a different one. Also the original came out in an exhibition in 1888. (MFA:11.4962)

^{S}18. Yoshitsune and Benkei on the bridge. Ikkei, one of the best Kioto artists of the last generation, a pupil of Totsugen. The manner of this is mostly in that of the Okio school. There is some Kano and a bit of Tosa element in it. The coloring is rather original. This is appreciated by a good deal of modern taste. The gradations are very pure. The interest of the picture does not lie in the faces and the expression of emotion, but in the color, touch, and gradations. The drawing of Benkei is rather spirited. It is a good picture for a modern. (MFA:11.4557)

^{S}19. Chinese mountain landscape. Taniu. This is roughly drawn, and is a fair specimen of Taniu's second class of landscapes, says Mr. Kano. It was formerly one of a set of three; as is known by the fact that Taniu painted the same or a similar subject many times over as one of a set of three. I have not yet been able to find the name of Chinese scenes from which these innumerable modifications are taken. The good landscape effect reached through such very careless touches is most characteristic of Taniu. I say third class.

^{S}20. A cluster of botan beaten by wind and rain. Sorin. This artist was formerly painter to the daimio of Owari. It is very finely conceived and executed. The grace of the curves of resistance is noticeable; the relief given to the petals of the flowers, as distinguished from the ordinary flatness of Japanese flower painting, and the variety of form and color in the leaves, all these qualities mark this as quite an original work. Its unity of lines and subject is perfect. Pictures of this artist are rare in Tokio. (MFA:11.4672)

S21. Colored painting of Sumidagawa at Mukojima in old times by Kano Yusen, or Sukenobu, the great grandfather of Kano Tomonobu. This is painted in that one of the Kano styles, which is nearest to Tosa in feeling, though the touch is different. Mr. Kano says this is the very best work of this artist, who was not especially celebrated. Tsukubayama looks natural rising at the north. (MFA:11.4802)

S22. A large picture of two carp leaping among the spray and waves at the foot of a large waterfall. Ranko. This artist is one of the greatest of modern times next to Ganku. (This is an exaggerated opinion.) This picture is much disliked both by foreigners and most Japanese critics, by the former, because it is too unnatural, by the latter, because it does not follow their narrow canons. They admit its strength. however, and power over the beholder. It has no gracefulness says Kano Yeitoku. True, but it has the higher quality of power. The artist knew what he was doing. He has deliberately sacrificed the actual lines of nature, and all graceful feeling, to an extraordinary composition of lines expressing his feeling in a most powerful manner, to one who will throw away his prejudices sufficiently to receive the impression, thus realizing most boldly the true artistic end. Everything I have seen of this artist is remarkably fine. Bought from Yamanaka. (MFA:11.4660)

S23. Landscape with dog and pups. Nanping. This is not so strong and beautiful as some of Nanping's work. But it has the merit of being genuine, according to universal consent at a time when thousands of imitations abound. Mr. Kano calls it a good specimen of the second class. Its subdued style is highly appreciated by Japanese. The painting of the dog has the best mild expression of animal painting from Nanping's brush, for which he is celebrated. The signature is undoubtedly genuine. The tree, flowers and grasses are characteristic of Nanping's best, delicacy of execution. The picture as a whole is weak in composition, and has no effect, like too many of the productions of this artist. It is painted on thick Chinese silk manufactured for the purpose. On the box is written "Nanping ga". Presented by Mr. Lyman. (MFA:11.4668)

S24. Large Buddhist picture, with many divinities in circles, red, blue, yellow, green &c. The artist is unknown, probably not more than a hundred years old. It has been retouched within a few years. Its execution has no value from a native point of view. Its general design shows something of the better qualities in recent Buddhist painting. The color is rich without being very good. On the whole it is better than the ordinary runs of later Buddhist paintings which foreigners buy up with eagerness. The porcelain ends are very fine, in old Japanese blue, and much appreciated by natives. On the box is written "Kiujo Kannon" meaning "many Kiujos." (MFA:11.4541)

S25. Large landscape of Mt. Yorozan in Mino. Sugawara Rankei. This was painted only 20 years ago by a descendant of an ancient noble house, though not greatly celebrated as an artist. It is rather in the manner of the Okio school. The perspective is faulty. It is contradictory in that it represents all seasons at once. This purposely done. The painting is excellent though not great. The distant mountain is the finest part of it. On the box is written "Yorozan Shinkei" "Sugawara Rankei." Kiosai says this artist attained the highest local celebrity in the province of Echizen. He afterwards came to Kioto and lived in Sanjo, very celebrated. (MFA:11.4759)

S26. A set of 3 by Taniu. His second quality of excellence, says Mr. Kano. Painted when he was 69 years old. Their excellence consists in their freedom and poetic expression. These served as models for the rapid work of later generations.
 1. Onagadori with Kaido flower.
 2. Rihaku looking at the waterfall. Rihaku was a noted poet of the To dynasty, who described in one of the most famous of his poems how in the heart of the mountains he discovered a great waterfall. In later Japanese art, any picture of a Chinese looking at a waterfall is said to be Rihaku. It was a favorite subject of old Chinese painters.
 3. Plum branch and moon. A common subject at this period. Painted in Taniu's most rapid yet fascinating manner. The touch is in the Giyo manner. Mr. Kano says this is a fine subject and shows good feeling.
Bought from King. Collection of ___.

S27. Chinese in villa gazing at mountain scenery: Kano Tanshin Morimichi, the grandfather of Kano Tambi Moriki. This is a direct copy from a famous picture by Oöki, a celebrated Chinese artist of the So dynasty. In Japan the works of this artist are exceedingly rare. This is charming in conception and treatment. The poets in the house are finely drawn, and the erratic trees have been a model for many good things of the Japanese. This artist was a little later than Bayen. A magnificent landscape of Eastern art. Highest ideality. Finest copy in existence. Probably, much better than in national museum.

S28. A set of 3 fine pictures by the same artist, the later Tanshin. For modern pictures these have very refined taste and execution. Among the best works of this artist, though not strictly original.
 1. Chinese mountain scenery, with hut in the foreground. Although this is not a direct copy from Motonobu yet all the parts of it are adapted from landscapes of Motonobu, and have combined anew into an original picture. The delicacy of finish is essentially from Motonobu in one of his landscape styles.
 2. A picture of Fukurokujiu, Keikaboku, and Saisho the servant. The design of this is directly copied from a famous picture of Motonobu, except that the original is in black alone, whereas this has Tanshin's color, and a certain weak delicacy of feeling added. Its execution is perfect in its way.
 3. Ideal Chinese landscape, rice fields &c. This, like No.1, is an adaptation from Motonobu, but not a direct copy. Its peculiarity of soft quiet brownish color is Tanshin's. Altogether these three form a charming work.
Bought from Kosho Kwaisha, who got them from Daizen.   (MFA:11.4254-4256)

S29. A set of 3 pieces by Taniu. These are good specimens of Taniu's third or ordinary style. They were painted at the age of 69. Their execution is careless, and lacks the inimitable technique of touch for which Taniu was so celebrated and which characterizes No.32 in the highest degree. They have power, but not noble and deep feeling.
 1. dragon and waves. The dragon of the typhoon has risen into the air, and the frenzied water from which he has emerged leaps after in tumultuous heaps. The water is here strongly drawn.
 2. Kanzan and Jittoku. These are not Sennin, but two servants of Bukkanzenji (*sic*). an ancient Chinese priest, who became his disciples. They studied the Zen sect of

Buddhism, and were noted among the Chinese for their learning. They are much honored by the Zen sect in Japan. They have been a favorite subject of the artists in all times. They communicated great thoughts to one another by secret gestures of hand and feature. For further facts about them, the book on such subjects must be consulted. These are executed in Taniu's coarsest style.

3. The storm dragon returning to the water. This one Mr. Kano says is the best of the three.

$30. A set of three by Kano Isen. These are said by his son Kano Yeitoku to be the finest specimens he has ever seen of this master. They were painted when he was from 48 to 50 years old. The style of the various parts of these most delicate landscape paintings is taken piecemeal from Motonobu and old Chinese artists of the So and Gen dynasties, notably the architecture from Sonkuntaku. The original Isen element is the composition of the parts into a peculiar feeling of colored beauty. The feeling is essentially Isenish. The coloring is so tender as to leave nothing to be desired. The structures represented are ideal or actual old Chinese palaces. There is a soft atmospheric effect about them, which establishes their excellence among the works of this period. The box in which they are kept is of the finest kiri wood, and must have belonged to a prince. The writing upon it is in the handwriting of his son Kano Seisen. On the outside is written "Sambukutsui" "Sansui Rokaku" i.e. Landscape of mountain palaces."Isen in Hogen". On the inside is written "Yoshin (Seisen) wrote this."

1. Shows a palace by a lake with a long distance lost amid gold clouds.
2. Shows in the foreground the terrace and part of the garden of a palace, a beautiful middle distance of shore, and fine overhanging peaks. The tree trunks are especially fine, and the finish is perfection.
3. Shows a winter scene, a villa in snow near a bamboo grove, with a shore of yellow grasses in the middle distance. There is no great strength in any of these pictures.

Bought from Kosho Kwaisha, who got them from Daizen.   (MFA:11.4212-4214)

$31. A set of three by Kano Tsunenobu. These are said by Yeitoku and Tomonobu to be the very finest work of Tsunenobu. The subjects are the most common among all artists, and Tsunenobu frequently painted them. But these specimens have far better line and color than ordinary, so that they present to a Japanese great nobleness of feeling. The delicacy of the suggested color is noticeable. The lines are very strongly drawn. Such large specimens of these gods are rare. The mounting is old. On the box is written Fukurokujiu, Yebisu, Daikoku, Sambuku, Hogen Kosen's painting.

1. Daikoku astride of his bag of wealth, pounding with a hammer. Several of his jewels have escaped on the ground. The combination of black and green in the drapery has almost the texture of velvet.
2. Fukurikujiu, deer, and stork. A very noble composition, well composed in line, with its grand pine tree.
3. Yebisu catching a red fish. Mr. Ninagawa says this is the best of the three, and with respect to the purity of the tones and gradations of the ink, he is right. The rock on which the figure stands is unequaled in tone by any of this style. There is the same refined atmospheric tone which characterizes all good Kano pictures from Taniu downward in all three pictures.

Bought from Kosho Kwaisha, 1st class.

S32. A set of three in black of Taniu. This is one of the most notable sets of Taniu in Japan. Mr. Kano says they are the best of his pictures executed with the So touch of the brush. The clouds are inimitable in their transparent black, rapid but perfect gradation, enormous sweeps, with broken bits of light scattered through them, where the impetuous sweep of the wet brush was checked by the firm hand. This effect has never been imitated or successfully copied by any other Kano artist. Indeed the method of execution is well-nigh inconceivable. The soulful quality of the pictures is however their greatest excellence. The spectator bows before their mysterious suggestions, their poetical rendering of the destructive powers of nature.

1. The storm dragon descending through the whirls of sulphurous cloud. This shows the peculiar excellence of the technique in the highest degree. The light spots in the midst of the black are wonderful. The identification of the mysterious and hideous dragon with the unearthly cloud is fine. The whirl of the lighter cloud below is full of power and mystery. The spectator stands awe struck at the exquisiteness of the thought which grasps the full grandeur and intensity of the subject in its colorless crystal vision.

2. The storm rolls far over the middle distance in the great gulf of Tsuruga (*sic*) Bay, as seen by the spectator on the heights of Idzu. In the midst of the forbidding clouds, the Kaminari, or thunder god Raiden, leaps with his circlet of rattling drums, while forks of red lighting radiates into the seething abyss below. Far above the troubled region of storm, calm Fuji lifts her reverent white head into the clear sky in magnificent contrast to the confusion of unequilibrated power below. The sweep of the brush in the lower cloud is stupendous. The Japanese usually like this the best of the three.

3. The storm dragon ascending from the abyss, high in air amid similar whirls and depths of lowering typhoon cloud. The feeling and touch are similar to No.1, but not so intense or wonderful.

Bought from Kosho Kwaisha, owned formerly by Daizen.   (MFA:11.4392-4394)

S33. A small set of three in black by Taniu. This is agreed by all to be the very finest specimen of Taniu's first class. Mr. Kano Yeitoku says there is nothing else of Taniu's to be compared with these, they are even better than the preceeding. They cannot be copied. They were painted at the age of from 30 to 40, when Taniu was possessed of his greatest vigor. Their excellence consists, according to Mr. Kano, in the harmony of the relations of every line to the others, the rich beauty of the black, the purity and tenderness of tone and effect. In style of touch they are between Giyo and Shin.

1. Branch of a plum tree with the kakessu bird. This illustrates most strongly the beauty of the black. When we remember that the effect is reached at a single dash, its transparency and richness is astonishing. The beauty of the simple lines too in their steady deliberate vital unsteadiness is most striking. This is a common subject, but has never been more finely treated.

2. Portrait of Yuima, a Hindoo philosopher, older than Daruma, who finally submitted to the Buddhist religion in his old age. He had been an independent thinker in the time of Shaka, with a system not greatly differing from the later's. It was Monju, the pupil of Shaka, who discussed with Yuima and converted him to the doctrines of Shaka, of whom he became a personal disciple. Mr. Kano says, and

I think it true, that this portrait may be called the finest in the whole range of Japanese art. The exquisite drawing of the features has been equaled in no other. The melancholy calm resigned features of the handsome old face, are wonderful in their power. The eye, though fixed in thought, is pregnant with life and soul. This is the highest point to which portrait painting can attain without the introduction of shadow. He holds in his hand the hossu, a wand used and waved by Buddhist chief priests in formal and other high ceremonies. In the Zen sect every priest has one.

3. Onagadori and kaido flower. This is very beautiful in arrangement and execution, having softer qualities than No.1. If these tender qualities do not touch the soul of the beholders, then there is no method of communicating appreciative feeling for them.

Bought from Kosho Kwaisha; formerly owned by Daizen.

S34. A set of three landscapes in black by Kano Seisen. These are in his second best style, according to his brother Yeitoku. They were painted when he was very young, perhaps only 20. He had been a great student of Sesshiu, and thus his early work reflects the style of the master, although there is an original element in it. Indeed the middle one is said to be adapted directly from a well-known design by Sesshiu. They are ideal landscapes. Their excellence consists in the beauty of their black contrasting with gold in the clouds, the grand drawing of the trees and rocks, which recalls the best period of the Kanos. The touch of the brush is not like that of Sesshiu. The mounting is old, especially fine, and suited to the dark refined tones of the pictures.

1. Ideal mountain landscape. The rock and trees in the ground are especially fine; the rocks of the mountain are very strong, and the effect of the picture is sharp and clear like that of an etching.

2. Ideal landscape with rustic bower in which are resting Fukurokujiu, and Keikaboku. Saisho the boy feeds the sacred deer. A strange tree rises above. The effect of the whole is powerful, beautiful, and full of the mystery of the ways of the gods.

3. Ideal winter mountain landscape. The tender tones of the black contrasting with the white of the snow are fine.

Bought from Kosho Kwaisha, owned by Daizen. I say they are 1st class of Seisen. (MFA:11.4330-4332)

S35. A marriage or New Year's set of three by Seisen. Mr. Kano calls them only second class, but they seem to me to be of a very great degree of excellence. They were probably painted to order by some prince at the time of his marriage. They contain all the lucky emblems. The artist was 30 years old when they were painted. Mr. Kano says that the fault of these pictures lies in their coloring, which is not harmonious and lacks dignity. The lines are tolerable. My own impression is that the drawing is poorer than the color, which is quite rich and fascinating. The mounting is princely and they are finished in the best of style; being types of those kakemonos prized by princes in later times.

1. This comprises the the elements of the stork and pine.

2. Jiurojin, the god of longevity and talents. The drawing of this is in the style of the older masters, but the coloring is Seisen's own, and very rich and striking. The figure seems to be against a soft background of sweet atmosphere.

3. Red plum tree and sacred turtle. From the mouth of the latter, in spiral form ascends

the sacred fortunate breath, or "good air" bearing its inspiration.
Bought from Yamanaka. 2d.class.

$36. A set of three large ones by Buncho. Mr. Kano says these are the best ones of the 2nd grade of Buncho. Mr. Setsuan agrees with him. In the execution of these, Buncho has been in some sort the follower of Sesshiu; but they are so individual, that the Sesshiu quality is lost in the good or bad genius of Buncho.
   1. Ideal landscape. The cliff overhead is strangely butting, and the touch careless in the extreme. Below amidst masses of rock, and in the shadow of lowering clouds, a palace is seen with its foundation in the water. This is the poorest of the three. Whatever excellences it has, are possessed in a much higher degree, by No.3.
   2. Jiurojin. This is an original figure of Buncho's in his own style, which here approaches that of the Kanos. Mr. Setsuan and Mr. Wakai think it is a fine figure. To me it possesses great coldness and lack of feeling. I cannot call it great. It possesses no genius.
   3. An ideal landscape, by far the finest of the three, and in some respects one of the most striking in the whole range of Japanese art. The body of the picture is occupied by an enormous outlandish double-horned cliff, which falling away toward the foreground ends in great heaps of sloping boulders from which mass of rubbish a long line of trees has sprung which stretch far up the sides of the cliff. Below nestled amid the boulders a mountain hut and a cleared space are seen, whence on the right a river stretches back around the base of the cliff till lost in the distance behind it. A wreath of cloud shrouding the bosom of the hill, half conceals the topmost pines, and, unusual thing, casts a shadowy gloom on all below it. The most extraordinary feature of the picture is its attempt to produce an effect of light, which plays with delicious gleam on the boulders and the trunks in the foreground, and upon the sides of the double cliff, where masses cast real shadows upon one another and the river below. The gradations are everywhere delicate and silvery, and the black touches exceedingly strong. This almost reaches the freedom of Kakei, without passing through the medium of Kano. 1st class.
Bought from a man to whom pawned.

$37. A set of 2 by Tsunenobu. These are very large and handsomely mounted. They are in Tsunenobu's second grade of excellence. They are both representations of a sacred lion, a bush of botans, and a cliff above. Monju rode on a lion, which was therefore considered a noble subject among Buddhists. Botans are always represented with lions, because these flowers grew and lions abounded in sacred Tendaiyama in China where Monju lived. The washes of ink are very crisp and beautiful, and the lions are better drawn than is usual with his school. What color there is in pleasant contrasting with the greys. On the box is written "Nipuku tsui, botan shishi. Hogen Yoboku". Bought from King -- collection of some kwazoku.   (MFA:11.4418-4419)

$38. A set of three remarkably large ones by Takanobu Yeitoku, the father of Kano Yeitoku's adopted father. He was not a very celebrated artist, but these are his best specimens. Probably painted to order for some prince.
   1. Waterfall and white flowers, mysterious and rather powerful.

2. Mr. Kano says this is adapted from old Chinese. A life size picture of a Sennin of Kuwan dynasty, who, first, as a common man, stole a magic peach from his friend Tobosaku a Sennin, which he ate, thus becoming a Sennin himself. It is rare to find such a large picture in later Kano painting.

3. Waterfall with red flowers.

Bought from King -- Collection of the same Kwazoku.

S39. A copy of a famous large mountain landscape of Bagenkin of Gen, by Gentan an as yet unknown Japanese artist. I have seen another copy of the same picture at Hasegawa's. The composition is very fine and bold. The touch and style of coloring show well the transition from the noble style of So to the weaker feeling of Min. This copy probably has not the harmony of color and softness of atmosphere of the original. The coloring is not so pure. The character of the touch, the composition, and the general conception of the color, are all that this picture can be said to illustrate. It is striking however, and such a large one is rarely found.   (MFA:11.4792)

S40. A very curious picture of 10 Rakan. No name is attached, and the painter is unkmown. It is clear by the touch that the artist belonged to no known school of painter. As Mr. Kano says, "it was not an artist who painted it." But that depends upon what we mean by artist. It was probably a priest, perhaps of Kioto, at first an amateur, but who developed a style of his own in his love for the art. Surely the sweep of the brush in the outlines is like that of no other artist. This settles that it is not a copy, though the lines of the bush above in their great strength might have been from the brush of Cho Densu. The figures too utterly lack that grace which is common to the professional Buddhist painter. The design is evidently earnest but not graceful, the features are distorted, and there were many things the artist did not know. But he was filled with his conception, and was blessed with a love and knowledge of color vouchsafed to but few Japanese artists. In this the color lies the greatness of the picture. I have seen but few things which equal its dazzling tones. It needs only to place it beside any other thing we have praised for brilliancy to see its extraordinary excellence. From the fact of their being 10 Rakan only, it seems probable that this was one of a set of 50 pictures of 500 Rakan. The simplicity of the whole is primitive and touching. One must forget the distortion in contemplation of the excellencies. Bought from King.   (MFA:11.4646)

S41. Large picture of peacock, white plum tree, and flowers. Wunkin. This gorgeous picture was painted for the national exhibition at Uyeno in 1878. The paralyzed artist was occupied 3 months upon it. He considered it his masterpiece. It was his last important work. The drawing is not strong, but this we can excuse the unfortunate artist. The composition too is a little confused toward the foreground. But the execution of details is masterly, and the color of the whole and of the parts is very beautiful. The artist and his friends considered it his masterpiece from the care and accuracy with which each detail of flower and leaf is rendered. Indeed Wunkin considered the lower part of it to be the best. There is no one left in Tokio who can equal it, and no one in Japan with such a feeling for color. My appreciation of this picture made bright Wunkin's last year. This thing must be considered as a refined symphony in beautiful color. I cannot consider it Wunkin's best work, or equal in quality of imagination and power to his earlier sketches. See No.45. Mounted to my order.   (MFA:11.4674)

^{S}42. A set of 2 large pictures of deer, by Taniu. These are reckoned by every Japanese artist who see them as the best of Taniu's first class, or at least just closely following No.33 in excellence. They were painted when the artist was 66 years old. The distortion of the drawing displeases foreigners, and it is at first difficultly (*sic*) to appreciate the ground of the raptures of native beholders. Mr. Kano says one excellence consists in the overcoming of the difficulties of execution. The color of the deer is exactly right. The red one is slightly better than the white. The chief excellence lies in the dignity of the soft yet strong, delicate yet simple, touch, pose, color, and general atmosphere. This quality no artist can copy says Mr. Kano. "We admire these pictures because they give us the noblest ideal impression of a deer." This appreciation undoubtedly depends upon the possession of a "classic" taste; just as our cultivated feelings at once granted to that which bears the stamp of ancient Greece, whatever be its peculialities or deformities. The whole picture is filled with what Japanese or Chinese must at once recognize as peaceful nobleness. The study of Chinese poetry may enable us to appreciate this Eastern classical feeling.
 1. White deer and green banboo.
 2. Red deer and white cherry tree. This deer is much the better of the two; and the drawing of the cherry tree is magnificent. The branches and blossoms also are most feelingly rendered in the highest classical style. The touches on the tree trunk every tree artist will recognize as marvellous. Even the weeds in the foreground are full of spiritual excellence to the Japanese aesthetic souls.
Mr. Kano Yeitoku knew these pictures by reputation, having in his own collection copies made by his ancestors, on which is written "In possession of the Tokugawa family." They may have been lost in the ruin of the Shogun's fortunes. There are no other Taniu's of their stamp known to be in existence.   (MFA:11.4796, 11.4825)

^{S}43. A set of two landscapes, by Kano Motonobu. These are large and in every way a most extraordinary work. No critic to whom I have shown them has ever seen anything equal to them before, or even of their kind. They represent a hunting scene in the mountain of China by the Royal or Mandarin's huntsmen. They probably were painted originally upon a two panelled screen, which explains the fact that they are but two halves of one picture. The conception is grand in the extreme, almost equal to old Chinese in feeling. The drawing is in Motonobu's strongest. The stratification and other formation of rocks is most impressively given. The drawing of figures and horses is most spiritual, the action actual. The drawing of the trees is unique and powerful. Mr. Hasegawa had never seen trees drawn in such a manner. The color is glorious what there is of it, deep violet and golden and gray. The contrast of the yellow hues and the lingering traces of gold, throws into a soft charming violet the masses and lines of the neutral ink. These may be called the finest landscapes of Motonobu, and they certainly have qualities which the work of no other artist possesses. Their last excellence of course lies in their spiritual power over the beholder, who gazes in amazement at their impressive panorama filled with unearthly beauty, knowledge, and life. I have since discerned that these were formerly on the sliding doors of Daitokuji. Kioto. See Note book of Biography. Sold about 40 years ago. In highest decorative style of Motonobu. (MFA:11.4265-4266)

^{S}44. Three large monkeys on a tree. Sosen. This is in the style of Sosen. The color is richer than is usual, and the drawing more accurate. There is as usual a lack of the divine fire and imagination. But this realizes the highest perfection to which the noted style of this painter could attain. But see No.59. The faces of the monkeys are the central point.

^{S}45. Branches of plum trees and blue bird. Wunkin. This is perhaps the finest of this artist's work, and yet it is only a sketch. The composition of the several branches in radiating lines with the bird at their focus is great. The touch also is very powerful, and in some respects original. The beauty of the grey and black is considerable. But the color is the point where the artist has impressed his originality. The red, grayish, and greenish plum blossoms make an extraordinary passage of subdued and varied color, which culminates in the perfect colors of the bird. Imagination and strong feeling make this picture, and it was struck off according to the artist's own fancy, not to fulfil an order, in the heat of inspiration. It was painted when Wunkin was a rising young artist, 20years old or so, and had not been seized with the fatal paralysis which so early put an end to his wonderful growth. The feeling in this may be compared with the fine things of the old masters, being altogether beyond the conventionalities of the later Nanping school. It is a fresh addition to Japanese conceptions.

^{S}46. Red plum blossoms and moon. Hoitsu, the prince and painter, who renounced his rank and fortune, and traversed the country on foot sketching. He followed in the style of Korin, as being striking and easily conveying impressions. This is a fair specimen of this artist. The stem and blossoms are painted in the Korin manner, though with a more modern, appreciative, and less hard and grotesque feeling. The moon is original being outlined only with a circular sweep of gold cloud. It is the type of Hoitsu's feeling at its pleasantest. He is far inferior in greatness of soul and strength to Korin. But see Nos.___.

^{S}47. Small simple mountain landscape. Taniu. This is in his commonest or poorest manner, and yet is not bad. After seeing his better works it may be compared, but need not here be dwelt upon. The scene seems to be similar to that of many others of his landscapes.

^{S}48. White eagle on a rock. A copy from Kiso Kotei, the Chinese Emperor of So. This is old, painted on Chinese silk, and according to Ninagawa the antiquarian, and also Mr. Kano, must have been executed in China 350 or 400 years ago. Very few genuine works of Kiso Kotei were in existence. This copy probable (*sic*) lacks the great strength and vigor of the original. It is beautiful however in its simplicity, and should be compared with the similar subject by Taniu. Bought from Tazawa.

^{S}49. A single branch of Fuyo. Tsunenobu, This simple work shows well the ordinary style of flower painting of the Kano school at this period. It has a delicacy and artistic meaning, without ever appreciating the side of flower beauty realized by the Nanping school. It is directly derived from old Chinese flower painting, as may be seen from a copy by Taniu in my album.   (MFA:11.4420)

^{S}50. Eagle on a pine branch covered with snow. Wunkin. This was about the last painting from his brush, being executed the month before he died. It has no special qualities, but is a common specimen of Wunkin's later style.

from here sent April 1881.

S51. A large picture of Shioki about to kill a green devil which he has under his foot. Bunrin of the Shijo or Okio school. In fierceness, force, and grotesqueness, this outranks all other Shiokis. The weight and pose of the massive figure is well rendered. The flying folds of drapery are conceived with an unintelligent brutal strength. Bunrin aimed evidently to render the powerful and horrible as such, and to make a sensation. The foreshortened drawing of the foot is rather unique, and the strength of the left arm and hand is praiseworthy. As a piece of painting the face with its masses of hair must be considered quite wonderful. The devil however is not so executed and conceived as to add to the picture. What color there is is poor, and after the manner of Buncho. The style in general is of the Okio school, but modified to imitate the grosser features of Ganku and Buncho. It probably succeeds well in rendering the impression the artist desired. Mr. Kano says it is good, but not very great, since it is only strong. It is coarse and has no refined artistic feeling. Mr. Hasegawa says the picture is not interesting, and shows the corruption of the Ganku style. Mr. Kano says this reminds him of Hokusai. Whenever the Okio style degenerates, he thinks, it always tends toward Hokusai. To the foreign eye, it is certainly an interesting, if not an admirable picture. Bought from Yamanaka. (MFA:11.4692)

S52. The female Sennin Seyobo (*sic*), with her two female attendants, one carrying a dish of sacred peaches, the other the long fan-screen. They are floating through the clouds, with gleams of light breaking here and there through the suggested mists. By Kowin, of the Okio school. The figures are graceful in their drawing, and dignified in pose. The drapery, decidedly Okioish, is very finely managed, especially the long mantles which float on the wind in yielding twisted broken curves. The touch in every part is firm and clear. But the chief beauty of the picture lies in its color, which, while quiet and less obtrusive than that of the great colorists of the Kano, Tosa, and Buddhist schools, is perhaps more charming and subtle. The brilliant key is reached only once in the handle of the wing-shaped fan which the principal figure carries. The execution of the beam of light which falls across the figure on the left is striking in the technical knowledge it displays. The weakest thing in the picture is the faces, which are all alike, and though dignified, possessing no great character. This however may have been the intention of the artist, to represent the unaffected calmness of such exalted minds. As a whole, though not strong, it is among the most beautiful of its school, which generally is quite lacking in color. Mr. Hasegawa says of it, that it is very good, and the artist must be put in the same rank with the great Keibun. As a picture this is as good as the large Ippo No. 84, described later on, he thinks. Mr. H. met this artist in Kioto 53 years ago. He was then about 40 years old. Mention of the composition should not be omitted, achieved by the position of the large fan-banner nearly over the head of the chief figure. Bought from Yamanaka. (MFA:11.4740)

S53. Small picture of a badger sitting on the snow with a few sprays of grass. Ippo. This is one of the best things of the Okio school, although one of the simplest. The badger is erect on his hind legs with his fore-paws in the act of beating his chest, while his cunning suspicious head looks off through the cold misty air, as if his attention had been attracted by some noise. The whole pose of the animal is the perfection of naturalness. The execution however is that which most astonishes. The drawing with no outlines in the first place is perfect. In the second the execution of the hair all over the body is microscopic, every individual hair white, gray, black and brown being represented with skilful fidelity. The spirit however is not lost in this detail. From a distance the figure stands out with almost the clearness of an etching, the black of the paws and face giving character and force to all the gradations. According to Japanese mythology the badger possesses a soul, and, like the fox, is able to bewitch the unwary among men. This picture therefore must be considered as more than the mere representation of an animal, since it attempts to render the spiritual power and realistic weirdness which the native sees underneath its animal nature. Mr. Kano says of this picture that its excellence shows that Ippo is next to Okio in the Shijo school. The sprays of grass are very fine in execution and feeling. Mr. Hasegawa says it is better than Okio's fox No.79. In this he is clearly wrong, and is regarding only what is mechanical in the picture. When the badger strikes his chest or his belly, it gives out a sound like a drum. Bought from Yamanaka. (MFA:11.4724)

^{S}54. Landscape in black. Renzan, best pupil of Ganku. This is good in conception, fine in composition, and unique and picturesque in execution. Two men stand in the foreground on the bank of a river, calling for the ferry boat which lies half concealed among the sedge and rocks. The ferryman's house lies behind a fine clump of trees in the middle distance. A cliff rises behind with the new moon at its edge. The tones in this are original and tender, masses taking the place of lines. There is an original element added to that of Ganku, somewhat influenced perhaps by bunjinga. So soft and pure on the gradations that they almost represent color. Renzan is perhaps the finest landscape painter of modern times. Mr. Kano and Mr. Hasegawa had never seen his work before, but thought it fine. He is not known outside of the Kioto district.

^{S}55. Bust of Monju in black, Cho Densu. The face is kinder and more spiritual than is usual in all Buddhist paintings. The touches in the drapery are very strong and characteristic of this artist. The hair is finely painted for the old style and with a fine effect of black. Clouds obscure the bust below; thus probably the figure is meant to be flying through the air. This picture has been much reduced in size, but originally had no other figure beside this. Mr. Hasegawa says that, although the picture bears no signature, yet it so well bears the stamp of the master that there is little doubt of its genuineness, Mr. Kano said it was a very fine picture and probably a genuine Cho Densu. Its fineness consists in its mild, kind, nobleness of expression, and well befits the supposed bearer of glad teachings from India to China. Bought from Yamanaka. (MFA:11.4497)

^{S}56. Blue Onagadori on a branch of a tree -- kaido or kind of cherry -- with red flowers. Minenobu, younger brother of Chikanobu. This represents the later form of the Taniu period. It is very pure and pretty, but has no element of greatness in it. The coloring is good, and the picture well unified in the darker mass of the bird. Mr. Kano Tomonobu says that Minenobu is the ancestor of his branch of the Kano house, i.e. the one into which he is adopted. And Mr. Yeitoku says it is a very good specimen of this artist, who was not greatly celebrated.

^{S}57. A red fox dozing beside a spray of purple asters. Sketch by Tetsuzan, one of the great pupils of Okio. The method of coloring the fox is fine as is the whole expression of rest and muscular relaxation. The tail which sweeps into the foreground is a mere blurr (*sic*) of color, while the head, upon which the attention is to fall, is clearly cut against the light background, thus displaying the artist's knowledge of the optical law of the focus. The sketch of the asters behind is pleasant. This shows finely the union of the naturalistic and picturesque qualities of the Okio school, which is not always as successfully achieved. Mr. Hasegawa says it is as good as Ippo's badger. Mr. Kano, while he thinks is good, calls it inferior to the Shioki of the same artist. See No.88, a most artistic sketch.   (MFA:11.4772)

^{S}58. Shioki and tiger in black. Kingiokusen. This artist is one of the early ones who painted in the black style in Japan. His pictures are very rare, Mr. Hasegawa or Mr. Kano having never seen one before. This is the only one I have seen. The figure is quite grotesque, but powerful in its drawing. It is cold and material, in this respect resembling the common work of Sesshiu. The difference between this and Sesshiu to the foreign eye would be slight, since it appears to be mostly technical. Mr. Hasegawa says that "it probably shows this artist at his best. He lived about the time of Masanobu." He says further that "below the waist the form is rather poor; but then," he says "in old pictures the form was generally not good. He cannot be called one of the finer Japanese painters." Mr. Kano says it is like the style of Doan the pupil of Sesshiu, but not so good. It must be genuine, for the artist being unknown, and not being a very great picture, no one would copy it. It is a pretty good picture however. Bought from Yamanaka. He was a very famous pupil of Motonobu.   (MFA:11.4228)

^{S}59. A black dragon in whirling descent through the cloud masses of a typhoon by Sosen, the famous painter of monkeys. This is one of the notable pictures of modern times, for several reasons. First, no one in Tokio, or in Osaka so far as I can learn, had ever seen or heard before of a dragon painted by Sosen. It is therefore perhaps a unique work of this artist. Second, in comparison with the many other works of Sosen I have seen, it is by far the finest. In his monkey and deer pictures realism seemed to be his chief object, and his composition and drawing of accessories was (*sic*) generally weak. Thus I had placed him in the modern schools as quite inferior to Okio and Ganku. But this picture exhibits a height of ideality, a possession by the spirit of beauty, a magnificent composition, and a strong sure drawing, such that he becomes at once lifted up to the level of the greatest reformers of the last century. Third, it is quite original in conception and manner. It owes nothing to Taniu, the great painter of dragons in storm. Its method of gradation is quite different from that of the Kano school. It is not rough and picturesque like the Ganku style; and while its touch approaches somewhat to the Okio manner, its feeling is quite peculiarly its own. Moreover it is what no dragon before has been, positively realistic in its drawing. The great scaly serpentine body actually curves and looks solid, now projecting forward into the light of its attendant flames, now retreating back into the shading mass of the cloud. One is prompted to ask from what natural model this was studied; and the answer is suggested, from some enormous serpent which must have reached Japan as a curiosity during Sosen's life. The fourth remarkable thing about the picture is the fact that it is one of the finest dragons ever painted by any artist, ancient or modern, Chinese or native. This is shown first in the conception which is evidently grand and powerful, next in the gradations of black which are as exquisite in their beauty as they must have been difficult of execution, but chiefly, as is sure at first glance, in the magnificent composition of curving lines, in which respect this picture almost stands alone in all Eastern art. The dragon himself forms a system of complicated spirals, against which the terrific strength of clawed limbs break in straighter masses of harmonious divergence, while the shifting lines of the curling flame play like luminous bands of wind-lifted shroud, before, around, and behind the rolling forms of the glorious monster, the mantle of its unearthly majesty. If we add to this the whirling masses of the cloud itself, and picture these several elements as fused into the transcendental unity of the artist-poet's conception, until lines and spirit are one in significance and actuality, we may then realize the exalted character of this work. If Ganku with all his power had been so true to himself, as Sosen in this picture, he might have attained the height of the great artists of the climactic period of old Chinese painting. Bought from Yamanaka. Sosen is a very great artist in other subjects than monkeys. In his great works he rivals any artist of modern times.   (MFA:11.4155)

^{S}60. Three quail and grasses. Tosa Mitsuoki. This is the subject for painting which this artist for 250 years has had the highest reputation. It is thought very much of by Japanese even of the present day. This is in his fine simple style of painting this subject. The excellences and weaknesses are apparent, first among the former the microscopic fidelity in the painting of the quail's plumage, and second the soft melting poetic satiny tone which characterizes character of the whole picture, seeming to be at once with the style of drawing and the character of composition, thus realizing a certain unity and delicate feminine refinement of feeling. Its weaknesses are, of course, this very femininity which seems almost unworthy of a man, rather clumsy and woodeny (*sic*) outlines, and the lack of significant masses. Nevertheless I can appreciate what the Japanese mean when they speak of the superior artistic beauty of Mitsuoki. This is far weaker than the Benten No.10, before mentioned, this being his more common style, and that his uncommon. From Yamanaka.   (MFA:11.4558)

^{S}61. A small picture of Shioki on a mule. Sesshiu. It is surprising how much is suggested by this meagre sketch. The two trees on the right and the lines of the ground are a mere scratch. The mule is done with a few vigorous touches of deeper tone; but Shioki is sketched with great power in firm angular black lines, his whole fly-away attitude and fierce expression well exhibiting the eagerness of his search. The use of black is masterly. Mr. Hasegawa says that 40 years ago this picture was brought to his house for criticism, and after considerable discussion by the artists of the day, it was decided to be genuine, and bought by one of the Tokugawa cabinet officers for 21 Rio, a sum near equal to 140 yen. Still it is of course not one of the great things of Sesshiu. From Yamanaka. Miniature copy by Tanyu exists in collection of Mr. Kuki. (MFA:11.4137)

^{S}62. A small picture of Quannon on a rock in black. Kawo. This is so darkened by age as to give no effect at a distance. Quannon is drawn simply with graceful outlines. The drawing of the rock and water is in very strong Chinese style. The expression of the face is not very noble. The feeling on the whole is something like that of Mokkei. Mr. H. says this is surely genuine, and a good specimen. He considers this artist as great as Ganki and greater than Motonobu. Motonobu may be more original, but not so great he thinks in execution. He became very celebrated after his death, His pictures were very rare. Mr. Kano says of it, that while he does not feel absolutely sure of it, yet it is what would be usually accepted by artists as Kawo. From Yamanaka.

^{S}63. The seven gods of happiness. Tanshin, the son of Taniu. This is an ordinary representation of this subject. Fukurokujiu is dancing with a child. Tanshin was not a great artist, simply copying his father's style. Four of the gods are acting the part of musicians. Bisyamon sits haughtily above, while Hotei sits watching with a childish grin. The arrangement is very good for this subject. Mr. Kano says it is a common specimen of Tanshin. Mr. H. thinks it a good picture for Tanshin. My own opinion is that it is rather a superior specimen.   (MFA:11.4727)

^{S}64. Dragon ascending on a storm cloud. Nikka of Shijo-school. This is very simple, but mysterious. Its peculiarity is that while other dragons have been painted with strongly outlined form, this has no outline, but is melted into the mass of the cloud in such a manner that one must use his imagination to see it, <u>as in nature</u>. The upward sweeping motion is fine, while a jet of lightening like flame sweeps downward. This shows the Okio style of sketching in some degeneracy of execution, though still retaining power in conception. The artist has no great celebrity. Mr. Kano thinks it approached to Hokusai. The artist is one of the good pupil of Toyohiko.   (MFA:11.4749)

^{S}65. Portrait of Yuima. Tsunenobu. This is one of the best portrait of the Kano school, next to Taniu. The simplicity of it is remarkable. The lines are not hard, but executed with a broad yielding touch of the pen, such that they represent the curves rather than the boundaries of surfaces. Thus there is a tender, melting sympathetic treatment which is in complete unity with the pathetic face of the old man. To my mind, there is more artistic feeling and power than in Tsunenobu's later and harder, even if prouder, mannered style. All effect is realized something like that which Ganku consciously sought after and attained. Mr. Kano says that the artist was not perhaps much over 20 when it was pictured. He considers it very good for his pictures at that age, but not equal to his later ones. 1st class.

^{S}66. A small heron on a rock. Sketch by Sesson. This is simple and rough, It is what the Japanese of taste greatly admire. Tones of the ink and the execution are considered perfect. It has not so much feeling to the foreign eye. The bits of bamboo are peculiarly striking and Sessonish. Of course it does not exhibit Sesson's great style. Mr. H. says, certainly genuine, at first glance, but a common specimen. Mr. K. says, good, and belongs to Sesson's middle class. From Yamanaka.

^{S}67. Chinese philosopher or Sennin among the rocks of a mountain, by Goshosen, a

Chinese artist of the middle (early first) Min Dynasty. He was a very noted artist, Mr. Kano says; and this, he assures me, is a fine specimen. It is a picture which Japanese artists would always consider great, and worthy to rank with the great productions of earlier days. It has none of the sickly weakness of most of Min work. The execution of the rocks is regarded as especially fine, the masses and wild strong touch reminding me strongly of Shohaku. The figure is drawn with great knowledge of the use of the brush. The simplicity, directness, and force of the whole feeling are grand. Still to my mind, it is colder and less deep in feeling than the great works of To and So, being good indeed for Min. From Yamanaka.

^{S}68. ~~Birds of paradise~~ Chinese pheasants on a rock, with bamboo, roses and a large peach tree. Chinnanpin. A characteristic specimen of this artist, whose pictures are much sought after at the present days. Its chief beauty is its delicacy of drawing and coloring. That of coloring is hardly surpassed by any artist. It is not perfectly harmonious however. Nanping's (*sic*) coloring was a revelation to the Japanese at Nagasaki. The rose blossoms and leaves are in the perfection of his delicate style. The peaches also are carefully painted. The execution of the principal bird is remarkable. This picture also shows Nanping's faults, his overfinish, his lack of composition, of strength of drawing, and of harmony in tone. Mr. Kano is inclined to doubt its genuineness, but he does the same of any noted Nanping in Tokio. Mr. Hasegawa is certain it is genuine, although he is inclined to think the signature was afterward put in when the old had been cut off. He says it is a fine specimen, uncommonly so, the coloring being Nanping's best, but the strength of drawing not to his greatest. My own opinion is that there is little doubt of its genuineness. Mr. Miyatsuka is certain it is genuine. All other critics whom I have consulted say likewise. From Yamanaka.

^{S}69. Lotus flower and leaves. Wunkei, a pupil of Sesshiu. This is certainly simple and beautiful in its drawing, although meager in masses and in color. Far weaker than anything of Sesshiu. For this reason it is especially <u>liked</u> by "bunjin". It is finely preserved, and its cloth mounting is splendid and old. Mr. H. says that it is a very good specimen of Wunkei, who was the direct student of Sesshiu, and whose paintings are now very rare. Mr. K. says it is good, but does not consider the artist as anything remarkable. It shows the more feminine development (*sic*) of the Sesshiu influence, as Sesson and Shiugetsu represent the masculine. From Yamanaka.   (MFA:11.4157)

^{S}70. Small mountain landscape. Okio. This is a notable work, chiefly because genuine landscapes of this epochal artist are very rare. In the second place it merits attention from its own peculiar excellencies, and signs of originality. Its most notable excellence is its beautiful soft atmospheric effect, showing the world as shining through the crystal ether of genuine mountain air. This is a new quality. Again there is an attempt at perspective, even among such difficult altitudes. There is an absence of the throwing up of the horizon line, so that the distant hills give their true feeling of altitude above us. Third the rocks are drawn with that realistic touch which Okio had discovered, showing their solidity, hardness, planes of cleavage, and ragged edges. Similar qualities are developed to a less degree in the pine tree. The cloud effects and distant hills are also finely rendered. It is discoverable at once however that Okio had studied from the

Ming artists. The composition and arrangement is more or less theirs, and the tree suggests them. In fact, if we compare the Ming landscapes with those of the later Okio school, we shall see that this distinctly exhibits the transition from the former to the latter. We may see moreover in this the distinctive weaknesses of Okio's pictures as pictures, namely their lack of any distinctive and significant masses of dark and light. The secret of this quality, Okio, with all his scientific observation of nature, never learned, and in this essential element fell far below the level of the old masters. Mr. Kano says this is undoubtedly genuine, and a very rare subject, so rare indeed that no one would have a motive to forge it. Mr. Hasegawa says that this was painted perhaps after seeing Bayen or Baki, but he is mistaken. for, as said, it is more like Ming work. He says further that it is a very fine specimen of Okio's landscape, its purity being very prominent.

^S71 View in the celebrated bay of Wakanoura in Kii, by Ippo. This is a simple bit by our reckoning, but is remarkable for a Japanese. Perspective, aerial and linear, are well rendered. The gleam of the water on the beach is a bit of naturalism new to Eastern art. The bending pine trees with insecure sand-bound root are common on every Japanese low shore. The blue is regarded rather as a quality of gray than as a positive color. The poem above says, "Who would not come to the Bay of Wakanoura to behold the gem of his soul?" This is a place renowned in Japan for its scenery. This was painted in the period of Tenmei, when ~~Ippo~~ was about ___ years old.

^S72. Tokei. Sketch of crows and moon.   (MFA:11.4773)

^S72. ~~Group of flowers, plum tree and 28 birds of different species. Shiuki. This painting although too crowded and too little unified as a picture, is especially valuable as a specimen of bird drawing. The small birds chiefly in the upper part of the picture are very finely and picturesquely drawn and colored. The branches and flowers of the plum tree as also the bits of bamboo are a fine specimen of the painting of the later Nanping school. There is a fresh deliciousness about the coloring which appears again in Wunkin, and is the only distinctive excellence of the artists of this century. This must be regarded as a group of studies, rather than as a picture. Mr. K. says this is much like Nanping, especially in the flowers, but far less noble than the picture of the Sangi No.___. Mr. Hasegawa said this was painted in the finest style of Nanping, this being even better than the Sangi in many respects, which latter is more in the style of Rioki.~~

^S73. Riotobin the Sennin teaching his magic arts to Shioriken another Sennin, the one who frequently is represented as floating on a fan. Design of Ganki copied by Taniu. First as a copy I judge this to be pretty good, since it is better than Taniu himself could paint in his own design. It probably is inferior to the original in gradation, and in the drawing of parts especially the feet. But it retains the deep intensive expression of the great period of Chinese painting, and well illustrates Ganki's conception and composition, if not his execution. The chief excellence of this, as of the old Chinese school as distinguished from the Japanese in general, is that the drapery, though skillfully executed, is not so done as to draw attention to its manner from the central motive of the subject, In this case the attitude and countenances of the two figures. On

the contrary the execution, strong without being exaggerated, is rather a pure mirror through which the artist's thought is seen. It is not necessary to describe what is so patent, the power of the faces and the nobleness of the attitude. Mr. Kano says this is one of the very fine designs of Ganki. It has nothing of the peculiarities of Taniu in it. From Yamanaka.

^{S}74. Large Quannon as fisherman's daughter. Tozan of the Shijo school. This isolated figure has some merits, but is not so interesting as many works of this school. There is a cold unsympathetic manner and tone about the whole which repels. The face is the weakest part, being quite Japanese in type rather than fine old-time Chinese. The lower part of the drapery is however quite fine both in its flowing folds and in its color, while the basket and fish is really a good piece of painting. This, of course, is the degenerating of the Okio school, but it still retains elements of greatness. Mr. K. calls it ordinary, of not sufficient nobleness, and inferior to the work of Kowin No.52. Mr. H thinks it noble enough for Quannon in this capacity. Its color he considers pretty good, but its drawing of lines not great. Its proportions are those of an ordinary Japanese woman. Tozan is pupil of Tetsuzan.   (MFA:11.4779)

^{S}75. Group of people sheltered from a sudden shower under a gateway. Icho (*sic*), son of the first Icho. This subject gives good opportunity for displaying the genre painting peculiar to the Icho school. Here ladies, and servants, artisans and carpenters, pilgrims and farmers, climbing boys, cake sellers, and nursemaids with babies have huddled together to escape a wetting. A group of blind musicians are hurrying along the street on the right, and in the foreground two boys are hurrying on a packhorse. It is one of the finest and most comprehensive specimens to be found of this style. Mr. Kano at first thought that it might be by the first Icho, but if so, he said it was not a good specimen of Icho's execution being too weak. If it be a copy, he said it must be from one of Icho's finest designs. Mr. H. however, said at once that it was by the second Icho, a very fine picture, though not so strong as his father. The son painted under the same name and signature; so many have thought his designs to be merely copies, when they were really independent works. This shows the popular painting of Japan 100 years before Hokusai was born. The three kinds of cloth in the mounting are magnificent. (MFA:11.4218)

^{S}76. Botans, bamboo, and queer waterworn rock. Bayitsu. This is the style admired at the present day, something between the Nanping style and Bunjinga. The artist is considered very expert in the use of his brush; but while his bamboo is well drawn, there is no very great artistic feeling in the picture. It is at best, clever. Mr. Hasegawa however, says of it, "the height of power is in this picture, and it is to be classed with Ippo's best work." He considers him one of the best of the recent artists. Says he died something more than 10 years ago. Mr. Kano says this artist was the teacher of Katei, now living in Tokio, and is not so good as Shiuki. Mr. Kano is speaking from the narrow point of view which regards all "bunjin" element as evil.

^{S}77. White falcon on a rock by the ocean. Taniu. This is rather better than the ordinary specimens of Taniu. Its chief excellence is the majesty of the bird's attitude, and noble independence of expression as it gazes off over the mist-hidden sea. The rock is also very strongly painted, and the water has a power of whirl and shock peculiar to the drawing of Taniu. The contrast also of the white of the bird with the dark of the rock adds purity and further grandeur to the whole. The fault lies in the hasty execution, and careless reliance upon a mannerism, which in Taniu's old age, too often served him as an infallible receipt for inspiration. The red orb of the sun, rolling through clouds above hardly gives the suggestion of light, and is never intended to do so in Eastern painting. The mounting is very old. The subject of this was undoubtedly suggested by Kiso Kotei. The bird is inferior to Sanraku or Chokuan. Bought from King.

^{S}78. Fujiyama seen from one of the mountain passes. Tanzan, pupil of Taniu. Mr. Kano says this is genuine and a common specimen. Mr. H. says it is rather poor, and that Tanzan's pictures are so rare, because nobody cared to order from such a common artist. On the other hand Mr. Setsuan said he considered Tanzan one of the best pupils of Taniu. This is the only one I have ever seen, and since it was painted at the age of 67, it undoubtedly exhibits a mature but hasty mannerism in which the best genius of the artist is far from appearing. The low natural slope of the mountain is far more impressive than the common exaggerations of its angle. It is degenerate Taniu. (MFA:11.4407)

^{S}79. White fox sitting out in the night mist. Okio. This is in the first class of Okio. It is not the drawing of the animal alone which rendered this great, masterly and accurate though it is. It is not the foreshortening of the head which seems to project from the background. Neither is it the technique which casts semitransparent mists across the figure. But it is the spiritual and supernatural meaning of the whole thing, which is a step beyond the mere naturalness which was too often the sole aim of Okio. The mysterious white fox, most knowing and dangerous in this bewitching powers of all animals, sits in the weird moonlight like a ghost half hidden behind a ghostly shroudy screen, casting his cold piercing glance into the very heart of the startled beholder, until the fascination of his gaze enables one to understand the superstitious fears and legends of a simple unscientific people. This is great art, to render a nation's belief of fear, in its strongest essential imaginative power, in a concrete force which renders unnecessary abstract description or story. This was painted in the period of Ainyei(*sic*). The sprays of grass, mysterious, almost without beginning or end, add form and give tone to the picture. Mr. Hasegawa says, strangely enough, that this reminds him of Taniu. He is referring evidently to the studies from Nature, such as Kano Moriki possesses. Mr. Kano says it is undoubtedly genuine and very impressive; still it does not show Okio's greatest power of drawing. Mr. Miyatsuka said it was the finest Okio he had ever seen. It is certainly the greatest I have yet seen with the exception of Mr. Nishimura's screens at Kioto. From Yamanaka.   (MFA:11.4900)

^{S}80. Tiger peering over the edge of a cliff. Ganku. This is the next best of Ganku's tigers, so far as I have seen, to the one on my pair of screens. Its excellences are many and great. Its conception, powerful, solid, intense. Its unity and composition of line simple, unconscious, and great. Its execution in Ganku's greatest picturesque, powerful style. The striped fur is well rendered, but all force is concentrated in the tiger's eager, cruel face, and in the half curved, projecting supporting leg and claw. The body as a whole seems to be thrown forward out of a mysterious misty background. The bit of bamboo on the left is perfect, and reminds one somewhat of Sesson. In all great qualities this must be compared with the old masters of Japan and China, with the additional merit of being original in style. One of Ganku's most vigorous productions. From Yamanaka.   (MFA:11.4698)

S81. 1.&2. Birds and flowers. Yosen. This is almost the best flower painting of the Kano school. The gradations in the flowers are so pure and the color in the greens is such that they seem almost like tinted ivory. The rocks also are very strongly drawn. Only secondary to the masses of flowers are the birds which enter into the composition of each. No.1 has botans and golden pheasants. The composition and coloring is less pleasing than in No.2, which shows sort of white pheasant and flowers like hollyhocks. Mr. Kano says that these are the very best specimens of Yosen's work. In many respect they are like the pictures of Ojakusui, though some of the flowers are like Shunkio. He says artists of this period took their subjects from the great Chinese painters of So and Gen, especially in flowers, although they had a style of their own. They are not direct copies, but adaptations. Their color is the richest ever used by Kanos, and probably shows us what the great old Chinese flower pieces looked like when they were nearly new. If I remember correctly, they are almost exact copies of designs by Shunkio in Shomu Kioku. From Yamanaka.   (MFA:11.4452-4453)

S82. The great waterfall in Mino. Richo of the Shijo school. This is one of the fine things which show the power in the new style. The old Kano waterfalls had fallen in gentle sliding curves as if in a lazy tumble. This curves on the brink, and then falls at once in almost straight lines with tremendous force and weight, the impression of which is heightened by the splash and seething of the foaming mass as it strikes in two projecting rocks near the bottom, where the seething spray has been rendered in attempt by a thoroughly new method. The side sprays of the fall leaping in tiny streams from crag to crag, like exquisite lace-work, add to the beauty and break the monotony of the great central mass. All the lines of white water are well brought out against the masses of rock and dark foliage. We may say that this artist has not been content to copy, but has been studious in receiving new fresh impressions from nature. Mr. H. says this is a good specimen, but its execution is not equal to Toyohiko's. Mr. K. says it is very fine, Mr. Tomonobu admiring it as I do. From Yamanaka. Probably a pupil of Toyohiko. A great picture.   (MFA:11.4762)

S83. Pine tree and two peacocks in black. Okio. This, not so good as the fox, is a fine specimen of Okio. The pine tree is in Okio's original strong peculiar style. The peacocks however are the best in drawing, the noble pose and unity of mass of the one on the tree being especially impressive, while the mere execution of the female below is even finer. Thus the head of the latter half turned on one side, is drawn with such knowledge, that it projects from the picture with solidity, although it is relieved by no shading. The execution of all the feathers, especially the smaller ones about the neck, is very fine, and exhibits Okio's peculiar masterly technique. As a whole the picture impresses by its simple lines, and as a Japanese suggested, its greys and gradations are so managed as to give the impression of positive color. This is the only attempt I have ever heard of, of painting a peacock in ink alone. Mr. Kano says there is no doubt that this is genuine, and must be ranked in the second class of Okio, the composition being especially fine. Its fault is a certain stiffness which is always visible in Okio's work. Mr. Hasegawa said it was genuine, as also Setsuan who greatly admired it. Bought in Tokio. Remounted by myself.

S84. Group of large pine trees in the snow landscape. Ippo. One of the finest landscapes of the Okio school. The conception is admirable, but the execution, in full harmony with it, is even greater, realizing winter to the full. The glorious masses of the ancient trees covered heavily with snow stand out in relief from the background of snow hills, as if seen through a stereoscope. The black edges of the trunks under the snow are so given as to help to produce this lively effect. Perhaps the greatest wonder is the execution of the snow lying on the pine foliage, which is merely the white ground of the silk, yet seeming to lie upon the outspread branches. Altogether the execution of this is so wonderful that one may fairly doubt if a European artist could begin to reproduce such an effect in water colors at all. Certainly it could not be done with any such simple direct means. This picture cannot be praised too highly, and with the badger No.53, it proves the greatness of Ippo, as almost the rival of Okio. Mr. K. thought it very fine. He said Ippo was far greater than Sosen and almost equal to Okio. Mr. H. called it in the best style of the Okio school, far greater than the Richo waterfall. From Yamanaka. (MFA:11.4728)

S85. Quannon seated on a rock. Black drawing by Yasunobu. A very good specimen for this artist. The lines of the drapery are quite beautiful, and the expression of the face is really sweet and feminine. The masses of the rock are subdued and refined, the only deep black in the picture being on the head and shoulders. Altogether there is a unity and a refined feeling in this picture and a style of finish, which I have nowhere else seen equalled by this artist. Mr. Kano calls it a very good one of the 2nd class. From King.

S86. Mountain landscape with rain. Yosen. This is hardly more than a sketch, and needs no description. The mountain dome above is noble with light on its edge. Mr. Kano said it was painted when the artist was young, that it is a common specimen, and more in the style of his father. 3rd class. (MFA:11.4455)

S87. Female tiger and young. Ganku. Not so good as the preceding, No. 80. This is much milder in expression and in drawing, less distinct, and less well composed. The rocks above are not strong either. The artist was less in earnest when he painted it. Still it is not a bad specimen for his common ones.

S88. Sketch of Shioki in red. Tetsuzan. In outlines merely, yet strongly put together and finely executed in lines of varying thickness. The expression of the face is very strong and peculiar, and the management of the drapery is original. Mr. Kano considered this to be a very good work of the Okio school, and a good typical specimen of this artist. (MFA:11.4390)

S89. Tiger coming down between two rocks to drink. Ganku. Very curious picture. Drawing distorted, face of tiger poor, stripes not blended, rocks bold but tremblingly executed. This is the poorest of my Ganku tigers, and it shows well the weakness of the old man in his last years. The manner of painting still however retains much of his former glory, the giant inside of the artist refusing to die.

S90. 1 & 2. Portraits of the two famous Gama & Tekkai Sennin. Chikanobu. These are painted in a rough shapeless style, hard and without inspiration. Yet Mr. Kano says that they are remarkably good specimens of this artist, being his 2nd class. If this be so, it shows that Chikanobu had degenerated to a level far below his father. No.2, the left one, is the best in every respect. To show the poorness of these, they should be compared with Ganki. No.2 has some individuality worth noticing. Bought from King. Collection of same kazoku as before.

S91. Mt. landscape in bunjinga style. Buncho. This exhibits well attractive qualities bunjinga possesses. Soft grays make a background for a few black queerly shaped touches and some trees of darker wash. This is meant to be hardly more than symbolical painting, still it contains a picturesqueness and free artistic execution recognizable by the unprejudiced eye. Mr. Kano called it a good one of the 2nd class of Buncho, and in the style of Taigado. All bunjin greatly admire it. Bought from Shimoda.

S92. Sangi and karassu on a branch of a tree crowned with snow. Hanabusa Icho (*sic*). A very odd picture in Icho's clever unexpected style of composition. The two birds one pure white and the other pure black stand one above another but facing in opposite directions. A vine with red berries winds round the branches and falls from above, these spots of blood red, giving the only color in the picture. The picture is striking and bold, and full of genius. Mr. Kano says it is undoubtedly genuine, although its execution is not very masterly for Icho.

S93. Portrait of the Sennin Oshitsu. By Gido of the Shijo school. This is a hasty sketch, but has the excellencies of the Okio rapid manner. The man sits leaning against a rock, an axe in his hand, and with a rapt upward gazing face. This somewhat approaches bunjinga, in manner. Mr. Kano called it good; and it is such as Japanese of modern taste admire.

S94. Tobosaku. Ranko. This picture, though small is excellent in all respects, drawing, shading, artistic touch, and expression. Especially well is the avaricious delight of the robber shown, as he lifts to his lips the coveted form of the magic peach. Mr. Kano thought it fine.   (MFA :11.4659)

S95. Birds & flowers. Banzan. A little better than this artist's ordinary work. In his 2nd class perhaps. Shows the increasing weakness of the Nanping school. The colors rather good.   (MFA:11.4666)

S96. Branch of cherry tree and water. Mochizuki Giokusen, the son of Ganku's pupil. This is a sketch made for me at Kioto in 1880. The artist seems to have left the Ganku style, and to have been absorbed into the commonplace of the degenerate Okio.

S97. Plum tree and roses. Kowun the young daughter of Wunkin. Childish, but interesting on that account.   (MFA:11.4658)

S98. Eagle on a rock with water below. Wunkin. This is strong for Wunkin, but shows that strength is not Wunkin's strong point. The color is harsh, and the waves are thin and splashy. Still it is original among modern productions.

S99. Narrow mountain landscape in black. Tameichi. This is common, but good and honest in effect. Shows the commoner sort of good painting (?). Since found that this is Hokusai.

S100. Eagle on pine tree by Kano Utanosuke. This is one of the most celebrated paintings of Utanosuke, and perhaps the best of the few now remaining. Kano Moritaka has in his collection a copy of this made by Taniu. It was celebrated through this copy for years in the Kano family; but they never knew what had become of the original. I bought it in the summer of 1881, at Yamanaka's, Osaka. Utanosuke rarely painted such large pictures, Mr. Kano says. The bird is the finest eagle I have seen in Japanese art. It seems to have the nobleness and keenness of a supernatural being. The pine tree is very powerful, and somewhat in the style of his father. The spikes of the leaves however have been retouched by a later hand, according to Kano Yeitoku, who took the greatest interest in examining it. The rest of the work is finely preserved. This picture almost reaches the simplicity and unconscious grandeur of the great works of So. Indeed it is not impossible that it may be a copy of a great Chinese work, but this is unfounded conjecture. The seal is genuine. Facsimiles of the two seals are to found *(sic)* in Honcho Gashi. It is considered by all the Tokio critics one of the finest of old Japanese paintings. It is believed to have come from the Konoke *(sic)* collection, Osaka. The grandeur of it consists. Possibly it belonged to the Hachisuka collection. One of the finest kakemonos in existence. All Japanese are carried away by it.

From here on sent March 1883.

S101. Monkeys on a cherry tree swinging in the wind and rain. Sosen. Of all the finely i.e. minutely executed pictures of monkeys by this artist, this is on the whole the best I have ever seen. The criticisms made on Nos.13 & 44 must in this case be taken back. Sosen here reaches great artistic height. The cherry tree is considered by Jap. artists to be a splendid piece of painting. The composition with its lines of repetition is perfect. As for the rest the picture describes itself. Bought in Kioto summer of 1881. All Japanese to whom I have shown it considered it to be the best of Sosen's first class. Formerly belonged to the collection of a Kioto gentleman.

S102. Small Chinese landscape. Shubun. In his characteristic style, with his strange scratchy etchinglike touches. Its goodness lies in an elevation of poetic sentiment approaching the Chinese. A copy of this picture by one of the descendants of Taniu is in the collection of Kano Moritaka. All the Tokio artists agree that this is a genuine Shubun. To me it is certain that this is the genuine work of this artist. No other touch is just like it in the history of Eastern art. In comparing Moritaka's copy with this, it was clear the former was copied from this identical picture. Obtained from an Osaka dealer who bought it from the collection of the Konoke (*sic*) family. Mr. Kanda had never seen such a fine specimen of Shubun. Some critics think that the seal was put in afterward.

^{S}103. Chinese landscape and palace. By Bun-o, son of Buncho. This is one of the finest specimens of Bun-o's original style, which is more regular if weaker than his father's. This landscape is very impressive, and gives one a pure Chinese impression. This is remarkable for a style which is not itself derived from the Chinese as the Kano is. But indeed Mr. Kano Yeitoku says that the foreground including the trees and man are almost copied from a design by Kakei. The touch of the brush however is somewhat different and more stiff. Its magnificence of composition is undoubtedly from Kakei. As for the palace, the style of it is derived from Kuntaku or Kameiyen. The upper rocks however are much in the Buncho manner, rather artificial, and lacking the freedom and blending of the great Chinese masters. The gradations throughout the whole picture are extremely beautiful, and though not managed at all like the Chinese, yet are so fine as to make up for some lack of strength in the drawing. Indeed then the work is notable, since it is an original conception of the very Chineseness of Chinese, recalling the very masters themselves, yet not like them. It is like perfect moonlight after the sun. This artist has not been so celebrated in Japan as he deserves. He is one of the best of modern times. Bought from King. (MFA:11.4790)

^{S}104. Mountains and mist in moonlight. Bunrin. Remarkably poetic. Style of Giok Ran with Bunrinish modifications. The writing on the picture says this is the night before the full moon. The nearest approach to the effect of moonlight breaking through clouds in Jap. art. The Kanos admired it. Fr.Yamanaka. (MFA:11.4688)

^{S}105. Hotei, by Keishoki. This though small is most characteristic of Keishoki's touch, and can be put in his second class. He is tickling his nose to make himself sneeze. On the box is written "Picture of Hotei about to sneeze." The cloth mounting is very old. Bought in Tokio. Criticized as genuine by Kano Yeitoku & Kano Tomonobu. All Tokio gentlemen consider fine. Kawasaki thinks first class. Sumiyoshi thinks cloth remarkably fine.

~~X? 106. Small landscape in rain. Toyohiko. Simple and characteristic of the artist's style. The silvery tones on the foreground water as of sun shining through the shower were intended for this, and are simply beautiful. It is in Toyohiko's ordinary style,~~

^{S}106. Tosa Mitsushige. Rakan.

^{S}107. Kaido flower and shijukara bird. Matsumura Keibun. The most beautiful painting by Keibun I have ever seen. Bought in Osaka. This shows the greatest height reached by flower painting by the pure Okio school. Lightness of touch, grace of form, and beauty of color are very notable. In the first class of Keibun. Bought from Uyemura, who in former years bought many first class things from good families, that had been pawned. All the Tokio artists consider it 1st class of Keibun. In the box is preserved a letter signed by Keibun acknowledging to the owner the receipt of the price of this picture which had just been painted for him, 5 bus (at that time).

S108. Bamboo in snow and sparrows. Keibun. Mostly in grey. Almost as beautiful as the preceeding. The box is not the true one belonging to this picture, therefore the writing on it has no significance. This is perhaps the finest black flower and bird painting of the Okio school. From Osaka. Considered by artists to be 1st class of Keibun. It was one of a set of 3, belonging to Nishio Bankichi which he broke.

S109. Keishoki. Small colored landscape, A beautiful little bit of Chinese scenery in the more angular style used by Geiami in his colored pictures, and partly borrowed from Shubun. Mr. Kano considered this genuine, and a very interesting fine and rare landscape. It recalls the landscape feeling of the Sento period in China. The color is thin & harmonious. Uneasy roughness of stroke is the sign of its freedom. & feeling. (MFA:11.4127)

S110. Buddhist painting of Monju on a lion. Kose Toshihisa. The lines of the figure are very delicate, though the lion is too stiff. The coloring however is very rich, and still shows the influence of Kanawoka. It says on the back of this that it is by Bunkan Shonin. Kano by himself consider the picture 900 ys. old. This writing however is of a much later date, (Kawasaki says time of Tsunetaka) and by no means to be trusted. The present Sumiyoshi of Tokio, the most able critic of such pictures in Japan, assures me it is by Kose Toshihisa, and his opinion is probably correct. I can see myself that it shows all the characteristics of the later Kose school, somewhat weakened by an admixture of Tosa element. On the outside it says that this picture was dedicated (to some temple) on Dec. 25th, 9th year of Anyei. The box does not belong to the picture. Bought in Osaka, A very fine specimen of middle age Buddhist painting. Mr. Kano considers this better than Jizo, No.1. He thinks inside cloth as old as the picture.

S111. Choso sitting on a pine tree. Ganki. This is declared by every one to be genuine. I saw it in Kodaiji Kioto in summer of 1880, where it was the property of the priest. We could not then agree about the price. In the summer of 1881 I saw it again., and finally bought it for 50 yen, the priest considering that he presented it to me as a favor. The certificate accompanying is a genuine one by Taniu, his handwriting being at once identified by the Kanos. Mr. Kano Tomonobu criticized it as genuine before my buying it. Kano Yeitoku confirmed it. No one dissents. The perfection of powerful simple stroke is in it. But the greatest point is the face with its intensive expression, and magnificent drawing. The very soul of this second St. Simon Stylites, with his magical Sennin power, gleams through his eyes. He sits on a nest in a pine tree, which can just be discerned below. A cloud obscures part of the picture on the right. It has probably been reduced a little in size, though not greatly Mr. Kano thinks. (MFA:11.4003)

S112. Fine Shaka on a throne. Takuma Tamehisa. The lines of this are considered very fine. Kano Tomonobu criticized it to be by Tamehisa. Yeitoku is sure it is Tamehisa. Matsuura, Ninagawa, & Kiosai agreed it was Tamehisa. Sumiyoshi, on the other hand, at first sight, said it was not very good, not Japanese at all, probably some unknown Chinese. In Dec.1882, about a year after, he saw it again, and at once pronounced it to be Japanese & by Kose Arihisa, considering it quite fine. This contradiction takes away much of the weight his criticism would otherwise have had. To me it appears clear, that the strokes are not at all in Kose style, but decidedly in that of Takuma. It was bought from the magnificent collection of the priest of Daiyoji, Tokio, and has always been considered to be by Tamehisa. Its ends are rock crystal. Sumiyoshi said the cloth was very fine, though of course comparatively new. Kawasaki says silk not older than 600 yrs. Yamana says Chinese.   (MFA:11.4093)

^{S}113. Picture of the banks of Sumidagawa. Sukoku. Very characteristic. Temple of Ushi no Gozen in the distance. It is spring. Mists are over the rice fields. Cherry trees are in blossom. Farm houses peep from under clusters of trees. Ferry boats and fishing boats are plying in the river. This is perhaps the purest of Japanese landscapes in Kano style, the Main Kano school chiefly painting Chinese landscapes or in a Chinese manner. This gives almost the exact appearance of the scene, but with high artistic generalization. The pleasure parties in the boats and the scenes on the banks are interesting. Crows fly away on the fields. This is in the first class of Sukoku. The box has nothing to do with the picture. This well shows Yedo suburbs 200 years ago. Mr. Kano, and all artists say this is the finest small work of Sukoku.   (MFA:11.4369)

^{S}114. 1-2. A set of 2 snow landscapes, by Genki, by some considered the best pupil of Okio.
No.1. Shows a small farming hamlet high on the mountain side and half buried in snow. The tone and execution of this are most tender and pure. All is most beautifully and simply rendered. The effect is less bold than in Ippo's landscapes, but more poetical and refined. Indeed this realizes in the Okio manner landscape feeling of the best Chinese period.
No.2. Shows a ravine in the side of a mountain. This is more clever than deep feeling. Snow and ice are in the ravine, but a stream falls out below. On the pictures it says Genki copied this, wh. undoubtedly means that it was copied from nature. It also says it was done in the autumn. The snow falls early on the heights around Kioto. The pure tone of the mounting cloth harmonizes with the soft delicacy of the picture. Mr. Kano considers this better than Ippo, indeed one of finest things of Shijo school. First class of Genki.   (MFA:11.4770-4771)

^{S}115.1-2. A set of 2 small landscapes. Buncho. These are characteristic of the artist, with their high rocks, half shadows, wild mists, and vigorous foregrounds. These have true atmospheric tone. There is some element of Kakei in China, and a little of Okio.
No.1 has a palace built over a brook in the immediate foreground, a Chinese scene.
No.2 has a man crossing a bridge in the immediate foreground. These have more freedom than any Japanese modern painting, except the best of Ganku. Both are autumn scenes. Kiosai doubted if they were genuine. Kano says they are fine for his youth, 30 yrs. old. The idea much like Sesson. He says it is a good specimen of his ordinary work. Matsuura considered them genuine.

^{S}116. Kano. Kanzan & Jittoku.

S117.1-2. A set of 2, dragon & tiger, by Goshun. These are queer specimens, especially the tiger. The dragon is in Goshun's ordinary manner, when he is painting after Okio style. This dragon is No.1. The upward whirl of cloud with its black opening is Okioish. The dragon himself has original power, and his soft greys look as if he were clothed in an armor of steel. The plum branch is in his own rapid manner. No. 2, the tiger, is probably an experiment of his, with a very soft hair brush such as is used in some kinds of bunjinga. I have never seen any other picture of any artist painted in the same touch. The Japanese artists do not like it, for it does not fall into any of their categories. Foreigners do not like it, because it looks unnatural. I alone see the artist's intent, and his high degree of success. The tiger is half sleeping in the sun. The touches of bamboo are masterly. The beauty of black and white is high. Kano considered the touch in tiger very original. I have since found that this use of soft brush was one of Goshun's regular methods. Undoubtedly genuine & good specimens. Bought in Kioto, at Sagakichi's.

S118. A small painting of a group of monkeys. Sosen. This is in his middling rough style. The hair is mostly in broad washes. The faces are most artistically painted. The composition is not striking, but the monkeys themselves are interesting in action. The box does not belong to the picture. All critics consider them genuine. Remounted by me.

S119. Three wild ducks standing on the edge of a frozen pond, by Manju. There is no composition here, and the picture is extraordinarily simple. But the interest centres in the ducks themselves which are most beautifully painted with soft greys. The legs are a little weak. Mr. Kano and others say this is so fine in execution, it might almost be mistaken for Okio. Indeed there is hardly any difference between these and Okio's ducks. The tones of grey in their plumage are almost unsurpassed. The box tells the subject on the outside. Box says "Two wild ducks on a snowy shore design." Manju must be one of the pupils of Okio.   (MFA:11.4746)

S120. Kano Motonobu. Large black pine & birds.   (MFA:11.4271)

S121. Rough landscape. Ganku. This is in the rugged picturesque manner of Ganku's later years. This probably represents the summer house of rustic build belonging to some man who loves tea ceremonies, by the side of a lake. Two men are starting off for an aesthetic picnic with their lunch baskets. The faces are dots and blurs like Turner's. The box does not belong to the picture. Kano considers it is Ganku's ordinary style. This is Chinese scene & Kano confirms it is picnic, box different.

S122. Small landscape, Oguri Sotan. The works of this artist are extremely rare, and this is an especially fine one. The crystalline rocks, and the pine trees are painted in a style of his own, though somewhat reminding of Bayen. The distance reminds quite strongly of Shubun. The bit of clouded sky beyond the mountain is a touch of naturalism not often found in old pictures. The effect of distance is finely rendered. Indeed the whole work is superior to that of Shubun No. 102. The cloth is very old. The following poem is written above the picture. "The mountains are blue and the water green. How old is that temple?! The mist is hanging from the top of the pagoda." On the inside of the box is written a certificate of genuineness, by someone whose name cannot be easily read. It says the poem was written by Made no Osho, and his seal is on the picture. The outside of the box mentions Made Koji as the writer of the comment. Made no Koji or Manri no Koji was priest of Sokokuji, where Sotan lived: also called Shitsuto Osho, and also Baiyan. Common name Dzuikiu. Lived in the era Onin. Both Kano Yeitoku & Tomonobu, criticize it to be a fine specimen of Sotan. His works very rare. Formerly in Konoke (*sic*) collection in Osaka. Nomura and Kashiwagi considered it fine.

^{S}123.1-2. Landscape by Bunrin. No.1.is a winter or early spring landscape. The snow is melting away from the foreground under the genial sun. The fresh green of bushes and young verdure is appearing beneath the late snow. A plum tree is just breaking into blossom. Others are not yet ready for it. A fisherman is spreading his net on the river in the foreground. Beyond rises the as yet unbroken dome of snow. The atmosphere is filled with damp which for the moment half obscures the sun. This is the most delicate and delicious painting of Bunrin I have seen, without any unnatural stirrings after effect, and yet showing his original genius in its purest phases. No.2. is far less successful. The artist failed to realize fully what he aimed at, having broken up the unity of the whole. Yet parts are interesting. He intended to represent the sun shining through the clouds of a breaking storm, the rain still falling, the mountain stream falling like a cataract, trees & rocks wet; the whole scene lying on the side of a mountain, and some foresters just about to cross the swollen stream and dangerous bridge. The sun shows the upper mountain white against a fragment of dark storm cloud. When looked at in the light of this original attempt the picture becomes interesting. He failed chiefly through attempting to introduce color. This represents a fall scene.

^{S}124. 1-3. A set by Taniu. No.1. is a landscape of powerful composition, No.2. a Fukurokujiu, No.3. a landscape still more powerful. The letters on the black box are written in silver. This is a very powerful set, bought from Yamanaka. When the two Kanos' saw it, they at once called it very bad and imitated by some ignorant fellows, much to my surprise. Of course great weight is due to their testimony. On the other hand Matsuura the antiquarian went into raptures over them, and said that they were the finest set he had ever seen, such hardly ever to be found again. Hasegawa Settei also, after careful inspection pronounced them to be in the 1st class of Taniu. Kiosai thought them fine, tho' not quite up to 1st class. My own impression is that they are genuine & fine. The roughnesses about them are frequent on other Taniu's declared genuine by the Kanos, and in very (*sic*) (every?) quality they are better than some they endorse. Sumiyoshi in presence of the two Kanos, could not help contradicting them, and calling them quite fine. Sumiyoshi thinks signatures good.

^{S}125. Yoshinobu. Yoshitsune on horseback. This is one of a former set of three, of which two were sold to Mr. George Emery. It is a good 2nd class specimen of the artist, and is almost a copy from a famous design of Tanyu. The coloring is well done. (MFA:11.4183)

^{S}126. Sosen Akinobu. Chinese pheasants. (MFA:11.4356)

^{S}127. Seiko. Bridge of Tofukuji in fall. This is quite beautiful. Good for recent Shijo. The subject is interesting on account of association with Cho Densu's life. (MFA:11.4765)

^{S}128. Tsuruzawa Tansen. Stork, sun & waves.   (MFA:11.4382)

^{S}129. Tansetsu. Storks and plum. This is a common specimen. Already is far toward the uninspired degeneration of the Tanyu style.   (MFA:11.4328)

^{S}130.1-3. Large paintings by Seisen. These are very handsomely mounted, and were undoubtedly painted to the order of some prominent man. The leaves on the botan are probably the crest of some Daimio. They are in Seisen's finest style of execution, and almost recall the strong days of Chinese painting. Altogether they make one of the handsomest sets of kakemono in existence, though their subjects are not especially interesting.
   No.1. is a group of botan and a rock. This is a pure Chinese style, and if not copied directly, is in close imitation of of some painting by Ojakusui or Chosho. The rock is finely painted, showing the best work of later Kano style, and the small botan shoots, the bamboo, and dandelion at the bottom are nearly perfect in their way. The upper leaves are almost exactly copied from Ojakusui.
   No.2. The Buddhist lion, sitting with Rakan-like contemplation at the entrance of his den. A Corean friend said he looked like Daruma. This is quite in the style of Isen, but the color is more muddy. It is one of the strongest paintings of the latest Kano. The finest points are the leaves and grasses hanging from the rocks, and the broken foreground under the signature. These points remind one of Chinese So & Gen painting. Indeed it is possible that this design is taken wholly from a Chinese original, now lost.
   No.3. This is another botan picture, but less well composed than the other, and fewer interesting points. It is copied either in whole or part from some Chinese flower picture, and shows just what Chosho must have looked like, when he was new. There is a decided nobleness about these pictures in spite of their defects.
These three represent subjects symbolical of Monju. Kano considers them 1st class of Seisen. Yeitoku says about 30 years old, when painted.   (MFA:11.4334-4336)

^{S}131.   Kionobu. 4 sleepers.   (MFA:11.4231)

^{S}132. Josen Yukinobu. Tobosaku. Not a celebrated artist. His works are rare. Ancestor of Tomonobu, who says this is a very fine specimen of him. It is indeed better than most post-Tsunenobu work, being nearly up to that master. Indeed Josen is already full of the new excellence which was lighting up Yeisen, and founding the fourth movement in the Kano school.   (MFA:11.4465)

^{S}133. Yukinobu. Figures.

s134. Torin Yoshinobu. Willow & sangi.   (MFA:11.4806)

^{S}135. Shubun. 2 small landscapes in circle.

^{S}136. Kano Yusen --- nobu. Kiku. The nounting of kiku cloth is in harmony with the picture. Formerly one of a set of 3 owned by Yamanaka. Tomonobu praised it as very good for this artist. It is tender, and the coloring is soft. A representative specimen of the work of the subordinate Kano of the day.   (MFA:11.4468)

^{S}137. Yusei. squirrel & chestnuts.

^{S}138. Ganki. Sennin.

^{S}139. Hunter seaking deer. Hokusai. This is a rare specimen, H.'s painted work being extremely scarce. The strange color, like oil, and the peculiar method of drawing are easily recognizable. (Many bad forgeries of Hokusai are now being made for foreigners?) His true touch is fine though grotesque. Every critic says this is genuine. Not so good as Kowin picture. Signature "Hokusaio." Very characteristic of Hokusai's later manner. (MFA:11.4601)

^{S}140. Scene on Lake Seiko, by Wunkoku Togan, the so called 6th from Sesshiu (including S. as No.1). Sumiyoshi says subject is Seiko. Signature says 6th from Sesshiu. Box says Wunkoku Hogen. Sumiyoshi says good picture.   (MFA:11.4509)

^{S}141. Quiet winter scene. Kiho. This although executed in rough style, and therefore not so well appreciated by Japanese, is really a fine work of genius; since what degree of dark and light and what color there is, is so managed, as to give at the distance of 25 feet a strong realistic impression. This is a simple farm among the mountains. The plum blossoms are almost coming out under the snow. The half frozen brook feels its way along its bed. This is a Chinese landscape.

^{S}142. Group of growing flowers. Hoitsu. This is one of the most splendid specimens of the Korin style. The grace of form and richness of color speak for themselves. The method of grading leaves is quite like Korin. Sumiyoshi says genuine, tho' not great specimen. Kano thinks fine.

^{S}143. Large picture of a Rakan. Kawo. This is very powerful, the expression of face intense. The hand is too small. Mr. Kano says this is surely not Nen Kawo, the touch being different; and thinks perhaps it may be by another Kawo at the time of Sansetsu. On the other hand Matsuura says it is genuine Kawo, made with soft brush; Hasegawa said it was Kao (*sic*) after taking it home to criticize; Kiosai guessed it was Kaosic from a distance, without seeing box or seal. It is a question hard to determine. Kano says it is nothing very good. Every body else thinks it a very fine thing, whether it be by Kaosic or not. The seal appears to be a genuine old one. It is true, that it appears to me to be unlike Kao's ordinary work, although very fine. Kiosai said that the rocks are drawn like Kaosic, and no one else would do such a Daruma. This, he says, is the Ranbioshi, style of touch like vine leaves. This is Kao's usual style, and this is finest specimen of Kaosic, he says. Kashiwagi said that seal looks genuine, and the only reason for not calling it Kaosic would be its unusual style. He considered it a fine work. So also Nomura. Sumiyoshi thinks not older than 300 yrs. I think really Kaosic.

^{S}144. Peach blossoms, willow, and yellow birds. Bayitsu. Firm scratchy drawing. Coloring delicate and striking. Fine composition. Everybody admires this, Matsuura calling it the finest specimen of Baiitsu. Birds are Ocho. Kanos think fine. Teacher of Katei of Tokio.   (MFA:11.4648)

^{S}145. 1-2. by Raisho. No.1. is pheasants and cherry blossoms. The color on the neck of the bird is good. No.2 is deer and flowers. This is soft and tender, but not great. These are the finest specimens of Raisho I have ever seen, and came from Kioto. All critics consider these to be in the first class of Raisho. They were originally exhibited at a government loan collection made for me in Kioto.

^{S}146. Fujiyama, clouds, & landscape. Tangei. This was presented to me by Mr. Kodera's uncle of Himeji, to whom I sent an oil painting of the Franconian old man on his 70th birthday. He was the teacher of Yutei. A rare thing, & characteristic, though not very great, -- subject, Fuji, Okitsu, Seikenji temple, Miwo coast. Box says "Spring Fuji." The gate below is Kiomigaseki on Tokaido, famous poems made there by courtiers.   (MFA:11.4293)

^{S}147. 1-3. Hotei & 2 flower pieces. No.1. is plum. No.3. bamboo. Taniu. No.2. Hotei. Kano Eitoku called them common specimens of Taniu, painted at about the age of 50. This is correct. They are not great, but they are simple and pure, and well represent the type of those sweet fine things, wh. spread through Japan, gave Taniu his hold of the common appreciation, and dominated the practice of artists. Genuine, but only 3rd class. No.3 is of miyama hojiro bird (whitecheek). Tomonobu says very likely painted at a dinner.

^{S}148. 1-3. Taniu. 2 storm dragons, & Shoki on a tiger. The Kanos say of them that they are 1st class of Taniu. Should say on general ground that they are next best to my Yuima set (No.33); but the Fujiyama set is in rarer style. Hasegawa thought them first class. Kiosai called them first class. Matsuura thinks them fine, but not equal to Fukuroku set (No.124). The transparency of the ink, and purity, and high tone is what the Kanos admire in them. Inside of box certified by Kohitsu, professional judge of handwriting.

^{S}149. 1-3. Chokuan the 2nd.
This is a very fine set of a very fine artist. 1 is the hawk on willow branch. 2 the hawk grasping heron, 3 the hawk pouncing on duck. Greatest hawk painter of Japan. Ink & strokes tremendous & artistic. Matsuura said he had never seen a painting of willow so fine as No.1. Hasegawa said they were so fine that they seemed to be by his father the 1st Chokuan. No.1 indeed has elements of the 1st Chokuan. Kiosai never saw so fine a specimen before. The drawing & ink on No.1 is stupendous. Both this artist and his father were as celebrated for hawks and eagles, as Sosen is for monkeys. Kano Y. says a very fine specimen. Artist famous at his time, afterwards forgotten, for more careful school. He is decidedly inferior in power to his father. Mr. Nomura says very black touches are characteristic of Soga school (?). No.2 is reproduced in Gonse from a printed copy. Famous design. Bought from Yamanaka.

^{S}150. 1-3. Kimura Nagamitsu.
Yeitoku says works of this artist are very rare. This is a very fine specimen. His style is peculiar to himself. All Japanese of pure literary taste admire it. Kashiwagi & Nomura considered it among the most striking of my collection. In the homely unadorned design, the fine pure depth of feeling comes forth. The very carelessness of the execution is in harmony with its special ideality.
  No.1. Sennin lying in boat, poorest of the three. Signature above man sleeping.
  No.2. Kinzanji temple on Lake Seiko. Meagre strange, and great. Touch has greatest power in a style afterward much used by Sanraku.
鄂州巖頭山
No.3. Kantashi in banishment. Noblest original expression of figures, equal to Motonobu. Horse is also splendidly conceived and executed. These are a good test as to whether one really perceives the high excellence of Japanese. No other such striking work of the artist is known to exist. From Yamanaka. Title "Mt. Gantôzan, in Gakushû" written on this picture. (MFA:11.4274-4276)

^{S}151. 1-2. Chikudô (Chikutô), both of dragons and water. The outlines of dragons are taken from designs by Shoô, so it says on pictures. But the forms are quite different from Shoô's, and the whole touch and style are original. Particularly the waves of No.2 are noticeable as rendering frothy mass and not outline of splashes. Clouding is pure and grand. The touch of brush is half bunjingaish, & half Okioish, especially in washes. Very grand, pure, pictures, high, original feeling, approaching great Chinese. Mr. Kano says that this method of painting foam is not entirely original, since Taniu sometimes did it. Matsuura says much better than ordinary bunjinga landscapes of Chikuto. Can be considered as among his best works. He is a Kioto artist, half of Shijo school. Bought in Kioto. (MFA:11.4650-4651)

^{S}152. Quannon. Motonobu.
Mr. Kano said that Motonobu's portrait of Buddha sold by Shosen to Okurasho has been considered the best of Motonobu, but this can now be said to be better, therefore the greatest Motonobu in existence. It is not a copy from Godoshi as some supposed. An original work. M's best in color and drawing. The Kanos in Tokio have a copy of this by Taniu; and they have been studying and copying this design for ages, without ever having seen the original, or knowing where it was. A greater work than the colossal Nehanzo of Mot. at Miokakuji, Kioto. For so old a picture on silk, this is well preserved. Has noblest feeling. Kano calls it the finest picture in my collection! The execution of the rocks is considered by Kano to be unsurpassed. The whole effect really rises to the simple grandeur of Godoshi. The starry effect of the white would not have been noticeable when new. The double halo is effective & original. Lines in drapery most powerful. The calm unearthly grandeur grows on one. Matsuura offered me 150 yen for it. It formerly belonged to the collection of the daimio Hachisuka of Awa. The touch in the rocks of this is absolutely uncopiable. In this Motonobu's style is merely the clearest form of expressing his idea of rock, instantaneous, inspired, not a manner. Of Motonobu's middle period. Kashiwagi said it was finest picture in my collection. Yamanaka sold me this cheap thinking it or calling it Cho Densu. Tanyu's copy of this afterward (1883) sold in Tokio for 350 yen. Has now become a celebrated work in Tokio, having been several times exhibited. (MFA:11.4267)

ˢ153. Shaka. Yeiken. Mr. Kano says this is very fine and well painted. Done he thinks about the period of Taniu. The coloring is the best part of it. He says it is quite possible that the design is taken from old Chinese.

ˢ154. Large tiger. Ganku.
Kiosai says this is equal to Ganku's peacock. Matsuura says good, but others as good can be found. Kashiwagi considered almost equal to deer (No.). The fur is wet, & thus the usually blurred stripes are stippled, also the wet gleam is well brought out on the top of the head. The air is full of driving mist. Some Japanese consider the bamboo especially fine. As Kano said, it is almost like Sesson. Probably in Ganku's later years. About best tiger of Ganku. Bought in Kioto. Such large powerful tigers of Ganku are now very rare.

ˢ155. Yojo. Kwazan. This represents Shin no Yojo, in the famous historical scene in which he attempts the life of the Chinese Emperor. It is a very large and remarkable specimen of figure painting. Its style is between that of Okio, and that of Ganku. The power of the picture is unmistakable, and Japanese immediately exclaim at it. Coloring is also well done. Yokoyama Kwazan, who must be distinguished from Watanabe Kwazan, must be considered as one of the greatest artists of modern Kioto. The mtg. is old and splendid, and harmonizes with the picture.   (MFA:11.4731)

s156. 1-3. Kano Yasunobu. Set of 3. 2 landscapes and Fukurokuju.
Kano Yeitoku and all agree that these are absolutely 1ˢᵗ class of Yasunobu - drawing firm and clear, and color beautiful. Only equalled by the Kuanon of Yasunobu in Chishakuin Kioto.
  1. Best landscape. Clear pure atmosphere, delicious foreground. Total feeling very much like Sesshiu. Yet touch characteristic.
  2. Fukuroku, deer, and stork made into a circular design. This is done with the utmost cleverness, no circular outline being given. The lines in drapery here are the best of Yasunobu, the face also is most characteristic of his best work; also the color in its ivory softness is unsurpassed.
  3. Snow landscape. This is poorer, and seems more like the degenerate works of the immediate descendants of Yasunobu.
The whole set is very noble and beautiful, and illustrates well the essential differences between this artist and his two brothers.

ˢ157. Peacocks. Hoyen.
Kiosai says this is very fine, but not equal to Ganku's peacock. Matsuura says very fine. Kanos also admire it. The drawing of the flower petals, and the delicate gradations of the leaves are noticeable. Whatever stiffness there may be in the birds, is derived from Okio. Composition fine. Such a carefully deep colored large bird piece of Hoyen is very rare. Yamanaka.   (MFA:11.4722)

ˢ158. Rough monkeys. Sosen. Kiosai says this is the finest picture of the Shijo school he has ever seen. Matsuura says this style of Sosen is very rare. This is finer, he thinks, than 101. I have never seen any other one in such a rough style. Kanos call it first class.

All admire its amazing artistic power of execution. The fur is representing (*sic*) by coarse grading melting touches with a wide soft haired brush. What knowledge is contained in such a hand that can bring out such a thing by such means. This has a deep tone like the old masters, quite unlike Sosen's ordinary work. Really to be ranked with old masters. Bought in Kioto. All critics admire it. The best of Gonse's illustrations of Sosen are in this style. It is among his most powerful and artistic works. 1st class.

^{S}159. Peacock. Ganku. This is one of the most extraordinary of Japanese paintings. In it the wild genius of Ganku reaches high power. The bird with spread wing perched on the edge of the cliff, is like a demon bird. The leaves are finely painted, the two bits of red coming in with effect. This is unlike any other Eastern painting. The composition, subject and drawing spring from original vigor and idea. The Kanos considered it very great. Ganku's style is unlike any Chinese. Such a picture of a peacock is unique they say. It impresses one with great feelings. Hasegawa says that this is better than Nanping's; although usually Nanping is better than both Ganku & Okio. Kiosai thought it magnificent. It is in Ganku's sketchy style on paper. Greater I think than Ganku's celebrated careful peacock in Kioto. Yamanaka. Probably toward the end of Ganku's middle period.

^{S}160. 8 gods of happiness. Kwazan. The 8th one on the left is Otafuku, not the name of any particular person; any ugly woman is called Otafuku. This is a most clever picture. and well sustains the reputations of Kwazan. The gods are slightly hilarious with saké. Benten pours more, with smiling face. Bisyamon is already overcome. It is very comical. The execution in the faces, and in the rich flowing drapery is beyond all praise. It is not exaggeration to say that this is one of the best drawn pictures Japan ever produced.   (MFA:11.4730)

^{S}161. Flower and birds. Rioki.
Yeitoku says this is poorer than Koyoshin, not Rioki, or a copy. But a genuine unknown Min. Few know the genuine Rioki. Most called so are false. Hasegawa calls this a good genuine specimen of Rioki. My own opinion is that it is not genuine Rioki. All Tokio Riokis are false. Only 1 or 2 in Kioto are genuine. This is a good specimen of the Tokio Rioki. Since writing the above, Mr. Nomura has criticized this to be surely of Gen. The method of shading the rock shows it. There is an old seal on the side, not yet deciphered. I also think it to be of Gen, and quite fine.

^{S}162. Donshu. Wild mountain landscape. This is inferior to Donshu's greater works, still it retains a measure of the artist's strange unearthly genius. It is half like Buson and the macaroni school; but the strange silvery lights play through it, and it has true landscape power.   (MFA:11.4695)

^{S}163. Fukurokuju. Ganku.
Kano Yeitoku says this may be called next best to Ganku's peacock. As to the subject, he says that children are considered a fortune. Fukuroku then with child is God of Fortune. I think this is doubtful. It is perhaps some forgotten legend of a child being carried off to the Sennin heaven to have long life conferred upon him. It was probably

to hang up at a birth. Some think it may have been tried in imitation of a Christian painting. If not a legend, it is the genial expression of a hope or well wishing to a child. Kashiwagi thinks this theory is correct. Kashiwagi says surely genuine. It is in Ganku's later style, and somewhat affected in drapery by Okio influence. Such foreshortening of a child's leg is a unique thing in Japanese art. Even a naked child is unique. Yamanaka.

^{S}164. 2 deer. Ganku.
Yeitoku calls this very greatest of Ganku, far greater than Okio. Hasegawa says finest of Ganku, Okio more mild & noble, but not so strong. Matsuura says there is no other such Ganku in existence. Painted probably when about 40. The mountain is the finest part. Every body is struck at the sight of this; and all say "we never knew Ganku could paint like that." Mr. Wakai admired it so much, that he carried it to Kioto to be copied by process on silk, but it could not be done. Bought in Tokio from King. Kashiwagi, Mr. Nomura, Mr. Sano all called it Ganku's finest work. The greatness lies first in natural conception of deer, in management of hair and spots, so as to bring out form in relief without shadows; the hair itself executed neither too fine nor too coarse; the Mt. behind, which may be considered equal to Sesshu in force & simplicity; the soft warm swimming atmosphere behind the deer; in which the mt. side seems to quiver. Japanese say this is equal to Okio, but it is far ahead of Okio. It is the greatest picture of modern times in Japan probably, Ganku being the only modern artist who in knowledge, vigor, & ideal feeling approaches Sesshiu. Some Japanese consider the mountain the finest part of it. It is undoubtedly a work of Ganku's middle age, say about 35 or 40. Austin Robertson raved over it as the finest kakemono he had ever seen, and far ahead of Landseer. It is one of the greatest animal paintings in the world.   (MFA:11.4701)

^{S}165. Tree, flowers, & bird. Koyoshin
Mr. Kano Yeitoku says this is in the regular style of the famous bird painter at the beginning of Min. Hasegawa says the idea is better than Rioki, the execution not so good. All artists admire its grandeur of conception. The birds are the hahacho. I consider it one of the very finest of the Min bird pictures, equal to the finest genuine Rioki's. Its grandeur is almost unsurpassed in bird pieces. Its execution is not the greatest, but simple, vigorous direct. Bought from Yamanaka. The strong dominating dark branch of the tree is grandly painted.

^{S}166. 1-2. Toyohiko. Set of 2 landscapes.
These are in the middle class. They are good and clear in execution.
(MFA:11.4777-4778)

^{S}167. 1-2. Tsukioka Sessai. Set of 2 figure pieces.
These are not so strong as the works of his father Settei; but they are of much the same character. The coloring is careful and good.   (MFA:11.4626-4627)

^{S}168. 1-3. Naonobu. Set of 3. Daruma, heron and lotus.
39 yrs. old. First class Kano Yeitoku.

ˢ169. 1-3. Tanshin Morimasa. Set of 3, Rihaku, birds and flowers. 1st class of Tanshin, according to everybody.

s170.1-3. Tanyu. Copy from Masanobu. set of 3. Confucius and 2 disciples. (MFA:11.4399-4401)

ˢ171. Suyeyori. Black flowers and bird. First class. In fine, Kano Yeitoku.

s172. Motonobu. Painted fan -- figures.
Box says Kohogen, really Suyeyori in all possibility. no seal. Good average picture of Motonobu school, and interesting as showing the prevalent style of gift fans. (MFA:11.4270)

ˢ173. Morikage rough landscape, river scene.
Yeitoku thinks signature is not genuine, and as to painting very risky. Tomonobu thought it one of finest landscapes ever seen, almost up to Sesshu. My own opinion is that it is surely genuine, clever and good; but too grotesque and meagre to be considered of high rank. It is typical however of a great deal that Morikage did, and was admired for in his day.

ˢ174. Kano Yeino. Small landscape.
"Scenery a poem in early spring in Royei" on box. Yeitoku says fine. Works of this artist very rare. This retains traces of the pre-Tanyu style of Kano painting. Tomonobu thought it very interesting and good.   (MFA:11.4429)

ˢ175. Kano Yosen. Shuko. portrait, Shuko Tan. Middle class, 50 yrs. old, says Yeitoku. A good typical specimen of Yosen's style in painting faces, and of later Kano work. Its excellence goes beyond mere form, and even reaches the sphere of high soulful expression.   (MFA:11.4454)

ˢ176. Shoyei. Sprays of botans, colored, genuine certificate by Yeishin. Otherwise Yeitoku would hardly think it genuine, lowest of middle class he says. He thinks paper repaired. Sumiyoshi thinks fine. I say, one of the most splendid flower paintings of early Kano. Tomonobu admired, color peculiar, rich and surprising, of a most original and decorative tone. Most artistic. Bought in Nagoya 1882.

ˢ177. Chinese boys at palace gate. Hoyen.
This is one of the most delicate, pure, and carefully thought-out and finished works of this master.   (MFA:11.4717)

ˢ178. Kaihoku Yusetsu. Jurojin.
Very rare says Yeitoku. Box says "Jurojin" but both Kanos say surely Yuima. A very striking picture, having something of the power of Sesshu in it.   (MFA:11.4534)

ˢ179. Geiami, small landscape.   (MFA:11.4124)

s180. Soga Shotei. 2 horsemen. Small.
Another name for Shohaku undoubtedly, say (sic) Kano. "Jasokken" on picture. Very fine.

This is one of the most delicate works of Shohaku. Ink magnificent, drawing of horses fine. A great work worthy of a great European artist. Every one admires. (MFA:11.4520)

^{S}181. Kano Ko-Yeitoku, birds and flowers, colored, genuine, in good, says Yeitoku. picture only a little larger in beginning. Camellia flower, bird probably pigeon. Middle class, about 30 yrs. old says Yeitoku. A good rough specimen, I think. It does not have the great qualities of Yeitoku. 3rd class.

^{S}182. Choriusai. 2 young hawks small. (MFA:11.4120)

^{S}183. 1-2. Tanyu. Set of 2. Carp & waterfalls. Yeitoku says first class of Tanyu.

^{S}184. Hoyen. Fine landscape with waterfall. (MFA:11.4718)

^{S}185. 1-3. Tanyu. Set of 3. Yokihi, birds & flowers, small.
 1. "Hakukan bird" & botan" on back. They (the Kanos) say sanko bird.
 2. Yokihi, usually subject connected with botans.
 3. Sanko bird & botans
Yeitoku says these are first class of Tanyu. Such fine lined ones of Tanyu are very rare indeed. Designs are his own, not Chinese. Done as early as 30 years old. Sumiyoshi says "worth 150 yen." Kanos say these and Yuima set are best of Tanyu.
(MFA:11.4395-4397)

^{S}186. Tsunenobu. Branch of tree.
Fine, 1st class of his youth say Kanos. Subject parasitic cherry, Signature genuine. 20 years old. (MFA:11.4417)

^{S}187. Yofu. Small black landscape.
Kanos & Sumiyoshi think fine. (MFA:11.4159)

^{S}188. Giokuraku. Bird & branch, colored.
Shijukara bird. Yeitoku says genuine. Middle class. Flower is Mokugen. Certificate by Yeishuku genuine. (MFA:11.4190)

^{S}189. Yokoyama Kwazan. Colored landscape. Chinese scene, box says "Good harvest." Men are drunk in congratulation of good times.

^{S}190. Hokusai. Colored landscape.

^{S}191. Sukoku. Copy of flowers & bird fr. nature.
Kawarahiwa bird. Upper flower Mokugen. All say a very medzurashii thing.
(MFA:11.4367)

^{S}192. Cho Densu. Seated Rakan colored.
"12th Rakan, Kadaka Daisa Sonja" on box. Writing on box by Tanyu. Yeitoku says middle class. Sumiyoshi says genuine. (MFA:11.4067)

S193. Kano Sansetsu. Dragon.
Good, Sumiyoshi says. Yeitoku says 1st rank of middle class.

S194. Kano Tohaku. Hotei.
Name Tohaku Chikanobu, Kano thinks.   (MFA:11.4180)

S195. Buzen. Night landscape. Small.   (MFA:11.4791)

S196. Goshun. Landscape.   (MFA:11.4716)

S197. Kaihoku Yusho. Kinko Sennin
Yeitoku says middle class. Sumiyoshi says good.

S198. Tosa Mitsuoki. Figure piece. Wide.
One of the 6 brooks famous in poetry, Tamagawa Ide of Yamashiro. Man horseback is Shunjei, the court poet who made the poem about the river, The poem itself is written on the picture, "I will stop my horse, and make it drink of the Tamagawa, where clean water gives dews to this yamabuki." (yellow flower). Box different.   (MFA:11.4567)

S199. Seiki. Landscape.
Subject is Togen sennin of peach valley. Box different.   (MFA:11.4764)

S200. Kano Chikanobu. 3 happy gods.
Middle class says Yeitoku, formerly one of set of 3. 40 yrs. old says Kano. Subject Hotei, Yebisu & Daikoku.   (MFA:11.4175)

S201. Gido. Daikoku.   (MFA:11.4709)

S202. Gido. 8 Sennin.
Kanos don't know what the sennin are doing. But the small circles above are stars. (MFA:11.4708)

S203. Oguri Soritsu. Birds and flowers.

S204. Yamada Doan. Bird on branch.
Bird is Jutaicho. Kanos & Sumiyoshi say good. His pictures rare. Jutaicho means "longevity-carrying bird."

S205. Tosa Mitsunari. Female figure.
1st class of Mitsunari says Sumiyoshi. Box says "Court lady under cherry," comment by an imperial relative."   (MFA:11.4816)

S206. Kano Juseki Atsunobu. The 3 Founders.
Pictures of Sosen's ancestor are very rare. This is good & interesting. Sumiyoshi says fine. Poem says "Dries when touched by the lips. There is no taste to the sweet dew." Kanos never saw before.   (MFA:11.4171)

S207. Ikkiu. Sketch of tree and bird.

S208. Nikka. Charcoal burning.   (MFA:11.4751)

S209. Tanyu. Portrait of Chinese Emperor.
Yeitoku says middle class, so Sumiyoshi. Emperor is Bunno of Shu. Signature good. Hogen about 50 years old.

S210. Yosai. Kuanon(*sic*)
Yosai when old. Kanos & Sumiyoshi say genuine.   (MFA:11.4780)

S211. Nagaku (*sic*). Monkey on rock.   (MFA:11.4748)

S212. Tsukioka Settei. Group of women.
Box says "Prostitutes of 3 cities." Yeitaku thinks middle figure is Tokio. Sumiyoshi thinks left is Kioto. Age 67. Sumiyoshi says interesting thing.

S213. Toyokuni. Figures & screen.
Subject "Popularized Genji." This is 2nd Toyokuni, whose former name was Kunisada. He was artist who illustrated the novel of Genji Interesting & fine thing, all say. (MFA:11.4610)

S214. Yukinobu. Figures and boat.
Subject, Hanrei & Seishi. Yeitoku says middle class. Sumiyoshi says better than Genji. Box says Yokihi -- is wrong.   (MFA:11.4464)

S215. Tosa Mitsutada. Horai.
Sumiyoshi says genuine, painted about Tempo.

S216. Ganrei. Landscape with canal.

S217. Kano Takanobu. Rihaku.
Yeitoku thinks that style not so modified by time of Takanobu, perhaps by Koi's son. (MFA:11.4372)

S218. Bunrin. Large snow landscape.

S219. Tosui. Great waterfall.   (MFA:11.4776)

S220. Soshiseki. Rooster and flowers.   (MFA:11.4820)

S221. 1-2. Tanshin, Morimasa. Set of 2. Chinese landscapes.
Subject four seasons. Kanos say genuine.   (MFA:11.4386-4387)

S222. 1-2. Nishikawa Tsukenobu (*sic*). Set of 2, female figures.
Sumiyoshi thinks later and false. Yeitoku thinks fine. Tomonobu surely genuine & fine. Sumiyoshi is mistaken about his age that he was pupil of Matahei. Much later I say. The girls are portraits of those who wrote the annexed poems.

S223. Shokado. Portrait of Yamabe no Akahito and 6 poets.   (MFA:11.4518)

S224. Ashikaga Yoshimochi. Toba.
Some say subject is Toshimi, --probably Toba says Yeitoku. Yeitoku says genuine. Formerly had Isen's certificate says box. Certificate by Kohitsu Riôhan. (MFA:11.4161)

S225. Towun. Heron and lotus.
1st class say both Kanos & Sumiyoshi, rare thing equal to Tanyu. Chajin would like it, the most chajin thing.   (MFA:11.4238)

S226. Morikage. Toba.
Middle class say Sumiyoshi & Yeitoku. Genuine. Yeitoku has copy. Cloth fine. This is a tea man's picture says Sumiyoshi.

S227. Shohaku. Horse.
Sumiyoshi thinks interesting.   (MFA:11.4505)

S228. 1-2. Kano Mitsunobu. Set of 2 landscapes.   (MFA:11.4472-4473)

S229. Tosa Mitsubumi. 7 gods.
Good for him says Sumiyoshi but not much of an artist. Name to be pronounced Mitsuaya.   (MFA:11.4559)

S230. Donshu. Tengu and birds.
"Made in Kayei." Subject King of Tengus, and the birds are attendant Tengus. (MFA:11.4696)

S231. Morikage. Botans.
All say first class, rarest thing. No critic would know it. "Mugeisai" is name.

S232. Kwakei. Burning of Eastern Hongwanji.
"Higashi Honganji fire" on box.   (MFA:11.4735)

S233. Copy of Chinese landscape, falsely said to be by Isen.   (MFA:11.4215)

S234. Maruyama Oshin, wide landscape.
On box says "Green trees & spring rain Arashiyama."   (MFA:11.4755)

S235. Kano Kiuyen. heron and lotus.
Sumiyoshi things (sic) rather interesting, good for Kiuyen. A rare thing. Kano says genuine. This Kiuyen he thinks is about Genroku period.   (MFA:11.4373)

S236. 1-3. Kano Yosen. Set of 3. Jurojin and dragons.
Upper class of middle rank, very good, says Yeitoku. Sumiyoshi thot (sic) very fine. Middle subject of Juro taken fr. Sesshu's design with modifications.

^{S}237. Hiakkoku. Botans and bird.
Finely painted, by Tomonobu & Sumiyoshi. Box is different, the name is same. (MFA:11.4655)

^{S}238. 1-3. Kano Yeishuku. Set of 3. Jurojin and landscapes.
1. Spring & summer. 2. Jurojin. 3. Autumn & winter. Waterfall is sign of summer, because then liked best. First class of Yeishuku says Yeitoku.   (MFA:11.4440-4442)

^{S}239. Seisen. Copy of Chinese landscape by Sonkuntaku.
Original owned by Tokugawa Moyei Hitotsubashi. Good copy.   (MFA:11.4333)

^{S}240. Kano Chikanobu. Willow & swallows.
First class say all. Painted at same time as Minenobu, 242, about 30 yrs. old. Swallows migrate hither when willows are green.   (MFA:11.4174)

^{S}241. Kano Tsunenobu. Fukurokuju.
Yeitoku thinks painted when young, 30 yrs. or so. 3rd class.

^{S}242. Kano Minenobu. Bamboo, snow & sparrows.
Very good says Yeitoku. Middle class says Tomonobu. Sparrow is an honest bird, thus only likes worms that grow on bamboo.   (MFA:11.4247)

^{S}243. 1-2. Genya. Set of 2. Small landscapes.
Very fine say Yeitoku & Sumiyoshi. Probably 2 of an original hakkei.
   (MFA:11.4188-4189)

^{S}244. 1-2. Kawo. Set of 2. Kanzan & Jittoku.
Yeitoku thinks false, that is, very old copies. Sumiyoshi thinks genuine & fine.

^{S}245. 1-2. Hasegawa Tohaku. Set of 2, landscapes.
Very fine copies of Choshiu Motonobu screen, Middle class of Tohaku.

^{S}246. 1-2. Tobun. Set of 2, figures.
Subject is the preservation of healthy sennins, by sneezing No.1. & shampooing. No. 2, Yeitoku thinks surely older than Motonobu & by the original Doki Tobun, pupil of Shubun. Sumiyoshi says fine & rare.

^{S}247. 1-3. Kano Toshun set of 3, plum &c.
Yeitoku says by old Toshun. Sumiyoshi says cloth very fine & rare. Pine & plum arranged in style of flower arranging art. Good for that artist. Set used for congratulation. Pine is young pine. Surely a New Year's set. No.3. is the best one says Yeitoku.

^{S}248. 1-3. Kano Yusei Teranobu (*sic*). Set of 3. Sun & waterfalls.
Yeitoku says middle class of him.

  1. of Kegon waterfall at Nikko.
  2. middle. Sun & water. Sumiyoshi says finely done.
  3. Jakko waterfall, Nikko.
Sumiyosi says fine set. (MFA:11.4411-4413)

S249. 1-2. Kano Tamboku. Set of 2. Storks.
Man who painted very little. Said to have spent his life in playing go. Sumiyoshi thinks a fine set, good mounting. (MFA:11.4374-4375)

S250. Kano Isen. set of 2. Botans.
Isen 20 years old, says Yeitoku. First class for his young years Used in congratulating occasions, very fine. His own design, not copied from Chinese says Yeitoku.
(MFA:11.4210-4211)

S251. 1-2. Kano. Set of 2, flowers in ink. He (Yeitoku & Sumiyoshi) think seal on 2 is genuine, on 1 is false. Perhaps from screen. Sumiyoshi says by some pupil using Yeitoku's seal.

S252. 1-3. Tosa Mitsuyoshi. Set of 3.
Storks and quail. Very good set for him but not very good in itself. Except quail, the subjects signify happiness & good wishes. 1. kiku & quail. 2. storks & pine. 3. corn & quail. (MFA:11.4570-4572)

S253. Kano Naonobu. Toenmei.
Painted when about 20 says Tomonobu, good rough, not tea picture. But his rough pictures ordinarily loved because he was a great tea man himself, and for simplicity.

S254. Hoyen. Landscape of Biodoin.
Box different. (MFA:11.4720)

S255. Icho. Piper and boys.
Seller of cake & midzuame says Sumiyoshi. Box has cake, & barrel ame, umbrella. Large fan is his sign. Man has dress of foreigner with false beard, blows pipe to attract children. Yeitoku thinks a copy. Sumiyoshi thinks fine. Kano Tomonobu thinks fine.
(MFA:11.4222)

S256. Yogetsu. Hotei.
Yeitoku says signature is very fine. Very good. Signature "Shiakushin Yogetsu." Yeitoku says first class. (MFA:11.4160)

S257. Kano___. hawk and bird.

S258. Minenobu. Sparrows & ricefield.
Yeitoku & Tomonobu say first class. (MFA:11.4246)

S259. Tangen. Pine branch.
Mounting very fine. Kano says picture genuine, pretty good. Name Morihiro. Certificate by Okura Kosai, a Kioto critic who lately died. (MFA:11.4376)

S260. 1-2. Toyeki. Set of 2. Landscapes.
Chinese landscapes in style of Sesshiu. Genuine says Kano, but not first class. Cannot identify the landscapes.   (MFA:11.4528-4529)

S261. Yukinobu. Female in house.
One of subjects in Genji Monogatari, box says "Ishiyama scene" of author. Probably is not so says Sumiyoshi. Probably one of the 2 seaside chapters.

S262. Kano Shosen. Group of storks.
A common specimen says Kano. Hogen between 30 & 40 years old.   (MFA:11.4346)

S263. Sukoku and son. Fukuroku & children.
Son's name Sukei. There's a seal. Kano Tomonobu says very fine & interesting. Perhaps almost first class of Sukoku, box different.   (MFA:11.4368)

Atsunobu 3 founders	206
Bagenkin Copy, Gentan	39
Baiitsu botans	76
Baiitsu peach & bird	144
Banzan kwacho	95
Buddhist Rakans	40
Buddhist Monju	110
Buddhist Shaka	112
Buddhisr Shaka Yeiken	153
Buncho landscape	4
Buncho hawk	7
Buncho waterfall	11
Buncho 3 Jurojin	36
Buncho Bunjin sansui	91
Buncho 2 landscapes	115
Bun-o landscape	103
Bunrin Shoki	51
Bunrin moon sansui	104
Bunrin 2 landscapes	123
Bunrin snow landscape	218
Buzen landscape	195
Chikanobu 2 Sennin	90
Chikanobu 3 Gods	200
Chikanobu willow	240
Chikuto 2 dragons	151
Chinese sennin Ganki	138
Chinese flowers	161
Chinese tree & birds	165
Cho Densu Monju	55
Cho Densu Rakan	192
Chokuan 2nd 3 hawks	149

Choriusai hawks	182
Donshu landscape	162
Donshu Tengu	230
Ganki Choso	111
Ganku tiger & tree	12
Ganku tiger & cliff	80
Ganku tiger & young	87
Ganku rough tiger	89
Ganku landscape	121
Ganku tiger & bamboo	154
Ganku Fukuroku	163
Ganku deer	164
Ganku peacock	159
Ganrei landscape	216
Geiami landscape	179
Genki 2 landscapes	114
Genya 2 landscapes	243
Gido Oshitsu	93
Gido Daikoku	201
Gido 8 sennins	202
Giokuraku flowers	188
Giokusen Kanzan & J.	9
Giokusen 2nd cherry	96
Goshosen	67
Goshun 2 tiger & dragon	117
Goshun landscape	196
Hoitsu plums	46
Hoitsu flower	142
Hokusai hunter	139
Hokusai landscape	190
Hokusai landscape	99

Hoyen peacocks	157
Hoyen karako	177
Hoyen waterfall	184
Hoyen Biodoin	254
Icho heron & snow	92
Icho piper	255
Icho 2nd people in rain	75
Ikkei Ushiwaka	18
Ikkiu tree & bird	207
Ippo badger	53
Ippo landscape	71
Ippo snow pine	84
Isen 3 landscapes	302
Isen copy Chunese, false	332
Isen 2 botans	501
Josen Tobosaku	322
Kaisen botans	371
Kano Kanzan & J.	161
Kano pine & birds	201
Kano squirrel	371
Kano fan	722
Kano 2 bl. flowers	512
Kano hawk	57
Kawo Kuanon	621
Kawo Rakan	432
Kawo 2 Kanzan & J.	441
Keibun kaido	107
Keibun snow bamboo	108
Keisai heron	5
Keishoki landscape	109
Keishoki Hotei	105
Kiho landscape	141
Kingyokusai Shoki	58
Kionobu 4 sleepers	131
Kiso Kotei copy eagle	48
Kiuyen heron	235
Koin Seiobo	52
Koki rooster	6
Kose Jizo	1
Kowun plum	97
Kuazan Jizo	155
Kuazan 8 Gods	160
Kuazan landscape	189
Kwakei fire	232
Manju ducks	119
Minenobu bamboo	242
Minenobu sparrow	258
Minenobu bird	56
Mitsubumi 7 gods	229
Mitsunari female	205
Mitsunobu (Kano) 2 sansui	228
Mitsuoki Benten	10
Mitsuoki quail	60
Mitsuoki figures	198
Mitsutada Horai	215
Mitsuyoshi 3 storks	252
Morikage botans	231
Morikage Toba	220
Morikage landscape	173
Motonobu Kuanon	152
Motonobu 2 sansui	43
Motonobu horses	15

Nagaku monkey	211		Tanzan Fujiyama	78
Nagamitsu 3	150		Tetsuzan Shoki	88
Nanping dogs	23		Tetsuzan fox	57
Nanping pheasant	68		Tohaku (Has.) 2 sansui	245
Naonobu 3 Daruma	168		Tohaku (Kano) Hotei	194
Naonobu Toenmei	253		Tobun 2 figures	246
Nikka charcoal burning	208		Toho copy Ojakusui	3
Nikka dragon	64		Tokei crows & moon	72
Nishikawa Tsukenobu 2	222		Torin Yoshinobu sangi	134
Okio landscape	70		Tosa Rakan	106
Okio white fox	79		Toshun 1st 3 sun	247
Okio peacock	83		Tosui waterfall	219
Oshin landscape	234		Towun heron	225
Raisho 2 deer &c.	145		Toyeki 2 landscapes	260
Rankei landscape	25		Toyohiko 2 sansui	166
Ranko carp & water	22		Toyokuni figures	213
Ranko Toboaku	94		Tozan Kuanon	741
Richo waterfall	82		Tsukioka Sessai 2 figures	672
Renzan landscape	54		Tsukioka Settei women	12
Sansetsu dragon	193		Tsunenobu Benten	8
Seiki landscape	199		Tsunenobu 3 Gods	31
Seiko Tofukuji	127		Tsunenobu 2 lions	37
Seisen 3 landscapes	34		Tsunenobu Fuyo	49
Tanyu white hawk	77		Tsunenobu Yuima	65
Tanyu 3 Fukuroku	124		Tsunenobu pine	186
Tanyu 3 Hotei	147		Tsunenobu Fukuroku	241
Tanyu 3 Shoki	148		Tsuruzawa Tansen	128
Tanyu 3 copy Masanobu	170		Utanosuke eagle	100
Tanyu 2 waterfall	183		Wunkei Lotus etc	69
Tanyu 3 Yokihi	185		Wunkin peacock	41
Tanyu Emperor	209		Wunkin plums	45

Wunkin eagle	50
Wunkin eagle	98
Wunkin 6 flowers &c.	2
Wunkoku Seiko	140
Yamada Doan bird	204
Yasunobu 3 Fukuroku	156
Yasunobu Kuanon	85
Yeino landscape	174
Yeitoku 1st Bird	181
Yeitoku 2nd 3 Tobosaku	38
Yeishuku 3 Jurojin	238
Yofu landscape	187
Yogetsu Hotei	256
Yosai Kuanon	210
Yosen 2 kwacho	81
Yosen landscape	86
Yosen Shuko	175
Yosen 3 Jurojin	236
Yoshimochi Toba	224
Yoshinobu Yoshitsune	125
Yukinobu female	261
Yukinobu Seishi	214
Yukinobu female	133
Yusei Terunobu 3	248
Yusetsu (Kaihoku) Jurojin	178
Yusen 1st kiku	136
Yusen 2nd Sumidagawa	21
Yusho Kinko	197

Editor's Notes & Glossary

by Seiichi Yamaguchi

A

Ainyei   Correctly "Anyei".

Akamatsu   Art dealer, details unknown.

ame ([S]255)   See midzuame.

Anyei   安永. Era 1772-1781.

Arashihiyama   嵐山. Mountain in the west of Kyoto. Famous for cherry blossoms in spring and autumnal colors.

Ashikaga Yoshimochi ([S]224)   足利義持, (1386-1428). 4th Shogun of the Ashikaga Government, who learned painting under Chō Densu.

Austin Robertson ([S]164)   Richard Austin Robertson. American collector, who Stayed in Japan 1881-1886.

Awa   阿波. A province. Now Tokushima prefecture.

B

Baki   馬逵 (dates unknown). Chinese artist, Bayen's brother.

Banzan ([S]95)   Nakamura Banzan (中村晩山, 1834-?). Artist who died in the early Meiji era; details unknown.

Bayan ([S]122)   梅庵 Baian. See Made no Osho.

Bayen   馬遠 Baen (dates unknown). Chinese representative landscape painter ranking with Kakei (夏珪) in the Sung dynasty (late 12th century).

Bayitsu ([S]76,144)   Yamamoto Baiitsu (山本梅逸, 1783-1856). Nanga (南画) painter in the late Edo period.

Benten   弁天. Buddhist goddess of wealth.

Biodoin ([S]254)   平等院. Temple at Uji (宇治)

Bisyamon   毘沙門天. Bishamonten. One of 7 gods of happiness.

biwa   琵琶. A kind of lute which Benten always holds.

botan   牡丹 (peony).

Brooks, Mr. ([S]17)   Phillips Brooks (1835-1893). American preacher who visited Japan in 1889.

bu ([S]107)   分, equivalent to a fourth of one ryo (両) in the currency system of the Edo period.

Bukanzenji   豊干禅師. Zen priest in the Tang dynasty.

Buncho ([S]4,7.11,36,91,115)   Tani Bunchō (谷文晁,1763-1840). Nanga (南画) painter in the late Edo period.

bunjin   the literati.

bunjinga 文人画. Painting in the literati artist's style.

Bunkan Shonin 文観上人 (1278-1357). Priest artist in Daigoji temple (醍醐寺) in Kyoto.

Bunno of Shu (^{S}209)   Emperor 文王 of 周 (Zhou). Founder of Zhou dynasty (BC. 1066-BC.23.

Bun-o (^{S}103)   unidentified. Bun'yō? See Bun'yō.

Bunrin (^{S}51,104,123,218)   Shiokawa Bunrin (塩川文麟, 1808-1877). Pupil of Okamoto Toyohiko of the Shijō school.

Bun'yō (^{S}103)   Tōzaka Bunyō (遠坂文雍1783-1852). Artist of Nanga school in the late Edo period. Tani Binco's disciple and teacher of Yoshizawa Setsuan.

Buson   Yosa no Buson (与謝蕪村, 1716-1783). Artist of bunjinga in the middle Edo period.

Buzen (^{S}195)   Sumie Buzen (墨江武禅, 1734-1806). Pupil of Settei (月岡雪鼎).

C

chajin 茶人 (tea man). Expert in tea ceremony.

Chikanobu   See Kano Chikanobu.

Chikudo, or Chikuto (^{S}151)   Nakabyashi Chikutō (中林竹洞, 1778-1853). Nanga (南画) painter in the late Edo period

Cho Densu (^{S}55,192)   兆殿司 Minchō (明兆, 1352-1431). Priest artist of Tofukuji (東福寺) temple, Kyoto. ('densu' means sexton)

Chokuan (^{S}149)   Soga Chokuan (曽我直庵, dates unknown). Founder of the Soga school

Chokuan the 2nd (^{S}124)   Soga Nichokuan (曽我二直庵, dates unknown). Son of Chokuan.

Choriusai (^{S}182)   Chōryūsai (長柳斎, dates unknown). Artist in the middle Muromachi period (the 15th century)

Chosho Chōshō 趙昌 (dates unknown). Chinese painter in the North Sung dynasty (later 10th century).

Choso (^{S}111)   Mistake for Chōka (鳥窠). Another name of Dōrin (道林), a Zen priest in the Tang dynasty, always sitting on the branch of pine-tree.

D

Daikoku 大黒. One of 7 Gods of Fortune.

Daitokuji 大徳寺. Zen temple in Kyoto.

Daiyoji 大養寺. Temple in Tokyo.

Daizen 大善. Art dealer in Tokyo.

Daruma 達磨 Bodhidharna, (?-528). Founder of the Zen sect, born in India, active in China in n the early 6th century.

Doan   See Yamada Dōan (山田道安).

Donshu, Ohara (^{S}162,230)   Ōhra Donshū (大原呑舟, ?-1857). Artist of the Shijō school in the age of the late Edo to early Meiji era.

Dzuikiu (^{S}122)   瑞九. See Made no Osho.

E

Echizen, province of   越前国. Now Fukui prefecture.

F

4 sleepers (^{S}131)   四睡図. A subject of a Zen picture, representing Bukan accompanied by a tiger, and Kanzan & Jittoku sleeping together.

Fukurokujiu or Fukurokuju   福禄寿. One of the 7 gods of happiness.

fuyo   fuyō 芙蓉 (confederate rose).

G

Gama & Tekkai Sennin   蝦蟇仙人 & 鉄拐仙人. Two sennins in ancient China, both well-known for using supernatural arts.

Ganki (^{S}73,111,138)   顔輝 (dates unknown). Chinese artist in the late 13th century.

Ganku (^{S}12,80,87,89,121,154,159,163,164)   岸駒 (1749-1838). Artist in the late Edo period; founder of the Gan school

Ganrei (^{S}216)   岸礼 (1816-1883). Grandson of Ganku (岸駒).

Geiami (^{S}179)   芸阿弥 (1431-1485), also called Shingei (真芸). Son of Nōami (能阿弥) and father of Sōami (相阿弥); they worked as artist under the Muromachi government.

Gen   Yuen (元). Chinese dynasty (1271-1368)

Genji (^{S}213)   *Nisemurasaki Inaka Genji* 『修紫田舎源氏』. A novel by Ryūtei Tanehiko 柳亭種彦, 1783-1842).

Genki (^{S}114)   Komai Genki (駒井源琦,1747-1797). Artist in the middle Edo period; one of Ōkyo's most distinguished pupils.

Genroku   元禄. Era 1688-1704.

Gentan (^{S}39)   Shimada Gentan (島田元旦,1778-1840)? who some say is Bunchō's brother.

Genya (^{S}243)   Kano Genya (狩野玄也, dates unknown). Pupil of Motonobu.

George Emery, Mr. (^{S}125)   American collector (1853-1933). The period of stay in Japan unknown. Later one of the founders of Saco Museum, Maine.

Gido (^{S}93,201,202)   Shibata Gitō (柴田義董,1780-1819). Artist in the late Edo period; pupil of Goshun.

<u>**Gio**</u>   Gyō (行). An art style in Japanese calligraphy, flower arrangement, gardening and other arts. 行 is characteristic of "cursiveness". See Shin (真) and So (草)

Giokuraku (^{S}188)   Kano Gyokuraku (狩野玉楽,dates unknown). Pupil of Motonobu.

Giokuran   Ike no Gyokuran (池玉瀾、1728-1784). Wife of Taiga (池大雅).

Giokusen (S9)   See Mochizuki Giyokusen (望月玉川).

Giokusen 2ⁿᵈ (S96)   See Mochizuki Giyokusen (望月玉泉).

Godoshi   呉道子 or 呉道元. Chinese artist in the Tang dynasty (8ᵗʰ century).

Gonse (S149)   Louis Gonse. Author of *L'Art Japonais* published in 1883.

Goshosen (S67)   呉小仙 (1459-1508). Chinese painter in the Ming dynasty. A pseudonym of Goi (呉偉)

Goshun (S177,196)   Matsumura Goshun (松村呉春,1752-1811). Artist in the late Edo period; the founder of the Shijōha (四条派).

H

Hachisuka, Prince   Hachisuka Mochiaki (蜂須賀茂韶,1846-1918). Former lord of Tokushima clan; appointed to the post of ambassador to France in 1882

hakkei   八景?, 8 beauty spots.

Hakukan   白鵰. A bird of luck.

Hahacho   八八鳥 (hahachō). Bird, a kind of starling.

Hanrei & Seishi   范蠡&西施. Chinese loyalist & his sweetheart. (BC. 5ᵗʰ century).

Hasegawa, Mr.   Hasegawa Settei (長谷川雪堤,1819-1882). Contemporary artist.

Hiakkoku (S237)   Oda Hyakkoku (小田百谷, 1785-1862). Another name for Oda Kaisen (小田海僊). Artist in the late Edo period.

Himeji   姫路, a city in Hyōgo prefecture.

Higashi Honganji   東本願寺. The main temple of Jōdoshinshū Ōtani school (浄土真宗大谷派) in Kyoto.

Hogen   法眼 (Hōgen). A title conferred on excellent painters, next to Hōin (法印); higher rank of Hokkyō (法橋).

Hoin   法印 (Hōin). Highest title given to the most excellent painters. See Hogen.

Hoitsu (S46,142)   Sakai Hoitsu (酒井抱一, 1761-1828). Artist in the late Edo period, who strove for revival of Kōrin (光琳) style in his later years

Hokusai (S99,139,190)   Katsushika Hokusai (葛飾北斎 1760-1849). Ukiyo-e artist in the late Edo period

Honcho Gashi   『本朝画史』*Art History of Japan* (5 vols), edited by Kanō Einō (狩野永納) and published in 1678.

Horai   蓬莱 (Hoōrai). Isle of Eternal Youth (Chinese legend).

hossu   払子. A kind of flapper, a brush of long white hair (one of priest's belongings)

Hotei   布袋. One of the 7 Gods of Fortune.

Hoyen (S157,177,184,254)   Nishiyama Hōen (西山芳園, 1804-1867). Artist of the Shijō school, who studied under Matsumura Keibun (松村景文)

I

Icho, 1ˢᵗ (S92, 255)   Hanabusa Itchō (初代英一蝶1652-1724). Genre painter in the middle Edo period. In his youth he was a popular aitist called Taga Chōko (多賀朝湖), but in 1693 he was arrested because of satirical drawings and exiled to Miyakrjima island. Seven years later when returning to Edo by acquaintance, he changed his name to Hanabusa Itchō.

Icho,2nd (^{S}75) Hanabusa Irchō (二代英一蝶1676-1773). Son of Itcho,1st Painter of the same style as his father's.

Idzu 伊豆. A province, now a part of Shizuoka prefecture.

Ikkei (^{S}18) Ukita Ikkei (浮田一蕙, 1795-1859). Artist who studied under Tanaka Totsugen (田中訥言) in the late Edo period.

Ikkiu (^{S}207) unidentified, 一休?

in 印 (Seal).

Ippo (^{S}53,71,84) Mori Ippō (森一鳳, 1798-1871). Artist in the Edo-Meiji period; pupil and later son-in-law of Mori Tetsuzan (森徹山).

Isen See Kano Isen.

J

Jakko waterfall Jakkō waterfall (寂光の滝). A waterfall at Nikko (日光).

Jasokken 蛇足軒. Pseudonym of Shōhaku (蕭白).

Jiso Jizō (地蔵菩薩). Buddhist god of mercy.

Josen Yukinobu (^{S}322) Kano Jōsen Yukinobu (狩野常川幸信,1717-1770). Son of Yoshinobu(甫信);the 3rd master of the Hamachō Kano family (浜町狩野家).

Jurojin 寿老人. One of the 7 gods of happiness.

jutaicho 綬帯鳥. A bird of congratulation.

K

Kadakadaisa Sonja 迦諾迦代蹉尊者 (the 12th Rakan).

kaido 海棠. Crab apple,

Kaihoku Yusetsu (^{S}178) Kaihō Yūsetsu (海北友雪 1598-1677). Son of Kaihō Yūshō

Kaihoku Yusho (^{S}197) Kaihō Yūshō (海北友松1533-1616). Pupil of Kano Eitoku; Founder of the Kaihō school.

Kakei 夏珪. Chinese painter in the Southern Sung dynasty. See Bayen (馬遠).

kakesu 懸巣, a kind of jay.

Kameiyen (^{S}103) 夏明遠 (dates unknown). Chinese artist of the 17th century.

Kanawoka See Kose no Kanawoka.

Kanda, Mr. 神田□□? Not identified: contemporary critic?

Kano (^{S}116,251,257) 狩野□□? Not identified.

Kano Chikanobu (^{S}90, 200, 240) 狩野周信 (dates unknown). Son of Tsunenobu.

Kano Isen Kano Isen Naganobu (狩野伊川栄信, 1775-1828). 8th master of the

Kobikichō Kano family (木挽町狩野家).

Kano Juseki Atsunobu ([S]206)　狩野寿石敦信　(1639-1718). 3rd Master of the Saruyachōdaichi Kano family (猿屋町代地狩野家).

Kano Kiuen ([S]225)　Kano Kyūen Kiyonobu (狩野休円清信, 1641-1717). Artist in the early Edo period; the founder of the Azabu-Ipponmatsu Kano family (麻布一松狩野家).

Kano Ko-Yeitoku　狩野古永徳 i.e. Kano Yeitoku Kuninobu (狩野永徳州信, 1543-1590). 5th master of the Kano Head family, sometimes called Ko-Yeitoku (Yeitoku the senior), distinguished from the 12th master Kano Yeitoku Takanobu (狩野永徳高信,1740-1794).

Kano Masanobu　See Masanobu.

Kano Minenobu ([S]242,258)　狩野岑信　(1662-1708), 2nd son of Tsunenobu; Founder of the Hamachō Kano family (浜町狩野家).

Kano, Mr.　See Kano Yeitoku (狩野永慮).

Kano Mitsunobu ([S]228)　狩野光信　(1656-1608), 6th master of the Kano head family.

Kano Moritaka　狩野(探美)守貴　(1840-1893). Contemporary artist. A descendant of the Kajibashi Kano family (鍛冶橋狩野家).

Kano Sansetsu ([S]193)　狩野山雪　(1589-1651). Adopted son of Sanraku.

Kano Seisen ([S]34,35,130,239)　Kano Seisen Osanobu (狩野晴川養信, 1796-1846), 9th master of the Kobikichō Kano family.

Kano Sukenobu ([S]21)　狩野友川助信　(1810-1831), 2nd son of Kano Yūsen Hironobu (狩野融川寛信)

Kano Takanobu ([S]217)　狩野孝信　(1571-1618)?. Father of Tanyu and his brothers.

Kano Tanbi Moriki　狩野探美守貴, correctly "Moritaka". See Kano Moritaka.

Kano Tanshin　Kano Tanshin Morimasa (狩野探信守政,1653-1718). Tanyu's son; the 2nd master of the Kajibashi Kano family ((鍛冶橋狩野家)

Kano Tanshin Morimichi ([S]27)　狩野探信守道　(1785-1835). 7th master of the Kajibashi Kano family (鍛冶橋狩野家). Tanshin Morimasa's great-grandson

Kano Tanyū　See Tanyu (探幽)

Kano Terunobu ([S]248)　Kano Yūsei Terunobu (狩野祐清英信,1717-1763). Artist in the middle Edo period, the 4th master of the head Kano family

Kano Tohaku ([S]194)　Kano Tōhaku Naganobu (狩野洞白愛信,1772-1821). 5th master of the Surugadai Kano family (駿河台狩野家)

Kano Tomonobu　狩野友信(1842-1912). Contemporary artist; the last master of the Hamachō Kano family (浜町狩野家).

Kano Tsunenobu ([S]8,31,37,49,65,186,241)　Kano Yōboku Tsunenobu (狩野養朴常信,1636-1713). Son of Kano Naonobu (狩野尚信). Said one of the 4 great masters of the Kano school.

Kano Utanosuke ([S]100)　狩野雅楽助　(dates unknown). Another name of Kano

Yukinobu (狩野之信), young brother of Motonobu.

Kano Yasunobu (^{S}85)　　Kano Eishin Yasunobu (狩野永真安信, 1613-1684) Tanyū's younger brother; the 8th master of the Kano head family.

Kano Yeino (^{S}174)　　狩野永納 (1631-1697). Artist in the early Edo period. Son of Kano Sansetsu (狩野山雪). After Sansetsu died, he studied under Kano Yasunobu (狩野安信). In 1697 he published "Hionchō Gashi (本朝画史), the first painting history in Japan, based on his father's manuscripts.

Kano Yeishuku (Morinobu) (^{S}238)　　狩野永叔主信 (1675-1724). 9th master of the Kano head family.

Kano Yeitoku (^{S}181)　　See Kano Ko-Yeitoku.

Kano Yeitoku Takanobu (^{S}38)　　狩野永徳高信　See Takanobu Yeitoku.

Kano Yeitoku　　狩野永悳 (1815-1891). Contemporary artist, master of the 15th Kano head family.

Kano Yosen (^{S}81,86,175,236)　　Kano Yōsen Korenobu (狩野養川惟信, 1753-1808), the 6th master of the Kobikichō Kano family (木挽町狩野家).

Kano Yusen (^{S}136)　　Kano Yūsen Hironobu (狩野融川寛信,1778-1815). 5th master of the Hamachō Kano family (浜町狩野家).

Kantaishi　　韓退之 or 韓愈 (768-824). Chinese poet, once banished by slander when young.

Kanzan & Jittoku　　Hanshan & Shide (寒山・拾得). Chinese Zen-hermits in the late Tang dynasty.

Kao　　可翁. See Kawo.

Kashiwagi　　Kashiwagi Kaichirō (柏木貨一郎, 1841-1898). Art critic.

Kato Kiyomasa　　加藤清正 (1562-1611). General under Taikō Hideyoshi, who invaded Korea under Taikō's order towards the end of the 16th century.

Kawarahiwa　　河原鶸, bird, a kind of goldfinch.

Kawasaki　　Kawasaki Chitora (川崎千虎,1835-1903). Contemporary artist.

Kawo (^{S}62,143,244)　　可翁 宗然 (Kawō Sounen, ?-1345). Priest artist.

Kayei　　嘉永 Kaei. Era 1848-1854.

Kegon waterfall (^{S}248)　　華厳の滝 at Nikko (日光).

Keibun　　See Matsumura Keibun.

Keikaboku　　邢和璞 (correctly Keikahaku). Chinese hermit in the Tang dynasty.

Keishoki　　啓書記 (dates unknown). Priest-artist Shōkei (祥啓) in the15th century. ('Shoki' means secretary).

Kiho (^{S}141)　　Kawanura Kihō (河村琦鳳, ? -1852). Artist in the late Edo period; adopted son of Kawamura Bunpō (河村文鳳). Pupil of Ganku (岸駒).

kiku　　chrysanthemum.

Kimura Nagamitsu (^{S}150)　　木村永光 (dates unknown). Father of Kano Sanraku. (16th century).

King Art dealer, details not identified.
Kingiokusen 金玉仙 Kingyokusen (dates unknown). Pupil of Kano Motonobu.
Kinko Sennin 琴高仙人. Sennin depicted as standing on carp.
Kinzanji 径山寺. Temple in Hangchou, China.
Kionobu (^{S}131) Kano Kiyonobu (狩野休円清信,1641-1717). Artist in the early Edo period, grandson of Kano Shōei (狩野松栄).
Kiosai Kawanabe Kyōsai (河鍋暁斎,1831-1889). Contemporary artist; the highest award-winning painter at the 2nd Domestic Industrial Exhibition in 1881.
Kiri 桐 (paulownia).
Kiso Kotei Kisō Kotei 徽宗皇帝 (1082-1135). Last emperor of Northern Sung and all-round artist, poet.
Kiujo Kannon (^{S}24) not identified. Misreading of Kokuzō?
Kiyomigaseki 清見関. Checking station before the Meiji era in Shizuoka prefecture, famous for viewing spot.
K. K. K. Not identified. Kiryū Kōshō Kwaisha?
Kodera (^{S}146) Not identified; Perhaps Kōdera Shinsaku (国府寺新作, dates unknown), one of Fenollosa's pupils at University of Tokyo.
Kohitsu 古筆. Family of professional judges of old handwriting.
Kohogen 古法眼, i.e. Motonobu. (狩野元信). See Hogen.
Konoke Mistake for Kōnoike (鴻池)? Kōnoike Zen'emon (鴻池善右衛門1841-1920); one of the magnates in the economic world of Osaka. Zen'emon (鴻池善右衛門1841-1920) ; one of the magnates in the economic world of Osaka.
Ko-ōki, or Koki 公紀(1648-1670). Pseudonym of Tokugawa Tsunakata (徳川綱方), adopted son of Tokugawa Mitsukuni (徳川光圀) the load of the Mito clan.
Korin Ogata Kōrin (尾形光琳, 1658-1716). Artist in the middle Edo period; Founder of the Rinpa (琳派) style.
Kose Arihisa 巨勢有久 (dates unknown, 13th to 14th century). Artist of the Kose school in the Kamakura period. Buddhist painter in his later years.
Kose no Genkei (^{S}1) 巨勢源慶. Painter of the early 13th century.
Kose no Kanawoka (^{S}1) 巨勢金岡 Kanaoka. Artist of the 9th century; founder of the Kose school.
Kose Toshihisa (^{S}110) 巨勢俊久 (dates unknown, 14th century). Artist of the Kose school in the Nanbokuchō period.
Kosen 古川, one of Tsunenobu's pseudonyms.
Kosho Kwaisha Kiryū Kōshō Kaisha (起立工商会社), established in 1874 by the government as manufacturing and trading company.
Kowin (^{S}52, 74, 139) Nagayama Kōin (長山孔寅, 1765-1849). Artist of birds and flowers in Ōsaka.
Kowun Kamei Kōun (亀井香雲, dates unknown). Daughter of Wunkin.

Koyoshin   Chinese artist unidentified.

Kuakei (^{S}232)   Yokoyama Kakei (横山崋渓, 1816-1864). Son of Kazan (横山華山).

Kuki, Mr.   九鬼隆一 Kuki Rryūichi (1852-1931). Art administrator of the Meiji government.

Kunisada   国貞 See Toyokuni.

Kuntaku   See Sonkuntaku.

Kuwan dynasty   漢代, China in BC.292-AD.8.

Kwatei   Taki Katei (滝和亭, 1830-1901). Contemporary artist of Nanga (南画).

Kwazan (^{S}155,160,189)   Yokoyama Kazan (横山華山, 1784-1837). Artist of the Shijōha in the late Edo period.

Kwazan   渡辺崋山, See Watanabe Kwazan.

<u>**Kwazoku**</u>   華族 (families of former daimyō or court nobles).

L

Landseer (^{S}164)   Edwin Landseer (1802-1873). English painter of animal subjects.

Lyman, Mr. (^{S}23)   Benjamin Smith Lyman (1835-1920). American geologist, employed by the Japanese government in 1872, and engaged in geological surveys till 1881.

M

Made no Osho   和尚 of 萬里. Priest of Shōkokuji Temple (相国寺) in Kyoto, whose common name is Zuikyū (瑞九), also called Made no Kōji (萬里の小路), Shittō Oshŏ (漆桶和尚), or Baian (梅庵).

Manju (^{S}119)   萬寿 (dates unknown). 吉岡茂喬. Artist of the Shijō School.

Marblehead   Port situated to the east of Salem, Massachusetts.

Maruyama Oshin (^{S}234)   円山応震 (1790-1838). Adopted son of Ōzui (応瑞). Son of Ōkyo (^{S}70,79,83) (応挙).

Masanobu (^{S}170)   Kano Masanobu (狩野正信,1434-1530). Motonobu's father; founder of the Kano family.

Matabee   Iwasa Matabee (岩佐又兵衛, 1578-1650). Fenollosa confused Matabee with Matahei (又平) whom he thought as the founder of Ukiyo-e.

Matsudaira (^{S}11)   Matsudaira Sadanori (松平定教, 1857-1899). Goverment official in the early Meiji era (son-in-law of the former daimyo), who exhibited Buncho's Illustrated Scrolls of the Sagami Bay scenes to the first Kanko Bijutsukai Exhibition (観古美術会) at Ueno Park in May 1880.

Matsumura Keibun (^{S}107, 108)   松村景文(1779-1843). Goshun's younger brother who founded the Shijīōha (四条派) with Goshun.

Matsuura   松浦□□, not identified. (松浦久兵衛?). Connoisseur, staff member in the Imperial Museum.

Matsuwo, Mr.   Matuo Gisuke (松尾儀助, 1837-1902). President of Kiryū Koshō

Kwaisha (起立工商会社).

medzurashii (^{S}191)　rare.

midzuame (^{S}255)　millet jelly.

Min　明 (Ming dynasty, 1368-1643)

Minenobu　See Kano Minenobu

Mino (^{S}25)　美濃. A province (now Gifu prefecture).

Mino (82)　Minō 箕面. Hilly county in the north of Osaka prefecture, famous for its waterfall and autumn foliage.

Miokakuji　妙覚寺. Temple in Kyoto.

miyama hojiro　深山頬白. Bird, a kind of bunting.

Miyatsuka, Mr.　宮塚□□, not identified.

Miwo　三保 Miho. Sandspot in Shizuoka prefecture, famous for coastal pine grove.

Mochizuki Giokusen (^{S}9)　Mochizuki Gyokusen (望月玉川,1794-1852). Artist of the Shijo school; son of Gyokusen (玉仙), (4 generations of Giokusen; 玉蟾・玉仙・玉川・玉泉).

Mochizuki Giokusen (^{S}96)　望月玉泉 (1834-1813). Son of Gyokusen (玉川).

Mokkei　牧谿 (dates unknown). Chinese Zen artist in the late 13th century.

Mokugen (^{S}188)　Mokugenji (木樳子), a kind of soapberry.

Monju　文殊 (菩薩). Buddhist god of wisdom.

Morikage (^{S}173,226,231)　Kusumi Morikage (久隅守景, dates unknown, 17th century). Pupil of Tan'yū.

Motonobu (^{S}15,43,120,152,172)　Kano Motonobu (狩野元信, 1476-1559). 2nd master of the Kano school.

Mt. Yorozan in Mino　養老山 moumtain in 美濃. Famous for its waterfall.

mtg. (^{S}155)　mounting

Mukojima　向島. Town at the left bank of Sumidagawa river.

Mutamagawa　六玉川. Six rivers called "Tamagawa," often quoted in poetry.

N

Nangaku (^{S}211)　Watanabe Nangaku (渡邊南岳, 1767-1813). Pupil of Ōkyo, who taught the Maruyama style to painters in the Kantō district.

Nanping (^{S}23,68)　沈南蘋 Shen Nanpin (dates unknown). Chinese painter in the Qing dynasty, who stayed in Nagasaki (長崎) for 2 years from 1731.

Naonobu (^{S}168,253)　Kano Naonobu (狩野尚信,1607-1650), a brother of Tan'yū. Founder of the Kobikichō Kano family (木挽町狩野家)

Nehanzo　涅槃像, Image of Buddha immediately after his death.

Nen Kawo　然可翁. See Kawo.

nibuku tsui　二幅対, a set of 2 scrolls.

Nikka (^{S}54,208)　Tanaka Nikka　(田中日華, ?-1845). Artist of Shijō school in the late Edo period; a pupil of Okamoto Toyohi.

Ninagawa　　Ninagawa Noritane (蜷川式胤, 1835-1882). Contemporary antiquarian.

Nishikawa Tsukenobu (^{S}222)　　西川祐信 (Nishikawa Sukenobu, not Tsukenobu, 1671-1751). Ukiyoe artist in Kyoto.

Nishimura, Mr.　　西村□□, not identified. 西村治兵衛 (1860-1910)?, a kimono dealer in Kyoto; art collector.

Nishino-toyen Niudo (^{S}6)　　西洞院入道. Nishinotōin family was a Court noble in Kyoto. 入道 means priest. Nishinotōin Tokinari (西洞院時成, 1645-1724)?

Nishio Bankichi　　西尾□□, not identified.

Nishiyma Hoyen　　西山芳園. See Hoyen.

Nomura　　野村□□, Not identified. Nomura Jūji 野村重治?. Connoisseur and a staff member at the Imperial Museum.

O

Ocho (^{S}144)　　Ōchō 黄鳥 (Yellow bird) ?

Oguri Soritsu (^{S}203)　　小栗宗栗 (dates unknown, late 15th century). Priest artist. Pupil of Shūbun (周文).

Oguri Sotan (^{S}122)　　小栗宗湛 (1413-1481). Priest artist of Shōkokuji temple (相国寺) in Kyoto.

Ojakusui (^{S}3)　　王若水 (dates unknown). Chinese artist in the Yuen (元) dynasty.

Okio (^{S}70, 79, 83)　　Maruyama Ōkyo (円山応挙, 1733-17895). Artist in the late Edo period. Father of the Maruyama school.

Okurasho　　Ōkurashō 大蔵省, Ministry of Finance.

Onagadori　　尾長鶏 a long tailed cock.

Onin　　Ōnin 応仁, era 1467-1469.

Onishi Keisai (^{S}5)　　Ōnishi Keisai 大西圭斎 (1677-1724). Pupil of Tani Bunchō.

Oōki　　王輝 (dates unknown). Chinese artist of Sung dynasty.

Oshitsu (^{S}93)　　Ōshitsu 王質. Legendary woodman in ancient China, who spent hundreds of years watching children playing *go* in the mountain.

Otafuku (^{S}160)　　お多福, a merry lady.

Owari　　尾張, Name of a province before the Meiji era; the western half of today's Aichi prefecture (愛知県)

P

province of Echizen　　越前国, now Fukui prefecture (福井県).

Q

Quannon　　観音(菩薩) Kannon. Buddhist goddess of mercy.

R

Raiden 雷電 (thunderbolt).

Raisho (S145)　Nakajima Raishō (中島来章,1796-1871). Artist of the Maruyama school, who trained leading Meiji artists.

Rakan 羅漢 (lohan, or arhat). Disciple of Shaka (釈迦).

Ranbioshi (S143)　乱拍子. Term of Noh dance: some special performance.

Rankei (S25)　Sugawara Rankei (菅原蘭渓, dates unknown). Artist in the late Edo period. (This work, S25, was painted in 1859).

Ranko (S22,94)　Nakai Rankō (中井藍江,1766-1830). Artist of Kyoto Kano school in the late Edo period

Renzan (S54)　Kishi Renzan (岸連山,1802-1859). Pupil of Ganku.

Richo (S82)　Ishibashi Richō 石橋李長 (dates unknown). Artist of the Shijō school in the late Edo period).

Rihaku (S109)　李白 (701-762), LI Po. Chinese poet in Tang dynasty.

Rio　両 Ryō, former currency. See bu.

Rioki (S161)　呂紀 (dates unknown). Chinese artist in the Ming dynasty (late 15th century).

Riotohin　呂洞賓 (Ryodōhin). Chinese legendary person in the Tang dynasty. A legend says he received a book on supernatural arts from Shōriken (鐘離権), one of the 8 Sennins (the picture subject; Shōryo dendō 鐘呂伝道).

S

Sagakichi　嵯峨吉 or 佐賀吉. Art dealer?

St. Simon Stylites (S111)　Christian ascetic (ca.390-459), who is said to have spent about thirty years in preaching and contemplation on the top of a tall pillar near Antioch.

Saisho　崔曙. Chinese man of letters in the Tang dynasty, legendarily depicted as a friend of Keikaboku.

Sambukutsui　三幅対 (a set of three scrolls).

sangi and karasu　sagi and karasu (鷺 鴉, heron and crow).

Sanjo　Sanjō 三条, a street in Kyoto.

Sankobird　三光鳥, a bird like a magpie.

Sano, Mr.　佐野□□, not identified. Sano Tsunetami (佐野常民 1822-1902, Government official involved in art administration) ?

Sanraku　Kano Sanraku (狩野山楽, 1559-1635). Pupil of Kano Eitoku; later became the husband of Eitoku's daughter. The founder of the Kano family in Kyoto.

Sansetsu (S193)　See Kano Sansetsu.

Sansui　山水 (landscape with mountain and water).

Sansui Rokaku　山水楼閣 (Landscape with sansui and palace).

Seikenji　清見寺 Temple near Miho (美保). See Miwo and Kiyomigaseki.
Seiki (^{S}199)　Yokoyama Seiki (横山晴暉, 1793-1865). Artist of the Shijō school in the late Edo period; Keibnn' pupil
Seiko (^{S}127)　Okajima Seikō (岡島晴曠, 1828-1877). Artist of the Shijō school in the Edo-Meiji period; pupil of Seiki.
Seisen　See Kano Seisen.
Sennin　仙人. Transcendent. Superhuman hermit in ancient China.
Sento period (^{S}109)　Fenollosa's mishearing for 'Seito period'? (盛唐期 the golden period of the Tang dynasty).
Sesshiu, or Sesshu (^{S}16, 17, 61)　Sesshū (雪舟, 1420-1506). Artist priest in the Muromachi period.
Sesson (^{S}66)　雪村 (1504-1580). Artist priest who studied Sesshū.
Setsuan　See Yoshizawa Setsuan.
Setsuten Makiba (^{S}15)　雪天牧場 (pasture in snow).
Settei (^{S}212)　Tsukioka Settei (月岡雪鼎, 1710-1786). Artist of the Kano school, but later became a painter of genre pcture in Ōsaka (大阪).
Seyobo, or Seiobo　Seiōbo (西王母). Goddess in Chinese mythology.
Shaka　釈迦如来, Buddha.
Shiba Kokan　Shiba Kōkan (司馬江漢 1747-1818). Oil painter in the late Edo period
Shijō school　四条派, founded by Matsumura Goshun (松村呉春), who lived at Shijō street in Kyoto.
Shijukara　shujūkara (四十雀). Chickadee.
Shimoda, Mr.　下田某. Art dealer, not identified.
<u>**Shin**</u> (^{S}33)　真, a manner of drawing. See "Giyo" and "So".
Shin no Yojo　See Yojo.
Shioki, or Shoki　鍾馗 (Shōki). Chinese demon queller in the Tang dynasty.
Shioriken　鐘離権. Chinese sennin in the Tang dynasty.
Shitsuto Osho (^{S}122)　漆桶和尚. See Made no Osho.
Shiugetsu (^{S}14)　秋月 (Shūgetsu). Priest painter in the late Muromachi period (15th century); a pupil of Sesshū
Shiuki　Okamoto Shūki (岡本秋暉、1807-1862). Artist in the late Edo period, influenced by Ōnishi Keisai and Watanabe Kwazan.
Shohaku (^{S}180, 227)　Soga Shōhaku (曽我蕭白, 1730-1781). Artist in the middle Edo period, who surprised the world by an unrestrained style.
Shokado (^{S}223)　Shōkadō (松花堂昭乗, 1584-1639). Artist-calligrapher.
Shomu Kioku　商務局. Department of commerce in the Finance Ministry.
Shoō　所翁 (dates unknown). Chinese artist in the Southern Sung dynasty (13th century).
Shosen (^{S}262)　Kano Shōsen Tadanobu (狩野勝川雅信, 1823-1890). 10th master of the Kobikichō Kano family.

269

Shoyei (^{S}176)　Kano Shōei Naonobu (狩野松栄直信, 1519-1592). 2nd son of Motonobu.

Shubun (^{S}102,135)　Shūbun (周文, dates unknown). Zen priest artist at Shōkokuji temple (相国寺), Kyoto, in the 15th century. Teacher of Sesshū.

Shuko　周公 or 周公旦(Shūkōtan). Ancient Chinese statesman who helped found the Chou dynasty (BC.1066-BC.222).

Shunjei　Fujiwara Shunzei (藤原俊成, 1114-1204). Poet.

Shunkio　Sen Shunkyo 錢舜挙 (dates unknown). Chinese painter in the late 13th century.

So　宋 (Sung). Chinese dynasty, 960-1279.

So (^{S}32)　Sō (草). the most cursive manner of drawing. See Shin (真) & Giyō (行).

Soga Shotei　Another name of 曽我蕭白？ See Shohaku.

Sokokuji　Shōkokuji 相国寺. Zen temple in Kyoto.

Sonkuntaku　孫君澤. Chinese artist in the Yuan dynasty.

Sorin (^{S}20)　not identified. Shikō Sōrin (紫岡宗琳, 1781-1850, grandson of Soshiseki)?

Sosen (^{S}13,44,59,101,118,158)　Mori Sosen (森狙仙,1747-1821). Animal painter, especially strong in drawing monkeys. (狙 means 'monkey').

Sosen Akinobu (^{S}126)　Kano Sosen Akinobu (狩野素川彰信,1763-1826), the 6th master of the Saruyachōdaichi Kano family (猿屋町代地狩野家)

Soshiseki (^{S}220)　宋紫石 (1712-1786). Artist of the Nanpin school (南蘋派) in the middle Edo period.

Sugawara Rankei　See Rankei.

Sukoku (^{S}113)　Kō Sūkoku (高嵩谷,1730-1804). Second-generation pupil of Hanabusa Itchō (英一蝶).

Sumidagawa　隅田川. River running through downtown Tokyo.

Sumiyoshi Hirokata　住吉広賢 (1835-1883). Contemporary artist, master of the Sumiyoshi school.

Sumiyoshi, Mr.　See Sumiyoshi Hirokata.

Suyeyori (^{S}171)　Kano Sueyori (狩野季頼, dates unknown, 16th century). Son of Motonobu.

T

Taigado　大雅堂, i.e. Ike no Taiga (池大雅, 1723-1776). Nanga (南画) painter in the middle Edo period who accomplished bunjinga (文人画) of Japanese style.

Taiko　Taikō (太閤), another name of Toyotomi Hideyoshi (豊臣秀吉, 1536-1598) who unified Japan under a single authority after the age of civil strife. (Taikō: the honorific title for a regent).

Takanobu Yeitoku (^{S}38)　狩野永徳高信 (1740-1794). 12th master of the Kano head family. See Kano Ko-Yeitoku.

taki　滝 waterfall.

Takuma Tamehisa (^{S}112)　宅間為久 (dates unknown, 12th century). Artist of the Kamakura period.

Tamagawa Ide of Yamashiro (^{S}198) "玉川 of 井手" in province Yamashiro (山城). See Mutamagawa.

Tameichi (^{S}99) 為一. Pseudonym of Hokusai.

Tanaka Totsugen See Totsugen.

Tangei (^{S}146) Tsuruzawa Tangei (鶴沢探鯨, dates unknown). Son of Tanzan.

Tansetsu (^{S}129) Kano Tansetsu (狩野探雪, ?-1714). second son of Tanyū.

Taniu, Tanyu (^{S}19, 26, 29, 32, 33, 42, 47, 77, 124, 147, 148, 170, 183, 185, 209) Kano Tan'yūu Morinobu (狩野探幽守信,1602-1674). Artist in the early Edo period; Son of Takanobu (孝信), and elder brother of Naonobu (尚信) and Yasunobu (安信). At the age of 16 he moved from Kyoto to Edo and strove to revive the Kano school. Founder of the Kajibashi Kano family (鍛冶橋狩野家).

Tanshin Morimasa (^{S}63, 169, 221) Kano Tanshin Morimasa (狩野探信守政, 1653-1718). Son of Tan'yū.

Tanzan (^{S}78) Tsuruzawa Tanzan (鶴沢探山, ?-1655). Pupil of Tan'yū.

Tazawa 田沢静雲. Art dealer in Tokyo (dates unknown).

Tendaiyama 天台山, Mountain in the east of China. Fundamental seminary for the Tendai sect

Tenmei 天明, era 1781-1789.

Tenpo 天保, era 1830-1844.

Tengu 天狗, long-nosed winged goblin.

Terunobu (^{S}248) 英信. See Kano Terunobu (狩野祐清英信).

Tetsuzan (^{S}57, 88) Mori Tetsuzan (森徹山, 1775-1841). Sosen's nephew, son-in-law.

To Tang (唐). Chinese dynasty (618-907).

Toba Tōba 東坡 (1036-1101), another name of Soshoku (蘇軾). Chinese writer, also called Sotōba (蘇東坡).

Tobosaku 東方朔. Literati in China (ca.154-93 B.C.), who was later regarded as a sennin and legendarily said that he obtained 8000 years longevity by eating a magic peach which he had stolen from Goddess Seiōbo (西王母).

Tobun (^{S}246) Toki Tōbun (土岐洞文,1501-1582I), warrior painter in the Warring States period.

Tofukuji Tōfukuji 東福寺 Temple in Kyoto, where Chō Densu lived .

Togen 桃源 Peach garden, place of supreme bliss.

Togen no Sennin (^{S}199) Title of painting derived from a kind of Utopia story "Tōkagenki" (桃花源記) by Tōenmei (陶淵明365-427), a poet in ancient China.

Tohaku Chikanobu 洞白愛信. Misreading for "Naganobu"? See Kano Tohaku.

Toho (^{S}3) Murata Tōho (村田東圃, dates unknown). Artist of the Shijō school in the late Edo period.

Tokei (^{S}72) Bessho Tōkei 別所東渓 (Dates unknown). Artist of the Shijō school in the late Edo period.

Tomonobu (^{S}17)   See Kano Tomonobu.

Torin Yoshinobu (^{S}134)   狩野洞琳由信 (?－1820). Artist in the line of Kano Tōgen Kuninobu (狩野洞元邦信). One of Ko-Eitoku's disciples.

Tosa Mitsubumi (^{S}229)   土佐光文 (1812-1879). Descendant of the Tosa school.

Tosa Mitsunari (^{S}205)   土佐光成 (1636-1710). 1st son of Tosa Mitsuoki.

Tosa Mitsuoki (^{S}10,60,198)   土佐光起 (1617-1691). Artist who revived the Tosa school in the early Edo period

Tosa Mitsushige (^{S}106)   土佐光茂 (dates unknown). Court painter of the Tosa school in the 16th century.

Tosa Mitsutada   土佐光忠 (dates unknown). Artist of the Tosa school in the last Edo period

Toshimi   杜子美 (712-770), another name of Toho (杜甫). Chinese poet in the Tang dynasty.

Toshun   Tōshun Yoshinobu (狩野洞春義信) or Kano Tōshun Yoshinobu (狩野洞春美信)? 義信, the 2nd master; 美信, the 4th master; both of the Surugadai Kano family (駿河台狩野家).

Tosui (^{S}219)   Kubota Tōsui (久保田桃水, 1841-1911). Contemporary artist of the Shijō school

Totsugen   Tanaka Totsugen (田中訥言, 1767-1823). Artist in the late Edo period. The father of the Fukko-Yamato-e school (復古大和絵派).

Towun (^{S}225)   Kano Tōun Masunobu (狩野洞雲益信1623-1694). Pupil of Tan'yu; the founder of the Surugadai Kano family (駿河台狩野家)

Toyeki (^{S}260)   Unkoku Toyeki 雲谷等益 (1591-1644). Son of Unkoku Togan (雲谷等顔)

Toyohiko (^{S}166)   Okamoto Toyohiko (岡本豊彦, 1773-1845). Artist of the Shijō school in the late Edo period

Toyokuni (^{S}213)   Utagawa Toyokuni (the 3rd Toyokuni) i.e. Utagawa Kunisada (歌川国貞1786-1864). Ukiyo-e artist.

Tozan (^{S}74)   Ishigaki Tōzan (石垣東山 1806-1876). Artist active till the beginning of Meiji era

Tsukioka Sessai (^{S}167)   月岡雪斎 (?-1803). Artist in the middle Edo period; adopted son of Settei (雪鼎).

Tsunenobu   See Kano Tsunenobu (狩野常信, 1636-1713).

Tsunetaka   Tosa Tsunetaka (土佐経隆)?. Artist of the 14th century.

Tsuruga Bay (^{S}32)   Mistake for Suruga Bay (駿河湾).

Tsuruzawa Tansen (^{S}128)   鶴沢探泉 (dates unknown). Descendant of Tanzan (探山).

Turner (^{S}121)   J. M. William Turner (1775-1851), English landscape painter.

U

Ushi no Gozen   牛御前, now Ushijima shrine (牛島神社).

Ukita Ikkei   See Ikkei.
Uyemura   上村(植村？) □□. Aart dealer in Osaka, details unknown.

W

Wakai, Mr.   Wakai Kanesaburō (若井兼三郎, 1834-1908). Vice president of the Kiryū Kōshō Kwaisha (起立工商会社).

Wakanoura in Kii   和歌浦 in 紀伊, famous for fine views in Kii (紀伊) province.

Watanabe Kwazan   Watanabe Kazan 渡辺崋山 (1793-1841). Artist and scholar of Western learning in the last years of the Edo period.

Wheeler, Prof.   William Wheeler (1851-1932). American civil engineer who taught mathematics and civil engineering at Sapporo Institute of Agriculture (1876-79).

Wunkei (^{S}89)   Unkei 雲渓 (dates unknown). Priest painter in the middle 16th century. Pupil of Sesshū (雪舟).

Wunkin Oguchi (^{S}45,50,98)   尾口雲錦 (dates unknown). Contemporary painter.

Wunkoku Togan (^{S}140)   雲谷等顔 (1547-1618). Painter in the Momoyama period who revived the Unkoku-an (雲谷庵 Sesshū's hermitage at Yamaguchi).

Y

Yamabe no Akahito   山部赤人 (dates unknown). Poet in the early Nara period (8th century). One of 36 great poets selected in the early Kamakutra period

Yamada Doan (^{S}204)   Yamada Dōan 山田道安 (? - 1573). Warrior-painter in the Civil War period (戦国時代)

Yamana   Yamana Tsurayoshi (山名貫義, 1836-1902). Contemporary artist of the Sumiyoshi school (住吉派), later appointed as professor at Tokyo Art College (東京美術学校)

Yamanaka   山中. Art trading company managed by the Yamanaka family in Ōsaka.

Yamato style   大和絵様式. Japanese traditional style of painting since the 9th century.

Yasunobu   See Kano Yasunobu (狩野安信).

Yebisu   Ebisu 恵比寿, one of the 7 Gods of Fortune.

Yeiken (^{S}153)   Eiken, 栄賢 Buddhist painter in the early Edo period.

Yeino (^{S}174)   See Kano Yeinō.

Yeisen   Kano Eisen Michinobu (狩野栄川典信, 1730-1790). 5th master of the Kobikichō Kano family (木挽町狩野家).

Yeishin   Eishin 永真. See Kano (Yeishin) Yasunobu (狩野永真安信).

Yeishuku (^{S}238)   Eishuku, See Kano Yeishuku (狩野永叔).

Yeitoku (^{S}181)   Kano Eitoku (狩野永徳). See Kano Ko-Yeitoku.

Yeitoku (^{S}38)   Kano Eitoku (狩野永徳). See Takanobu Yeitoku.

Yeitoku   See Kano Yeitoku (狩野永悳).

Yofu (^{S}187)   Yōfu 楊富, Priest-artist (dates unknown, early 16th century).

Yogetsu (^{S}256)   Yōgetsu (楊月, dates unknown). Priest artist of Kasagidera temple (笠置寺) in Yamashiro province (15th century); pupil of Sesshū.

Yokihi   Yōkihi (楊貴妃,710-756). Mistress of Emperor Gensō of Tang.

Yojo (^{S}155)   Yojō 豫譲. Loyalist of Shin (晋) in BC 5th century China, who tried to revenge his lord Chihaku (智伯) killed by Joshi (襄子).

Yorozan Shinkei   養老山真景 (real landscape of Mt. Yōrōzan).

Yosai (^{S}210)   Kikuchi Yōsai (菊池容斎, 1788-1878). Artist who studied the practices and usages in ancient court and samurai families; and published *Zenken Kojitsu* 『前賢故実』 50 vols (Biography of about 50 great men with their portraits).

Yusei   Not identified, 祐清, 友清, or 友盛?

Yosen   See Kano Yosen.

Yoshinobu (^{S}125)   Kano Yoshinobu (狩野随川甫信, 1692-1745). 3rd son of Tsunenobu; the 2nd master of the Hamachō Kano family.

Yoshitsune & Benkei   Minamoto no Yoshitsune (源義経,1159-1189) & Benkei (弁慶 ?-1189), Lord & Vassal. Their first encounter was the fight on Gojō bridge, in Kyoto.

Yoshizawa Setsuan   吉沢雪庵 (1819-1889). Contemporary artist and connoisseur of old paintings.

Yuima   維摩 (Vimalakirti), Legendary Buddhist scholar in ancient India.

Yukinobu (^{S}214)   Kiyohara Yukinobu (清原雪信,1643-1682), female artist of Kano school.

Yukinobu (^{S}133,214,261)   Not identified. 之信 (狩野之信1513-1574, Motonobu's brother ? or 幸信(狩野幸信1717-1779) or 清原雪信1643-1682?

Yusei Terunobu   See Kano Terunobu.

Yusei Sukenobu   See Kano Sukenobu.

Yutei   Ishida Yūtei (石田幽汀, 1721-1786). Artist in the middle Edo period, known as Ōkyo's first teacher.

アーネスト・フランシスコ・フェノロサ著
『日本絵画蒐集作品解説付総目録』
邦 訳

山口静一 訳

訳者序文

日本絵画総合目録の構成

　このフェノロサ自筆ノートブックはタイトルに『日本絵画蒐集作品解説付総目録』アーネスト・フランシスコ・フェノロサ　東京・本郷・加賀屋敷一番館　1880年12月と記され、内容は序文2ページ、本文190ページ、索引5ページで構成されている。「総目録」と言っても序文に述べられているように、本ノートブックは「区分A 掛けもの編」であって、他に「屏風編」「画題編」「落款編」等が存在していた。

　本文「掛けもの編」は263点の作品が大凡入手順に配列されている。スペンサリアン社会学者であったフェノロサは、作品の優劣好悪にこだわらず、各流派系統を追い絵画盛衰史の標本として蒐集した。各作品を specimen（略号 s.）と呼んだ所以である。本文では作者名と画題を紹介し（※順序等不同、翻訳では適宜修正した）、構図、彩色、筆使いなどについて忌憚の無い批評を加え、さらに鑑定者として雇った同時代の著名な画家や古物学者の批評を添える。時には彼ら助言者さえ批判の対象となる（「狩野氏は文人画的要素をすべて悪とみなす狭い見解で物を言う人だ」s.76）。また、彼自身の作品評をのちに修正することもやぶさかではなかった（s.101）。最後に購入元、時には購入価格が記される。購入元の過半数は起立工商会社と山中商会。前者は全額政府出資の国策会社で輸出工芸品の製造と販売が本業だったが、古美術をも蒐集売却して外貨獲得に一役買っていた。

　この解説目録は明治期美術批評の有りようを示す点でも興味深いが、フェノロサ出版物の大部分が翻訳者ないし編集者によって潤色されているなかで、彼の見解が生の声で語られている点が特色であると言えるだろう。

　タイトル下段の「加賀屋敷一番館」は現在本郷東大キャンパスとなっている旧加賀藩別邸の敷地に建設された旧東京大学の外国人教師館で、フェノロサはその一番館に居住し、一ツ橋の校舎に通勤していた（担当学科は文学部の主要学科たる政治学・理財学・哲学）。日付「1880年12月」はこの解説目録を書き始めた時期を示すもので、蒐集活動を停止してから3年後1889年の加筆も見受けられる（s.17）。

　文末の索引は将来の日本絵画史研究のため検索の便を考え私的に作成したものと思われる。原文は蒐集作品の作者名をアルファベット順に配置し各作品の掲載番号を記したものだが、翻訳では作者に加えて文中に引用された固有名詞についても簡単なプロフィールや註解を加え、アイウエオ順に配列した。

「掛けもの編」の続編

　フェノロサ没後11年余り経った1920年1月、未亡人メアリは亡夫の書斎にあった蔵書（約200点）と草稿類（35編に雑編300枚）をニューヨークのウォルポール・ギャラリーズでのオークションに出品した。その『オークション目録』No.271に、本総目

録シリーズ「掛けもの編」の続編が掲載されていた。ノートブック No.2 とも言うべきこの続編には 69 ページにわたって作品 264 から 517 までの 254 点が収録され、付注によれば「詳細な解説付きのものもあるが、多くは画題のみ。落款と印章を模写したものも数点ある」という。

　オークションに出品された蔵書・草稿類の大部分を落札したのはニューポートの医師スティルマン（Ernest G. Stillman）だった。彼はのちにこれらを母校のハーバード・カレッジに寄贈。ハーバードではワイデナー図書館やフォッグ美術館に分置されていたが、草稿類は現在同大学ホートン・ライブラリーが所蔵している。しかし、同ライブラリーのフェノロサ資料にこの Notebook No.2 は含まれていない。オークションで他者が落札したか、或いは売れ残ったかは不明だが、何れにせよ行方不明である。また Notebook No.1（「掛けもの編」（前編））が『オークション目録』に載っていないのは 1920 年以前に既に逸失していたことを物語っている。

『日本絵画総合目録』の発見と現状

　1929 年 12 月から 1931 年 6 月まで、当時東京帝室博物館（現東京国立博物館）鑑査官だった美術史学者秋山光夫（てるお）（1888-1977）は欧米における日本美術調査のため出張中だったが、たまたまボストンの古書店でこのノートブックを見つけ、購入して持ち帰った。この件を最初に報じたのは秋山の友人松岡譲が第一書房発行の文芸雑誌『セルパン』（1933 年 5 月号）に載せた「フェノロサと明治文化」であった。「この古色蒼然たるノオトブックは」で始まる文章はその内容を詳細に紹介したのち「こうした興味深き根本資料を広く世間に出すのは、其の道の学者が喜ぶのみでなく、今日の美術思想の上からいって極めて意義あることと思われるので、私は極力秋山君にすゝめて、それに解説を加え、ボストン所蔵の名画の写真をどっさり入れて出版してくれるよう、頼んでいる」と記している。しかしこのノートブックは翻訳されることもなく数十年が過ぎた。「写真をどっさり」がネックとなったのであろう、該当する図絵をボストン美術館（以下 MFA と略す）コレクションから探し出すのは容易な仕事ではなかった。

　1970 年代の中頃、訳者は光夫氏の長男秋山光和（てるかず）氏（1918-2009、当時東京大学教授、美術史学）よりノートブック全文のコピーを頂き 1980 年までには翻刻と翻訳がほゞ完成した。秋山光和氏はこの翻訳の出版に尽力されたが、やはり「写真をどっさり」が祟って実現を見ぬままに他界された。光和氏の子息秋山光文（てるふみ）氏（お茶の水女子大学名誉教授、美術史学）はこのノートブックを、フェノロサに傾倒し同じく奈良を愛した會津八一の記念館（早稲田大学）に寄贈された。このたび念願の出版が可能となったのは秋山光文氏と早稲田大学會津八一記念博物館のご好意によるものである。

ウェルドにコレクション譲渡

　1884年末頃からフェノロサは絵画（浮世絵版画を除く）の蒐集活動を自粛している。この頃フェノロサは東京大学在職のまゝ文部省図画調査会委員を依嘱された。この委員会は小学校図画教育を洋式（鉛筆画）から和式（毛筆画）に移行させる件、国立の美術専門学校創設の件のほか、美術品の海外流出防止の件が諮問されていた。おそらくそれが自粛の理由だったと思われるが、フェノロサと共に蒐集に熱中し、既に数万点に及ぶ日本の美術品を入手していたボストンの富豪ビゲロウ（William Sturgis Bigelow, 1850-1926）も、同じ頃蒐集を中止している。所謂美術国益論に乗じて、貴重な古美術が湯水のように海外に流出する惨状を憂えたものと思われる。（ビゲロウの場合、とくに1885年9月フェノロサと共に三井寺の律僧桜井敬徳に受戒して仏教に改宗したことが、仏教文化の育んだ日本美術への認識が改まったことも契機となったかもしれない。）以後両人共熱心な伝統文化財保護論者に変身している。

　フランス留学中にジャポニスムの洗礼を受けたビゲロウはMFAを日本美術の府たらしめようとする強い意志をもっていた。1886年、ビゲロウの後輩にあたるボストンの医師で蒐集家のウェルド（Charles Goddard Weld, 1857-1911）が自家用ヨットで来日、ビゲロウ宅に来泊した折り、ビゲロウはウェルドとフェノロサを説得し、ウェルドにフェノロサ蒐集品を譲渡すること、ウェルドは「フェノロサ」の名を冠するコレクションとしてMFAに寄託すること、ウェルド死去の際はMFAに遺贈すること、の三条件を承諾させた。この条件は忠実に守られ、ウェルド死去でMFAの有となった1911年の11を冠し、アクセッション番号11.4000（平治物語絵巻《三条殿夜討》）から始まる1000余点がFenollosa-Weld collectionと呼ばれ、厖大なビゲロウ・コレクションと共に日本美術の中核となっている。（一説に25万ドルと伝えられるウェルドへの譲渡金について、当時森有礼文相の顧問格であった木場貞長は晩年の回想で「惜しげもなく某所に寄贈された ― 『朝日新聞』1934年10月25日 ― と述べている。当時のフェノロサが国立の美術専門学校創立に腐心していたことを思えば寄贈先もおおよそ推定できる。）

　フェノロサは1886年8月、4期8年間勤務した東京大学（最後の年は帝国大学と改称）から宮内省（帝国博物館理事）・文部省（東京美術学校幹事）両省雇いの美術行政官に任命され（四年契約で年収6000円）、海外視察、畿内宝物取調、東京美術学校（現東京藝術大学美術学部の前身）創設に関わって1890年6月末日契約満期となって辞任する。同年9月からビゲロウの推挙でMFAに新設された日本美術部キュレーターとなり、自ら蒐集した作品やビゲロウ寄託作品等の管理に当たることになる。五年契約で年俸2500ドル（在日中の年俸6000円 ― 当時の為替レートで4620ドル ― が如何に高額だったことが分る）、同部寄託作品解説目録の作成が主要任務だった。

フェノロサのボストン美術館勤務と解雇

　しかし、この5年間は毎年の企画展に加え各所からの講演や原稿の依頼、加えてシ

カゴ万博に際しての詩集 " EAST AND WEST " の出版など、多忙を極め、MFA は目録発行を促進するため助手（メアリ・スコット夫人 Mrs. Mary Scott, 1865-1954）を雇ったが、目録発行は遅々として実現しなかった。一方フェノロサは、契約切れを機に日本再訪の希望を捨て切れずにいた。フェノロサ夫人リジーは日本行きに賛同しなかったが、メアリは理解を示し、彼の研究意欲に敬意を抱いた。メアリ夫人は別居中の夫スコットとの間の娘アーウィンと、前夫チェスターとの間の遺児アランを養育する女性作家だった。1895 年 3 月、夫のスコットは娘を取戻すための離婚訴訟に勝訴、その際フェノロサとメアリの不倫説が広まってスキャンダルとなり保守的なボストン市民の非難の的となった。彼がメアリと結婚し共に日本再訪を企てたのはこの時だったのであろう。それには妻に離婚訴訟を提起させることが必要だ。画策はマンマと成功し、同年 10 月彼は妻に財産の半額を提供し、年額 2600 ドルの慰謝料・養育費を負担する条件を甘受して離婚判決に署名した。MFA は解説目録の完成を待って雇用契約を延期したがフェノロサは出勤せず、ニューヨークに転居して同年 12 月メアリと結婚。翌年四月欧州経由日本に向かう船上から MFA に辞表を送った。解説目録は失われ、MFA は激怒して彼を解雇、勿論ビゲロウとの交遊も断絶した。以後 MFA ではフェノロサの名は禁句となり、「フェノロサ・コレクション」も「ウェルド・コレクション」と改称された。（甚大な代償を払った日本再訪だったが、既に外国人を重用する時代は過ぎ去り、フェノロサは前妻への送金にも苦しむ苦境に陥った。）

その後のフェノロサ＝ウェルド・コレクション

　MFA 日本美術部はその後適任のキュレーターを欠いたまゝ十年近くが経過、1904 年岡倉覚三をエキスパートに迎え「中国日本美術部」と改称して第二の発展期を迎える。ビゲロウやフェノロサの蒐集した絵画の目録作成を依頼された岡倉は、約 5000 点のコレクション中十カ月で 3642 点の目録を作り、そのうち「真作は 2889 点、残りは贋作 476 点、模写 277 点」と報告している（清水恵美子『岡倉天心の比較文化史的研究』）。美術史盛衰の標本として、評者により真偽に異説ある作品や摸写をも排除しなかったフェノロサ・コレクションに「偽物」の烙印を推された作品が少なくなかったのは当然だった。これらは後に整理されたのであろう、1974 年訳者が MFA にて調査した際、当時の目録カードには収蔵番号 11.4577（酒井抱一）、11.4580（同）11.4647（山本梅逸）、11.4702（岸駒）、11.4703（同）などが「偽筆のため売却」と記され、番号のみで該当作品が空白となっているカードも少なからず目についた。(MFA では必要に応じて優品をも売却して他の作品を購入することもあったようで、1932 年国宝級とされた《吉備大臣入唐絵巻》入手の際は、ビゲロウ・コレクションより浮世絵・四条派の逸品数十点と事実上交換する形で納入されている。)
　いずれにせよ収蔵番号 11.4000 から 11.5009 まで数えられるフェノロサ＝ウェルド・コレクションで現在データベースに登録されている作品は 759 点のみである。（尤も収蔵番号は、例えば三幅対は 3、六曲屏風は 6 と数えられていることを考慮しなければならない。）

総合目録「掛けもの編」収載作品とMFA収蔵番号

　訳者は予ねてより、この目録に収載された作品の収蔵番号を照合する作業を試みていた。最初は岸田勉「ボストン美術館蒐集の日本美術調査報告」（佐賀大学『研究論文集』1956~1973年）を、次いで戦後十数回にわたって開催された同美術館の里帰り展図録や、『在外日本の至宝』（毎日新聞社1980年）など各種美術全集を参考に作業を進めたが、判明数は極めて少なかった。1998年に至りMFAと講談社が発行した『ボストン美術館日本美術調査図録』（アン・ニシムラ・モース、辻惟雄共編）によって数十点の収蔵番号を確認することができた。さらに数年前からインターネットでボストン美術館収蔵作品の検索が可能となり、「掛けもの編」263点中150余点の収蔵番号が判明。本編ではこれを明記し、収蔵番号から図版を検索し、フェノロサ時代の評価とは異なる新しい研究によるコメントを読むことが可能となった。（ボストン美術館 Museum of Fine Arts, Boson の公式サイト〈https://collections.mfa.org/advancedsearch〉上の収蔵品検索画面に収蔵番号 Accession Number を入力すれば図像の鑑賞に加え、寸法、コメント等を知ることができる。）

　残念ながら収蔵番号を照合するに足る情報を得られなかった作品も半数に近く、また収蔵番号が判明しながら該当作品の欠落したものもある。後者の場合は上記の事情によって売却ないし交換されたものと推定される。

　なお、フェノロサが特に熱心に解説した数点を選んで口絵とし、関連事項を補足した。

謝辞

　本書刊行に当り、原文翻刻で難読文字解読に助力された John T. Carpenter 氏、旧訳稿全文の WORD 入力作業を代行した孫の須田珠希、翻刻のチェックならびにフェノロサ＝ウェルド・コレクションのデータベース調査に協力を賜った畏友三好彰氏に謝辞を捧げると共に、前述の秋山光文氏、早稲田大学會津八一記念博物館長肥田路美氏に改めて感謝申し上げたい。

フェノロサ蒐集作品日本絵画解説付総目録　目次

※は Fenollosa=Weld collection 収蔵番号を付した作品

s 001	人物図（地蔵）	※
s 002	花鳥図　六幅　雲錦筆	
s 003	花鳥図　東圃（王若水の模写）	※
s 004	山水図（雪景）文晁	
s 005	花鳥図（紅梅に白鷺）大西圭斎	※
s 006	花鳥図（鶏に百合）公紀	※
s 007	花鳥図（岩に鷹、松の一部）文晁	
s 008	琵琶を持つ弁天　常信	
s 009	寒山拾得図　望月玉川	※
s 010	弁天図　光起	※
s 011	山水図（山中の滝）文晁	
s 012	樹下に虎、小鳥　岸駒	※
s 013	断崖の樹木に猿の親子　狙仙	
s 014	寿老人に鹿　秋月	
s 015	雪景に野馬　元信	
s 016	雪舟　山水図（漁村図）模写	※
s 017	雪舟「寿老人」（狩野友信模写）	※
s 018	橋上の義経と弁慶　一蕙	※
s 019	中国の山水　探幽	
s 020	牡丹に風雨　宗琳	※
s 021	向島隅田川　狩野友川助信	※
s 022	大滝に鯉　藍江	※
s 023	親犬と仔犬　南蘋	※
s 024	仏画（五大虚空蔵菩薩か）	
s 025	養老山真景　菅原蘭渓	※
s 026	李白観瀑図（三幅対）探幽	
s 027	王輝「唐人山荘景観図」狩野探信守道摸写	※
s 028	福禄寿・邢和璞（三幅對）狩野探信守道	※
s 029	寒山拾得に龍（三幅対）探幽	
s 030	山水楼閣（三幅対）狩野伊川	※
s 031	恵比寿大黒福禄寿（三幅対）狩野常信	
s 032	龍・雷神（三幅対）探幽	※
s 033	維摩・花鳥（三幅対）探幽	
s 034	山水墨画（三幅対）狩野晴川	※
s 035	寿老人・花鳥（三幅対）晴川	
s 036	寿老人・山水（三幅対）文晁	
s 037	牡丹に獅子（双幅）常信	※
s 038	山水・人物（三幅対）永徳高信	
s 039	馬元欽「山水」模写　元旦	※
s 040	十羅漢図　作者不明	※
s 041	花鳥（孔雀・白梅・花）雲錦	※
s 042	鹿図（双幅）探幽	※
s 043	山水・狩猟風景（双幅）元信	※
s 044	樹木に猿　狙仙	
s 045	花鳥（梅の枝に青い鳥）雲錦	
s 046	紅梅に月　抱一	※
s 047	山水図　探幽	
s 048	徽宗「岩に白い鷲」模写	
s 049	芙蓉の枝　常信	※
s 050	雪を置いた松の枝に鷲　雲錦	
s 051	青鬼を踏み潰す鐘馗　文麟	※
s 052	西王母　孔寅	※
s 053	狸図　一鳳	
s 054	山水図水墨　連山	
s 055	文殊菩薩半身図　兆殿司	※
s 056	枝に泊まる青い尾長鶏　岑信	
s 057	狐図　徹山	※
s 058	鐘馗に虎　金玉仙	※
s 059	龍図　狙仙	※
s 060	鶉に草　土佐光起	※
s 061	驢馬に乗る鐘馗　雪舟	※
s 062	岩上の観音　可翁	
s 063	七福神図　探信	※
s 064	龍図　日華	※
s 065	維摩図　常信	
s 066	岩に鷲　雪村	
s 067	岩山の仙人図　呉小仙	
s 068	岩上に雉、竹、薔薇、桃の大樹　沈南蘋	
s 069	蓮華図　雲渓	※
s 070	山景図　応挙	
s 071	名所紀伊和歌浦景観図　一鳳	※
s 072	鴉に月　東渓	※
s 073	顔輝「仙人図」探幽模写	

s 074	漁師の娘となった観音（魚籃観音） 　　　　　　　　　東山　　　　※	s 114	雪景山水図（双幅）源琦　　　※
s 075	驟雨を避け雨宿りする人々 　　　　　　　　二代一蝶　　　　※	s 115	山水図（双幅）文晁
s 076	牡丹に竹、奇岩　梅逸	s 116	寒山拾得図　狩野派
s 077	海を臨む岸壁に白い隼　探幽	s 117	龍虎図（双幅）呉春
s 078	峠の富士　探山　　　　　　　※	s 118	群猿図　狙仙
s 079	夜霧の中の白狐　応挙　　　　※	s 119	野鴨図　萬壽　　　　　　　※
s 080	断崖を覗く虎　岸駒　　　　　※	s 120	松に鳥図　狩野元信　　　　※
s 081	花鳥図（双幅）養川　　　　　※	s 121	粗放な山水図　岸駒
s 082	箕面の大滝図　李長　　　　　※	s 122	山水図　小栗宗湛
s 083	松に孔雀　応挙	s 123	山水図（双幅）文麟
s 084	雪景に松林　一鳳　　　　　　※	s 124	福禄寿、山水（三幅対）探幽
s 085	岩に座す観音　安信	s 125	義経騎馬図　美信　　　　　※
s 086	山水雨景図　養川　　　　　　※	s 126	雉図　狩野素川彰信
s 087	母子の虎　岸駒	s 127	東福寺通天秋景図　晴曠　　※
s 088	赤鍾馗図　徹山　　　　　　　※	s 128	鶴に日輪に波　鶴沢探泉　　※
s 089	虎図　岸駒	s 129	梅に鶴図　探雪
s 090	蝦蟇仙人鉄拐仙人　周信	s 130	獅子に牡丹図（三幅対）晴川　※
s 091	山水図　文晁	s 131	四睡図　キオノブ 　　　　（キヨノブ狩野清信の誤り）　※
s 092	雪の枝に泊まる鷺と鴉　英一蝶	s 132	東方朔　常川幸信　　　　　※
s 093	仙人王質図　義菫	s 133	人物図　ユキノブ
s 094	東方朔　藍江　　　　　　　　※	s 134	柳に鷺図　洞林由信　　　　※
s 095	花鳥図　晩山　　　　　　　　※	s 135	円中に山水（双幅）周文
s 096	櫻の枝に水　望月玉泉	s 136	菊図　融川□信（寛信）　　※
s 097	梅に薔薇　香雲　　　　　　　※	s 137	栗鼠に栗　ユウセイ
s 098	岸壁の鷲　雲錦	s 138	仙人図　顔輝
s 099	山水図　墨彩　為一	s 139	鹿を追う狩人　北斎　　　　※
s 100	松に鷲図　狩野雅楽助	s 140	西湖景観図　雲谷等顔　　　※
s 101	桜に群猿　狙仙	s 141	山水冬景　琦鳳
s 102	中国山水図　周文	s 142	花卉図　抱一
s 103	中国山水楼閣図　文雍　　　　※	s 143	羅漢図　可翁
s 104	月光の中の山と霧　文麟　　　※	s 144	桃花、柳に黄色の小鳥　梅逸　※
s 105	布袋図　啓書記	s 145	雉に桜、鹿に花（双幅）来章
s 106	羅漢図　土佐光茂	s 146	富士山、雲　探鯨　　　　　※
s 107	花鳥図（海棠に四十雀）松村景文	s 147	布袋に花（三幅対）探幽
s 108	花鳥図（雪中の竹に雀）景文	s 148	嵐に龍、虎に乗る鍾馗（三幅対）探幽
s 109	山水図　啓書記　　　　　　　※	s 149	鷹図（三幅対）二直庵
s 110	仏画　文殊騎獅図　巨勢俊久	s 150	山水人物図（三幅対）木村永光　※
s 111	松の木に坐る鳥窠　顔輝　　　※	s 151	龍図、波濤図（双幅）竹洞　※
s 112	台座に坐る釈迦　宅磨爲久　　※	s 152	観音図（白衣観音）元信　　※
s 113	隅田川堤防図　嵩谷　　　　　※	s 153	釈迦図　栄賢
		s 154	虎図　岸駒

283

s 155	豫譲の図　華山		s 196	山水図　呉春	※
s 156	福禄寿、山水（三幅対）狩野安信		s 197	琴高仙人図　海北友松	
s 157	孔雀図　芳園	※	s 198	人物図　土佐光起	※
s 158	猿の図　狙仙		s 199	山水図　晴暉	※
s 159	孔雀図　岸駒		s 200	三福神　狩野周信	※
s 160	八福神の図　華山	※	s 201	大黒図　義董	※
s 161	花鳥図　呂紀		s 202	八仙図　義董	※
s 162	荒山風景図　呑舟	※	s 203	花鳥図　小栗宗栗	
s 163	福禄寿　岸駒		s 204	枝に鳥　山田道安	
s 164	二頭の鹿　岸駒	※	s 205	女人図　土佐光成	※
s 165	花鳥図　コヨーシン（不明）		s 206	三聖図　狩野寿石敦信	※
s 166	山水図（双幅）豊彦	※	s 207	木に鳥　一休	
s 167	人物図（双幅）月岡雪斎	※	s 208	炭焼きの図　日華	※
s 168	達磨、鷲、蓮（三幅対）尚信		s 209	中国皇帝図　探幽	
s 169	李白、花鳥（三幅対）探信守政		s 210	観音図　容斎	※
s 170	孔子と弟子（三幅対）正信原図		s 211	岩に猿　南岳	※
	探幽模写	※	s 212	婦人図　月岡雪鼎	
s 171	花鳥図　墨彩　季頼		s 213	屏風に人物　豊国	※
s 172	扇面人物図　元信	※	s 214	舟に人物図　雪信	※
s 173	川景色　守景		s 215	蓬莱図　土佐光忠	
s 174	山水図　永納	※	s 216	運河景観図　岸礼	
s 175	周公図　狩野養川	※	s 217	李白図　狩野孝信	※
s 176	牡丹図　松栄		s 218	雪景山水　文麟	
s 177	宮門で戯れる唐子たち	※	s 219	大瀧圖　桃水	※
s 178	寿老人　海北友雪	※	s 220	雄鶏に花（柳に鳥？）宗紫石	※
s 179	山水図　藝阿弥	※	s 221	中国山水図（双幅）探信守政	※
s 180	騎馬人物　曽我蕭亭	※	s 222	女人図（双幅）西川ツケノブ	
s 181	花鳥図　狩野古永徳		s 223	山部赤人に六歌仙　松花堂	※
s 182	二羽の幼鷹　長柳斎	※	s 224	東坡図　足利義持	※
s 183	鯉に瀧図　探幽		s 225	花鳥図　洞雲	※
s 184	瀧に山水図　芳園	※	s 226	東坡図　守景	
s 185	楊貴妃に花鳥（三幅対）探幽	※	s 227	馬図　蕭白	※
s 186	木の枝　常信	※	s 228	山水図（双幅）狩野光信	※
s 187	山水図（水墨）楊冨		s 229	七福神図　土佐光文	※
s 188	枝に小鳥　玉樂	※	s 230	天狗に鳥　呑舟	※
s 189	山水図　横山華山		s 231	牡丹図　守景	
s 190	山水図　北斎		s 232	東本願寺炎上図　華渓	※
s 191	花鳥写生図　嵩渓	※	s 233	中国山水図　伊川模写	※
s 192	羅漢坐像　兆殿司	※	s 234	山水図　円山應震	
s 193	龍図　狩野山雪		s 235	鷺に蓮　狩野休圓	※
s 194	布袋図　狩野洞白	※	s 236	寿老人に龍（三福対）狩野養川	
s 195	夜景図　武禅	※	s 237	牡丹に鳥　百谷	※

s238　寿老人に山水（三幅対）狩野永叔　※
s239　中国山水図　孫君澤原図（晴川模写）
　　　　　　　　　　　　　　　　　　※
s240　柳に燕　狩野周信　　　　　　※
s241　福禄寿図　狩野常信
s242　竹、雪、雀　狩野岑信　　　　※
s243　山水図（双幅）玄也　　　　　※
s244　寒山拾得図（双幅）可翁
s245　山水図（双幅）長谷川等伯
s246　人物図（双幅）洞文
s247　梅など（三幅対）狩野洞春
s248　瀧に日輪（三幅対）狩野祐清英信※
s249　鶴図（双幅）狩野探牧　　　　※
s250　牡丹図（双幅）狩野伊川　　　※
s251　花卉図（双幅）　狩野□□
s252　鶴に鶉（三幅対）土佐光芳　　※
s253　陶淵明図　狩野尚信
s254　平等院景観　芳園　　　　　　※
s255　笛吹きと唐子　一蝶　　　　　※
s256　布袋図　楊月　　　　　　　　※
s257　鷹に小鳥　狩野□□
s258　稲田に雀　岑信　　　　　　　※
s259　松の枝　探原　　　　　　　　※
s260　山水図（双幅）等益　　　　　※
s261　屋内婦人図　ユキノブ
s262　群鶴図　勝川　　　　　　　　※
s263　福禄寿に唐子　嵩谷父子　　　※
（s264〜s517 第2冊に続く）

アーネスト・フランシスコ・フェノロサ蒐集作品
日本絵画解説付総目録

東京市本郷加賀屋敷一番館
1880 年 12 月

※は訳者註
MFA 11.XXXX はボストン美術館の収蔵番号 (Accession Number) を示す

目　録

区分 A
掛けもの

ナンバーは単幅連幅を問わず各作品に付した。連幅の補助ナンバーは各幅を示し、掛け順、落款については多くの場合はここでは触れないが、ときに箱書きの翻訳を添えることがある。落款については別稿「落款集稿本」を照合のこと。文中に記した画家の伝記については同じく「画人伝稿本」を参照されたい。ただし興味ある話題を折りに触れて紹介することもある。東京在住の指導的画家、批評家による特別批評をも加えた。構図細部の叙述は、鑑定や画題あるいはすぐれた特質を理解する上で必要な最小限に留めた。画題一般については「画題稿本」を参照のこと。年代は仮に記しておくが、おおよそのものに過ぎない。場合により日本人の見解と外国人の見解を併記して作品の特質を述べたことがある。全体的には他の諸稿本がコレクション解説に役立つよう配慮して、ここではできるだけ簡単に記述した。

作品1　人物図、小品。仏教の神、地蔵。
みごとなスタイルを持つかなり古い日本仏画。巨勢金岡筆で1000年ほど前のものと言われるが、蜷川氏、狩野永悳、雪庵の説によればいささか独特の大胆なタッチに欠けるところがあり、金岡自身の手になるというよりむしろその息子ないし孫の作品で900年ほど前のものという。金泥を塗布して耐久性を持たせる秘伝はこの時代を境にやがて消滅した。一方シモダ氏や逸名氏は金岡筆と断定。このような古い絵画になるといずれの証言も信を置けない。線と色彩の優美さでは後代の仏画をはるかに凌ぐものがあるものの、線の大胆さや色彩の壮麗さでは、現在京都にあり金岡の真筆とされる数点に較べて見劣りがする。結局のところ東京在住の現存画家住吉の鑑定により巨勢源慶の作とされる。赤松より購入。以下1880年秋送付された分。（MFA:11.4080）

作品2 (1-6)　花鳥図、1877年か78年。雲錦筆。
六幅もの、あるいは四幅（一、二、三・四、五・六）かとも考えられるが、便宜上六幅ものとして扱っておく。
　　　第一図。葦原から飛び立つ野鴨二羽。情調・色彩とも繊細だが全体として強さに欠ける。
　　　第二図。松の曲がった幹にとまる孔雀二羽。美しさは主として構図にある。
　　　第三図。桃の花に雉一羽。きわめて豊かな色彩を持つが、それほど純粋な情調が伝わってこない。
　　　第四図。黄色の花をつける草むらの中の鶉。真に高雅な日本的情調を持ち、日本人の目から見て、また事実その通りだが、六幅中最高の作。
　　　第五図。岩上の青鷺二羽と松。純粋なグレーの色調において卓越し、六幅中第二位の作。
　　　第六図。紅梅の枝に青鷺二羽。雲錦が大晦日の夜に見た夢の図という。幸福の象徴という三題を描くが、迫力に欠ける。

作品3　［※花鳥図］。
岩に雄鶏、雌鶏、数羽の雛、上部に紫の花を配す。元の画家王若水の逸品を東圃という画家が模写したもの。狩野氏は画家の手腕が所期の効果を挙げるに成功していない拙い模写と言うが、他方長谷川氏は実にみごとな模写と評す。かなりの技量によりきわめて柔和で趣きに富んだ中国的色彩効果の域に到達している点で、私としては後者の意見に賛成したい。情趣の点では南蘋をはるかに凌ぐ。独特の畝のある中国製絹地が色彩効果を増している。まさに中国的情調を完全に伝え、岩の線、デリケートな色彩、軽やかなトーンが際立った要素となっている。山中より購入。（MFA:11.4664）

作品4 ［※山水図］。文晁筆。小品。

色調はグレー。岩、凍結した川、落葉樹、屹立した崖を配した冬景色。雪が空に舞う。冷たくかすむような効果がこの画家独特の手法で描かれている。凡作で、とくに注目に値する作例ではない。

作品5 ［※花鳥図］。大西圭斎筆。小品。

紅梅の枝に庭の白鷺、梅には残雪。圭斎は宋紫石の弟子、秋暉の師。この作品は圭斎の作としてはかなりすぐれたもの。圭斎の描く鳥は頭が大き過ぎることで有名だが、この作でもそれが言える。とくに色彩のフィーリングが純粋で、中国的というより日本的な情調を伝える。描法は独特で、南蘋およびその流派の一般的作品に見られる手法を全く離れ、明らかに岸駒派の手法を継ぐもの。紅梅の枝や幹を描く筆さばきは岸駒によく似ている。箱書きには「鷺紅梅」と書かれ、掛けものの裏面に「大西圭斎」、表面上部に「圭斎」とある。単純明解な色彩と威勢よく書かれた複雑な大枝の量感が見どころ。（MFA:11.4793）

作品6 ［※花鳥図］。公紀筆。小品。

雄鶏、雌鶏、雛、上部に百合。この作者の名は画人伝では不明。箱書きには「西洞院入道」［※フェノロサはニシノトウエンと発音］と書かれている。狩野氏の考えでは京都の公卿の名という。様式がいずれの流派の影響をも受けておらぬ点に興味がある。彩色は力強く粗豪で情調の純粋さに欠けるが、後代の日本花鳥図にはめったに見られぬ力の効果を持つ。大阪でこの画家の作品数点を見たことがあるが、いずれも同様の特徴を持っていた。あるいは専門の画家ではなかったか。（MFA:11.4741）

作品7 ［※花鳥図］。文晁筆。

岩に鷹、松の一部。ほとんど墨一色だが全体に褐色味がかったトーンがありセピア風。雪庵は落款が文晁初期のものでありながら画風を晩年のものと見て作の真偽を疑う。逆に狩野氏は画風を文晁若年のものとし、偽物ではないが文晁としては二級品と見る。私見では後者の見解に賛成だが、これは三級すなわち凡作にランクさるべきもの。真物であることに疑いは持たぬが、文晁の手法としては未熟である。

[原注]（以下すべての画家に関し、その作品ないし画風に一級、二級、三級の評語を用いる場合はつねに下記の規準によるものとする。第一級にはその画家独自の画風が大まかに鑑定して最高度の暢達を示し最大の迫力を発揮している、ごく少数の作品、全作品の2パーセントないし5パーセントの逸品のみを含める。第二級とはその画家の力量の最高限度にまで到達してはいないがとくに優秀さを示す作品のすべて。一作家の作品の15ないし20パーセント、少なくとも現在鑑賞し得る原作の15ないし20パーセントとする。以上の比率で評価を下すに当たらない第三級とは凡庸な画で、過半数の比較的よく見かけられる作例をいう。この等級とパーセンテージは、実際上便

宜的なものとして、かつ大体穏当なものとして、狩野永悳氏に教示されたものである。)

作品8　琵琶を持つ弁天。常信筆。小品。
真に常信的な筆致を持つが、その一連の凡庸作に伍するものと言わざるを得ない。その中では良い方に属する典型的な作。箱書きには「弁財天」「常信」とある。

作品9　寒山拾得図。佳品。望月玉川筆。
優品。玉川は岸駒の高弟。狩野永悳氏の説では近世日本画中最高傑作のひとつ。画想、画法ともきわめて独創的。岸駒の精神を受け継ぎながら全く新しい形で作品を包みこんでいる。描法は外国人の目から見ても日本ではまず最高のもの。手足とくに手の表現が実に写実的。顔は表情に富み蓬髪は岸駒を受け継いだ手法でみごとに表現されている。姿態、四肢、衣服の流れるような線は驚嘆に値する。線の統一は画中人物の心中に存する感情の統一を表出したもの、画面を超越して目に見ることの出来ぬある実体への熱烈な憧憬を表現したものにほかならない。その憧憬の対象を画中に彷彿させることによって鑑賞者の注意を人物の表情にみなぎる理念から逸らさぬようにする筆写のなみすぐれた才能を、この作品は示している。岸駒の描く線とはタッチが異なり、より軽やかで曲線的である。色彩は薄く無きに等しいが構成は非凡。どこか応挙風の名残がみられる。山中より購入。（MFA:11.4712）

作品10　弁天図。土佐光起筆。
現存弁天図中最高傑作の一つ。光起は土佐派最大の画家の一人。狩野氏の評では気品と純粋さを持つ光起の最高作品。いわゆる土佐風ではなく、後世の諸流派によって堕落し奇怪な作風となる以前の、古様大和絵最高作に即して制作されたもの。岩の描法は金岡風で中国唐朝様式から出ている。人物は純粋な金岡風に近い。K氏によれば琵琶の持ち方を斜めにする常例を破って水平に保つところに光起の異才があると言う。そのため弁天はまことに平和な気品を与えられている。ところが画家ではなく古物学者である蜷川氏は、なんとこの作を高尚と気品に欠けるとして凡作なりと言うのである。長谷川氏によれば光起秀作の一つ、また雪庵も極めて高尚かつ純粋な作とする。私見では色彩に光起の特徴がうかがえると思うが、これは狩野氏の見解と異なる。設色は光起の優品のすべてに認められるのと同様、爽快かつ繊細、繻子の如くなめらかなトーンがある。デリケートな描法でも他を圧している。鶉や草花を描かせると細部はあたかも顕微鏡で見る如くになる。作品60参照。だが光起には大きな覇気ある主題を扱う力がない。しかしこの作品に見られる描線と画想は私の見たうち最も雄壮で力強い。技巧の点でも土佐派のうち彼の右に出るものはいない。線描、設色ともその筆法を完璧に示すのがこの弁天図である。水の描写がやや弱い。工商会社の岩井氏より贈呈されたもの。個人的見解だがこの作品は金岡とは全く無関係、むしろ探幽を仲介とする元朝中国画に近いように思われる。（MFA:11.4565）

作品 11　山中の滝。文晁筆。

日本絵画としてはきわめて特異な作。これに類するものは見たことがない。日本の批評家諸氏もこの作を見て他に類例がないという。もっとも注目すべき特徴は第一にキアロスクーロ［※明暗を基調とする画法］の試みである。これはいかなる画家の作品にもいまだかつて見ることのなかったもので、文晁の他の作品でもごく少数に限られている。第二は力強い描法とタッチのおおらかなこと。これは文晁としても異例の事である。第三に彩色法。文晁独自の感覚をもって描かれた部分がとくに文晁的である。もっとも文晁は、偉大な画家たるものあらゆる流派の描法に通じていなければならぬと説いた。しかも実際の作はその言説に背馳するものではなかった。長崎でオランダ人に学んだ司馬江漢に教えられて若き日に油絵を研究、やがてこれを廃したという雪庵説の生ずる所以である。もしその説が事実であれば、後年の文晁画に見られる独特な色彩法、陰影法の説明がつく。この作品の場合とくにそのことが言える。まさに油絵のように、20乃至30フィート離れてこの作を眺めたときもっとも効果を発揮するのである。同じ彩色法を有する文晁の他の作品といえば、私の見る限り、1880年5月大名・松平によって上野の展覧会に出品された東海道風景の画巻のみである。私のこの所蔵品については、狩野氏を始めすべての評者によって文晁第一級の秀作と考えられている。狩野氏、雪庵、共に制作年代を作者40歳ごろと説く。箱書きに「滝、山水」「谷文晁」とある。画中落水の迫力は京都の西村が所蔵する応挙の二枚屏風のそれに匹敵し他に類例がない。また明白なことだがそのタッチは規則に縛られたものではない。キング［※金か？］より購入。

作品 12　樹下に虎、枝に小鳥。岸駒筆。

いわゆる岸駒風の佳品。この手のものは今なお売りに出されており、京都のコレクション中でもよく見かけるが、彼の秀作とは比較にならない。Y・狩野氏［※狩野永悳］は偽作と考えているらしい。雪庵は真作に間違いないと保証している。京都でも何点か当地のどの評者も真作と太鼓判を押す作品を見たことがあるが、それらに較べてはるかに良いので、私は真作であると確信している。岸駒特有のタッチをもつが岸駒的理念が最高の力を発揮したものとは言えない。岸駒は生きた虎を実見したことがある。応挙の習作よりすぐれている。落款はまぎれもなく岸駒。晩年の作。（MFA:11.4698）

作品 13　断崖に生ずる樹木と樹間に戯れる猿の親子。狙仙筆。

狙仙第二級品のうちではまさに最上位にあるとするのが評者の一致した見解。猿を微細に描くことでは彼の力が最高に発揮されている。構図は狙仙通例の作をはるかに凌駕しているが、山水は独創性に欠け描写も強くない。猿を描写して気品ある作とする画家は多いが、狙仙ほど迫真的に描く者はいない。彩色法についての知識はほとんど持っていない。K・K・Kより購入。

作品 14　寿老人と鹿。秋月筆。

秋月の作は珍しいがその佳品のひとつ。狩野永悳によれば秋月第二級の最高作。蟹川は凡作というが彼はいつも私の蒐集品を貶し自分のものを褒める。現存雪舟派の代表者長谷川雪堤は秀作という。雪庵と神田氏の評も秀作。現在（1880年）まで私の目に触れた秋月のものでは最高の作品である。屏風絵の中にはさらにすぐれたものがあるに違いない。この寿老人はその時代のすべての画人が同様の構図で描き、また数百年後にも受け継がれた主題だが、真に秋月的スタイルを持っている。その簡素さは当時の画家の高尚な気品を伝えるものである。印影は真物。画法は雪舟に酷似するが雪舟ほどの力強さ、のびやかさに欠ける。箱書きには「寿老人」「秋月」とある。田澤より購入。（MFA:11.4967?）

作品 15　荒山雪景中の野馬二頭。元信筆。

稀品だが元信第二級の作。この種のものはあまり見られない。押された印影には元信の息子松榮の名が読める。従って蟹川、神田その他何人かの評者は一致して松榮作とする。工商会社役員松尾、若井の両氏は注目すべき特異の作と見ている。しかし狩野永悳氏は狩野家の巨匠たちから伝来された模写、原図を数多く所蔵しており、その中に元信の六曲屏風を模写したものがあってその一枚の原図がまさにこの作品であると認めているのである。従ってこの作品が元信の自筆であること、もとの屏風があるいは一部破損したため切り離して掛けものに表装したものであることがわかる。のちに松榮の印章を所持していたおそらく狩野派の画家がその謬見に従って押印したものであろう。黒の扱いはまさしく元信のもの。タッチは通例の作と較べて緊張感がある。雨の凍りつくような印象は意図的に描かれたものか。画面全体のすばらしさ、それが日本人の美意識に訴えかける所以はその荒涼たる風景、その中にある生命の尊厳なる無常観によって与えられる感情の高揚にある。馬の表情までがおのれの立場の醸し出す孤独な悲壮感を噛み締めていることを伝えるが如くである。我々は科学者ぶった態度を忘れ得ぬかぎり、そして東洋絵画の深遠霊妙な情感に心を開き得ぬかぎり、中国絵画や日本絵画の偉大さを理解することはできない。箱書きには「雪天牧場」「狩野松栄法眼」。東京にて購入。

作品 16　雪舟筆漁村図の模写。

単純だが魅力的な小品。近代ヨーロッパ風景画の情趣とすぐれた日本古画のそれとが共通の基盤に立つことをみごとに示している。たとえばマーブルヘッドその他ニューイングランド沿岸の町と見做しても一向に差支えない。画法はまぎれもなく雪舟のもの、それに雪舟の落款も入れてあるが、狩野永悳氏と長谷川雪堤は真作ではないと断定する。両者の見解では落款は明らかに偽筆、それに筆致もとくに家屋の描き方が生硬に過ぎ、絵画性と迫力に欠けると言う。他方蟹川氏は真物であることに疑いなしとし、雪庵氏も真物であるとする以外の説には一切耳を傾けないであろう。落款も真筆

と見るのが彼の説である。単なる一証言に過ぎないが永悳・雪堤両画家が雪舟の秀作に詳しいことを考えて前者の見解の方に重みがあることは当然である。また私の見解も前者に傾いている。すなわち落款は私にも偽筆と見えるし、雪舟通例の山水画と較べてタッチも明らかに弱い。しかしながらみごとな作ではある。仮に雪舟でなくても、かなり早い時期の模写、あるいは雪舟生存中の模写ではないかとするのが、評者全員の一致した見方。同様にすぐれた画家の作であろう。欠点は外国人には、教えられないとちょっと分からない。少し離れて眺めて得た印象はまぎれもなく雪舟山水画の印象なのである。この作品の長所は明らかに風景情趣の純粋さにある。（MFA:11.4139）

作品 17　寿老人。雪舟筆、1880 年狩野友信模写。

まず友信の模写が原図に忠実であることを強調しておかねばならない。この原図は日本で最も重要な絵画のひとつ。現在知られている雪舟作では最秀作と評されている。この作品には変わった歴史がある。雪舟中国滞在中に描かれたことは確かで、その後朝鮮の首都ソウルの王宮にもたらされていた。日本のタイラント太閤の名において加藤清正が侵略軍の先頭を切って首都に攻め入ったとき、王宮略奪のあと他の重宝とともにこれを奪取し日本に持ち帰った。現在は（最近まで）蜂須賀侯爵家の家宝、日本絵画の至宝のひとつと見做されている。狩野氏もすぐれた模写を一枚所持している。作の秀逸な所以は、見るものの心にきわめて霊妙な効果を与えるところにある。その理由はまず寿老人の顔と姿態である。顔は神格をそなえて人間の顔ではなく、画面から神秘的まなざしでこちらを見据える。姿態も独特で、体躯は湾屈し、奇妙で不均衡、あたかも逡巡するがごとき形状を持つ。顔や体の色彩もまた独特で神秘性を加えている。しかしながら画中の他の要素をうまく描写するにはどう説明したらよいだろうか。神人に従う玄鹿も主人とそっくりである。左側の松の大幹が寿老人の頭の背後にある光輪の中に突き出しておのずから一場の夢の世界を現出する。その伸びた枝は崇高な神秘性を湛えて白梅の幹枝と混じり合い、厄除けのように張りめぐらされた枝があるいは光輪を突き抜け、あるいは寿老人の頭を覆う。その描法は驚異的である。光と翳の線描の作り出す銀の色調はほとんど他に比類がなく、このような形状との組み合わせにいたっては絶無である。かくのごとき枝の描写はいったいいかなる規準に拠ったものであろうか。他の規準など無いのだ。驚異的な思いもよらぬ構図であって、まさに力と神秘と超自然的魔力の啓示にほかならない。白梅の小枝はまるで蛇のように、生きた指のように画面を這う。老人は節くれた仙杖を手にし、その先端はさらに深い重々しいカーブを描いて交錯した線と翳の中に伸びる。その独創性は完全かつ偉大であり、それ自身の法則に従うのみで他の基準からは判断できない。理想的絵画の分野ではこの作品こそまさに最も独創的創造のひとつと見るべきである。主題、描線、量感が混然一体となってひとつの理念を構成する。それは実に深遠で、形而上学的で、かつ超自然的であり、超人間的精神にしてはじめて養想し得るものであろう。残念ながら今日の日本人はこれを興味ある古代の遺物としか見ることができない。この、より深遠な意味が理解できるのは狩野派の画家のみである。長谷川さえ、自ら描いた拙

劣な模写を見る限り、それを理解してはいないと思う。画中のいかなるものも、いかなる形状も、いかなる陰影も、変えることはできないのである。（札幌のホイーラー教授が大阪で購入し1880年自宅の火災で焼失したのが、おそらくこの模写の原画と考えられる。）（1889年にブルックス氏から聞いたところによると、ホイーラー教授の焼失したのは全く別の作品という。また、この原画は1888年開催のある展覧会に出品されたとのことである。）（MFA:11.4962）

作品18　橋上の義経と弁慶、一蕙筆。
一蕙は前代京都画壇の逸材のひとり。訥言の弟子。この作は、画風はおおむね応挙派的だが狩野派的なところもあり、いくぶんか土佐派的趣きを持っている。彩色は独創的といってよく、多分に近代的味わいが見られる。濃淡が実によく出ている。注目すべきは人物の顔や感情の表現ではなく、やはり色彩、タッチ、それに濃淡である。弁慶の描線はかなり強い。近代画としては佳品。（MFA:11.4557）

作品19　中国の山景。探幽筆。
素描であり探幽の山水画としては第二級のものと狩野氏は言う。もと三幅もののひとつ。これと全く同じ、またよく似た主題を探幽は三幅対のひとつとして繰り返し書いていた。何枚となく写されたこの中国の景観の名を私はまだ知らない。このようにさりげない筆致でよく山水画の効果を挙げる点がきわめて探幽的である。私見では第三級のもの。

作品20　牡丹に風雨。宗琳［※宗紫岡］筆。
この画家はもと尾張藩の大名付きの絵師だった。構想も描写もみごとである。吹き折られまいとする力がみごとな曲線で描き出される。日本の画では花は通常平面的に描かれるのと違って、ここでは花弁がレリーフのように浮き立って見える。葉の形と色にもバラエティーがあり、それらの特色がこの作を独創的なものとしている。描線と主題の統一は完璧である。この画家の作品は東京ではあまり見られない。

（MFA:11.4672）

作品21　昔日の向島隅田川。狩野友川助信筆。彩色画。
友川は狩野友信の曽祖父。かの土佐派的情調に極めて近い筆法だが、それとは異質の、狩野派の一様式で彩色されている。友川は特に有名にはならなかったが、彼としては最高の作だと狩野氏は言う。北に筑波山が実景そのままに聳えている。（MFA:11.4802）

作品22　大瀧の波しぶきに跳ねる二匹の鯉。大作。藍江筆。
藍江は岸駒に次ぐ近代画巨匠のひとり。この作は外国人にも多くの日本の評者にも評判が悪い。外国人は不自然すぎると言って嫌い、日本人は日本的な狭い規範に従って

いないとして貶す。しかし彼らもその筆力、見るものに与える迫力は認めている。優雅さに欠けると狩野氏は言う。確かにそうだが、この作には迫力というさらに高度の特性がある。作者はおのれの描法を意識しているのだ。彼は故意に自然の実際の形状や優稚な情趣を犠牲にし、自己の感情をきわめて力強く表現するために並外れた形体を作り出そうとする。見る側はおのれの偏見を捨ててその印象を十分に受け止める。その結果、真の芸術的目的はきわめて大胆に達成される事になるのだ。この画家の作品は今まで目にした限り、いずれも際立ってすぐれたものばかりである。山中より購入。（MFA:11.4660）

作品23　親犬、仔犬のいる風景。南蘋筆。
南蘋の何点かの作品のようにとりわけ美しく、迫力に満ちた美しい作ではないが、模造品が何千と出回っている折から、偽物でないのがメリットとするのが評者の一致した見解。狩野氏は第二級に属する佳品と見ている。その控えめな画法を日本人は高く評価する。犬の色描は高名な南蘋的筆法から生まれた動物画としては最高のおだやかな表現を持つ。落款は疑いなく真物。木と花と草に南蘋のもっともデリケートな描法がよく表れている。全体として構成は弱く、この画家のあまりにも多い作品と同様、効果を挙げていない。とくにこのために製造された清国製の厚手の絹布に描かれている。箱書きには「南蘋画」とある。ライマン氏より贈られたもの。（MFA:11.4668）

作品24　仏画。大作。
それぞれの円陣内に赤、青、黄、緑などの神々を描く。作者は不詳。せいぜい100年ほど前の作。近年補修したあとが見られる。日本人は描法に価値を認めないが、全体的な構図には近年の仏画としてはややましな特色がある。色彩は華麗だがとくにすぐれているわけではない。総じて、外国人が熱心に買い漁るたぐいの凡庸な近年の仏画よりは出来がよいと言ったところ。磁器製作の軸先が実にすばらしく、日本古代のブルーで、日本人が感心する。箱書きには「キウジョー［※コクーゾーの誤読か］カンオン」とあり。［※五大虚空蔵菩薩か。］（MFA:11.4541）

作品25　美濃国養老山の景観、大作。菅原蘭溪筆。
20年前の作。作者は平安貴族の末裔だが画家として特に著名ではない。作風は応挙派的。遠近画法は成功していない。四季のすべてを描出するという矛盾もあるが、これは意識的なもので、画描は偉大と言えないまでも卓越さを示す。遠山がとくによい。箱書きには「養老山真景」「菅原蘭溪」とある。暁斎によれば作者は越前国ではもっとも著名、のちに京都に出て三条に住み、かなり有名の由。（MFA:11.4759）

作品 26　三幅対［※李白観瀑］。探幽筆。

狩野氏いわく第二級品。作者69歳の作。奔放さと詩的表現にすぐれ、後世画家の速筆の規範とされる。

　第一図。雄鶏と海棠。
　第二図。滝見をする李白。李白は唐朝の高名な詩人。もっとも有名な詩のひとつに深山で大滝を発見した状況を述べている。その後日本画で中国人が滝見をするのは必ず李白とされる。昔の中国の画家には好まれた画題である。
　第三図。梅の枝に月。この時代にはよく見られる主題。探幽としてはきわめて速筆だが魅力ある描法。筆致は行書風である。狩野氏は主題と情趣にすぐれていると言う。

キングより購入。もと某氏蔵。

作品 27　唐人山荘景観の図。［※狩野探信守道摸写］

王輝筆の名画。狩野探信守道が原画より模写したもの。王輝は宋代の著名な画家。探信は狩野探美守貴の祖父。日本で王輝の作はきわめて稀。この作は着想とその処理法に魅力がある。山荘内の詩人たちの線描がみごとで、風変わりな樹木は多くの日本画のモデルとされてきた。王輝は馬遠より少し後の画家である。東洋美術出色の風景画。最高の理想的作品。現存する第一級の模写で、おそらく国立博物館の所蔵するものよりはるかに優れている。

作品 28　探信後期の三幅対。［※山水・邢和璞］。秀作。

近世画としては情趣描法が非常に洗練されている。厳密な意味で独創性があるとは言えないが、作者最高作のひとつ。

　第一図。中国山水、前景に陋屋。元信からの直接の模写ではないが、あらゆる部分を元信の山水図から改作して新しく独創的なものとしている。繊細な仕上げは特に元信山水図の筆法が顕著。
　第二図。福禄神、邢和璞、及び従者崔曙。元信の著名な作から構図を写したものだが、原作が墨一色であるのに対しこの作には探信の色彩が施され、いくぶんか繊細な情感が加わっている。それなりに完璧な出来栄え。
　第三図。理想的な中国山水、田園風景。図一と同じく元信を改作したものだが直接の模写ではない。柔らかくもの静かで褐色がかった色彩は探信独自のもの。総じて三作とも魅力ある作品。

工商会社より購入。工商会社は大善より入手。（MFA:11.4254-4256）

作品29　三幅対。[※寒山拾得・龍]。探幽筆。

探幽第三級すなわち通常作の画風をよく示している。60歳の作。描法は粗放。探幽の筆さばきの妙技は他の追随を許さぬことで著名であり、作品32ではそれが最高の特色となっているが、この作にはそれが見られない。力はあるが高尚深遠な情感に欠ける。

　　第一図。龍に波浪。嵐の中を空中に翔け昇る龍。龍の飛び立ったあと激しくうねる怒涛。波の描線が強い。
　　第二図。寒山と拾得。二人は仙人ではなく唐僧豊千禅師の従僕でその弟子となった。禅宗を学びその学徳は中国人の間で知られる。日本の禅宗の間でも深い尊敬を受け、あらゆる時代の好画題となった。寒山と拾得とは手の動き顔の表情だけで人知れず高邁な思想を語り合ったという。それ以上の両人の事蹟については、関係する書物を参照されたい。探幽の描法としては最も粗放である。
　　第三図。嵐の中を水に戻る龍。狩野氏は三点の中では最良と言う。

作品30　三幅対。[※山水楼閣]。狩野伊川筆。

実子狩野永悳の評ではこの絵師のもので彼の見た最高のものと言う。48歳乃至50歳の作。きわめて繊細に山水の各部を描くがその様式は元信や、宋・元の中国画家とくに孫君澤の楼閣図などから部分部分を学び取っている。伊川独自の要素は各部分をまとめて独自の情調を持つ色彩美を作り出した点にある。情調こそ本質的に伊川的であり着色も優美で非の打ち所がない。描かれる楼閣は空想上の乃至現実の古い中国の宮殿だが、その周囲には何とも柔らかな雰囲気が漂い、それがこの作を時代に傑出した優品たらしめている。これを納めるのは最高級の桐箱で、高貴な人物の所有であったに違いない。箱書きの書は息子狩野晴川の筆。外側に「三幅対」「山水楼閣」「伊川院法眼」、内側に「養信（晴川）書之」とある。

　　第一図。湖畔の宮殿。湖の対岸は遠く金色の雲の中に消えている。
　　第二図。前景にテラスと庭園の一部、中景に美しい湖岸、上部は覆いかぶさるような山の連なりが見事で、樹木の幹がとくによい。仕上げは完璧である。
　　第三図。冬景色。雪の中の別荘、隣に竹林。中景には黄色い枯草のある湖岸。

三図とも特別な迫力はない。工商会社より購入。工商会社は大善より入手。

(MFA:11.4212-4214)

作品31　三幅対。[※恵比寿・大黒・福禄寿]。狩野常信筆。

永悳、友信とも常信最高の傑作と言う。この画題はすべての画家が決まったように描くもので常信もしばしば試みたが、この作の描線と色彩はほかの通常作をはるかに抜きんで、日本人にきわめて高雅な情感を伝えている。それとなく示された色彩のデリケートな感じは注目に値し、描線の筆力も大変強い。福神をこのように大きく表わす作品も稀である。表装は古い。箱書きは「福禄寿・恵比寿・大黒」「三幅」「法印古川画」。

第一図。米俵に跨がり打出の小槌を振るう大黒。打出された財宝が下に散らばっている。衣服は黒と緑の配合を持ち、さながらベルベットのように見える。
第二図。福禄神、鹿、鶴。描線の構成がよく、巨松を配して気品の高い構図となった。
第三図。鯛を釣る恵比寿。蜷川氏は三作中最高と言うが、色調と墨の濃淡の点でその見解が当っている。恵比寿の立つ岩の色調はこの情景を描く如何なる作も及ばない。探幽から常信のこの三作にかけて、狩野派の秀作にはすべてこの種の精緻な・情趣的色調が特徴となっている。

工商会社より購入。第一級品。

作品32　三幅対。[※龍、雷神]。探幽筆墨画。
日本で最も著名な探幽三幅対のひとつ。「草書」風の筆致で描かれた探幽最高作と、狩野氏は言う。雲の独特で透き通るような墨色、速筆だが完璧な濃淡、豪快な筆勢、墨をたっぷりと含んだ激しい筆の一閃が確実なる手並みで抑えられたとき、墨の間際に生ずる光の分散、こういった雲を描いては全く他の追随を許さないものがある。狩野派の如何なる画家といえども、この技法を真似たり、また写し取って成功した者はいない。実際その技法にはほとんど想像を絶するものがある。しかしながらこの作の最大の長所はその情熱性にある。それが与える神秘的な暗示、自然の破壊力に対する詩的な処理に対して、見る者は頭を下げざるを得ない。

第一図。渦巻く雷雲の中を降る嵐の中の龍。独特の卓越した技法が最高度に発揮されている黒一色の中の光の点在がすばらしい。神秘的で恐ろしい龍とこの世ならぬ雲とが同一不二であるところもよい。下方に描かれる浮雲の渦には力と神秘性が溢れている。色彩を施さぬ水晶のような光景の中で壮大激烈な主題をすべて捉え得た絵師の強烈な構想は、これに接する者に畏敬の念を生ぜしめるものである。
第二図。中景に伊豆の山から見える駿河湾。そのはるか上空に嵐が吹き荒れている。見るも恐ろしい雲の中を、雷音を発する小鼓を輪につないでこれを背にした雷神が飛び跳ね、赤い稲妻がはるか下方に煮えたぎる地獄の深淵を照らし出す。騒々しい嵐の世界のはるか上方には澄み切った空に富士が悠然とその崇高な白雪の頂を見せ、下界の混乱した不均衡な力の世界とみごとな対象をなしている。下方の雲を描く筆力は驚くべきものがある。日本人は誰でも、これを三幅中でもっとも称賛する。
第三図。深淵から同様に渦を巻きながら収まり行く乱雲の中を、空中高く翔け登る嵐の龍。筆致、情感は第一図と同じだが迫力と驚異性に欠ける。

工商会社より購入。大善旧蔵。（MFA:11.4392-4394）

作品33　三幅対。[※維摩・花鳥]。探幽筆。墨絵、小品。

衆目の一致するところ探幽第一級品の最優秀作。狩野永悳氏評では探幽作でこれと比較すべきものなく、前掲作品をさえ凌駕すると言う。模写はとうてい不能。30歳乃至40歳、探幽としては最大の力を発揮した頃の作。狩野氏によればその秀作なる所似は各描線間の調和がとれている点、墨色が豊かで美しい点、明暗が柔らかく効果が純粋な点にある。筆致は行書風と真書風の中間。

　第一図。梅の枝にかけす。墨色の美がもっとも強く表われている。墨色の効果が唯の一筆で決まることを考えれば、その透明度と潤沢さは一驚に値する。危うげのない繊細さ、筆力の漲った奔放さをもつ簡潔な描線もまたみごとである。主題は平凡だがこれ以上美しく処理されたものはない。
　第二図。維摩像。維摩は達摩より古いインドの哲学者で晩年になってはじめて仏教に帰依した。もと釈迦の時代の独立した思想家だったが、思想体系は釈迦と余り違わなかった。釈迦の弟子文殊が維摩と問答を交わして仏教に改宗させ、以後釈迦の直弟子になったという。狩野氏も言い私も思うのだがこの肖像画は日本絵画のあらゆる分野を通じて最高の傑作といってよい。その表情描写のみごとさは他に比類がない。美しい老いたる顔にたたえられる憂愁に満ちた物静かな諦観が驚くべき筆力で表現される。目は思索に耽って一点を凝視するが、そこには生命力と精神力とが溢れている。陰影法を用いずに肖像画が行き着く最高点を示すのがこの作品である。維摩は手に払子を持つ。これは仏教の高僧が葬儀や重要な法要の際に打ち振る標識であって、禅宗ではどの僧侶も持っている。
　第三図。尾長鶏と海棠。花鳥の配置と第一図よりも柔和な描写がきわめて美しい。もしこの優美な特質を見て何ら感動を覚えぬ者がいるとするならば、もはや審美感を伝える方策はない。

工商会社より購入。大善旧蔵。

作品34　三幅対。山水墨画。狩野晴川筆。

弟永悳の評では作風は第二級。あるいは20歳くらいか、きわめて若手の作。雪舟を深く研究した画家で、初期の作には独創的要素も見られるが雪舟様式の影響が強い。実際、中央の作は雪舟のよく知られた構図を直接に攻作したものと言われている。三作とも想像上の山水。見どころは墨色と金色とが美しい対象をなす雲と雄渾な描線を持つ松と岩で、狩野派の全盛時代を彷彿させる。筆の扱いは雪舟とは違っている。表装は古く、またとくに見事で、暗色の洗練された画調にふさわしい。

　第一図　想像上の山景。前景の岩と木とが特に美しい。山の岩がきわめて強く、全体的にはエッチングのようにシャープでクリアーな効果を与える。
　第二図。想像上の風景にあずまやを配し、中に福禄寿と邢和璞が憩う。侍童崔曙が玄鹿に餌を与えている。奇妙な形の樹木が上方に聳える。全体的効果は壮麗で、

霊妙な神仙的気配に満ちている。
　第三図。想像上の冬の山景。冬の白さと対照する墨色の優美なトーンがみごとである。

工商会社より購入。大善旧蔵品。私見では晴川の第一級品。（MFA:11.4330-4332）

作品35　三幅対。婚礼ないし新年の祝賀用。晴川筆。
狩野氏は二流品に過ぎぬというが私見ではきわめて秀作の域に達したもの。ある貴人の婚礼に際しての注文作と思われる。あらゆる幸福の象徴が描きこまれている。作者30歳の作。狩野氏が欠点として挙げるのは、着色が不調和で気品にかける点だが、形状はまずまずの出来。私自身の印象では、線描が色彩に較べて劣るとは云え、色彩は実に豊かで魅力的である。豪華な表装はまさに近世の貴人に愛蔵された掛け物らしく、最高の様式で仕上げがなされている。
　第一図。鶴と松を描く。
　第二図。寿老人。長寿と才能の神。線描は往時の巨匠の様式だが彩色は晴川自身のもの。豊潤で印象的。寿老人の姿が甘美な趣きをもつ柔和な背景に対して、対照的に描き出されているように思われる。
　第三図。紅梅に神亀。亀の口から渦巻き状に霊感を伝える吉祥の気が立ち上る。

山中より購入。第二級品。

作品36　三幅対。[※寿老人・山水]。文晁筆。大作。
狩野氏いわく文晁第二級品中の最高作。雪庵氏も同意見。描法にやや雪舟を受け継いだあとも見られるがかなり個性的で、良否は別として文晁的特質の中にその要素は埋没している。
　第一図。想像上の山水。上部の断崖が奇妙に突き出し、きわめて無造作な筆致で描かれる。下方、重なり合った岩の間、垂れ込めた雲の蔭に宮殿が見え、床下の柱を水中に没している。三作中最も悪く、見どころはほとんど第3図に奪われている。
　第二図。寿老人。文晁自身の様式による独創的人物画で狩野派に近い。雪庵氏と若井氏は人物画として称賛するが、私見によれば寒々として情調に欠け、傑作とは呼び得ない。才能の閃きが見られないのである。
　第三図。想像上の山水。三作中ずばぬけて良い。ある点では日本絵画の全領域においてもっとも驚嘆すべきもののひとつである。画面の主要部に巨大な断崖が描かれ、其の頂きは二つの円い山に分かれて異国的風趣を添える。断崖の下は画面の前方にかけて大きな丸い岩がうず高く積み重なって傾斜し、その重なりの間から樹木が一列に伸びて崖の中腹まで続く。下方、岩の間に山小屋と拓かれた空き地が望まれ、その右手に谷川があって、上流は断崖の麓を回り遠くその背後に消

える。渦をなす雲が山腹を包み、上端の松の梢を隠す。雲の下は一面に暗い無気味な雰囲気が漂う。この作品のもっとも際立った特徴は、一種の光の効果を生み出す努力である。それは前面に描かれた岩や樹幹を、また断崖の中腹にある松を照らす微妙な光によって表される。一連の松は相互に、また下の谷川にその陰を投じている。どの部分も明暗がデリケートで銀のように美しく、墨色の筆使いは甚だ強い。奔放さにおいては狩野派を介在せずに夏珪の域に到達していると言ってよい。この第三図は第一級作。

質流れ品、所有者より購入。

作品37　双幅。[※牡丹に獅子図]。常信筆。

大作でみごとな表装。常信としては第二級品。両幅とも聖なる獅子と牡丹を表す。獅子は文殊の乗物であり仏教徒の間では高貴な画題と考えられている。牡丹が獅子と一緒に描かれることが多いのは文殊の住居と言われる中国の天台山には牡丹が咲き獅子が群棲したからという。墨の薄塗りが引き締まって美しく、獅子の描法も狩野派の常道を抜いている　色彩もグレイの色調と快い対象を示す。箱書きは「二幅對　牡丹　獅子　法眼養朴」。キングより購入。もとさる華族の所蔵品。（MFA:11.4418-4419）

作品38　三幅対。[※山水、人物]。永徳高信の際立って大きな作品。

高信は狩野永悳の養父の父。高名な画人ではないがこれはその最高作。おそらくある貴人の注文に応じて描いたもの。

　　第一図。龍に白い花。神秘的趣があり、迫力は感じられる。
　　第二図。狩野氏は中国古画からの改作と言う。漢代仙人の等身図。はじめ普通の人間だったが友人の仙人東方朔から仙桃を盗み、これを食して自ら仙人になったという。後世の狩野派にこれほど大きな人物画は稀である。
　　第三図。龍に赤い花。

キングより購入。前作と同じ華族の旧蔵品。

作品39　元代[※清代の誤り]の画人馬元欽の著名な山景図大作の模写。作者は未だに知られざる日本の画家元旦。

彼の同じ模写を長谷川の家で見たことがある。構図は実にみごとで大胆。筆致や彩色のスタイルは宋代の貴族的様式から明代の柔弱な情調への変化をよく示している。この模写はおそらく原作のもつ調和のとれた色彩と柔和な雰囲気を伝えてはいないと思う。彩色も原作ほど純粋ではなかろう。この作が伝えていると言い得るのは筆使いと構図と色彩に対する全体的構想に見られる特徴のみである。しかしその特徴は顕著に示されており、またこのような大作は稀にしか見ることができない。（MFA:11.4792）

作品40　きわめて風変わりな十羅漢図。

落款を欠き作者不明。筆使いから見て著名な流派に所属しておらぬ画家だったことは明らかである。狩野氏は「この作者は画家ではない」と言うが、それは画家の定義の問題。おそらくは僧侶、それも京都の僧侶で、はじめ素人だったが絵が好きで、ついに自分なりの画法を作り上げた人のように思われる。輪郭を描く筆勢は明らかに独特のもので、上方の藪を描く強烈な描線は兆殿司の筆法を学んだふしも見られないではないが、模写ではないと結論することができる。人物はまた、プロの仏画作者なら誰にも見られる優雅さが全くなく、構図も気まじめだが気品に欠け、人物の表情も歪んでおり、作者の無知による描写も少なくなかった。しかし作者は豊かな構想力の持ち主であり、色彩に対する愛情と知識においては、日本の画家として稀に見る天分に恵まれている。この色彩の点にこそこの作の良さがある。その眩しい程の色調に匹敵する作を私はまだ見たことがない。かつてその優美さが称賛された如何なる作品と並べてみるだけでも、この技群のすばらしさが理解できるであろう。羅漢が10人しかいないところから、おそらく五百羅漢五十幅ものの一枚だったと考えられる。全体的な素朴さが古様の感じを与え人の心を打つ。人物の歪みを無視すればすぐれた特質がみえてくる。キングより購入。（MFA:11.4646）

作品41　孔雀、白梅、花。雲錦筆。

この華麗な大作は1878年［※1877年の誤り］上野で開催された官営展覧会に出品のため描かれたもの。作者は中風を病み、制作には三ヶ月を要したという。本人は傑作と自賛しており、最後の重要作となった。線描は強さに欠けるがこれは作者の病気のせいである。構図も前景にかけてややぼやけている。しかし細部の仕上げは巨匠の域に達しており、全体や各部の色彩は大変美しい。花や葉の細部を一々丹念にかつ正確に写し取っている点で、作者もその友人もこれを傑作と称するのである。雲錦自身、とくに作品の下半分を最高の出来と考えていた。色彩に対するこのような情感にかけては、東京でもまた日本でも、彼に匹敵する画家はすでに存在していない。私はこの作品を見て雲錦の晩年が決して衰退したものではないことを知った。この作品はまさに美しく彩られた優雅なシンフォニーと考えられるべきである。私見では雲錦最高作と評することはできない。想像力、迫力の点で初期の素描に比肩し得るものではないのだ。作品45参照。表装は私の注文によるもの。（MFA:11.4674）

作品42　鹿図。双幅。探幽筆。大作。

その秀逸さは探幽第一級品中の最高作、少なくとも作品33のすぐ後に位置するものとするのが、すべての日本人評者の見方。作者66歳の作。線描の歪みが外国人には気になるところで、日本人評者が狂喜する根拠がまず理解し難い。狩野氏の言によれば制作の難しさを克服した点が長所のひとつ。鹿の色は正確そのもので、赤い鹿のほうが白鹿よりややまさっている。主たる長所は絵の「気品」に、すなわち、柔和であ

りながら力強く、繊細でありながら簡潔な筆致、姿態、色彩、全体的雰囲気にあると言う。この特質は他の画家の模倣し得ぬところ、「我々がこの作に感心するのは鹿に備わるもっとも高貴な理想的な印象を伝えるからだ」と、狩野氏は言うのである。この評価は無論一種の「古典」趣味を抱懐することによるもので、ちょうど西洋の洗練された心情が古代ギリシア的要素をもつものに、優劣を問わず惹かれて行くのと全く同じである。この作品のもつ全体的印象は、日本人か中国人ならば直ちに平安高尚と受け取るに違いない要素に満ちている。漢詩を学べばこの種の東洋の古典的心情が理解できるかもしれない。

　第一図。白鹿と緑の竹。
　第二図。赤い鹿と白の桜樹。この鹿の方が前者よりずっとすぐれている。樹の線描がすばらしく、枝や花も最高度の古典的様式をもってきわめて感情豊かに描かれる。幹の部分の筆使いは、樹木を描く真の画家なら誰でも驚嘆すべき出来ばえと思うであろう。前面の雑草さえ日本人の美的精神にとっては霊妙な特質に満ちている。

狩野永悳氏がこの作品の名声を知っているのは、その蔵幅中に先祖の描いた模写画を所持するからである。その模写には「徳川家所蔵」と記されている。幕府崩壊のときに散佚したものかもしれない。印影は現在知られている探幽のものでは唯一のもの。

(MFA:11.4796, 11.4825)

作品43　山水図。双幅。狩野元信筆。（※韃靼人狩猟図）
大作。しかもあらゆる点で驚嘆すべき作品。評者はいずれも、これに匹敵する作を、またこれに類する作をも見たことがないと言う。画題は中国山地、王侯の猟人たちによる狩猟風景。二幅でひとつの絵を構成しているところから、おそらくはもと二枚屏風に描かれたものか。構想はきわめて雄大、中国古画の情調に迫るものがある。線描は元信としてはもっとも強く、岩石層、岩石形状の描き方はとくに印象的。人馬の描線もきわめて霊的で動きも活発。樹木の描写も独創的で力強く、長谷川氏はこのような描法の樹木を見たことがないと言う。色彩は紫紺、金色、灰色、そのすべてにおいて華麗である。黄色と、たゆとうような金色の筆跡とが対象をなし、そのために柔らかい魅力的な紫の色調の中に中間色の墨で描くマッスと線とが強調される。元信山水画の最高作と呼ばれるにふさわしく、事実他の画家の作品には見られぬ特色を持っている。最後に挙げる特質はもちろん鑑賞者に伝わる精神的な迫力。彼らはこの世ならぬ美と知識と生命力とを描き込んだこの印象的なパノラマを驚愕の目をもって見つめるのである。私はこの作品がもと京都大徳寺の襖絵だったことを知っている。「画人伝稿本」を参照されたい。40年ほど前に大徳寺から売却されたもの。元信最高の装飾画。(MFA:11.4265-4266)

作品 44 木に三匹の大猿。狙仙筆。

いわゆる狙仙風の作。彼の他の作品に較べて色彩が豊か、線描も正確。この画家は通常宗教的情熱と想像力に欠けているが、これはその高名な画風が到達し得る最高の完璧さを示す。(但し、作品 59 を参照のこと。) 猿の顔が中心的見どころ。

作品 45 梅の枝に青き鳥。雲錦筆。

雲錦最高の作かもしれぬが素描に過ぎない。数本の枝が放射線のように広がり、焦点に小鳥を配する構想図がみごとである。筆使いも非常に力強く、独創的な箇所も見られる。灰色と黒の墨色の美が注目に値するが、雲錦自身その独創性を強調するのは色彩である。赤や灰色がかった、また緑がかった梅の花が、抑えの利いた多様な色合いの独創的な部分を生じ、そのまま小鳥の完全な色調を作り出している。この作品を支配するのは想像力と強い情感であり、それが依頼者の注文を満たすためでなく作者独自の空想力によって、インスピレーションの高まりのままにみごとに描き出されているのだ。雲錦が新進画家として活躍した 20 歳前後の作。その後致命的な中風にかかり、その驚異的成長は早くも挫折してしまった。この作の持つ情調は往昔の巨匠の優品にも比すべく、また平凡な近年の南蘋派をはるかに凌賀するものである。日本絵画の構想に新たなる一作を加えたもの。

作品 46 紅梅に月。抱一筆。

抱一は城主の子に生まれて画家になった人。地位と財産を捨て、全国を行脚して写生をしたという。光琳風を継ぎ、注目すべき印象的作品を描いた。この作品は抱一のものではかなりよいもの。幹や花の描き方は光琳風だが、光琳より近代的で観察力に秀れ、生硬さ怪奇さのない情調を持つ。月は独創的で、金色の雲をさっと円く描いて縁取りをしただけ。まさに抱一のもっとも軽快な情趣を表わす描法である。生気、迫力の偉大さでは光琳に遠く及ばない。但し作品 □□ 番［※番号空白］を参照のこと。(MFA:11.4577［※本作品は売却され、現在はビゲロウ・コレクションの能面に代わっている。］)

作品 47 山水図。探幽筆。

簡素な小品。探幽としてはごく普通の凡庸な画風だが悪くはない。これ以上の作を見てから比較することがあるかもしれぬが、ここで論ずる必要はない。この景観は探幽の他の多くの山水図によく見られる。

作品 48 岩に白き鷺。模写。

原作者徽宗は中国宋代の皇帝。かなり古く、中国製絹布に描かれており、古物学者蜷川や狩野氏によれば 350 年乃至 400 年前中国で模写されたものという。徽宗皇帝の作

で現存する真物はきわめて少ない。模写であることには多分間違いのないこの作には、原作の持つ強い筆力、迫力に欠けている。しかしその簡潔さは美しく、探幽の扱った同種の画題と比較すべきである。田澤より購入。

作品49　芙蓉の枝。常信筆。
当時の一般的狩野派花卉図様式はこの簡単な作品によって十分に示されている。そこでは上品さと芸術的意義が重視され、南蘋派の表現した花そのものの美しさという面を評価することがない。私のアルバムに収められた探幽模写の画作からも分かることだが、それは古い中国花卉図の系統を直接に受け継いだものである。（MFA:11.4420）

作品50　雪を置いた松の枝に鷲。雲錦筆。
雲錦死去の1ヶ月前に描かれた、絶筆に近いもの。特に際立った特徴は見られない。雲錦晩年の画法を伝える一般的な作例。

作品51　青鬼を踏み潰す鍾馗。文麟筆。大作。
文麟は四条乃至応挙派の画家。鍾馗の荒々しさ、迫力、形相の凄まじさは抜群。がっしりとした体躯の重量感と姿勢が巧みに描かれ、衣服の襞の翻る様に、如何にも無知獰猛な力が表わされている。文麟がかくの如き強さと恐ろしさとの表現を狙って評判を得ようとしたことは明らかである。遠近法を用いた足の描線は独創的と言ってよく、左腕、左手の力は称賛に値する。顔の表情、振り乱した髪の毛も、部分的描法としては実にすばらしい出来と考えなければならない。しかし鬼の方はこの作品に付言するほどの描写も着想もない。用いられた色もすべてが貧弱で文晁の亜流を行くものである。総じて画法は応挙派的だが、岸駒や文晁の描く粗豪な容貌を真似て修正したところがある。おそらく作者の狙った印象を与える点では成功したものであろう。狩野氏の評では、悪くはないがただ力を強調するばかりで、特にすぐれた作ではない。粗野で、洗練された芸術的情調に欠けていると言う。長谷川氏も、この作には人の関心を惹くところがないばかりか堕落した岸駒風の見本であると評している。狩野氏はこれを北斎に通ずるものとも言う。応挙的画風が堕落すれば必ず北斎に近くなるとするのが彼の考えである。外国人の眼から見れば、この作は称賛すべきものではないとしても興味ある作品であることには間違いない。山中より購入。（MFA:11.4692）

作品52　西王母。孔寅筆。
仙女西王母と二人の侍女。一人は聖なる桃を盛った皿を捧げ、一人は長柄の宝扇を持つ。三人とも雲中に浮かび、そこかしこに洩れる光が薄靄の中を照らす。孔寅は応挙派の画家。人物の描法が優雅で姿態にも気品がある。衣裳は紛れもなく応挙風で実に手際よく処理され、特に長い衣が或いは捻じれ或いは途切れるカーブを描いて風になぶられる様がみごとである。あらゆる部分で筆致は的確明快だが、この作の主たる美

点はその彩色である。狩野、土佐、仏画系の偉大な色彩画家に較べれば控えめでとくに目立ちこそしないが、より魅力的かつ繊細なところがあると言えるだろう。その美しい色調は西王母の手にする翼形の扇の柄を見れば分かる。左側の人物に射しかかる光の描写は、それが示す技術的知識の点で一驚に値する。作品のもつ最大の弱点は顔の描写である。みな似たような顔で、気品はあるが大きな特色をもたない。もっともこれは、他から心を動かされることのない高貴な人々の寂静の境地を表そうとする作者の意図であったかもしれない。全体として強さこそないが、一般に色彩美に欠けるこの派のものでは、もっとも美しい作のひとつである。長谷川氏の評では大変よい作、作者は偉大なる景文と同列におかれるべきだと言う。絵画としては後に述べる一鳳の大作（作品84）に比肩するものと彼は考えている。H氏は53年前に京都でこの画家に会ったことがあり、当時40歳位であった由。西王母の頭部を覆わんばかりの大きな宝扇の位置が作品の構図を決定していることも付言しておかねばならない。山中より購入。（MFA:11.4740）

作品53 狸図。一鳳作。小品。

雪の上に狸が坐り、数本の草が見える。きわめて簡単な図でありながら応挙派最高作のひとつである。狸は後三脚で体をまっすぐに支え、前脚で胸を叩く。狡猾で疑い深そうな顔が、何か物音に気を取られたかのように、雪にかすむ彼方を見つめる。狸の姿勢は全体として如何にも写実的だが、その画法には人を驚かすものがある。まず輪郭のない描法が完璧の域に達している点。第二に体全体を覆う毛の一本一本が、まるで顕微鏡で覗いたように、白色、灰色、黒色、褐色と、忠実な技術をもって表現されていること。しかも細部を描いて活気の失われることがない。離れて見ると狸はまるでエッチングのようにはっきりと浮き立って見え、前脚と顔の墨色が画面の濃淡に特色と力を添える。日本の伝説では狸は人の魂に取り憑き、狐と同じように用心しないと人を騙すと言う。従ってこの作品も、日本人がこの動物の本性たる霊的な力と現実の気味悪さの表現を狙ったものである以上、単なる動物の描写と考えてはならない。狩野氏はこの作を評して、その特質は四条派中応挙の次に位置するものと言っている。長谷川氏評では作品79の応挙筆狐図に勝るとする。この点は明らかに長谷川氏の誤りで、彼は即物的側面のみを見て絵画の精神的要素を見落している。狸が胸や腹を叩くと太鼓のような音がするという。山中より購入。（MFA:11.4724）

作品54 山水図。水墨。連山筆。

連山は岸駒の高弟、着想がよく、構図がみごとで、独創的かつ鮮やかな描法。前面の土手に二人の人物が立ち渡し船を呼ぶ。船は岩と菅との間に半分姿を隠している。中景に美しい木立があり、そのうしろに船頭小屋が見える。背後に断崖が聳え、その端に新月がかかる。その明暗が独特で柔らかい感触を持ち、線描によらずマッスとして表現されている。岸駒の特色の上にさらにオリジナルな要素を加味するが、やや文人画的影響も考えられる。濃淡が実に柔らかく純粋なため、墨に色彩を感じさせるほど

である。連山は近世山水画家のうち、或いは最高の存在かもしれない。狩野氏も長谷川氏もこれまで連山の画を見たことがなかったが、この作を優品と評している。京都近辺以外では知られていない画家である。

作品55　文殊半身図。兆殿司筆。水墨画。
顔は一般の古い仏画に見られるより優しく精神的な深味がある。衣服の筆致は非常に強く、この画家の特色を示している。髪の毛は古い画法にしてはみごとに描かれ、墨色の効果がみごとである。雲が胸の下を包んでいるところから、おそらく文殊は空中を飛来するものとして捉えられているのであろう。画のサイズは大分縮まっているが、もとは一尊形式だったもの。落款はないが作者の印章から真物にまず疑いないとするのが長谷川氏の言。狩野氏も、実によい作でおそらく兆殿司の真筆と言う。その優美さが優しく穏やかで気品のある表情にあり、インドから中国へ福音を伝えたと言われるにふさわしい顔立ちである。山中より購入。（MFA:11.4497）

作品56　木の枝に泊る青い尾長鶏。岑信筆。
樹木は赤い花をつける。桜の一種、海棠か。岑信は周信の弟。探幽時代末期の形式を示す。純粋に狩野派的で美しいが崇高美に欠ける。彩色は巧みで、濃色の鶏を大きく描いて画の統一もよくとれている。狩野友信氏によれば岑信は彼の系統の狩野家の先祖。友信はそこへ養子に入った由。永悳氏の評では岑信は高名な画家ではなかったが彼の作としては大変よい作例だと言う。

作品57　狐図。徹山筆。素描。
紫苑の小枝の横で居眠りする赤い狐。徹山は応挙高弟のひとり。狐の彩色法はいかにも安心しきって筋肉の弛んだ全体的表情と共にみごとである。尾は前面にさっと描き、色がぼけたようにしか見えないが頭の部分は人の注目を惹くところで、明るい背景の前に明確に描出され、作者が焦点に関する光景的法則を知っていたことを示す。背後にある紫苑の素描も好ましい。これは応挙派の特色である自然的要素と絵画的要素の結合をみごとに実証したもので、応挙派の画家でも必ずしもうまく到達し得なかった境地である。長谷川氏評では一鳳の狸図に比肩する作。狩野氏は佳作としながらも、同じ作者のきわめて芸術的な素描鍾馗図（作品88）程ではないと言う。（MFA:11.4772）

作品58　鍾馗に虎。金玉仙筆。水墨画。
金玉仙は日本の初期墨絵画家のひとり。その作は非常に少なく、狩野氏も長谷川氏もこれまで目にしたことがない。私にとっても初見の作。人物は異様だが描線に迫力がある。冷たく即物的でその点雪舟の通常作に似ている。雪舟との違いは、主として技術的な問題であるため、外国人の目にはほとんど分からない。長谷川氏は「おそらくこの画家最盛期の作風を示すもの。正信のころの人」とし、さらに「腰から下の形状

がやや弱いが古い画では一般的に形状はよくない。傑出した日本画家のひとりに数えるわけには行かぬ」と言う。狩野氏は「雪舟の弟子道安の作風に似ているがそれほどよくはない。有名な画家ではないし秀作とも言えぬので、模写を試みる者もいなかったであろう。従ってこれは真筆に違いない」と評する。しかし、私はかなり佳い作だと思う。山中より購入。筆者［※MFAでは官南］は元信の高名な弟子であった。

(MFA:11.4228)

作品59　龍図。狙仙筆。

嵐の雲の中を旋回して下降する黒い龍。狙仙は猿の絵で有名。つぎの理由で近世画として注目すべき作のひとつと言える。まず第一に、私の知る限り東京・大阪の誰一人として狙仙の描く龍など見たことも聞いた事もないこと。従ってこれは狙仙のユニークな作である点。第二に、私の知る狙仙の多くの画作と比較してこれがはるかに優れていること。猿や鹿を描く場合彼の主たる目的は写実にあると思うが、それらの構図や付属物の描写は概して弱く、その点が彼をして近世諸派のうち応挙や岸駒よりもかなり低いランクに位置せしめられる所以である。ところがこの作品の示すものは高邁な理想、美の精神による支配、雄大な構図、それに強く確実な線描であり、これにより狙仙は一挙に前世紀最大の革新的画家の地位に引き上げられる。第三は構想、画法が全く独創的であること。嵐の龍に巧みな探幽の影響も受けておらず、その濃淡法も狩野派のそれとは全く異なっている。岸駒の画風に見られるような粗放さ、派手やかさもなく、応挙風の筆使いにやや近いようだがその情調は全く狙仙独持のものである。その上、龍もこれまで全く見られなかったもので、その描写もきわめて迫真的である。鱗で覆われた蛇のような大きな胴体がまるで生き物のようにうねり、立体感をもって迫り、出ては自ら吐く紅蓮の炎の中に身をくねらせ、退いては暗い雲の団塊の中に身を隠す。人は如何なる自然のモデルについてこれを学んだかを問わずにおれないであろう。答えはおそらく、狙仙在世中に見世物として日本にもたらされたに違いない大蛇を研究した成果と思われる。この作品の第四の特徴は、龍が古代近世を通じ、また中国日本を通じ、およそ画家によって描かれた諸龍のうちもっともみごとな龍の一つに数えられることである。それが示されるのはまず構想が極めて崇高で迫力に満ちている点、次に墨の濃淡が描法の難しさに比して実に優美に表現されている点だが、やはり一番重要な点は一目で看取されるように曲線の形づくる壮麗な構図である。その点、この作品はすべての東洋絵画の中で唯一の地歩を占めるものと言えるであろう。龍自体は一定の法則に従って複雑に旋回するが、それに逆らうように恐ろしい力を持つ爪の生えた脚が、直線的に開いて左右に分岐する。一方、渦巻く炎の変化して止まぬ曲線は、まるで風に煽られた幕の光の帯のように、旋回する壮麗な怪獣の前、横、うしろに翻り、まさにこの世のものと思えぬ龍神の衣の如くである。もしこの上に渦巻く雲塊そのものの描写を加えるならば、そしてこれら各要素が渾然として詩的絵画的構想の理想的統一に達し、描線と作者の心とが重要性においても現実においても一体のものとなっていることを述べるならば、この作品のもつ高邁な特性を理解しても

らうことができるかもしれない。もし岸駒が、狙仙のこの作のように全力を尽して己に忠実な作品を描いていたとするならば、中国古画全盛期の巨匠たちの域にまで到達したかもしれない。山中より購入。

狙仙は猿以外の絵を描いても実に偉大な画家であった。この傑作は近世の如何なる画家にも引けを取らない。（MFA:11.4155）

作品60　三羽の鶉に草。土佐光起筆。

鶉の画家として光起は過去250年の間もっとも有名だった。現代の日本人にも高く評価されている。この作では鶉は彼独自のみごとな簡略画法で描かれている。長所短所は歴然としている。長所ではまず鶉の羽毛が顕微鏡で覗いたように忠実に描かれていること。つぎに画面全体の特徴でもある柔らかで優しく詩的で繻子のように滑らかな色調。これは描法のスタイルでもあり同時に構図の特徴でもあるようだが、これらがある種の統一と繊細で女性的に洗練された情調を作り出している。短所は当然ながらまさにその女っぽさ。ほとんどが男性画家にふさわしいところがなく、輪郭も覇気に欠けてぎこちなく、大切な量感が全く出ていない。しかしながら日本人が光起のすぐれた絵画美を語るとき、私はその気持ちを理解することができる。この作は前述作品10の弁天図よりはるかに劣る。これは彼の平凡な画法、弁天図は非凡な画法である。山中より購入。（MFA:11.4558）

作品61　驢馬に乗る鍾馗。雪舟筆。小品。

貧弱な素描だが暗示するところは大きい。右手の二本の木と大地の描線は走り書きの程度。驢馬は活気あるタッチを何度か加えてより深い味わいを持つ。しかし鍾馗は角ばった墨線をもってしっかりと力強く描かれ、その如何にも敏捷な姿勢、激しい表情が敵を追求する意欲を十分に表わしている。墨色の使い方が巧妙。長谷川氏の話では40年前にこの作品が鑑定のため長谷川家に持ち込まれ、当時の画家たちの間でかなりの論議があった後ついに雪舟の真筆と断定され、幕閣に列する役人に21両、今の金額にして140円で納入されたとのこと。もちろん今でも雪舟の偉大な作品に数えられているわけではない。山中より購入。探幽による縮写が九鬼氏蔵幅の中にある。

（MFA:11.4137）

作品62　岩上の観音。水墨画。可翁筆。小品。

年代を経て画面が暗く、離れて見ると判然としない。観音の線描は簡単だが優美、岩と水は中国画風で非常に強い。観音の表情はあまり高貴ではない。全体の画調はどこか牧谿に似ている。H氏評では可翁の真筆にして佳品。顔輝に比肩し、元信に勝ると言う。元信は独創性では勝るが描写がそれほどでない、というのがH氏の意見。死後に有名になり作品数は非常に少ない画家の由。狩野氏は断定こそしないが、多くの画家が通常可翁の作と認めているものであろうと言う。山中より購入。

作品 63　七福神図。探信筆。

探信は探幽の子。ごくありふれた図柄。福禄寿がひとりの子供を相手に踊っている。探信は偉大な画家ではなく、ただ父の画風を模倣するのみだった。四神が楽人の役を演じ毘沙門天のみ傲然と構え布袋が子供のような笑みを浮かべてそれを眺めている。この画題としてはなかなかのよい配置である。狩野氏は探信の凡庸作と評し、H氏は探信としてはよい作と言うが、私はなかなか秀れた作品だと思う。（MFA:11.4727）

作品 64　龍図。日華筆。

日華は四条派の画家。嵐の雲に乗って昇る龍。極めて単純だが神秘的趣きがある。特色としては、龍は強い線で輪郭を描くのが普通であるのにこの龍は輪郭がなく、雲塊の中に溶け込んでいてこれを実物のように見分けるには、観る者の想像力が必要とされるような描き方である。上向きに撥ねた筆勢が美しく、それに対して勢いのよい稲妻に似た炎が下向きに描かれる。これは応挙風の素描がやや衰えた描法だが、それでも構想には力が残っている。日華は著名な画家ではない。狩野氏は北齋に近い描法と考えている。豊彦のすぐれ門弟の一人である。（MFA:11.4749）

作品 65　維摩図。常信筆。

狩野派では探幽の維摩図に次いで最高の肖像画の一つとされる。その簡潔さが特色である。描線は堅牢でなく、輪郭を示すと言うより曲線を表わすような柔軟で太い筆致で描かれている。従ってもの柔らかで心和む好ましい画面処理が見られ、それが老維摩の感動的面持ちと完全に融合している。常信後期のより堅牢な、荘重ではあってもマンネリ化した画風に較べて、この作にはより芸術的な情感と力とが感じられ、岸駒が意図的に追求し達成した効果と似たものが実現されていると私は思う。狩野氏の評では常信が20歳をそれほど超えていなかった頃のもの、その年代の作としては大変よいが後期の作には較ぶべくもないと言う。第一級品。

作品 66　岩に鷲。雪村筆。小品。

簡潔粗豪の作。画趣を解する日本人の称賛するところ。墨調、描法は完璧だが、外国人の眼には情趣がそれほどではない。竹の描写がとくによく、雪村的だが、もちろん雪村の偉大な画風を出し切ってはいない。H氏いわく、一目にして真筆たることに間違いないが凡庸作。K氏いわく佳品、雪村の中級品に属すると。山中より購入。

作品 67　岩山の仙人図。呉小仙筆。

呉小仙は明代中期（の始め）の中国画家。狩野氏の言によれば非常に有名な画家でこの絵もすばらしい作と保証する。日本の画家が常に称賛し古画の秀作にランクする価値ありと認める要素を持つ作品で、明代の作によく見かける感傷的弱さがない。岩の

描写がとくに秀逸と見なされ、その量感と荒々しく強い筆使いが著しく蕭白を思わせる。人物の書き方に深い筆法の知識が認められ、簡潔で直接的で、全体的情調に力強さも感じられる。しかし、私見で唐宋の名画に較べて情感が冷たく、深みがない。明代としてはかなり優れた作という程度。山中より購入。

作品68　岩上の雉に竹と薔薇と桃の大樹。沈南蘋筆。
作者の典型的作例。沈南蘋の作は今日でも渉猟されている。主な見所は繊細な描線と彩色。彩色のデリカシーは如何なる画家も及ばないと思われるが、完全な調和がとれているわけではない。南蘋の設色法は長崎の日本人には一種の啓示であった。薔薇の花と葉はその繊細な画風の完璧さを示し、桃の彩色も綿密であり、主題の雉もすぐれた描法を示してはいる。しかし同時にこの作品は塗り過ぎや、画面構成の欠如、筆力の弱さ、不調和な画調といった南蘋の欠点をも露呈しているのである。狩野氏はこれが真筆であるかどうかについて疑念を持つようだが、彼は東京にある南蘋の著名な作はことごとく同じ眼で見る。長谷川氏は真筆と確信するが、古い落款を削り取って新しく落款を入れ直したのではないかと言う。長谷川評では南蘋の優品、とくに彩色が最高だが筆力が出し切れていないとする。私見では真筆たることまず疑い無し。宮塚氏も真筆に相違ないと言うし、私が意見を求めた他の評者もすべて同じ見解。山中より購入。

作品69　蓮華図。雲渓筆。
雲渓は雪舟の弟子。この作品は量感、色彩に乏しいが、簡潔にして優美なことは確実。雪舟のいずれの作に較べてもはるかに力が弱く、いわゆる「文人」にとくに愛好される所以である。保存状態は大変よい。布表装が美しく古色を帯びる。H氏いわく、雪渓図の秀作。雲渓は雪舟の直弟子でその作品は現在では極めて少ないとのこと。K氏いわく、佳品ではあるが作者は特色ある画家ではない。雪舟風を女性的に展開したものであって、雪村や秋月が男性的なものを表わすのと対比されるという。山中より購入。(MFA:11.4157)

作品70　山景図。応挙筆。小品。
この作の注目すべき理由はまずこの画期的作家の山水図真筆が非常に少ないこと、次に作品自体の秀逸さ独創性から言って注目に値すること。優美にして穏やかな大気の与える効果が特筆すべき見所であり、それが水晶のように清澄な山の空気を通して映し出される世界を示している。これは新たなる特色である。またこのような扱いの難しい山地にも透視画法の試みがなされ、水平線が目立たぬために遠山の描写は如何にも高山の趣きを観る者に与える。第三に岩の描線が応挙の創見になる迫真力ある筆致で処理され、その立体感、堅牢さ、そいだような岩肌、ぎざぎざした山嶺が如実に示される。同様な特徴は、それほど強くないが松の描写にも表われ、また雲の印象、遠

山の描出もみごとである。しかしながら同時に、応挙が明代の画家から学んだ点も看取される。構成や配置は多かれ少なかれ明画的であり樹木描写もそれを思わせる。事実、もし明代山水図と後期応挙派のそれとを比較してみれば、明らかに前者から後者への移行の跡を見ることができるであろう。この作品ではさらに応挙画の特徴たる絵画性の弱さ、すなわち独特かつ重要な明暗の広がりに欠けている点も見られるかもしれない。この種の絵画性の奥義を、応挙は科学的自然観察力をそなえていたにも拘らず知らなかったのであり、この最も重要な点において、往昔の巨匠たちの遥か下の段階に留まらざるを得なかったのである。さて狩野氏評ではこれは疑いなく真筆。きわめて珍しい画題で、そのために贋作を作ろうとする者はいなかったであろうとのこと。長谷川氏によればこの作は馬遠乃至馬逵を見て制作した節があるが、こと志と違い前述のごとく明画に似たものとなったものと言う。彼はさらにこの作の卓越した清浄さを挙げ、応挙山水図の傑作と称している。

作品71　名所紀伊和歌浦景観図。一鳳筆。

我々西洋人の判断では簡略な作だが日本人は注目する。直線遠近画法と色遠近画法とが巧みに用いられている。浜辺の水の煌めきは東洋画には目新しい自然主義的なところがある。下がり松が砂地に不安定な根を張るのは日本の海浜ならどこでも見られる風景。青はブルーというよりむしろグレーの特質のひとつとして考えられている。画の上部には「誰か和歌浦を訪れる者で我が魂の宝玉を見ぬものがあろうか」という意味の賛がある。和歌浦は日本で風光名媚の地として知られたところ。この作品は天明期、一鳳□歳※頃の作。[※年齢不記。]

作品72　鴉に月。東渓筆。

[※作品72はもと秋暉筆花鳥図「花卉、梅樹、28種の鳥」を扱い、南蘋や雲錦との関係を述べたのち例によって永悳や雪堤の批評を添えたものだが、何故か全文を横線で抹消し、上記のように別作の題名と作者名のみを挙げてある。]　(MFA:11.4773)

作品73　鐘呂伝道図。顔輝図、探幽模写。

呂洞賓が仙術を同じく仙人鐘離権に授けている。鐘離権はしばしば扇に乗って空中を飛行する姿に描かれる。まず模写として私はなかなかよい出来だと思う。探幽が独自の構図で描いたとしてもこれほどには至らなかっただろう。濃淡や身体の各部とくに足の線描ではおそらく原作より劣ると思うが、中国絵画黄金期の深味のある強い表現が保たれ、仮に顔輝自身の筆ではないとしてもその画想、構成を十分に伝えている。その主たる特質、これは十分に伝えている。その主たる特質、これは一般の日本絵画とは異なる中国古画の特質でもあるが、それは衣装の描法が熟練した筆致を示しながら決して衣装そのもののありように鑑賞者の心を惹きつけるに留まらず、あくまで主題の中心的モチーフ、この場合は二人の仙人の態度や表情を重視させるような描き方

がなされていることである。しかもその描法は雄勁でありながら誇張に陥らず、あたかも清浄な鏡のように作者の思想を反映している。両人の気品に満ちた物腰、力強い表情は歴然としており、これについては説明の必要もないだろう。狩野氏は原図は顔輝名品の一つで、探幽独自のものは混入していないと評する。山中より購入。

作品 74　漁師の娘の姿となった観音（※魚籃観音）。東山筆。大作。
東山は四条派の画家。この孤立する像には長所もあるがこの派の多くの作品が示すほど興味あるものではない。全体的な筆法、画調には冷たく共感を拒否するところがあって、それが鑑賞者に反発を感じさせる。最大の弱点は顔の表情。すぐれた中国古画ではなく典型的な日本画の顔である。しかし下半身の衣裳は流れるような襞やその色彩が大変美しく、また魚籃と魚は良く描けている。もちろんこれは応挙派の衰退を示すものではあるが、何点か長所も無いわけではない。狩野氏はこれを凡庸作で気品も十分でなく、孔寅の作品 52 よりも劣るものと言う。H 氏の評では魚籃観音としての気品をそなえ、その色彩もなかなか美しいが線描が余りよくない由。容姿のプロポーションはごく普通の日本女性のもの。東山は徹山の弟子である。（MFA:11.4779）

作品 75　驟雨を避け雨宿りする人々。二代一蝶筆。
二代一蝶は初代一蝶の息子。大勢の人物が驟雨を避けて軒下に佇む。この主題は一蝶派の特徴たる風俗画を示す好機を与えてくれる。軒下には貴婦人や下女、職人、大工、巡礼に農夫、梯子乗りや飴売りや子守り女たちが雨を除けようとひしめいている。右手の道路から盲目の琵琶法師の一団が駆けて来る。手前の道を荷馬車に乗った二人の男が駆け抜ける。この種の様式としてはもっともみごとで内容の豊富な作例のひとつと考えられる。狩野氏は最初これを、あるいは初代一蝶の作かとも考えたが、それにしては迫力がなく佳品とは言えぬと評し、もし模写だとすれば原図は一蝶の秀作に違いないと言う。しかし H 氏は一見して一蝶二世筆と断じ、父親ほど強い筆力はないがその秀作に数えられるものと評した。息子も父と同じ名前同じ落款を用いて制作したため、別箇の作品なのにその構図を単に模写だと考える人々も多かったのである。北斎の生まれる百年前の日本の流行画様式を伝えるもの。表装に使われた三種の布が豪華である。（MFA:11.4218）

作品 76　牡丹、竹、奇岩。梅逸筆。
この様式は南蘋風と文人画風との中間をいくものとして現在賞美されているもの。作者は筆法の熟達者として知られ、竹の描法も達者だが、画面の芸術的情趣はそれほどでもない。せいぜい、画法の巧者と言ったところ。しかし長谷川氏は「高度の筆力があり一鳳の最高作と比肩すべきもの」とし、作者を近世画家の巨匠の一人に数えている。10 年以上前に死去したという。狩野氏の話ではこの画家は現在東京在住の和亭の師。秋暉ほどよくないと言う。狩野氏は常に、すべての「文人」的要素を悪ときめつ

ける狭量な見方で物を言う人だ。（MFA:11.4647 但し偽物として売却）

作品77　海を臨む岩壁に白い隼。探幽筆。

探幽の一般作に較べると良い方。主たる長所は威厳に満ちた隼の姿勢と遠く霧にかすんだ海を疑視するその自立的な気品ある表情。岩の描写も強く、波の逆巻いて岩にぶつかる力は探幽の線描に独特のものである。白い隼と黒い岩とが作り出す対象も画面全体に清浄さと、さらに威厳とを加えている。短所は速成画であることと無造作にマンネリズムへ依存していること。これが探幽の晩年にあっては霊感を作り出すための絶対的処方として用いられることが余りにも多い。上部の雲間を進む赤い球形の太陽はほとんど明るさを思わせない。東洋絵画にあっては太陽が明るさを表わすよう意図されることはないのである。表装は大変古い。画題は明らかに徽宗皇帝の作からヒントを得たもの。隼は山楽や直庵のものに劣る。キングより購入。

作品78　峠の富士。探山筆。

探山は探幽の弟子。狩野氏いわく、真筆だが凡作。H氏もどちらかと言えば貧弱な作だと評し、凡庸な画家であったため揮毫を乞う者もなく、そのために作品が少ないのだと言う。他方雪庵氏は探山を探幽の高弟の一人と考えている。私の見た唯一の探山。67歳の作であるから円熟はしているが速成画のマンネリズムを露呈し、そのために作者の天才が全く表われていないことは疑いの余地がない。富士の弱い傾斜が写実的で、よく描かれる誇張した角度のものよりはるかに印象的。探幽風の退歩した作。

(MFA:11.4407)

作品79　夜霧の中の白狐。応挙筆。

応挙の第一級品。巧妙精緻に描かれているが、この作を秀逸ならしめているのは単に白狐の描法のみによるのではない。白狐の頭が背景から浮き出して見えるのも遠近法のせいではない。また白狐を包む半透明の霧も単なる技巧ではない。すべてが霊妙かつ超自然的な意味あいを持っており、応挙の唯一の目的になっていることが余りにも多かった単なる写実の世界から一歩を踏み出したものである。神秘的な感じの白狐、これは人に取り憑く魔力にかけては最も狡知にたけた危険な動物なのだが、これがこの世の物とも思えぬ神秘の幕に半身を隠した亡霊のように、無気味な月光の中に坐っている。その冷い突き刺すような視線が、驚異の念をもって見入る鑑賞者の心臓を貫き、その目に魅入られているうちに、これが愚かで非科学的民族の作り出した迷信的な恐怖、伝承に過ぎないことを理解できなくなってしまう。これこそ一民族の信仰や恐怖心を最も強烈な基本的想像力をもって捉えた、また抽象的描写や解説を不必要ならしめるほどの具体的な力をもって表わした、偉大なる芸術作品である。安永年間の作。草の小枝も神秘的でどこで始まりどこで終わるかも定かでなく、それが作品に格調を添え趣きを与えている。長谷川氏は不思議なことにこれを見て探幽を想起すると言う。明らかにこれは、狩野守貴氏所蔵の粉本に見られるような自然描写のことを言っ

ていると思う。狩野氏の評では疑いなく真筆、しかも極めて印象的な作品だが、応挙の最大の描写力を発揮したものではないと言う。宮塚氏によれば、今まで見た応挙のうち最高作の由。私見では京都の西村氏所蔵屏風絵を除いて、かつて見た応挙のうち最高作たることは確実と思う。山中より購入。（MFA:11.4900）

作品80　断崖を覗く虎。岸駒筆。
私の見る限り岸駒の虎としては私の所蔵する二曲一双屏風に次ぐ秀作。見るべき点も多く、かつ秀れている。まず画想に迫力があり、重厚で緊張感が漲る。画面の統一と描線の構成は簡潔で気取りがなく美しい。描法は岸駒最高の絵画的迫力のある様式。縞模様の毛もよく描けているが激しく獰猛な顔とやや湾曲して突き出し体を支える脚と爪の描写に全力が集中している。神秘的な霧に包まれた画面から虎が体ごと飛び出して来るように感じられる。左側に描かれた竹も完璧で、どこか雪村を思わせる。これらの特性に独創的画風が加われば、優に日本中国古画の名匠に比肩されるに違いない。岸駒の最も生気ある作品の一つである。山中より購入。（MFA:11.4698）

作品81　花鳥図。[※双幅]。養川筆。
狩野派の花卉図としてはおそらく最高作。花の濃淡は純粋、草の色はまさに象牙に色取りを施したごとくである。岩の線描も極めて強い。鳥は花の量感にわずかに劣るが、両図各々の構成要素となっている。第1図は牡丹と金色の雉。構成、彩色の点では第2図の方が面白く、それには白い雉のような鳥と立葵に似た花が描かれる。狩野氏の評ではこれは養川秀作のうちに入る。花は舜挙に似たところもあるが、多くの点で王若水の作に似ている。狩野氏によれば、この時代の画家は独自の様式を持っていても、とくに花は宋・元の偉大な中国画家から画題を教えられるところが大きかったという。それも直接の模写ではなく翻案であった。色彩は従来の狩野派では用いなかったほど絢爛たるものとなり、中国の古花卉図が制作当初、如何に豪華なものだったかを想像することができたほどだという。しかし私の記憶に間違いがなければこれは、商務局にある伝舜挙の意匠をほとんど正確に模写したものである。山中より購入。

（MFA:11.4452 - 4453）

作品82　箕面大滝図。李長筆。四条派の画家。
新しい様式で迫力を示す佳品の一つ。従来の狩野派の描く滝はまるでのろのろと転がるような緩やかなカーブを描いて落下するが、この滝は崖っぷちでカーブするが、一気に、ほとんど直線をなして猛烈な勢いで落下する。その印象は滝壺近くに突き出した二つの岩に激突して飛び散る水しぶきによってますます高められる。滝壺のたぎるような飛沫は全く新しい手法の試みによって描かれている。本流の横にいくつもの細流が岩から岩へと、美しいレース編みのように伝い、それが作品の美しさを増幅すると同時に中心の大滝の持つ単調さを破る。一面の岩と暗い樹葉を背景に、真白な水流のすべての描線がみごとに浮かび上がっている。作者は写生に満足する画家ではな

かったが自然の新鮮な印象を受け容れることに真剣な人だったと言えるであろう。佳作ではあるが豊彦に匹敵するほどの描写ではないとするのがH氏の評。K氏は非常に良いと評し、友信氏は私と同程度にK氏の意見に賛成。山中より購入。作者はおそらく豊彦の弟子であろう。秀作である。（MFA:11.4762）

作品83　松に孔雀二羽。応挙筆。水墨画。
白狐図［※作品79］ほどではないが応挙佳作の一つ。松も応挙の独創になる強い独自な描法だが、孔雀の線描が特に優れている。枝にとまる孔雀の気品あるポーズと統一の取れたマッスが特に印象的だが、下にいる雌孔雀の簡単な描写の方がさらに良い。後者の頭部は半分ほど一方に傾いているが、精緻な観察力をもって描かれているため別に陰影法によって浮き出すような手法を用いているわけではないが画面から今にも実際に飛び出してくるように感じられる。羽毛の描写、特に頸の周りの細かい羽毛がすばらしく、応挙独自の巧みな技巧を示す。全体として簡単な描線によって強い印象が与えられ、日本人の言うように、その薄墨色と濃淡が実際の色彩を思わせるほど巧みに用いられている。孔雀を墨一色で描く試みとしては、私の聞いた範囲では唯一のもの。狩野氏いわく、真筆に疑いなく、応挙の第二級品に属するべきものだが、特に構図がよい。欠点は応挙の作品によく見かけられる或る種の堅さに有るとする。長谷川氏も雪庵も真筆とするが、雪庵はこれを大変褒めている。東京で購入。表装は私が作り直したもの。

作品84　雪景に松林。一鳳筆。
応挙派山水図秀作の一つ。画想もみごとだが描法がそれと完全に調和してさらに美しく、如何にも冬を実感させる。壮麗な量感を持つ古木は雪を重そうに載せ、雪山を背景に浮き出して見える様はあたかも立体写真鏡で望むが如くである。雪の下に見える黒々とした幹の先端が、この鮮烈な効果を生み出すのに役立っている。もっとも驚嘆すべきものは松の葉に積もる雪の描写かもしれない。それはまさに白地の絹布を広げて突き出た枝を覆っているように見える。総じてその描法はすばらしく、ヨーロッパの画家といえども水彩のみでこのような効果を再現することができるかどうかはかなり疑わしいものである。かくの如き単純かつ直接的な手段でそれを達成することは到底不可能であろう。いくら高く評価しても評価しきれぬのがこの作である。作品53の狸図と共に、これはほとんど応挙に匹敵する画家として一鳳の偉大さを証明するものである。K氏はこれを大変良い作品と考え、一鳳を狙仙よりはるかに優れ、応挙の域に達するものと評している。H氏もこれを応挙派画風の最高作に数え、かの李長の滝の図よりもはるかによいと言う。山中より購入。（MFA:11.4728）

作品85　岩に坐す観音。水墨画。安信筆。

安信としては非常によい。衣裳の線がまことに麗しく、顔の表情も実に優美で女性的。岩の量感も柔らかで優雅であり、画中唯一の深い墨色が顔と肩のあたりに見られる。全体として画面に統一があり、洗練された情調、独特の様式を持った仕上げは、他の画家で彼に比肩する者を知らない。狩野氏はこれを安信第二級品のうちの秀作としている。キングより購入。

作品86　山水雨景図。養川筆。

素描の域を出ず解説の要なし。上部山の円頂は稜線に光が当たって気品がある。狩野氏によれば作者若年の作。凡庸な作で父親［※狩野栄川院典信］の画風の影響が強いという。作者の第三級品。（MFA:11.4455）

作品87　母子の虎。岸駒筆。

前掲作品80ほどはよくない。表現、線描とも前作より穏やかで、特異性も少なく構成もよくない。上部の岩にも力が見られない。なかば座興の作。しかし同画家の通例作としては悪くない。

作品88　赤鍾馗図。素描。徹山筆。

輪郭のみだが構成力が強く、太さに変化を見せる描線がみごとである。顔の表情は極めて強く、徹山独特のもの。衣裳の処理も独創的。狩野氏はこれを応挙派の優品、徹山の典型的な佳作と評している。（MFA:11.4390）

作品89　虎図。岸駒筆。

水を飲むため岩の間から姿を現した虎。実に奇妙な作。描線は歪み、虎の顔は貧弱で、縞模様も崩れている。岩も大胆に描かれるが手の震えを感じさせる。私の所持する岸駒では最も悪く、老人晩年の弱さを露呈している。それでも描法にかつての栄光が多分に残り、死を拒否せんとする逞しい内心が感じられる。

作品90　蝦蟇仙人、鉄拐仙人。対幅。周信筆。

粗放な描写で明確な形を持たず、生硬でインスピレーションも感じられない。しかるに狩野氏は周信としては傑出した作と称しその第二級品に位置させる。もしそれに誤りがなければ、周信はその父［※狩野養朴常信］より遥か下の段階に位置した画家であることを証明することになる。左側の第二図がすべての点で秀れているというが、これらが貧弱であることは、顔輝と比較すれば一目瞭然である。第二図には注目に値するある種の独創性は認められる。キングより購入。さきに述べた某華族の旧蔵品。

作品 91　山水図。文晁筆。
文人画風。文人画が如何に魅力的要素を持つかを示す好例。柔らかいグレーの色調が背景をなし、それに風変わりな形の墨のタッチが少々加わり、さらに濃色の墨で何本かの樹木が描かれる。その意図するところは象徴的絵画の域を出ないが一種の絵画性と奔放な描法とを含み、偏見のない目で見た場合それが理解できる。狩野氏はこれを評して文晁第二級の佳品、大雅堂のスタイルに属するものという。文人はみなこの作を絶賛する。下田より購入。

作品 92　雪の枝に泊まる鷺と鴉。英一蝶筆。
一蝶の巧みで意想外な様式を持つ構成で描いた大変変わった作品。一は純白、一は漆黒の鷺と鴉が上下に並びそれぞれ反対方向に顔を向けている。赤い実をつけた蔓草が枝に巻きつき下にぶらさがる。その真紅の斑点が画面唯一の色彩である。特異かつ大胆な作で作者の天才が漲る。狩野氏いわく、描法は一蝶としてあまり秀れていないが真筆たることに疑いなしと。

作品 93　仙人王質図。義董筆。
義董は四条派の画家。速筆の素描だが応挙速筆法の長所を伝えている。王質は岩を背にして坐り、斧を持ち恍惚たる視線を天に向ける。手法はどこか文人画に近い。狩野氏はこれを佳作とする。近代的趣味を持つ日本人の称賛するもの。

作品 94　東方朔。藍江筆。
小品ながら線描、明暗、筆致、表現などすべての点で優れている。特に、欲しがっていた仙桃を盗んで口もとまで持ち運んだ東方朔の欲深な喜びの表現がうまい。狩野氏評でも佳品。（MFA:11.4659）

作品 95　花鳥図。晩山筆。
作者の通常作よりやや良い。あるいはその第二級品に入るか。南蘋派の衰退ぶりを示すが、色彩は良いほう。（MFA:11.4666）

作品 96　桜の枝に泉。望月玉泉筆。
玉泉は岸駒の弟子の息子。これは1880年京都で私の求めで描いた素描。作者は岸駒風を離れ、衰退した応挙派の凡庸の作家の中に吸収されているように感ぜられる。

作品 97　梅に薔薇。香雲筆。
作者は雲錦の娘。幼稚だが、それが面白い。（MFA:11.4658）

作品 98　岸壁の鷲。雲錦筆。
雲錦としては強い描写だが、その強さが雲錦の長所に繋がっていない。色彩が粗放で、波も描写が弱く見かけ倒しだが、現代絵画の中では独創的と言える。

作品 99　山水図。縦軸。墨彩。為一筆。
ありふれた作だが印象として好ましく、かつ誠実な感じを受ける。所謂佳品の部に入ると言えるか。後に北斎作であることが分かった。

作品 100　松に鷲図。狩野雅楽助筆。
雅楽助の作では最も有名なものの一つ。現存する少数のうち最高の作かもしれない。狩野守貴はその蔵幅の中にこの作の探幽模写を所持している。その模本によってこの作が何年もの間狩野家の所蔵だったことが判明したが、原本がどうなったかについては狩野家の人々は誰も知らなかった。私はこれを1881年の夏大阪の山中の店で購入したのである。雅楽助がこのような大作を描くことは稀だったと、狩野氏は言う。鷲は私の見た日本絵画のうちでは最も美しく、神秘的存在にふさわしい気品と強烈な力を持っているように見える。松にも強い迫力が張り、どこか雅楽助の父［※狩野正信］の画風を伝える。しかし、極めて熱心にこれを調査した狩野永悳によれば、松葉の先端部は後世の補修の手が加わっているという。その他はすべて原図がよく保存されている。ほとんど宋画の秀作に見られる簡潔さと無心の荘重さに到達していると言ってよい。中国画秀作の模写ではないかと想像することも不可能ではないが、それは根拠のない推測に過ぎない。印章は真物。「本朝画史」に複写した二つの印章が記載されている。東京在住の鑑定家は皆これを日本古画秀作の一つと考えている。この作品によって壮観をなした大阪鴻池のコレクションから出たものと信ぜられ、もと蜂須加家旧蔵の品と思われる。現存する掛け物中最高作の一つ。これを見る日本人で心を奪われぬ者は一人もいない。

作品 101　桜に群猿。狙仙筆。
風雨の中、枝にぶら下がる猿。猿をみごとに、すなわち微細に描いたものはこの画家に多いが、この作は私が見た中ではまず最高のもの。作品13および44で述べた批評はこの際引っ込めなければならぬ。狙仙はここで高い芸術的境地に到達している。桜の木の描写を日本人の画家たちはすばらしいと評しているが、その描線の繰り返しによる絵画構成は完璧。他の部分は画面の自ら語る通りである。1881年夏京都で購入。これを見せた日本人はみな狙仙第一級品の最高作と鑑定した。さる京都の名士の旧蔵にかかるもの。

作品102　中国山水図。周文筆。小品。

独特の引っ掻いたようなエッチング風タッチを持つ特徴的手法による。漢画的なるものを指向する詩的情感の高まりがよい。探幽の末裔によるこの作の模写を狩野守貴が所蔵している。これが周文の真筆であることは東京在住の画家全員の意見の一致しているところであり、私にも確信が持てる。これと少しでも似た筆使いは東洋絵画史の中にも見出すことはできない。守貴所蔵の模本と比較した結果、まさにこの作から模写したものであることが明らかだった。鴻池家コレクションから購入した大阪の美術商より入手したもの。神田氏はこれほどの周文秀作を見たことがなかった由。印章は後年押されたものと見る評者もある。

作品103　中国山水楼閣図。文晁の子ブンオウ［※谷文晁の弟子文雍の誤りか］筆。

ブンオウ独自の様式による秀作の一つ。筆力は父親ほどではないとしても整然たる趣きがあって実に印象的であり、観る者に純粋な漢画的印象を与える。注目すべきは、狩野派の如く漢画を元にした画風ではない点にある。しかし、実は狩野永悳評では、木と人物を含む前景はほとんど夏珪の構図を模したものという。筆致はしかしながら、やや夏珪とは違って生硬。壮麗な構図は明らかに夏珪のものである。楼閣の方は君澤乃至夏明遠の画風である。だが上部の岩は多分に文晁風でやや技巧的であり、漢画の巨匠に見られる奔放さと多様性に欠けたところがある。画面全体にわたる濃淡はきわめて美しく、漢画的処理は全くなされていないが、線描の弱さを補っている。以上、この作品は漢画の漢画らしさを具え、漢画の名匠を思わせながらしかもそれとは似ていないという独自の画想を有する点で注目に値する。あたかも陽光去りし後に冴え渡る月光の趣きが感ぜられる。作者は日本ではその実力に比してさほど著名ではないが、近世最大の画家の一人である。キングより購入。（MFA:11.4790）

作品104　月光の中の山と霧。文麟筆。

著しく詩的な作。玉瀾に文麟的修正を施したような画風。賛は「満月の前夜」の意。雲間を洩れる月光を描いて日本絵画中最も趣がある。狩野派の画家の称賛を得た。山中より購入。（MFA:11.4688）

作品105　布袋図。啓書記筆。

小品ながら啓書記の筆致を十分に示すもので、その第二級品に入れてよい。布袋は鼻を抑えくしゃみをしようとしている。箱書きは「くしゃみをしようとする布袋」の意。布表装は大変古い。東京にて購入。狩野永悳および狩野友信は真筆と鑑定。東京の識者はすべて佳品と見做す。川崎の鑑定では第一級品。住吉は画布をことのほか上質のものと考えている。

作品 106　土佐光茂筆　羅漢図。
[※原文は岡本豊彦の雨景図小品の解説であったが、何故か全文を×印で抹消し、上記のような題名と作者名を掲げるのみ。]

作品 107　海棠の花に四十雀。松村景文筆。
私の見た景文のなかでは最も美しい作。大阪にて購入。純粋な応挙派花卉図が到達した最高段階を示すもの。軽快な筆致、優雅な形態、美麗な色彩は特筆に値する。景文第一級作品に数えられる。ウエムラから購入したものだが、彼は以前格式ある家柄の所蔵する第一級品で抵当に入ったものを多く買収したという。東京在住の画家も皆、景文第一級品と考えている。箱書きに景文が依頼者に対し潤筆料として五分［※当時の金額。一分は一両の四分の一］を受領した旨の文字が残っている。

作品 108　雪中の竹に雀。景文筆。
ほとんどグレ一色。前作と同じくらい美しい。箱はこの作品のものではない。従って箱書きに意味はない。応挙派の水墨花鳥図としては最高の出来かもしれない。大阪から購入。画家たちは景文第一級の作品と考えている。もと三幅対だったものを所有者ニシオバンキチが分割した。

作品 109　啓書記筆。山水図。彩色。
中国山水の美しい小品だが、芸阿弥彩色図に見られるやや角ばった筆法と、一部周文的要素が加味されている。狩野氏はこれを真筆と鑑定し、大変面白い、みごとな、しかも稀な山水図と評価する。中国セントウ［※盛唐か］期の山水情調を彷彿させる。色彩は淡く調和がとれ、荒々しい筆力はまさにその奔放さと感情の表われである。
(MFA:11.4127)

作品 110　仏画。獅子に乗る文殊。巨勢俊久筆。
文殊の描線は実に繊細だが獅子は生硬に過ぎる。しかし彩色は非常に豊かで金岡の影響をいまだに留めている。裏に文観上人筆とある。狩野ひとりこれを九百年前のものと称するが、この裏書はかなり後世のもので（川崎は経隆の時代と言う）全く信用できない。東京の住吉はこの種の絵画にかけては最も有力な現存鑑定家だが、彼はこれを巨勢俊久筆と断定した。私もおそらくそれに間違いないと思う。私が見ても土佐派的要素の混入で弱められた後代巨勢派の多くの特徴が分かる。おもてに安永九年十二月二十五日奉納と記されており、箱ももとの物ではない。大阪にて購入。中世仏画の逸品。狩野氏も、作品1の地蔵図に勝ると言う。軸を包む布は作品と同時代のものと彼は見ている。

作品 111　松の木に坐る鳥窠仙人。顔輝筆。

真筆たることを疑う者なし。私がこれを初めて見たのは京都の高台寺で1880年夏のことだった。その住僧の所蔵だった。その時は売値のことで折り合いがつかなかった。翌1881年夏に再訪した際、住僧は私に贈呈することを考えたようだが、結局50円で購入した。付随する鑑定書は真筆で、その筆跡は狩野家の画家たちによって直ちに確認されている。私が購入する以前から狩野友信氏はこれを真筆なりと判定し、狩野永悳も確認して異論を唱える者はない。雄渾簡潔な筆勢の完璧さが漲っているが、特に偉大なところは強い表現力と勢いのよい線描をもつ主人公の顔である。サン・シモン・スティリテスの生まれ変わりのような、不思議な仙力を持つこの苦行者の魂がその両眼に輝いている。彼は松の樹上高く、鳥の巣の中に坐り、地上からは辛うじて見分けがつくほどである。画面右手の一部は雲に隠れている。周囲を切断して大きさをやや縮めたものと考えられるが、狩野氏はそれほど切ってはいないと言う。（MFA:11.4003）

作品 112　台座に坐る釈迦。宅磨爲久筆。

佳品。描線がことによいと思われる。狩野友信は鑑定の結果爲久と言う。永悳も爲久と確信。松浦、蜷川、暁斎も一致して爲久説。しかしながら住吉は一見して、あまりよい作ではない、日本の作とは全然違う、恐らく中国人画家の手になるものであろう、と評したが、一年ほど経った1882年12月、彼は再びこの作を見て言下に日本の作、巨勢有久の筆、なかなかの佳品、と明言した。この矛盾した言説により、彼の鑑定の信憑性も大分薄れた感じである。私には、その筆勢は巨勢風ではなく宅磨派風のものに間違いないことは明らかなように思われる。東京大養寺住職の立派なコレクションから購入したもので、そこでも以前から爲久と考えられていた由。軸は上下とも岩水晶。住吉いわく、表装の布はもちろん比較的新しいものだが極めて上質。川崎の説によればせいぜい600年前の絹地。山名は中国製と言う。（MFA:11.4093）

作品 113　隅田川堤防図。嵩谷筆。

極めて特色ある作。牛御前の社殿が遠くに見える。季節は春。霞が田園にたなびき桜は満開である。農家が木立ちの下から覗き、川には渡し船や釣船が行き交う。狩野派主流が主として中国山水図を描き、また漢画風に描くのに対して、これは狩野様式によりながら日本山水画の最も純粋なものかもしれない。ほとんど真景に近いが、細部に拘らぬ美術的包括性をもっている。船中の遊興客や堤の上の風景が面白い。鴉が田の上を飛んでいく。嵩谷の第一級品。箱は本図とまったく関係がない。200年前の江戸の郊外がよく示されている。狩野氏を始めすべての画家が嵩谷最高の小品と評している。（MFA:11.4369）

作品 114　雪景山水図。双幅。源琦筆。

源琦は応挙門弟の逸材と評する人もある。

　　第一図は高い山腹の、なかば雪に埋もれた狭い農村を描く。画調、筆法とも極めて優美かつ清浄な感じを与える。すべてが美しく簡潔に処理され、その効果は一鳳の山水図ほど際立ってはいないとしても、より詩的で洗練されている。まさに応挙的画法によりながら漢画最盛期の山水情調を実現したもの。
　　第二図は山腹の渓谷を示す。深遠というより巧妙といった感じを与える。渓谷は雪と氷に閉ざされているが、渓流が流れ落ちている。

両面ともに「源琦寫之」とあるが、まさに自然を写し取っている。また、季節は秋とあるが、京都辺の山地では雪の降るのが早い。狩野氏はこれを一鳳より良いと評している。実際、四条派最高作の一つである。源琦の第一級品。（MFA:11.4770-4771）

作品 115　山水図。双幅。文晁筆。

小品。高い断崖、薄暗さ、山の霧、力強い前景など、文晁的特徴を示して如何にもそれらしい雰囲気を伝える。南宋の画家夏珪風な要素もあり、またやや応挙的味わいもある。

　　第一図は前面の手前を流れる小川の上に築かれた楼閣の図で、中国的風景。
　　第二図は前面のすぐ手前にかかる橋を渡る人物。

二面とも、岸駒の最高作を別とすれば日本近世画のいずれよりも奔放な描写。ともに秋景。暁齋は真筆か否かを疑っているが、狩野は作者30歳の作とし、若年にしてはうまいと言う。画想は雪村によく似ているとのこと。文晁通常作としては佳品と評している。松浦は真筆と鑑定した。

作品 116　狩野 □□ 筆 ［※名前空白］。寒山拾得図。

［※作者は狩野とのみ記され名前は書かれていない。また解説文も空白。恐らく後に書き入れる積りだったのであろう。］

作品 117　龍虎図。双幅。呉春筆。

両図とも変わった作品だが、特に虎が面白い。龍は呉春通常の筆法、応挙派的な制作をしていた頃のもので、第一図がこの龍である。渦を巻き黒い風穴を作りながら上昇する雲はまさに応挙的。龍も独特な力を持ち、その柔らかいグレイの色調は鋼鉄の甲冑で身を堅めているかに見える。梅の枝は作者独持の速描。第二図は虎だが、ある種の文人画に用いられるような極めて柔らかい毛筆の筆法による実験作と思われる。同じタッチで描かれた如何なる画家の如何なる作品をも私は見たことがないのだ。日本の画家たちがこの作を好まないのは彼らの如何なるカテゴリーにも属していないからである。外国人がこれを好まぬ理由は、自然を写したとは到底思えぬからである。し

かし私だけは作者の意図とその偉大な成功を看取することができる。虎は陽光に照らされて半ば眼を閉じている。竹の描写は巨匠の域に入るもの。黒と白の作り出す美しさもみごとである。狩野も、虎の筆致は実に独創的と評している。私も、これを見て以来、柔らかい毛筆の使用こそ呉春の常套的画法の一つであることを理解した。真筆であり、しかも優品であることに疑いはない。京都サガキチにて購入。

作品118 群猿図。狙仙筆。小品。
狙仙としては中程度の粗放な筆法。体毛はほとんど幅の太い淡彩。顔は極めて技巧的に描かれる。構図は注目すべきものでないが、猿の動作は面白い。箱はもとのものではない。評者はすべて真筆と鑑定。表装は私がした。

作品119 野鴨図。萬壽（万寿）筆。
凍った池の端に佇む野鴨三羽。構図らしい構図があるわけでなく、極めて単純な絵だが、柔らかいグレイで非常に美しく描かれた野鴨そのものに惹きつけられる。脚の描き方がやや弱い。狩野氏らの評では描法のみごとさは応挙と誤解しかねないほどと言うが、実際、応挙の描く野鴨との違いはほとんどない。羽毛を描くグレイの画調に至っては、これを凌駕するものはまずいないであろう。箱書きの表には画題が書かれている。「二羽の野鴨、雪の池畔にある図」の意味である。萬壽は応挙の門弟の一人に違いない。（MFA:11.4746）

作品120 狩野元信筆。松に鳥図。水墨。大作。
[※解説欄空白]（MFA:11.4271）

作品121 山水図粗画。岸駒筆。
岸駒晩年の粗放な、趣きの豊かな画風で描かれている。湖畔に茶人などの使いそうな田舎風の小亭があり、二人の人物が弁当を入れた籠を手に風流な遊山に出かけようとしているところであろう。両人の顔はターナーの絵のようにおぼろにかすんでいる。箱はこの図のものではない。狩野は岸駒の通例作と考えている。中国の風景で、狩野も遊山の図だが箱は違うと断言した。

作品122 山水図。小栗宗湛筆。小品。
この画家の作品は稀少。中でもこれは逸品である。水晶のような岩と松は独自の手法で描かれ、どこか馬遠を思わせ、遠景は周文の感じが強い。山の背後の雲に覆われた空は実写的タッチで、古い絵には余り見かけられない。遠近の効果がよく出ている。全体として作品102の周文山水図に勝る。画布は非常に古い。つぎの様な意味の賛が画面上部に描かれている「・・・・・山は青く、水は緑。古寺は何年を経たものであ

ろうか。霧が塔頂から垂れこめている。」箱の内側に真筆鑑定の文字があるが、鑑定者の名はちょっと読めない。賛の作者は万里の和尚で、その印章が画面にある。箱の外側にも賛の作者名が万里小路であることが書かれている。万里小路は宗堪の住んだ相国寺の僧で、漆桶和尚とも、また梅庵とも呼ばれた。名は瑞九。応仁期の人。狩野永悳、友信とも、宗堪の傑作と評している。作例は非常に少ない。これはもと大阪鴻池コレクションにあったもの。野村も柏木も、よいものと言う。

作品 123 山水図。文麟筆。双幅。

第一図は冬または早春の風景。前景からおだやかな日射しに雪が溶け始め、残雪の間から新緑の木々や青草が顔を出す。梅もまさにほころびようとしているが、それ以外のものはまだ春の用意ができていない。前景の川で漁師が網を打っている。その向こうに、まだ雪の溶けぬ山の頂が見える。あたり一面に靄がおりて時に太陽もおぼろげである。私の見た文麟では最も繊細優美な作品。効果を狙った不自然な努力がなく、しかも文麟独自の天才が最も純粋な形で表われている。第二図は第一図と較べてかなり悪い。作者の目指すものを十分に実現しておらず、全体の統一も損なわれている。それでも部分的には面白いところがある。作者は嵐の後雲間から洩れる日光、まだ降り止まぬ雨、瀧のような渓流、雨に濡れた樹木や岩石を描きたかったのである。全景が山の中腹に収まり、水かさの増した渓谷とそれに架かる危い橋を渡ろうとする樵夫たちの姿が見える。日に照らされた山の上部が、ちぎれた黒雲を背景に白く光る。そのような作者の最初の意図を汲んで眺めると、この作品もなかなかに面白いが、主として色彩を表わす過程で失敗しているのだ。秋景色の図である。

作品 124 探幽筆。三幅対。[※福禄寿、山水]。

第一図は迫力ある構成の山水図。第二図福禄寿。第三図、さらに迫力ある山水図。黒い箱に銀で文字が書いてある。三点とも力作。山中より購入。非常に驚いたことに両狩野は一見してこれを大変な悪作だとなし、無知な画家の模写したものと評した。もちろん両人の証言は重要視すべきだが、一方、古物の専門家松浦はこれを見て感激し空前絶後の逸品と評する。長谷川雪堤も仔細に調べた結果探幽第一級品に入り得るものと断定。暁斎は第一級とまでは行かぬが優品と評価した。私自身の印象でも真筆の優品と思われる。筆法は粗豪だが、他の探幽作で両狩野が真筆と断言したものにもしばしば見られるところであり、質の点では両人の確証する探幽画を凌駕するものがある。住吉も両狩野に面と向って反論を唱え、これを優品として称揚した。住吉は落款も良いと評している。

作品 125 義信筆。義経騎馬図。

もと三幅対の一。他の二幅はジョルジュ・エメリー氏が購入した。この作者の第二級品中の佳品で、探幽の著名な構図をほとんど模写したもの。設色は巧みである。

(MFA:11.4183)

作品126　素川彰信筆。雉図。
［※解説欄空白］（MFA:11.4356）

作品127　清曠筆。東福寺通天橋秋景図。
大変美しい作。最近の四条派としては佳品。画題は兆殿司の生活が偲ばれて興味深い。
(MFA:11.4765)

作品128　鶴澤探泉筆。鶴に日輪に波。
［※解説欄空白］（MFA:11.4382）

作品129　探雪筆。梅に鶴。
凡作。探幽画法が衰退し、もはや何のインスピレーションをも感じさせぬ一例である。
(MFA:11.4328)

作品130　三幅対。［※獅子、牡丹］。晴川筆。大作。
実にみごとな表装で、大名などある要人の依頼によって制作されたものに間違いない。牡丹の葉は大名の家紋と思われる。晴川の最もみごとな画風で、漢画華やかなりし日を想起させる。全体としては、画題こそ平凡だが現存する掛け物としては最も華麗な作の一つである。

　第一図は岩に一群の牡丹。純粋な漢画様式。直接の模写でないとしても、王若水あるいは趙昌のある作品を線密に模倣したもの。岩の描写がみごとで後期狩野様式の最優秀作たることを示し、また小さな牡丹の新芽、竹、下部に描かれる蒲公英はそれぞれ完璧に近い。上部の葉はまさしく王若水の模写と言って差し支えない。

　第二図。仏に仕える獅子。おのれが洞穴の入口に坐り、まるで羅漢のように瞑想している。韓国の友人はこれを達磨のようだと評した。全く伊川の様式に依っているが、色彩は伊川より濁っている。後期狩野派では最も強い描法の一例。最大の長所は岩から垂れている葉と草、それに落款の下に描かれる起伏ある前景。これらは宋元画を思わせる。おそらく構図はすべて、今はなき漢画の原図から写されたものに違いない。

　第三図。またも牡丹図だが構図は第一図ほどでなく、興味を誘うところも多くない。全体乃至部分をある漢画花卉図から模写したもので、まさしく趙昌の絵が制作当時はこうであったに違いないと思われるような描きぶりである。以上の問題点はあるが、三図とも断固たる気品を具えている。

この三幅対は文殊を象徴する主題を表わすもの。狩野は晴川第一級品と評し、永悳は30歳頃の作と言う。（MFA:11.4334-4336）

作品131 キオノブ［※狩野清信か］筆。四睡図。

［※解説欄空白］（MFA:11.4231）

作品132 常川幸信筆。東方朔。

常川は高名の画家ではなく、作品も少ない。子孫の友信は常川の秀作と言う。実際、常信以後に描かれた作品のうちでは最も秀れ、常信の域にまで達するほどである。常川には栄川の名を高め狩野派第四期の運動の基礎を築いた新しい特色がすでに現れているのである。（MFA:11.4465）

作品133 人物図。ユキノブ［※前掲幸信か、清原雪信か、狩野之信か不明］筆。

［※解説欄空白］

作品134 洞琳由信筆。柳に鷺図。

［※解説欄空白］（MFA:11.4806）

作品135 周文筆。双幅。円中の山水。小品。

［※解説欄空白］

作品136 菊図。狩野融川 □ 信筆。［※□は寛］

菊色の布の表装が作品に似合う。もと山中の所蔵で三幅対の一幅だった。友信は融川作としては秀作と称賛する。優美で彩色も柔らかい。当時の狩野派支流の作として代表的な例。（MFA:11.4468）

作品137 栗鼠に栗。ユーセイ［※友清か祐清か不明］筆。

［※解説欄空白］

作品138 顔輝筆。仙人。

［※解説欄空白］

作品139 鹿を逐う狩人。北斎筆。

稀品。北斎の肉筆画は極めて少ない。油絵のような変わった色彩と独特な筆法のため、識別は簡単である。（現在では北斎の粗悪な偽物が外国人向けに作られているらしい。）異様ではあるが真筆のタッチはしっかりしている。いずれの評者も真筆と鑑定。孔寅の絵ほどよくない。落款は「北齋翁」。北斎後期の画法をよく示している。

（MFA:11.4601）

作品 140　西湖景観図。雲谷等顔筆。

等顔は雪舟派六代（雪舟を初代に数える）と言われる。住吉によれば画題は西湖。落款に雪舟六代とある。箱書きには雲谷法眼。住吉は佳品と言う。（MFA:11.4509）

作品 141　穏やかな冬景色。琦鳳筆。

粗放な筆法で描かれ、そのため日本人はあまり感心しないが、実は作者の天才のよく表われた佳品である。明暗の度合いといい、描かれた色彩といい、25フィート離れて眺めても強い実感的印象を与える素朴な田園。雪の間で梅がまさに花を開かんとし、雪溶けの小川が行く手を探るように河床を流れている。中国の風景。

作品 142　群生して咲き誇る花。抱一筆。

光琳様式による絢爛たる作例の一つ。優雅な形態と豊富な色彩が自ずから滲み出ている。葉を徐々に変色させる画法は全く光琳的。住吉鑑定では、秀作ではないが真筆。狩野氏は佳品と評している。

作品 143　羅漢図。可翁筆。大作。

大作。迫力があり、顔の表現も力強いが、手が小さ過ぎる。狩野氏は筆致が違うことを理由に然可翁の作と主張し、山雪と同時代の別の可翁ではないかと推測する。他方松浦は柔らかい筆で描かれた可翁の真筆と鑑定。長谷川は自宅に持ち帰って調べた結果、可翁なりと言う。暁斎は遠くから眺めただけで、箱書きも落款も見ずに可翁であると言い当てた。決定の難しい問題である。また、狩野はさしてよいものではないと言うが、他の評者はいずれも、可翁であるなしは別問題としてなかなか良い作だと称賛する。印章は古いもので真物らしい。私見では、秀作だが可翁の作例とは似ていないように思われると言うのが本当のところである。暁斎いわく、岩の線描は可翁的で、達磨は他の追随を許さない、特にこの作を彼は乱拍子すなわち蔓草の葉の如き筆法と称し、これこそ可翁の常奪的スタイルで、これはその秀作だと言う。柏木いわく、印章は真物に見えるが、通常画法との違いが可翁ならずとする唯一の理由。彼もこれを佳品と考えており、野村も同意見である。住吉鑑定ではせいぜい300年ほど前の作。私は可翁の真筆に間違いないと思っている

作品 144　桃花、柳に黄色の小鳥。梅逸筆。

しっかりした速描。色彩は繊細で印象的。構成もみごとである。誰もが称賛し、松浦は梅逸の最高作と言う。小鳥は黄鶯。両狩野も佳品と評す。梅逸は東京の画家和亭の師であった。（MFA:11.4648）

作品145　來章筆。双幅。[※花鳥図]。
　　第一図は雉に桜花。雉の首の部分の色彩がよい。
　　第二図は鹿に花。こちらは柔らかく優美だが崇高感に欠ける。
両図とも私の見た來章のうちでは最高のもの。京都より購入。評者はみな来章のものでは第一級品に入るものと言う。初め京都で開催された政府主催のフェノロサ所蔵品展に展示されたもの。

作品146　富士山、雲、風景。探鯨筆。
コデラ[※国府寺か]の伯父で姫路在住の人から贈られたもの。贈り主には70歳の誕生日を迎えたフランコニア地方の老人を描いた油絵を送った。探鯨は幽汀の師。あまり崇高な作ではないが、稀品であり、また特徴もよく出ている。主題は富士、興津、清見寺、三保海岸。箱書きには「春富士」。下に見える門は東海道清見ヶ関。大宮人たちによって数々の詩が詠まれた場所である。（MFA:11.4293）

作品147　三幅対。布袋に花二幅。探幽筆。
第一図は梅、第三図は竹、第二図が布袋。狩野永悳は探幽50歳のころの通常作と称するが、これは当たっている。気品はないが簡潔で清純。日本中どこでも見られる甘美美麗なるものの典型を巧みに描いて一般人の鑑賞を惹きつけ、かつ画家たちの画業に著しい影響を与えた。真筆だが第三級品に過ぎない。第三図にある小鳥は深山頬白。友信によれば宴席の揮毫にほぼ間違いないという。

作品148　探幽筆　三幅対　嵐に龍二幅と虎に乗る鐘馗
両狩野氏は探幽第一級品と言う。一般的立場に立てば私の所蔵する維摩図（作品33）に次ぐ秀作とすべきところ。しかし富士山図の方が画風の点では更に優れている。長谷川評では第一級品。暁斎も同意見。松浦は佳品としながら福禄寿図（作品124）には及ばぬと言う。透明な墨色、清浄さ、崇高な画調は狩野両氏の称賛するところ。箱の内側に筆跡鑑定の専門家古筆氏の証文がある。

作品149　二直庵筆。三幅対。[※鷹図]。
名匠の手になる優品。第一図、柳の枝にとまる鷹。第二図、鷺を捕える鷹。第三図、鴨を襲う鷹。作者は鷹の絵にかけては日本最高の画家であり、墨色筆勢がすばらしく、如何にも芸術的な味わいがある。松浦は第1図ほどみごとな柳の図を見たことがないと言う。長谷川評では、父直庵一世の要素が多い。暁斎もいまだかつて見たことのない作例と言う。第一図の線描墨色は驚嘆に値する。この画家は父子とも鷹と鷲の画で有名であり、狙仙の猿と対照するものである。Y・狩野[※狩野永悳]も非常にみごとな作と言っている。二直庵は当時有名な画家だったが、後により綿密な流派の出現

によって忘れられてしまった。迫力の点では明らかに父に劣る。野村氏はまさに墨のタッチが曽我派（？）の特色を示していると言う［※？は原文のまま］。第2図は印刷からの複写がゴンスの著書に収録されている。有名な構図である。山中より購入したもの。

作品150 木村永光筆。三幅対。［※山水人物図］。
永悳の話ではこの画家の作は至って少ないとのこと。大変みごとな作で様式は作者独自のもの。純粋な文学趣味を持つ日本人はみな称賛する。柏木と野村は私のコレクション中も最も注目すべきものに数えられると言う。素朴で飾り気のない構図だが、その中に束縛されぬ純粋な深みのある情緒が滲み出す。まさに描法の奔放さが、その持つ理想的雰囲気とみごとに調和している。

　　第一図は船中に横たわる仙人。三図のうちでは最も劣る。眠る人物の上に落款がある。
　　第二図。西湖に臨む径山寺。描線は細く、独特にして非凡。筆致は極めて力強く、後年山楽がよく用いた画法である。鄂州巖頭山と題す。
　　第三図、韓退之の追放。人物図の独創的表現は最高の気品に満ち、元信に匹敵する。馬の図に見られる画想、描法もすばらしい。これらは日本絵画の高度な特質を真に理解しているか否かの試舎石となるものである。

永光の作品でこれほど印象的なものは他に存在が知られていない。山中より購入。
（MFA:11.4274-4276）

作品151 竹洞筆。双幅。両図とも龍に波濤。
龍の輪郭は所翁の模写と画面に記されている。しかしその形態は所翁とは全く異なり、筆致、画法はすべて独創的である。とくに第二図の波は泡立つ水の量感表現が注目に値し、決して飛沫の線描にのみ留まるものではない。雲の表現も純粋かつ壮麗。筆致は半ば文人的、半ば応挙的で、特に薄描の部分にそれが顕著である。壮麗純粋を極めた画面、格調の高い独創的情調は漢画の傑作に迫るものがある。狩野氏は水沫の描法が必ずしも独創的でなく、探幽が時々用いたものと評するが、松浦は竹洞のよく描く文人山水画に較べて遥かに勝るものとする。おそらく竹洞の最秀作に入り得るものであろう。京都の画家で、半分ほど四条派的要素が加わっている。京都にて購入。
（MFA:11.4650-4651）

作品152 観音図。元信筆。
狩野氏によれば元信の最高作は大蔵省が勝川から買収した仏陀図だという。しかしこの観音図はそれに勝るもので、従って現存する元信の最高傑作ということになる。呉道子を模写したものではという者もあるが決してそうではなく、色彩線描とも元信の最高技量を示す独創的作品である。東京の諸狩野家にはこれを探幽が模写したものが

伝わっており、彼らは昔からこの模本を研究し模写し続けてきたが、その原図を実見したこともなく、その所在さえ知らなかった。京都妙覚寺にある元信筆大涅槃像を凌ぐ作。絹本でこれほどの古さのわりには保存がよい。情調は極めて崇高。狩野氏は私のコレクションでは最優秀品と言う。狩野氏によれば岩の描写は他の追随を許さぬとのこと。全体的効果としては呉道子の純粋なる壮重さに迫るものがある。白衣の輝くばかりの効果は、制作当時には気付かれぬものだったかもしれない。頭部の二重光輪も効果的かつ独創的。衣裳の描線は極めて迫力に富む。静かな、この世ならぬ荘厳感が観る者の心に広がる。松浦は150円でこの絵を譲り受けたいと申し出た。もと、阿波の大名蜂須賀家の蔵幅であった。岩のタッチに至っては到底他人の模写し得ぬものがある。元信のこの描法はまさに彼の岩の理念を最も明快に造形したものであって、瞬間的に成り、霊感に溢れ、決して単なる習癖によるものではない。元信中期の作。柏木も私のコレクション中最高と言う。山中はこれを兆殿司と考え、兆殿司として廉価で私に売却した。探幽による摸本でも、後に（1883年に）東京で350円で売買されたという。本図は東京で評判の名作となり、これまで何度も展覧会に出品されている。
(MFA:11.4267)

作品153　釈迦図。榮賢筆。

狩野氏の曰く、実にみごとで描法も良い、制作は探幽の頃で、特に彩色に優れ、構図は中国古雅風とのこと。

作品154　虎図。岸駒筆。大作。

暁斎評、作者の孔雀図に匹敵。松浦評、佳品だがこの程度のものは他にもある。柏木評、鹿図（作品□□）[※番号欠落] と比肩し得る作。毛を濡れたように描き、例のボケた縞模様が点描されている。虎の頭部も濡れた光が良く出ている。周囲は一面を覆う霧。竹が特に良いと評する日本人もある。雪村に近いと言う狩野の言には賛成。恐らく岸駒晩年の作。虎を描いたものでは秀作と言えよう。京都にて購入。これほど大作の迫力ある岸駒の虎図は最近では珍しい。

作品155　豫譲の図。華山筆。

晋の豫譲が皇帝の命を狙う有名な歴史的情景を描いたもの [※「鐘馗図」とされているものか]。人物画としては大変大きく、注目すべき作。作風は応挙と岸駒の中間。迫力は万人の認めるところ。日本人はこれを観て必ず驚嘆の声を挙げる。彩色もみごとである。横山華山は近世京都最大の画家の一人。渡邊崋山とは別人である。表装は年代物で豪華。作品との調和がとれている。(MFA:11.4731)

作品156　狩野安信筆　三幅対。山水二幅に福禄寿。
線描が確実明快、色彩が美しく、安信の作では第一級品というのが狩野永悳その他の評者の一致した見解である。これに匹敵するのは京都智積院の安信筆観音図のみ。

第一図。山水の秀作。明るく澄んだ雰囲気、快い前景。全体として雪舟的情緒が強いが独特の筆致。

第二図。福禄寿に鹿と鶴を円形の中に描く。極めて巧みな描写で、円形輪郭が無い。衣裳の描線は安信の作では最高。顔にも安信の逸品たることがよく表われている。同時に柔らかい象牙色の着色はこれに及ぶものがない。

第三図。雪景色。前二幅よりも劣り、安信直系の画家たちの衰退ぶりに似たところが多いように見受けられる。

全体としては気品高く美麗であり、作者と二人の兄［※探幽守信と主馬尚信］との間の基本的な違いをよく示している。

作品157　孔雀図。芳園筆。
暁斎によれば、なかなか良い作だが岸駒の孔雀には及ばぬと言う。松浦はたいへん良い作とし、両狩野も称賛する。花弁の線描、葉の繊細な濃淡に注目すべきである。孔雀の描写に固さが見られるようだが、これは応挙を学んだもの。構図が好い。芳園の作でこのような濃密細心の大作は非常に珍しい。山中より購入。（MFA:11.4722）

作品158　野猿の図。狙仙筆。
暁斎はこれまで見た四条派のうち最高の作と言う。松浦は狙仙のこの種の描法が珍しいこと、作品101よりも優れたものであることを述べる。私はこのように荒々しい描法のものを見たことがない。両狩野も第一級となし、評者も皆その驚くべき芸術的迫力を称賛する。猿の毛並みは大まかに色彩を変えて行く情緒的なタッチで表現され、太く柔らかい毛筆が使用されている。かくの如き手段でかくの如きものを描出し得るかくの如き技量には、一体如何なる知識が含有されているのであろうか。深みのある色調は往古の巨匠を偲ばせ、狙仙通常の作とは大いに趣きを異にしている。もちろんこれら巨匠たちと同列に扱うべきものである。京都にて購入。評者はすべて称賛。ゴンスの著書に掲載された狙仙の最優秀作はみな、この描法で制作されている。狙仙画のうち最大の迫力を持つ美術作品で、第一級品に属すもの。

作品159　孔雀図。岸駒筆。
日本絵画で最も特異な作品の一つ。岸駒の野生的天才が強い迫力を発揮している。絶壁の縁にとまり羽を広げた孔雀は、まさに魔鳥の感がある。樹木の葉は彩色がみごとで、とくに二ヶ所の赤色が効果的である。いわゆる東洋画的なところがなく、構成、主題、線描ともに独特の気力と着想から発している。両狩野とも偉大なる作と評した。

岸駒の画風には漢画と似たところがなく、このような孔雀を描いてもユニークであると両人は言う。鑑賞者に強い感動を与える印象的な作品である。長谷川評では、普通南蘋の方が岸駒や応挙より勝っているが本作品は南蘋以上とする。暁斎もすばらしい出来栄えと称賛した。紙本に描かれた岸駒のスケッチ風描法で、私見では京都にある岸駒の有名な孔雀の細密画よりも良いと思う。山中より購入。おそらく岸駒中期でもその終り頃の作。

作品160　八福神の図。華山筆。

左側の第八番目の人物はお多福。これは特定人物の名前ではなく、醜い女の通称。大変技巧的な作品で華山の名声を支えるに足るもの。神々は酒が入って少々浮かれている。弁天はにこにこしてさらに酒をついで回り、琵沙門はすでに酔いつぶれているといった実に滑稽な場面。神々の顔、豊かで流れるような衣裳の描写は称賛の言葉もないほどである。描写力の点では日本の生んだ最高作の一つと言っても過言ではない。

(MFA:11.4730)

作品161　花鳥図。呂紀筆。

永恵いわく、本図はコヨーシン［※不詳。作品165参照］に劣り、呂紀ないしその模写ではなく、明代無名画家のもの。呂紀の真筆を知る者はきわめて少なく、呂紀と称される作はほとんど偽物だと言う。長谷川は呂紀真筆の佳品と言うが、私も呂紀とは思えない。東京にある呂紀はすべて偽作であり、真筆は京都にある一、二点に過ぎない。この作も所謂「東京呂紀」の佳品であろう。最近、野村氏はこれを鑑定して元朝時代のものに間違いない、岩の描影法がそれを示していると言う。古い印章が横に捺してあって未だ解読していないが、私もこれを元代のものと思っている。なかなかの佳品である。

作品162　呑舟。荒山風景図。

呑舟の秀作に較べると劣るが、呑舟独特の神韻をある程度保っている。半ば蕪村や混交派［※四条派と文人画の混成派］に似たところがあるが、独特の銀色の光が画面に射し込み、真の山水画的迫力がある。(MFA:11.4695)

作品163　福禄寿。岸駒筆。

狩野永恵は岸駒の孔雀図に次ぐ秀作と言う。永恵の説によれば、この主題は子供を幸福の象徴とし、従って子供を連れた福禄寿は福の神であると言う。しかしこれは疑わしい解釈だと思う。長寿を授けるために子供を仙境に連れ去るという忘れられた伝説に拠るものではなかろうか。おそらく出産時に掛けられた画幅であったろう。ある種のキリスト教絵画の模倣だったかもしれぬとする説もある。伝説ではないとしても、子供に対する希望と幸福を優しく表現した主題であり、柏木もこの見解を是認し、さらに本図を岸駒の真筆に間違いないと評した。岸駒晩年の様式で、衣裳の襞にやや応

挙の影響が見られる。子供の脚をこのように遠近画法で描くのは日本絵画においてユニークなものである。裸の子供もユニークだ。山中より購入。

作品 164　二頭の鹿。岸駒筆。
永徳評、まさに岸駒最高の傑作で応挙より遥かに勝る。長谷川評、岸駒の最優秀作、応挙にはより優美高尚なところがあるがこれほど強い力はない。松浦評、岸駒現存の作では他に比類がない、おそらく40歳くらいの作。山の部分が最も良い、これを見て感動せぬ者はいないだろう、「岸駒にこのような作があったとは知らなかった」と言う。すべての評者が激賞する。若井氏など感嘆のあまりこれを京都に持参し、手順に従って絹布に模写せしめたがよくなし得るところではなかったと言う。東京にてキングより購入した。柏木、野村氏、佐野氏ら、すべて岸駒の最優秀作と見る。長所はまず鹿の迫真的描法。毛と斑点の扱いに見られ、陰翳を用いずにレリーフのように浮き立たせ、特に毛の描法は細密に過ぎずまた粗放に陥ったところもない。次に背後の山だが、その力と簡潔性においては雪舟に比肩し得るものと考えられる。さらに、鹿の背後の柔らかく暖かいゆらめくような大気の描出。その中で山腹がまるで打ち震えているように見える。日本人の評者は応挙に匹敵するものと言うが、応挙も遥かに遠く及ばぬ出来栄えである。恐らく近世日本絵画中最も偉大な作品であり、岸駒こそ制作に関する知識と気力と空想的情緒に関しては雪舟に接近し得る唯一の近世画家と言うことが出来る。山の部分最高だと評する日本人もある。疑いなく岸駒中年の作。35歳ない40歳くらいか。オースティン・ロバートソンはこの作品に感激し、今までに見た掛け物のうち最高のもの、ランシーアを遥かにはるかに凌駕するものと激賞した。まさに世界の動物画最優秀作に数えられる秀作である。（MFA:11.4701）

作品 165　花鳥図。コヨーシン［※不詳］筆。
狩野永悳いわく、作者は明代初期の著名な花鳥画家、これはその典型的な様式を示すもの。長谷川氏によれば着想は呂紀に勝るが描法は呂紀ほどではないと言う。壮大な画想は現代画家すべての称賛するところ。鳥はハハチョー［※叭々鳥］。私見では呂紀真筆の秀作と同格の明代花鳥図傑作に数えてよいと思う。鳥を描いてこれほどの荘重さを出し得る者はまずいない。描法こそ最高とは言えないが簡潔で生気に溢れ明快である。山中より購入。樹木の枝の墨色は明確で力強く、雄大な描法。

作品 166　豊彦筆。双幅。山水図。
中級品。描法は両図とも良好、明快。（MFA:11.4777-4778）

作品 167　月岡雪齋筆。双幅。人物図。
父雪鼎の作ほど力強くはないが、同様の風格を持つ。彩色は線密で優美。
（MFA:11.4626-4627）

作品 168　尚信筆。三幅対。達磨、鷺、蓮。
尚信 30 歳の作。狩野永悳の評、第一級品。

作品 169　探信守政筆。三幅対。李白、花鳥。
すべての評者が探信第一級品と見る。

作品 170　正信原図、探幽模写。三幅対。孔子と弟子。
［※解説欄空白］（MFA:11.4399-4401）

作品 171　季頼［※スエヨリ］筆。墨彩。花鳥図。
第一級品。印章が美しいと狩野永悳評。

作品 172　元信筆。扇面人物図。
箱書きに古法眼とあるが、あらゆる可能性から言って実は季頼作。印章なし。元信画法を継いだ平均作で佳品。当時流行した進物用扇子の様式を示していて面白い。
（MFA:11.4270）

作品 173　守景筆。川景色粗描。
永悳の言によれば落款は真物でなく描法は冒険的。友信は、これまで見たこともないほどの山水画の傑作で雪舟の域に達するほどだと言う。私見では真筆で手際のよい佳品と思うが、異様なところ貧弱なところがあって高いランクはつけられない。しかし守景の手法が大いに表われ、当時はそこが歓迎された。

作品 174　永納筆。山水図。小品。
箱書きは「ロエイ［※不詳］早春譜の叙景」の意。この作者の作は稀少。探幽以前の狩野画様式が跡を留め、友信評では大変興味ある佳品と言う。（MFA:11.4429　観桜山水図か？）

作品 175　狩野養川筆。周公図。
周公旦の肖像。中級品で養川 50 歳のときの作と永悳は言う。顔の描法に養川画の典型が見られ、後期狩野派作品の佳作である。単なる形態を超え、高度の精神的表現の領域にまで達しているのが長所。（MFA:11.4454）

作品 176　松栄筆。牡丹の花小枝。彩色。
永真の鑑定書つき。これがなければ永悳は真筆と言わなかったであろう。中級品の下と彼は評し、紙本が修補されていると言う。住吉評では佳作。私は初期狩野派の花卉

図では最もすばらしい作品の一つと思う。友信は、極めて独創的かつ装飾的トーンをもつ松栄独特の豊富で驚くべき色彩に感嘆している。芸術味豊かな作。1882年、名古屋にて購入。

作品177 社前で戯れる唐子たち。芳園筆。

芳園のものでは最も繊細かつ清純、しかも綿密に思考された上で仕上げられた作品の一例である。（MFA:11.4717）

作品178 海北友雪筆 寿老人

永悳は非常に珍しいものと言う。箱書きに「寿老人」とあるが、両狩野によれば間違いなく維摩図。どこか雪舟的迫力を具える驚くべき作品。（MFA:11.4534）

作品179 藝阿弥筆。山水図。小品。

［※解説欄空白］（MFA:11.4124）

作品180 曽我蕭亭筆。二人の騎馬人物図。小品。

蕭亭は蕭白の別名に違いないと狩野は言う。画面には「蛇足軒」とある。非常に良い作。蕭白のものでは最も繊細な作の一つ。墨色は壮麗、二頭の馬の線描がみごとである。ヨーロッパの巨匠にも比肩すべき優品。称賛せぬ人はいない。（MFA:11.4520）

作品181 狩野古永徳筆。花鳥図。

彩色画。真筆で、印章が好いと永悳。サイズはこれより大きかった、花は椿、鳥はおそらく鳩であろう、作者30歳ころの中級品、と永悳は評する。私見では略画体の佳品と考えるが、永徳の優れた特性が発揮されておらず、作者の第三級品と思う。

作品182 長柳斎筆。二羽の幼鷹。小品。

［※解説欄空白］（MFA:11.4120）

作品183 探幽筆。双幅。滝に鯉。

永悳評では探幽第一級に属するもの。［※以下空白］

作品184 芳園筆。滝に山水図。佳品。

［※解説欄空白］（MFA:11.4718）

作品185 探幽筆。三幅対。楊貴妃に花鳥。小品。

  第一図、裏書は「白鶺に牡丹」だが、両狩野は「三光鳥」と言う。
  第二図、楊貴妃。よく牡丹を配する画題。
  第三図、三光鳥に牡丹。

永悳説では三図とも探幽の第一級品、探幽のものでこれほど描線の美しい作は実に珍しい、構図は探幽独自のもので漢画的ではない、ごく初期のもので、30歳ころの作とする。住吉は「150円の値打もの」と評した。これと維摩図は探幽の最優秀作とするのが両狩野の意見である。（MFA:11.4395-4397）

作品186 常信筆。木の枝。

両狩野の評では常信青年期のみごとな第一級品。図はヤドリ木の生えた桜。落款は真筆。20歳の作。（MFA:11.4417）

作品187 楊冨筆　山水図。水墨。小品。

両狩野、住吉とも佳品となす。（MFA:11.4159）

作品188 玉樂筆。枝に小鳥。着彩。

小鳥は四十雀。永悳説では真筆、中級品。花はモクゲン［※モクゲンジ木槵子の誤り。庭木の一種、夏に黄色い花を付ける］。永叔による真筆鑑定書が付いている。
                   （MFA:11.4190）

作品189 横山華山筆。山水図。着彩。

箱書に「豊作」とあり、人々が祝い酒に酔っている。

作品190 北斎筆。山水図。着彩。

［※解説欄空白］

作品191 嵩谷筆。花鳥写生図。

河原鶸。上部に木槿。評者はみな、珍品と言う。（MFA:11.4367）

作品192 兆殿司筆。羅漢坐像。着彩。

箱書きに「第十二番　迦諾迦伐蹉尊者」とあり、探幽の筆跡である。永悳は中級品と言い、住吉は兆殿司の真筆とする。（MFA:11.4067）

作品193 狩野山雪筆。龍図。

佳品と住吉は言い、永悳は中級品の上と評す。

作品 194 狩野洞白筆。布袋図。
狩野は洞白を洞白愛信とする。（MFA:11.4180）

作品 195 武禅筆。夜景図。小品。武禅筆。
［※解説欄空白］（MFA:11.4791）

作品 196 呉春筆。山水図。
［※解説欄空白］（MFA:11.4716）

作品 197 海北友松筆。琴高仙人図。
永悳評では中級品。住吉は佳品と言う。

作品 198 土佐光起筆。人物図。横幅。
詩歌で有名な六玉川の一つ。山城国井手の玉川を写し、馬上の人物は玉川の歌を詠んだ宮廷歌人俊成。画面に書き添えた歌は「駒とめて猶水飼はん山吹のはなの露そふ井手の玉川」。箱はもとのものではない。（MFA:11.4567）

作品 199 晴暉筆。山水図。
画題は桃源の仙人。箱はもとのものではない。（MFA:11.4764）

作品 200 狩野周信筆。三福神。
永悳評では中級品。もと三幅対の一つで、40歳の作と彼は言う。布袋、恵比寿、大黒が描かれている。（MFA:11.4175）

作品 201 義董筆。大黒図。
［※解説欄空白］（MFA:11.4709）

作品 202 義董筆。八仙図。
仙人が何をしているか、両狩野にも不明。上部に散りばめた小円は星である。
（MFA:11.4708）

作品 203 小栗宗栗筆。花鳥図。
［※解説欄空白］

作品 204 山田道安筆。枝に鳥。
鳥は綬帯鳥［※尾の長い瑞鳥］。両狩野、住吉ともに佳品となす。道安の作は稀である。綬帯鳥は「長寿をもたらす鳥」という。

作品205　土佐光成筆　女人図。
住吉評では光成の第一級品。箱に「桜下宮女」「宮人の讃」を意味する書入れがある。
(MFA:11.4816)

作品206　狩野寿石敦信筆。三聖図。
素川の先祖の作は甚だ少ない。これは佳品で面白味があり、住吉もみごとな作と言う。賛は「唇に触れれば乾き、甘露にも味なし」の意。[※原画の賛は「嘩設唇邊　無味惟甘露」] 狩野も初見の作。(MFA:11.4171)

作品207　一休筆。木に鳥。素描。
[※解説欄空白]

作品208　日華筆。炭焼きの図。
[※解説欄空白]（MFA:11.4751)

作品209　探幽筆。中国皇帝図。
永惠評、中級品。住吉評も同じ。皇帝は周の文王。落款がみごと。法眼50歳頃の作。

作品210　容斎筆。観音図。
容斎晩年の作。両狩野、住吉とも真筆と言う。(MFA:11.4780)

作品211　南岳筆。岩に猿。
[※解説欄空白]（MFA:11.4748)

作品212　月岡雪鼎筆。女人図。
箱書に「三都の遊女」。永惠説、中央の女は東京。住吉説、左の女は京都。作者67歳の作。住吉は面白いものと言う。

作品213　豊國筆。屏風に人物。
題は「田舎源氏」。作者は二代豊國で、旧名は國貞。小説『源氏』の挿絵画家だった。おもしろい、またみごとな作とすべての評者は言う。(MFA:11.4610)

作品214　雪信筆。船に人物図。
范蠡と西施を描く。永惠評、中級品。住吉は「源氏」より良いと言う。箱書に「楊貴妃」とあるが、これは誤り。(MFA:11.4464)

作品 215　土佐光忠筆。蓬莱図。
住吉は真筆と言う。天保頃の作。

作品 216　岸礼筆。運河景観図。
［※解説欄空白］

作品 217　狩野孝信筆。李白図。
永悳の考えでは同時代の画風にそれほど左右されていないとのこと。或いは興以の息子の作かもしれない。（MFA:11.4372）

作品 218　文麟筆。雪景山水。大作。
［※解説欄空白］

作品 219　桃水筆。大瀧図。
［※解説欄空白］（MFA:11.4776）

作品 220　宋紫石筆。雄鶏に花。
［※解説欄空白］（MFA:11.4820）

作品 221　探信守政筆。中国山水図。双幅。
両狩野とも真筆と言う。（MFA:11.4386-4387）

作品 222　西川ツケノブ［※スケノブ　祐信か］筆。女人図。双幅。
住吉は後代の偽作と思っている。永悳は「佳品と思う」、友信は「佳品かつ真筆に間違いない」と鑑定した。住吉は作者の時代を勘違いしているようで、又平の門人と思っている。時代はずっと下がるのだ。女たちは添えられた歌を詠んだ歌人たちの肖像である。

作品 223　松花堂筆。山部赤人に六歌仙。
永悳、住吉はともに真筆と言う。（MFA:11.4518）

作品 224　足利義持筆。東坡図。
人物を杜子美とする者もいるが、永悳説では恐らく東坡。永悳はさらに真筆だと言う。箱書によれば、以前伊川の鑑定書がついていたと、古筆了伴が書いている。

（MFA:11.4161）

作品225　洞雲筆。花鳥図鷺に蓮。
両狩野も住吉も第一級品と言う。稀覯の作。探幽と比肩し得るもの。茶人好みの絵で、茶掛的性格が濃厚である。（MFA:11.4238）

作品226　守景筆。東坡図。
住吉と永悳評では中級品。真筆で、永悳がその模本を所持している。画布が美しい。住吉は茶人好みと言う。

作品227　蕭白筆。馬図。
住吉の感想では面白い絵。（MFA:11.4505）

作品228　狩野光信筆。山水図。双幅。
［※解説欄空白］（MFA:11.4472-4473）

作品229　土佐光文筆。七福神図。
光文としては佳品だが芸術的風格に乏しいと住吉は言う。名は、「ミツアヤ」と読むべきものという。（MFA:11.4559）

作品230　呑舟筆。天狗に鳥。
「嘉永の作」と記されている。大天狗と、鳥は従者の小天狗たち。（MFA:11.4696）

作品231　守景筆。牡丹図。
皆、第一級品と鑑定。極めて珍しいもので、この作あることを知る批評家はいないだろう。「無礙斎」と号す。

作品232　華渓筆。東本願寺炎上図。
箱書に「東本願寺の火事」。（MFA:11.4735）

作品233　中国山水図。
伊川模写と伝えられるが誤りである。（MFA:11.4215）

作品234　円山応震筆。山水図。
横幅。箱書に「緑樹に春雨の嵐山」の意が記されている。（MFA:1.4755）

作品 235 狩野休圓筆。蓮に鷺図。

住吉評では、なかなか面白い、休圓としては佳い出来で珍しい作。狩野は真筆となし、休圓を元禄ころの人ではないかかと言う。（MFA:11.4373）

作品 236 狩野養川筆。寿老人に龍。三幅対。

中級品の上位にあり大変良いものと永悳は言い、住吉も実にみごとな作とする。中央の寿老図は雪舟の構図に修正を加えたもの。

作品 237 百谷筆。牡丹に鳥。

友信、住吉とも、美しく描けていると評す。箱はもとのものではないが、作者は百谷とある。（MFA:11.4655）

作品 238 狩野永叔筆。三幅対。寿老人に山水。

第一図、春と夏。第二図、寿老人、第三図、秋と冬。瀧が夏の象徴であるのは、夏に最も好まれるため。永叔の第一級品と永悳は言う。（MFA:11.4440-4442）

作品 239 晴川模写。中国山水図。孫君澤原図。

原図は一ツ橋徳川茂榮旧蔵。模写の出来は好い。（MFA:11.4333）

作品 240 狩野周信筆。柳に燕。

評者全員第一級品と称す。作品242（岑信筆）と同時に制作されたもの。30歳ころの作。燕は柳が緑に色付くころ日本に渡って来る。（MFA:11.4174）

作品 241 狩野常信筆。福禄寿図。

青年期、30歳くらいの作と永悳は言う。第三級品。

作品 242 狩野岑信筆。竹、雪、雀。

永悳は大変好い作と言うが、友信評では中級品。雀は律儀な鳥で、竹に寄生する虫しか好まぬという。（MFA:11.4247）

作品 243 玄也筆。双幅。山水図。小品。

永悳も住吉も実にみごとな作と称賛。おそらく、もと八景図のうちの二幅。
（MFA:11.4188-4189）

作品 244 可翁筆。双幅。寒山拾得図。

永悳は極めて古い模写で偽筆とするが、住吉説では真筆佳品。

作品245 長谷川等伯筆。双幅。山水図。

チョウシュウ（※不詳。長州か）の元信屏風を模写した逸品。等伯としては中級品。

作品246 洞文筆。双幅。人物図。

仙人の養生を描く。第一図はくしゃみ。第二図は洗髪。永悳説では元信より古いことは確実、土岐洞文のものと言う。洞文は周文の弟子。住吉は佳品にして稀品と言う。

作品247 狩野洞春筆。三幅対。松竹梅図。

永悳は老洞春の作と言う［※ 駿河台狩野家第二代の洞春義信と第四代洞春美信との前者のこと］。住吉いわく、画布が大変みごとで珍しいと。松と梅が生け花様式に配置されている。この画家としては優品。祝儀用の画幅で、松は若松。年賀宴席用に違いない。永悳説では第三図が最秀作。

作品248 狩野祐清英信（テルノブ）筆。三幅対。滝に日輪。

永悳評、作者のものとしては中級品。

  第一図、日光華厳の滝。
  第二図、日輪に渓流。住吉はみごとな出来と褒める。
  第三図、日光寂光の滝。

住吉評、三図とも佳品。（MFA:11.4411-4413）

作品249 狩野探牧筆。双幅。鶴図。

探牧は寡作の画家。生涯碁を打って過ごしたという。住吉評、佳品で表装もよい。

（MFA:11.4374-4375）

作品250 狩野伊川筆。双幅。牡丹図。

永悳によれば伊川20歳の作。若年にしては第一級品。祝儀に用いられたもので非常に美しい。作者独自の意匠であって漢画を写したものではないと、永悳は言う。

（MFA:11.4210-4211）

作品251 狩野□□［※空白］筆。双幅。花卉図。墨彩。

永悳と住吉の考えでは、第一図の印章は偽物で、第二図が本物と言う。あるいは屏風絵を剥がしたものか。住吉は永徳の印章を使用した門人の作と言う。

作品252 土佐光芳筆。三幅対。鶴に鶉。

光芳としては大変よい出来だが、絵それ自体は秀作とは言えない。鶉別として、主題は幸福と祝賀の象徴。第一図、菊に鶉。第二図、松に鶴。第三図、粟に鶉。

（MFA:11.4570-4572）

作品253　狩野尚信筆。陶淵明図。

友信によれば作者20歳ころの作。略画体の佳品で茶室向きの絵ではない。しかし彼の略画はつねに、自身高名な茶人であったため、またその簡潔さの故に愛好されていた。

作品254　芳園筆。平等院景観。

箱はもとのものではない。(MFA:11.4720)

作品255　一蝶筆。笛吹きと唐子。

菓子と水飴を売る男、と住吉は言う。飴売りの箱には菓子と飴壺と傘が入っている。大きな扇が飴売りの看板である。彼は異国の服装につけ髭を生やし、笛を吹いて子供たちを集める。永恵は模写、住吉は佳品、狩野友信も佳品と認める。(MFA:11.4222)

作品256　楊月筆。布袋図。

永恵は落款が美しいと言うが、実にみごとである。「釋臣楊月」と記す。永恵評、第一級品。(MFA:11.4160)

作品257　狩野□□［※空白］筆。鷹に小鳥。

［※解説欄空白］

作品258　岑信筆。稲田に雀。

永恵及び友信評、第一級品。(MFA:11.4246)

作品259　探原筆。松の枝。

表装が大変美しい。狩野評、真筆でかなりよい作。作者の名は守広。最近死去した京都の評家大倉好斎の鑑定書つき。(MFA:11.4376)

作品260　等益筆［※雲谷等益］。双幅。山水図。

雪舟風の中国山水画。狩野評、真筆だが第一級品ではない。どこの景色か不明。
(MFA:11.4528-4529)

作品261　ユキノブ（※雪信か）筆。屋内婦人図。

源氏物語画題のひとつ。箱書に「石山」とあるが、恐らく作者の誤りで、海辺の章二篇のうちの一つであろうと、住吉は言う。

作品262　狩野勝川筆。鶴図。

狩野評、普通作。法眼（勝川）30乃至40歳ころの作。(MFA:11.4346)

作品 263　嵩谷父子共作。福禄寿に童児。

子の名は嵩溪で、印章がある。狩野友信評、佳品で面白い作。嵩谷の第一級品と称してよいか。箱はもとのものではない。（MFA:11.4368)

作者および引用人物等註解

※太字は掲載画の作者名と作品番号。

ア

赤松（アカマツ）　画商。詳細不明。

足利義持（224）　アシカガヨシモチ（1386-1428）。室町幕府第四代将軍。義満の子。兆殿司に画を学んだという。

イ

イッキュウ（207）　不明。（一休宗純 1394-1481）か。室町中期の禅僧。

一蕙（18）　イッケイ（1795-1859）。浮田（宇喜多）一蕙。幕末期、田中訥言に師事した復古大和絵派の画家で和歌・書道にも秀でた。尊攘の志厚く安政大獄に連座し出獄後間もなく没した。

一蝶（92、255）　イッチョウ（1652-1724）。英（ハナブサ）一蝶。江戸前期の画家。本名多賀氏。狩野安信門下で多賀朝湖と称した人気画家だったが筆禍事件に遭って流罪となり三宅島で12年を過ごした。58歳で赦免され江戸に戻った。配所の草庵で蝶が草花に戯れるのを見て改名したという。狩野派の画技をもとにし大和絵や菱川師宣の画風を取り入れ、軽妙な筆致で市井の風俗を描いた。

一蝶〔二世〕（75）　イッチョウ（1677-1737）。英（ハナブサ）一蝶二世。初代一蝶の長男。三宅島に生まれた。父の画風を継ぐ。

一鳳（53、71、84）　イッポウ（1798-1871）。森一鳳。幕末・明治初期の円山四条派の画家。森徹山の養子。《藻刈舟》の絵に一商人が「儲かり一方」と読んで購入し、米価高騰して儲けたことでその名を知られたという。

伊川（30、232、250）　イセン（1775-1828）。狩野伊川榮信（ナガノブ）。木挽町狩野家第八代．永悳は伊川の六男。

ウ

浮田一蕙 → 一蕙

雲錦（45、50、98）　ウンキン（生没年不詳）。尾口雲錦。明治初年の花鳥画家で第1回内国勧業博覧会（明治10年）に出品したことがある。後年岡倉天心がフェノロサ追悼談で野口雲錦として語った画家と同一人物と思われる。

雲溪（89）　ウンケイ（生没年不詳）。室町時代の画僧。画法を雪舟に学び、師と似た山水、人物画を能くしたという。俗姓土岐氏。

雲谷等益（260）　雲谷等顔の次男（1591-1644）で、父の画風を継いだ。

雲谷等顔 (140)　ウンコクトウガン（1547-1618）。安土桃山時代の水墨画家。雪舟の画風を慕い、その遺跡山口の雲谷庵を復興して雲谷を名乗った。長谷川等伯と雪舟五代を争ったという。

エ

榮賢 (153)　エイケン、法橋榮賢。江戸前期、京都の絵仏師。
H氏　不明。長谷川氏か。
永叔 (238)　エイシュク（1675-1724）。狩野永叔主信（モリノブ）。江戸中期、狩野宗家を継いだ祖父安信（探幽の弟）に育てられ宗家第9代となる。
永徳 (181)　エイトク（1543-1590）。狩野永徳州信（クニノブ）。信長、秀吉に用いられた安土桃山時代の画家。松栄の長男で元信の孫。安土城、大坂城、聚楽第などに豪壮雄大な障壁画を制作し、御用絵師としての狩野派の基礎を築いた。狩野宗家第五代。第十二代の永徳高信と区別して古永徳と呼ばれた。
永悳　エイトク（1814-1891）。狩野永悳立信（タチノブ）。木挽町狩野家伊川栄信の第六子で、江戸後期～明治の狩野宗家（中橋狩野家）第十五代を嗣いだ。維新後は宮内省にあって帝国博物館鑑査掛、博覧会・絵画共進会の審査官を務めた。またフェノロサの狩野派研究を助け、狩野永探理信の名号を授けた。狩野友信、住吉広賢らと共にフェノロサ蒐集品の鑑定に当った。
永徳高信 (38)　エイトクタカノブ（1740-1794）。狩野永徳高信。狩野宗家第十二代。

オ

王輝　オウキ（生没年不詳）。宋代の画家。左手で秀作を描いたという。
応挙 (70、79、83)　オウキョ（1733-1795）。円山応挙。江戸中期の画家。明清の写生画、西洋画の遠近法を研究し、伝統的な装飾画様式に融和させた新様式を創造した。円山派の祖。
王質　オウシツ。中国晋代蘭州の人。木を伐ろうと、斧を持って山に入ったが、2童子が棋を囲んでいるのを見て帰るのを忘れたという。
王若水 (3)　（オウジャクスイ、生没年不詳）。中国元代の画家。
応震 (234)　オウシン（1790-1838）。円山応震。江戸中期の画家。応挙の弟子木下応受の子。応挙の長男応瑞の養子となり円山家を嗣いだ。
大倉好斎　オオクラコウサイ（1895-1862）。紀州公に仕えた京都の古筆鑑定家。
オースティン・ロバートソン　Richard Austin Robertson。米国の蒐集家。1881~1886年日本に滞在した。
大西圭斎 (5)　オオニシケイサイ（1677-1734）。谷文晁門下とされ明・清から舶載される作を研究して花弁・羽毛の描写に巧みだった。
岡本秋輝　オカモトシュウキ → 秋暉。

小栗宗湛（122）　オグリソウタン（1413-1481）室町中期の画家。周文に水墨画を学んだ。足利将軍家の御用絵師。

小栗宗栗（203）　オグリソウリツ（生没年不詳）。室町中期の画僧。周文門下小栗宗湛の子で、周文の画法を得意とした。後年京都大徳寺に住む。

カ

海北友雪（178）　カイホウユウセツ（1598-1677）。江戸前期の画家．等伯、等顔と並び称された海北友松の子。フェノロサは海北をカイホクとしている。

可翁（62、143、244）　カオウ（生没年不詳）。南北朝時代の画家．「可翁」「仁賀」印の捺された作品があってその存在が確認されるが、実際は伝歴不明。仁賀可翁、可翁良詮、可翁宗然の諸説がある。可翁宗然（カオウソウネン）は元に留学した建仁寺の画僧で、フェノロサは然可翁（ネンカオウ）とみている。

夏珪　カケイ（生没年不詳）。宮廷画院に入り、馬遠と共に南宋院体山水画の双璧と言われた。雪舟など室町中期以降の水墨画に影響を与えた。

華渓　カケイ（1816-1864）。横山華渓。江戸後期の画家で応挙の門人横山華山の子。

華山（153、160、189）　カザン（1784-1847）。横山華山。江戸後期。岸駒、呉春について四条派を学び、特に人物画に長じた。幼いころ、家貧しく北野天神社の境内にて砂絵を描いて銭を乞い僅かに糊口をしのいでいた。或る日、一絵師これを見て凡庸ならざる才に驚き、家に連れ帰ってねんごろに画法を授けたという。この絵師が岸駒だったという説がある。

崋山　カザン（1793-1841）。渡辺崋山。三河の田原藩家老。家計を助けるために絵を学んだという。谷文晁の門に入り、また洋画を学んで写実的な肖像画を能くした。1839年の蛮社の獄に連座して逮捕され、国元蟄居中に自刃。

柏木　カシワギ。柏木貨一郎（1841-1891）。探古と号した明治期の古美術鑑定家、蒐集家、工匠。幕府御用の大工棟梁柏木家の養子だったが、町田久成の配下となって文化財保護行政に寄与した。

和亭　滝和亭。タキカテイ（1830-1901）。江戸末期から明治中期まで活躍した南画家。内国絵画共進会に出品、入選、のちに政府主催展覧会の審査官、帝室技芸員となる。美術史学者滝精一の父。

金岡　→ 巨勢金岡（コセのカナオカ）

迦諾迦伐蹉　カニャカバッサ。尊者。羅漢の一人。フェノロサはカナカダイサと誤読している。

狩野 □□（116）

狩野 □□（251）

狩野 □□（257）

狩野（氏）→ 永悳（エイトク）

狩野伊川　→伊川（イセン）
狩野雅楽助（100）　カノウウタノスケ（生没年不詳）。狩野派初代正信の子で、元信の弟と言う。狩野之信（ユキノブ）の別名。
狩野永徳（181）　→　永徳
狩野永徳高信（38）　→　永徳高信
狩野永悳　永悳
狩野永納（174）　カノウエイノウ（1631-1697）　江戸前期の画家。狩野山雪の長男。山雪没後、狩野安信の門に入って画法を学ぶ。元禄10年（1697）父の遺稿を撰して日本最初の画人伝・絵画史『本朝画史』を刊行した。
狩野孝信（217）　カノウタカノブ（1571-1618）　狩野永徳の次男で探幽・尚信・安信の父。長男探幽は江戸に出て幕府奥絵師鍛冶橋狩野家の祖、次男は同木挽町狩野家の祖となった。三男の安信は狩野宗家第8代を継ぎ、中橋狩野家の祖となった。
狩野休円（235）　カノウキュウエン（1641-1717）。狩野休円清信。江戸中期の画家。狩野松栄の末子休伯長信の末子。麻布一本松狩野家の祖。
狩野寿石敦信（206）　カノウジュセキアツノブ（1717-1778）。狩野永徳高信の門人。猿屋町代地狩野家第三代。
狩野助信（21）　カノウスケノブ（1810-1831）。浜町狩野家の融川寛信の次男。
狩野晴川（34、35、130、239）　カノウセイセン（1796-1846）。狩野晴川養信（オサノブ）。木挽町狩野家第九代。第八代伊川栄信の長男で永悳の祖父に当る。絵画のほか和歌に長じた。
狩野探信守道（27）　カノウタンシンモリミチ（1786-1835）。鍛冶橋狩野家第七代（探牧守邦の長男）。
狩野（探美）　守貴カノウタンビモリタカ（1840-1893）。鍛冶橋狩野家第十代。第八代探淵守真の次男。維新後宮内省などに勤務、また絵画共進会等の審査官を務めた。フェノロサとは狩野派の研究、粉本の譲渡などを通じて親交を結んだ。
狩野探牧　→探牧
狩野探幽　→探幽
狩野周信　→（チカノブ）
狩野常信　→常信（ツネノブ）
狩野洞春　→洞春（トウシュン）
狩野洞白（194）　カノウトウハク（1772-1821）。狩野洞白愛信。駿河台狩野家第五代。
狩野友信　→友信（トモノブ）
狩野尚信　→尚信（ナオノブ）
狩野光信（228）　カノウミツノブ（1565-1608）。安土桃山時代の画家、画をもって秀吉、家康に仕えた。狩野永徳の長男。狩野宗家代六代。

狩野岑信（56、242、258） カノウミネノブ（1662-1708）木挽町狩野家第２代常信の次男で、のちに浜町狩野家（幕府奥絵師）の初代となり随川院と号した。

狩野元信 →元信（モトノブ）。

狩野祐清英信 →英信（テルノブ）

狩野融川寛信（136） カノウユウセンヒロノブ（1778-1815）。本文中□は寛（ヒロ）。江戸後期、浜町狩野家第五代。城中にて老中阿部豊後守と画法を論じて逆鱗に触れ、帰路輿中にて自刃、享年46歳。

狩野養川 →養川（ヨウセン）

夏明遠 カメイエン（生没年不詳）。中国、明末清初の画家。楼閣図を能くした。

川崎 川崎千虎・カワサキチトラ（1835-1902）。幕末・明治の土佐派出身の画家で有職故実に詳しかった。内務省、大蔵省を経て宮内省博物館御用掛等を歴任し、のちに東京美術学校（現東京藝大）教授を務めた。フェノロサの蒐集古画鑑定メンバーの一人。

顔輝（73、111、138） ガンキ（生年不詳）。中国元初（13世紀末期）の画家。道釋画に秀作を残した。

岸駒（12、80、87、121、154、159、163、164） ガンク（1749-1838）。江戸後期の画家。金沢に生まれ京都で活躍。南蘋派、円山派、四条派を折衷して独自の新画体を創造した。岸派の祖。

神田 不明。神田孝平（カンダタカヒラ、1830-1898）か。幕府の蛮書調所に出仕、維新後明治政府の官僚として外国事情の調査に従事、また明六社に参加して西欧文化の啓蒙紹介に務めた。

韓退之 カンタイシ（768-824）。中国中唐の儒者・文人韓愈（カンユ）。白居易と並び称された詩人。憲宗皇帝の忌諱に触れ、地方の役人に左遷されたことがあった。

岸礼（216） ガンレイ（1816-1883）。江戸後期〜明治の画家。岸駒の長男岸岱（ガンタイ）の次男。

キ

徽宗皇帝（48） キソウコウテイ（1082-1135）。徽宗は中国北宋の第八代皇帝。書画・音楽を愛し、画院の充実に専念、自らも花鳥・山水画を制作した。政治には熱心でなく、北方の金軍に捕らえられて満洲で没した。

義董（93、201、202） ギトウ（1780-1819）。柴田義董。江戸中期の画家。四条派の祖松村呉春の高弟で山水画に長じた。

琦鳳（141） キホウ（?-1852）。河村琦鳳。江戸後期の画家。岸駒の弟子河村文鳳の養子。嘉永5年没。

木村永光（150） キムラナガミツ（生没年不詳）。豊臣秀吉の家臣で狩野山楽の父。狩野元信に学んで花鳥画を能くしたという。

暁斎 キョウサイ（1831-1889）。河鍋暁斎。幕末明治期の画家。駿河台狩野派の出身

で洞郁の名を与えられたが、単に狩野派に留まらず和漢すべての流派に通じた。浮世絵、風刺画も巧みで狂斎と号したが明治初年筆禍事件で逮捕収監されたのち暁斎と改めた。フェノロサ蒐集品鑑定メンバーの一人。

玉樂 (188)　ギョクラク (生没年不詳)。狩野玉樂。室町後期の画家。元信門下。画をもって北条氏政に仕えたという。一説に、元信の姪にあたる女流画家という。

清信 (131)　キヨノブ (1641-1717)。狩野休円清信。江戸初期の画家。狩野松栄直信の五男休白長信の子。

金玉仙 (58)　キンギョクセン (生没年不詳)。狩野元信を師として人物花鳥画を能くしした戦国時代の絵師。北条氏政の画師であった。

キング　不明。キン (金) か。古美術商。

ク

九鬼氏　九鬼隆一 (クキリュウイチ、1852-1931)。文部官僚で美術行政の中核。のちに岡倉覚三・フェノロサの上司として帝国博物館総長を務め文化財調査に携わった。

君澤　→孫君澤

ケ

藝阿弥 (179) ゲイアミ (1431-1485)。室町時代後期、足利義政に仕えた同朋衆で水墨画を能くした。法名真藝。能阿弥の子で相阿弥の父。

邢和璞　ケイカボク (正しくはおケイカハク) 唐代玄宗皇帝時代の仙人でしばしば死者を蘇らせたという。終南山に庵を結んで道を説いた。弟子に崔曙 (サイショ) がいた。

K・K・K 不明。起立工商会社の頭文字か．→工商会社

啓書記 (105、109)　ケイショキ (生没年不詳)。室町時代、鎌倉・建長寺の禅僧・画僧であった賢江祥啓。寺の書記だったので啓書記と呼ばれた。藝阿彌に師事し山水画に巧みであった。

景文 (107、108)　松村景文 (マツムラケイブン、1779-1843)。江戸後期、京都の画家。呉春の末弟。画法を父に学んで花鳥を写生し、四条派の発展に寄与した。

源琦 (114)　駒井源琦 (コマイゲンキ、1747-1779)。江戸中期の画家。姓は駒井、名は琦だが、氏が源なので源琦と署名した。応挙の高弟。

元旦 (39)　ゲンタン・島田元旦 (1778-1840)。江戸後期の画家で、一説に文晁の弟という。

玄也 (243)　ゲンヤ (生没年不詳)。安土桃山時代の画家、狩野元信の門人という。経歴不詳。

コ

興以　コウイ（?-1636）狩野興以。安土桃山〜江戸初期の画家。足利に生れ、狩野光信の高弟で、興甫、興也の父。紀州徳川家に仕え、後に法眼に叙せられた。

孔寅（52）　コウイン（1765-1849）。長山孔寅、秋田の人、大阪に出て松村月渓の門に入り花鳥画を描いた。

香雲（97）　コウウン（生没年不詳）。亀井香雲。明治期の女流画家。雲錦の娘。

公紀（6）　コウキ（1648-1670）。江戸後期、水戸藩主徳川光圀の養子徳川綱方（ツナカタ）の画号。家督相続前に死去したので弟綱條（ツナエダ）が藩主を嗣いだ。

古永徳　コエイトク → 永徳

呉春（117）　ゴシュン（1752-1811）。松村呉春。景文の兄。江戸後期の画家。与謝蕪村に南画を学び、のち円山応挙の影響を受けた。四条派の祖。

工商会社　起立工商会社（キリュウコウショウカイシャ）。明治9年政府出資で開設された美術工芸品製造輸出会社。参考品として古美術を蒐集したが外国人コレクターに売却してドル稼ぎに一役買った。

鴻池　鴻池善右衛門（コウノイケゼンエモン）。江戸時代からの大阪の豪商。十代目善右衛門（1841-1920）は版籍奉還・廃藩置県で貸金回収不能などの打撃を受け鴻池家をよく復興に導いた。

光琳　尾形光琳（オガタコウリン、1658-1716）江戸中期の京都の画家。光悦の風を慕い、また宗達に私淑して大和絵を革新し、琳派と呼ばれる独自の華麗な装飾画法を大成した。

呉小仙（67）　明代中期の画家呉偉（1459-1508）の号の一つ。中国明朝の画院に仕えた画家（小仙は号）。呂紀と並んで当時第一の山水画家だった。

巨勢有久　コセアリヒサ（生没年不詳）。鎌倉時代の巨勢派の画家。晩年には東寺の絵仏師となり、仏画を得意とした。

巨勢金岡（1）　コセノカナオカ（生没年不詳）。平安初期の宮廷画家。肖像画の名手だったと伝えられる。

巨勢源慶（1）　コセゲンケイ（生没年不詳）。鎌倉時代建仁年中（13世紀初期）の巨勢派の画家。

巨勢俊久（110）　コセトシヒサ（生没年不詳）。南北朝時代の巨勢派の画家。父惟久の業を継ぎ声明を堕さずと伝える。

コデラ氏　不明。国府寺新作（1855-1929）か。東京大学でフェノロサに習い明治13年卒業。哲学館、東京師範学校等で教壇に立った。

呉道子　ゴドウシ（生没年不詳）。玄宗皇帝に仕えた唐代随一と称される画家呉道元の別名。

古筆　コヒツ。古筆家は桃山時代末期の古筆了佐に始まる古筆鑑定の家柄。

古筆了伴　コヒツリョウハン（1790-1853）。江戸後期の古筆鑑定家、古筆家第十世。

嘉永6年没64歳。

コヨーシン（165） 不明。中国明代初期の画家か。

ゴンス Louis Gonse (1846-1921)。フランスの日本美術愛好家。『日本の美術』の著書（1883年刊行）あり。フェノロサは同年7月12日の英字紙"Japan Weekly Mail"にその絵画編について批評論文を寄稿している。

サ

崔曙 サイショ。中国唐代の文人。仙人邢和璞（ケイカハク）の友人だったと伝えられる。

サガキチ 不明。嵯峨吉？画商。

佐野氏 不明。佐野常民（サノツネタミ、1822-1902）か。政治家。大蔵卿、元老院議長等歴任。龍池会会頭で古美術蒐集家だった。

サンシモン・スティリテス （390?-459）。シリアの苦行者。アンティオキア附近で30年間、高さ16メートルの柱頭で苦行生活を営んだという。

山雪（193） サンセツ（1589-1651）。狩野山雪。江戸前期、京狩野家狩野山樂の養子。永納の父。

山楽 サンラク（1559-1635）。狩野山楽。安土桃山～江戸初の画家。秀吉にの小姓だったが画才を認められて狩野永徳の門に入り、狩野姓を与えられた。徳川幕府に仕えず、京都に留まって社寺の障壁画を描き、京狩野家の祖となった。

シ

司馬江漢 シバコウカン（1747-1818）江戸後期の画家。西洋画の影響を受けて油絵による風景画を描き、また日本で初めてエッチングを試みた。

下田氏 不明。

秋暉（72） シュウキ（1807-1862）。岡本秋暉。江戸末期の画家。大西圭斎、渡辺崋山に学んで柔らかな感じの花鳥画を描いた。

秋月（14） 秋月等観（シュウゲツトウカ、生没年不詳）。室町時代の画僧で雪舟の弟子。

周信 →チカノブ

周文（102、135） シュウブン（生没年不詳）。室町時代、京都相国寺の禅僧・画僧。兆殿司や如拙の築いた漢画的水墨山水を日本的様式に完成させた。室町幕府の御用絵師。雪舟の師。

綬帯鳥 ジュタイチョウ。吉祥の鳥。

松栄（176） ショウエイ（1519-1592）。室町末期、将軍足利義輝に仕えた狩野直信。薙髪して松栄と号した。狩野元信の三男。永徳の父。

松花堂（223） ショウカドウ（1584-1639）。松花堂昭乗。江戸初期、寛永三筆と称された書家。京都男山滝本坊の僧で、水墨画、大和絵にも長じた。

勝川 (262)　ショウセン（1823-1880）。狩野勝川雅信（タダノブ）。幕末〜明治初期の木挽町狩野家第十代。芳崖、雅邦らの師。

常川幸信 (132)　ジョウセンユキノブ（1717-1770）。狩野幸信。江戸中期の画家。浜町狩野家第三代。

蕭白 (180、227)　曽我蕭白（ソガショウハク、1730-1781）。江戸中期の画家。蛇足軒と自称し、自由奔放な画風で世人を驚かした。

所翁　ショオウ（生没年不詳）。中国南宋末期の画家陳容。所翁はその号。龍の画家として知られる。

ジョージ・エメリー　George D. Emery（1853-1933）。米国マサチューセッツ州生まれの美術品蒐集家。メイン州サコ（Saco）美術館創設メンバーの一人。材木輸入業で産を成した。訪日年代不明。

鐘離権　ショウリケン。唐代の仙人（八仙の一人）。呂洞賓に仙術の書を授けたと伝えられ「鐘呂伝道」として画題となっている。

ス

嵩溪 (263)　スウケイ（1762-1817）。高久（タカク）嵩溪。江戸中期の画家。高久嵩谷の長男。

嵩谷 (113、191)　高久嵩谷・タカクスウコク（1730-1804）。江戸中期の画家。英一蝶の門人佐脇嵩之に学び、英派の名手と称された。

季頼 (171)　スエヨリ（?-1557）。狩野季頼。室町時代末期の画家。狩野元信の次男。秀頼とも書かれるが、『本朝画史』では「スエヨリ」としている。

住吉　住吉廣賢（スミヨシヒロカタ、1835-1883）。住吉派第八代。フェノロサの大和絵・仏画研究に協力した。蒐集品鑑定メンバーの一人。

セ

西王母（セイオウボ）中国神話の仙女。周の穆王（ボクオウ）が西に巡狩した時、瑶池で宴会を開き、漢の武帝に降臨して不老長寿の仙桃を与えたという。（→東方朔）

晴暉 (199)　セイキ（1793-1865）。横山晴暉。江戸後期の画家。松村景文の門人で花鳥画に優れていた。

清曠 (127)　セイコウ。岡島清曠（1828-1877）幕末、明治初期の画家。四条派横山清暉の門人。

西施　セイシ（生没年不詳）。中国春秋時代（BC770-403）の越の美女。→范蠡（ハンレイ）。

晴川　→狩野晴川養信

雪庵　→吉沢雪庵か

雪舟（16、61）　雪舟等楊（セッシュウトウヨウ、1420-1506）。室町時代の画僧。備中に生れ京都相国寺で修行、周文に画技を習った。47歳の時明に渡り水墨画を学ぶ。帰国して雄渾な自然描写で個性的な山水画を描き、後世に多大な影響を与えた。

雪村　雪村周継（セッソンシュウケイ、1504-1589）。戦国・安土桃山時代の画僧。常陸国佐竹氏の出身。武家を継がず僧となる。雪舟を慕い，宋元画を学んで個性の強い動的画風を立て室町末期の代表的画家となった。

雪鼎（212）　セッテイ（1710-1786）。月岡雪鼎。江戸中期の画家。初め高田敬甫に狩野派を学んだが、のち大阪に住し、風俗画に転じて叙情的な美人画を描いた。

銭舜挙　センシュンキョ（生没年不詳）中国、宋末元初の画家銭選。元の朝廷に仕えず、在野の文人画家として山水花鳥を描いた。王若水と共に作品が室町時代に舶載された。

セント期（109）　不明。セイトウ（盛唐）期の誤りか。

ソ

宋紫石（220）　ソウシセキ（1712-1786）。本姓楠本氏。熊代熊斐（クマシロユウヒ）から南蘋風の写生画を学び、また1758年清国から来朝した宋紫岩に師事して漢名を名乗った。

宋琳（20）　ソウリン（1781-1850）。紫岡（シコウ）宋琳。南蘋の系統を継ぐ宗紫山の子。文政12年から尾張藩のお抱え絵師となった。

曽我蕭亭（180）　蕭白の別号という。

狙仙（13、44、59、101、118、158）　ソセン（1749-1821）。森狙仙。江戸中・後期の画家。長崎に生れ大阪に住んだ。性甚だ猨を好み、猿を飼ってその動静喜怒の態を観察写生した（「狙」は猨の意）。狩野派に円山派を加味した写生画、とくに動物画を得意とした。

素川　ソセン（1820-1900）。狩野素川寿信。江戸末期〜明治の画家。猿屋町代地狩野家の末裔。

素川彰信（126）　ソセンアキノブ（1763-1826）。江戸中期。のちに章信と改名。性格豪放、酒を好み、吉原流連して数か月帰宅せず、遊女らに絵を教えていたという。

孫君澤（239）　ソンクンタク（生没年不詳）。元代の画家。南宋の院体画風を学び、室町時代の日本で大いに称賛された。

タ

太雅堂　池太雅（イケタイガ、1723-1776）。江戸中期の南画家。すぐれた構想、彩色、用筆によって日本的文人画を大成した。

大善　ダイゼン。東京の画商（伊丹善蔵創始）。

宅磨爲久（112）　タクマタメヒサ（生没年不詳）。平安末期の画家宅磨爲遠の次男。源頼朝の命で鎌倉に下り、寺院障壁画を描いたという。

田沢　田沢静雲。タザワセイウン（生没年不詳）。古美術商。古筆了仲に鑑定を学んだという。

孝信（217）　狩野孝信

ターナー　Turner（1775-1851）。英国の風景画家。光の色彩化を研究し、印象派に影響を与えた。

田中訥言　タナカトツゲン（1760-1813）。鎌倉時代の大和絵を研究して江戸末期に特色ある大和絵を復興させた（土佐派中興の名手と言われる）。復古大和絵派の祖。浮田一蕙の師。晩年失明し、自ら食を絶って死去した。

爲一　→北斎

探鯨（146）　タンゲイ（1688-1769）。鶴澤探鯨。江戸前期、探幽の門人鶴澤探山の子。

探原（259）　タンゲン（1679-1776）。木村探原守広。江戸中期、探幽の子探信守政に学び、故郷薩摩に帰って藩の画員となった。

探山（78）　タンザン（?-1655）。鶴澤探山。江戸前期の画家。探幽の高弟。

探信（63、169、221）　タンシン（1653-1718）。狩野探信守政。江戸初期の幕府奥絵師。探幽の長男。鍛冶橋狩野家第二代を継ぐ

探雪（129）　タンセツ（?-1714）。狩野探雪守定。探幽の次男。

探牧（249）　タンボク（1761-1833）。江戸後期、狩野探牧守邦。鍛冶橋狩野家第六代。

探幽（19、26、29、32、33、42、47、77、124、147、148、183、185、209）　タンユウ（1602-1674）。狩野探幽守信。狩野孝信の長男で尚信・安信の兄。幼時狩野派衰微の折り、興以の指導を受けて同派中興に導いた。京都から江戸に出て幕府御用絵師となり、鍛冶橋に屋敷を拝領し鍛冶橋狩野家の祖となった。江戸初期、狩野派を新時代に即した新様式に再編し、狩野派四大家の一人と称せられた。

チ

周信（200、240）　チカノブ（1660-1728）。狩野周信、如川と号す。常信の長男で木挽町狩野家第三代）。

竹洞（151）　チクトウ（1776-1853）。中林竹洞。江戸後期、山本梅逸と共に尾張から京都に出て活躍した文人画家。

鳥窠　チョウカ　中国唐代の禅僧。つねに老松の樹上に座し、カササギの巣の傍にいたので鳥窠の通称で呼ばれた。フェノロサはチョウソウと誤読している。

趙昌　チョウショウ（生没年不詳）。中国北宋後期の画家。色彩の豊かな写生風の花鳥を描いた。その作品が室町時代に舶載された。

兆殿司（55、192）　チョウデンス（1352-1431）。室町時代の画僧、諱は明兆。京都東

福寺に住して殿司（殿堂の職務一切の責任者）だったので兆殿司と呼ばれた。宋・元の画風を学び、多くの仏画や頂相（チンソウ）を描いた。

長柳斎（182） チョウリュウサイ（生没年不詳）。室町中期の画家。揚月と似た絵を描いた。布袋の墨画が得意だった。

直庵（149） チョクアン（生没年不詳）。曽我直庵二世。江戸初期の画家。曽我直庵の子で二直庵と呼ばれた。

沈南蘋（23、68） チンナンピン、シンナンピンとも（生没年不詳）。1731年から2年間長崎に滞在した清国の画家沈詮。精緻な写生画の技法を伝え、日本の花鳥画技法に大きな感化を及ぼした。

ツ

月岡雪斎（167） ツキオカセッサイ（?-1803）。江戸中期の画家。雪鼎の養子。

月岡雪鼎 → セッテイ

経隆 ツネタカ（生没年不詳）。土佐経隆。鎌倉中期の画家。父藤原光長に学んだ春日派の画家だったが、土佐権守に任じられて土佐を称したという。

常信（8、31、37、49、65、186、241） 狩野常信（カノウツネノブ、1636-1713）。江戸前期、木挽町狩野家の画家。尚信の子。探幽以来の諸流派の画法を統合して時代に即する作品を描き、元信、永徳、探幽と共に狩野派四大家と称せられる。入道して養朴と号した。

鶴沢探泉（128） ツルサワタンセン（生没年不詳）。江戸後期の皇室御用絵師。鶴沢探山の家系（探山、譚鯨、探索、探春、探泉と続いた）。

テ

徹山（57、87） テツザン（1775-1841）。森徹山。祖仙の甥で、養子となった。応挙門下十哲の一人に数えられ、動物画に長じた。義子に一鳳、門人に森寛斎がいる。

英信（248） テルノブ（1717-1763）。狩野祐清英信。江戸中期、狩野宗家第十一代。第十代将軍徳川家治の厚遇を受けた。

ト

道安（204） 山田道安（ヤマダドウアン、生没年不詳）。室町時代の武人画家。大和筒井氏の一族。初め周文、雪舟の画風を慕い、のちに宋画の影響を受けた。

洞雲（225） トウウン（1625-1694）。狩野洞雲益信。江戸前期、狩野探幽の門下。探幽に実子が生まれるまでその養子だった。のちに分家して駿河台狩野家を開いた。

洞益（260） トウエキ。→雲谷等益

東溪（72） トウケイ。別所東溪（生没年不詳）。江戸後期、京都在住の四条派画家。

東山 (74)　トウザン (1806-1876)。石垣東山。敦賀出身の画家、江戸末期〜明治前期の画家・俳人・歌人。山水、花鳥画を能くした。大阪で没。

洞春 (247)　トウシュン。狩野洞春義信 (?-1723) 駿河台狩野家第二代。

桃水 (219)　トウスイ (1841-1911)。久保田桃水。江戸末期〜明治の四条派画家。芳園、晴暉に学んだ。

東坡　トウバ (1036-1101)。中国北宋代の詩人蘇軾の号。王安石の新法に反対してしばしば地方に左遷された。「赤壁賦」の作者。蘇東坡とも号した。

洞文 (246)　トウブン (1501-1582)。土岐洞文。戦国時代の武人画家。美濃鷺山城主土岐政房の子。足利幕府滅亡後諸国を流浪。和歌に長じ画に巧みであった。画は周文の弟子小栗宗湛の門下であったという。

東圃 (3)　トウホ (生没年不詳)。村田東圃。江戸末期、嘉永年中の京都四条派の画家。

東方朔　トウボウサク (BC154-BC90 頃) 中国前漢時代の文人。武帝に仕えたが後世仙人と見做され、西王母の植えた桃の実を盗んで食べ、8000 年の寿命を得た、などの説話を残した。フェノロサの解説とは齟齬している。

洞琳由信 (134)　トウリンヨシノブ (?-1820)。狩野由信。江戸後期、猿屋町代地狩野家の画家。

徳川茂栄　トクガワモエイ (1831-1884)。明治維新後、新政府と交渉した徳川氏の代表的存在。旧尾張藩主時代は茂徳 (モチノリ) と称したが、慶應2年一ツ橋家を継いで茂栄 (モチハルと読む) を名乗った。

土佐光文 (229)　トサミツアヤ (1812-1879)。幕末〜明治初期の土佐派の画家 (第二十五代)。光孚 (ミツザネ) の次男。川崎千虎の師。

土佐光起 (10、60、198)　トサミツオキ (1617-1691)。江戸中期、保守的な土佐派に狩野派の画風を加えて土佐派を再興。宮廷の繪所預を任じられた。江戸の探幽と妙を競ったという。

土佐光茂 (106)　トサミツシゲ (生没年不詳)。室町時代の土佐派を代表する画家だが、父光信を形式化した作品が多いとされる。

土佐光忠 (215)　トサミツタダ。江戸末期の画家。生没年、経歴等不祥。

土佐光成 (205)　トサミツナリ (1646-1710)。江戸時代土佐派中興の妙手土佐光起の長男。父の画法を忠実に守った。

土佐光芳 (252)　トサミツヨシ (1700-1772)。江戸前期、曽祖父光起、祖父光成と共に土佐派の名手と言われた。

杜子美　トシビ (712-770)。中国唐代の詩人杜甫。李白と共に中国の代表的詩人とされる。40歳を越えて仕官したが、のち官を捨て家族を連れて各地を放浪した。風雅沈痛の生涯がしばしば画材とされた。

訥言　トツゲン → 田中訥言。

友信 (17)　トモノブ (1843-1912)。狩野友信。幕末・明治期、浜町狩野家の後裔。開

成学校・東京大学予備門で画学の教員を務め、フェノロサ赴任以来同僚となって古画を模写し、その研究を助けた。フェノロサ蒐集品鑑定メンバーの一人。

豊国（213） トヨクニ（1786-1864）。浮世絵師歌川国貞（クニサダ）。初代歌川豊国の門人で豊国を襲名し亀戸豊国と呼ばれた。妖艶な美人画を描き幕末の浮世絵界をリードした。

豊彦（166） トヨヒコ（1773-1845）。岡本豊彦。江戸後期の京都の画家。呉春に学び、景文と共に四条派の双璧と称された。塩川文麟や柴田是真の師。

呑舟（162、230） ドンシュウ（?-1857）。大原呑舟。江戸後期、天保頃の画家。四条派の柴田義董に学び、山水・人物に巧みであった。北海道松前で客死した大原呑響の一子。

ナ

尚信（168、253） ナオノブ（1607-1650）。狩野尚信。江戸前期、狩野孝信の三男。兄探幽、弟安信と共に狩野興以に育てられた。江戸に出て幕府の御用絵師（奥絵師）となり、木挽町に屋敷を構えた。木挽町狩野家の祖。兄探幽と並び称される逸材であったが中年にて没した。

中井藍江 → 蘭江（ランコウ）

中島来章（145） ナカジマライショウ（1796-1872）。江戸後期、応挙の長男円山応瑞の門人となった京都の画家。当時横山清暉、岸連山、塩川文麟と共に平安四名家と称された。明治画壇の大家とされる幸野楳嶺、川端玉章らの師。

南岳（211） ナンガク（1767-1813）。渡辺南岳。応挙門下の京都の画家。光琳に私淑し、その装飾的画法を取り入れて円山派の一画風を作った。晩年江戸に出て円山派を関東に伝えた。

南蘋 → 沈南蘋（チンナンピン）

ニ

ニシオバンキチ 不明。西尾□□（?）

西川祐信（222） ニシカワスケノブ（1671-1751）。江戸中期、上方の浮世絵師。初め狩野派、土佐派に学び、のち菱川師宣の画風を取り入れて優美な美人画を描いた。

西洞院入道（6） ニシノトウインニュウドウ。西洞院家は京都の公卿。江戸時代初期の西洞院時成（1645-1724）か。享保9年80歳で没した。

西村 不明。京都の西村家か。西村治兵衛（1860-1910）は京都の織物業者。上賀茂神社社家の一つに西村別邸がある。

西山芳園 → 芳園

二直庵（ニチョクアン） → 直庵

日華（64、208） ニッカ（?-1845）。田中日華。江戸末期四条派の画家。岡本豊彦の高弟。

蜷川氏　蜷川式胤（ニナガワノリタネ、1835-1882）。太政官、内務省、文部省博物局等に勤務した古物学者。『観古図説』『徴古図説』などの著者。フェノロサ蒐集品鑑定メンバーの一人。

ネ

然可翁　ネンカオウ（?-1345）。可翁宗然。京都建仁寺の禅僧。→可翁

ノ

野村　野村重治（生没年不詳）か。柏木貨一郎と共に内務省博物局の職員だった。のちも終始博物館諸課を歴任した。

ハ

梅逸(76、144)　バイイツ（1783-1856）。山本梅逸。江戸後期の画家。尾張名古屋に生れ、中林竹洞と共に画業に励んだ。のち京都に出で南画を研究。花鳥、山水の文人画家として名声を得た。

馬遠　バエン（生没年不詳）。夏珪と並ぶ南宋の院体山水画の代表者。「残山剰水」と呼ばれるその画風は夏珪の「墨汁淋漓」と共に室町時代の画壇に大きな影響を与えた。

馬逵　バキ（生没年不詳）。中国南宋の画家。その作品は室町時代に明から舶載された。

馬元欽(39)　バゲンキン（生没年不詳）。清朝の画家。字は典欽。フェノロサは元代の画家としている。

長谷川氏　長谷川雪堤（ハセガワセッテイ、1819-1882）。雪舟派の末流。長谷川雪旦の子。父に学び、筆力また劣らずと称された。フェノロサ蒐集品鑑定メンバーだったが、明治15年に死去した（64歳）。

長谷川等伯(245)　ハセガワトウハク（1539-1610）。安土桃山時代の画家。京都で狩野派を学び、また雪舟に傾倒して宋・元の漢画を研究して一様式を開いた。

蜂須賀　蜂須賀茂韶（ハチスカモチアキ、1846-1918）旧阿波徳島藩主。維新後、英国留学から帰国し外務省、大蔵省を経て明治15年からフランス公使となった。侯爵。

晩山(95)　バンザン（1834-?）。中村晩山。江戸後期〜明治期の画家。経歴不明、没年不詳。

范蠡　ハンレイ（生没年不詳）。中国春秋時代の越の功臣。呉王夫差（フサ）と会稽で戦って敗れた越王勾践（コウセン）を助けて夫差を討った。勾践を滅ぼす手段として越の美女西施（セイシ）を夫差に献じ、夫差は色に溺れて国を滅ぼしたという。范蠡が西施を説得する面画が画題となった。

ヒ

百谷（237）　ヒャッコク（1785-1862）。小田百谷。小田海僊の別号。江戸後期、松村呉春に学び、また中国元・明の古画を研究して一家をなした。頼山陽の友人。

フ

武禅（195）　スミエブゼン（墨江武禅、1734-1806）。月岡雪鼎に学んだ画家。

蕪村　ブソン（1716-1783）。与謝蕪村。江戸中期の俳人・画家。池太雅と『十便宜図』を合作するなど、文人画家の代表者。

ブルックス　Phillips Brooks（1835-1893）。ボストン監督教会の牧師。モースの親日演説に刺戟され1889年に訪日した。

ブンオウ（103）　不明。文晁の弟子ブンヨウ（遠阪文雍）の誤りと思われる。

文観上人　ブンカンショウニン（1278?-1357）。鎌倉時代の醍醐寺座主、東寺の長者。能く仏像を描き筆跡非凡にして画家も及ばざるものありと伝えられる。

文晁（4、7、11、36、91、115）　ブンチョウ（1763-1840）。谷文晁。江戸時代後期の画家。諸流派の画法を取り入れ、独自の南画を完成して江戸文人画壇で重きをなした

文雍（103）　ブンヨウ（遠坂文雍、1783-1852）。江戸後期の南画家。谷文晁の門弟で吉沢雪庵の師。

文麟（51、104、123、218）　ブンリン（1808-1877）。塩川文麟。幕末・明治初期の画家。四条派の岡本豊彦に学び南画的手法をも採り入れて叙情的な山水画を描いた。

ホ

抱一（46、142）　ホウイツ（1761-1828）。酒井抱一。江戸後期の画家。姫路城主酒井忠以（タダザネ）の次男で本名忠因（タダナオ）。各種の才芸に富み、絵は特に尾形光琳に傾倒して『光琳百図』を刊行。37歳で西本願寺に入って出家し、画道に専念した。江戸琳派の代表格。

ホイーラー　William Wheeler（1851-1932）。マサチューセッツ農科大学出身。1876年（明治9年）クラークに従って札幌農学校に赴任、土木工学、数学を教えた（ホイレル先生の名で親しまれた）。79年11月まで滞日。

法印古川　ホウインコセン。古川は狩野常信の号の一つ。晩年、法印に叙せられた。

芳園（157、177、184、254）　ホウエン（1804-1867）。西山芳園。江戸時代後期の画家。松村景文に四条派を学び、人物・花鳥画に優れた。

北斎（99、139、190）　ホクサイ（1760-1849）。葛飾北斎。江戸後期の画家。隅田川の東岸葛飾に生れた。浮世絵師だが狩野派、土佐派、琳派、西洋画などあらゆる画法を学んで一家を成した。狩野派からは異端視される。

マ

正信　マサノブ（1434-1530）。狩野正信。元信の父。室町幕府の御用絵師となり狩野派の基礎を作った。

又兵衛　マタベエ（1578-1650）。江戸初期の画家岩佐勝以（カツモチ）。秀吉に仕えた武将荒木村重の子。土佐派・狩野派などを学び独自の画法による風俗画を描いた。フェノロサは又平（マタヘイ）と呼び、当時の説に従って浮世絵の元祖と思っている。

松浦　松浦九兵衛（生没年不詳）か。鑑定家。のちに帝国博物館（現東博）美術工芸部に勤務している。

松尾　松尾儀助（マツオギスケ、1839-1902）。起立工商会社社長。佐賀の茶商だったがウィーン万国博で副総裁だった大隈重信に同行して渡欧したのが契機となっての起用だった。

松平 (11)　松平定教（マツダイラサダノリ、1857-1899）。明治13年の観古美術会に文晁の『豆相海岸真景画巻』を出品している。桑名藩知事を経て明治7年から5年間米国留学、帰国後外務省書記官となった。

松村景文　→景文

萬里　マデの和尚、萬里小路（マデノコウジ）。江戸前期の公卿、葉室頼業。漆桶と号し詩文を能くした。別号を梅花無尽蔵と言った。延宝3年（1675年）没61歳。

萬寿 (119)　マンジュ（生没年不詳）。江戸後期（化政期）、京都の画家吉岡茂喬の画号。

ミ

三保（ミオ、ミホ）　静岡市南東部の海岸。白砂青松、羽衣伝説、冨士の景観で知られる景勝地。

岑信　→狩野岑信。

美濃 (25)　ミノ。旧国名。現在の岐阜県東南部

箕面 (82)　ミノオ。大阪府北西部の丘陵、箕面川渓谷の景勝地。紅葉・大滝などでなどが親しまれた。

宮塚　ミヤツカ。不明。

モ

望月玉川 (9)　モチヅキギョクセン（1794-1852）。江戸時代後期の画家。玉仙の子。幼くして父に死別し、岸駒に入門し、四条派を学び、かつ京都から江戸・長崎に遊学して研鑽。祖父玉蟾以来の望月派の画風を一変した。

望月玉泉 (96)　モチヅキギョクセン（1834-1913）。幕末明治期、京都の画家。画法を父の玉川に学び一家を成す。京都画学校の建設に尽力し、のちに帝室技芸員になった。

- **牧谿**　モッケイ（生没年不詳）。中国宋末元初の頃の画僧。日本では早くから知られ、水墨画に多大な影響を与えた。
- **元信**（15、43、120、152、172）　モトノブ　狩野元信（1476-1559）。室町後期の画家。狩野派の始祖正信の長男で狩野派第2世。漢画様式に大和絵技法を取り入れて新様式を大成し、桃山障壁画の基礎を確立した。
- **守景**（173、226、231）　モリカゲ（生没年不詳）。久隅守景。江戸初期、元禄年間に活躍した画家。探幽の門下で人物画、花鳥画に優れた。

ヤ

- **安信**（85、156）　ヤスノブ（1613-1685）。狩野永真安信。江戸初期の画家。孝信の第三子（長兄守信＝探幽、次兄尚信）、京都の狩野宗家第八代を継いだが、のち江戸に出て幕府から中橋（旧ブリッヂストン美術館の南西隣のあたり）に屋敷を拝領した。中橋狩野家の祖。
- 山田道安　→道安
- **山名**　ヤマナ。山名貫義（ヤマナツラヨシ、1836-1902）。幕末・明治の住吉派画家。住吉広賢の養父弘貫の門人で古画の鑑識にすぐれ、また1893年のシカゴ万博に源氏絵の金屏風を出品している。東京美術学校（現東京藝大）教授、帝室技芸員等に任じられた。
- **山中**　山中商会。大阪高麗橋に本店をもつ古美術商山中吉郎兵衛。のちに女婿山中定次郎（1866-1936）によって国際的古美術商社に発展する。

ユ

- **ユウセイ**（137）　狩野祐清（英信の別名）か、友清（狩野常信の次男、随川峰信の号）か不明。
- 友川助信　ユウセンスケノブ→狩野助信
- **幽汀**　ユウテイ（1721-1786）。石田幽汀。江戸中期、鶴澤探鯨に学び、緻密な装飾画風の作品を残した。応挙の最初の師と言われる。
- **雪信**（133、214、261）　ユキノブ（1642-1681）。清原雪信。江戸前期の女流画家。久隅守景の娘。狩野探幽の妹の孫。近古閨秀画家中第一と称された。

ヨ

- **揚月**（256）　ヨウゲツ（生没年不詳）。室町時代、山城笠置寺の画僧。画法を雪舟に学び墨画は牧谿の画風を修めた。山水花鳥画を能くし、筆法は粗放だが柔潤の体ありと言われた。百済に渡って日本の山水を描いたという。
- **容斎**（210）　ヨウサイ（1788-1878）。菊池容斎。幕末・明治初期の画家。有職故実を研究し、著書『前賢故実』（肖像入り歴史人物伝）によって歴史画に新生面を開いた。

養川（**81、86、175、236**）　ヨウセン（1753-1808）。狩野養川惟信（コレノブ）。伊川の父。江戸中期、木挽町狩野家第七代。

揚冨（**187**）　ヨウフ（生没年不詳）。室町時代の画僧。雪舟に学び、山水画、達磨を得意とした。

吉沢雪庵　ヨシザワセツアン（?-1889）。浅草在住の日本画家。遠坂文雍に学び山水花鳥図を描いた。明治13年にほゞ80歳という。

甫信（**125**）　ヨシノブ（1692-1745）。狩野随川甫信。江戸時代中期の画家。常信の第三子（浜町狩野岑信の弟）。

豫譲（**155**）　ヨジョウ（生没年不詳）。中国戦国時代（晋代BC5世紀）の義人。智伯に仕えて重用されたが、智伯が襄子に殺されたのち復讐を図り、身に漆を塗って癩者の姿となり、炭を飲んで聾唖者となって機会を窺ったが、捕えられて自刃した。

ラ

來章（**145**）　ライショウ　→　中島来章。

ライマン　Benjamin Smith Lyman（1835-1920）米国の地質学者、鉱山学者。1872年北海道開拓吏に招かれて来日し地質調査に当り、のち工部省に転じた。1881年帰国。

蘭溪（**25**）　ランケイ（生没年不詳）。菅原蘭溪（落款にば山陰邉史蘭溪菅原栄）。江戸末期の画家。本作は安政6年に描かれている。

藍江（**22、94**）　ランコウ（1766-1830）。中井藍江。江戸後期、京狩野の系統をひく画家。詩文、茶道にも長じたという。

ランシーア　Landseer（1802-1873）。英国の動物画家。

リ

李長（**82**）　リチョウ（生没年不詳）。石橋李長。江戸後期、京都派の画家。

呂洞賓　リョドウヒン（生没年不詳）　唐代の伝説的人物呂祖（リョソ）の別名。宋、元、明の各王朝に出現したと伝えられ、八仙の一人として尊崇された。→鐘離権（ショウリケン）

呂紀（**161**）　リョキ（生没年不詳）。中国明代孝宗帝頃（15世紀後期）の画家。桃山時代の装飾画に大きな影響を与えた。

レ

連山（**54**）　レンザン（1802-1859）。岸連山。江戸後期の画家。岸駒の女婿となって岸家を継いだ。明治期に活躍した岸竹堂は連山の女婿（養子）。

ワ

若井氏　ワカイカネサブロウ・若井兼三郎（1834-1908）。もと書画骨董商。起立工商
　　　会社副社長に起用され、のちに独立し林忠正と共に美術品輸出事業に携わった。

渡邊崋山　→崋山（カザン）

おもな参考文献

樋口文山編『日本美術　画家人名評伝』優美館（大阪）明治26年
狩野壽信 編『本朝画家人名辞書』明治44年　大倉書店（東京）
森　大狂 編 『近古藝苑叢談』巧藝社（東京）　大正15年
杉原夷山 編『日本書画人名辞書』秀文館（大阪）昭和15年改訂増補版
斎藤隆三 著『画題辞典』博文館（東京）大正10年
関　衛 著『大日本絵画史』厚生閣（東京）昭和9年
野間清六・谷信一 編『日本美術辞典』東京堂（東京）昭和27年
佐藤靄子著『日本名画家伝・物故篇』青蛙房（東京）昭和42年
細野正信 著『江戸狩野と芳崖』小学館（東京）昭和53年
秋山光和他 編『世界美術辞典』新潮社（東京）昭和60年

口絵について

《寿老人図》 作品番号 17
狩野春川友信 (1843-1912) 筆　174.2×86.3 cm　紙本墨画彩色　MFA:11.4962
　友信は幕府奥絵師浜町狩野家最後の当主、維新後は禄を離れ、東京開成学校・東京大学予備門の画学教師となっていた。大学文学部に赴任したフェノロサは予備門にも出講したので友信とは同僚であり、絵画史研究には絶好の指導者（フェノロサより10歳年長）となった。本作品は、「梅下寿老人」ないし「梅潜り寿老人」の名で知られた蜂須賀家所蔵の《寿老人図》を、1880年フェノロサの依頼で摸写したもの。作品の来歴、フェノロサの評価基準も興味深いが、フェノロサの聞いた秀吉朝鮮出兵の話は、この事件に対する当時の日本人の見解を覗かせるものとして注目される。
　雪舟の原作は重要文化財として東京国立博物館に所蔵されている。

《雲龍図》 作品番号 59
森狙仙 (1749-1821) 筆　104.3×38.2cm　絹本墨画　MFA:11.4155.
　狙仙は猿のさまざまな姿態を描いた画家。フェノロサも、優れた動物画家と認めていたが、写実の域を出ない、応挙や岸駒より一段ランクの低い画家と考えていた。ところがこの《雲龍図》を山中商会から購入して以来、狙仙評価が一変する。崇高で迫力に満ちた構成、墨の濃淡の優美な表現、曲線の形作る壮麗な構図、といった最大級の賛辞を連ねて激賞し「前世紀最大の革新的画家」と称揚している。
　狙仙は初め狩野派に学び、のちに円山派の写生的画風を採り入れて一家を成した（森徹山は狙仙の甥、森一鳳は徹山の養子、森寛斎は徹山の門人）。

《鹿図》双幅　作品番号 42
狩野探幽 (1602-1674) 筆　143.7×80.4 cm　絹本墨画彩色　MFA:11.4796 11.4825
白鹿に竹、赤鹿に桜を配した探幽の双幅。第1幅の賛により筆者60歳の作と知れる。フェノロサは蒐集品の出来栄えを第1級から第3級に分類したが、本作品を第1級の中でも最高の部類に入るものと激賞した。彼が感動したのは何よりも先ず作品に漂う「気品」にあった。
　友信はじめ狩野派の絵師たちに囲まれていたフェノロサは、自ずから狩野派の最も重視する「気韻生動」の有無を評価の基準とする画論に染まっていたようだ。探幽は江戸初期、幕府に招かれ最初に江戸に移って幕府莫専属の御用絵師（奥絵師）となった。本作は幕府の什宝として代々徳川家伝えられたが、幕府崩壊時に市中に流出したものという。

《韃靼人狩猟図》双幅　作品番号 43
狩野元信（1476-1558）筆　163.3×92.1 cm　紙本墨画彩色　MA:11.4265 -4266

フェノロサが元信山水画の最高作と絶賛し、鑑定した評者も全員賛同した作品。「韃靼」は「タタール」の中国語訳だが、古来「蒙古」の別称だった。騎乗の韃靼人が野馬を捉えようと山野を駆け巡る絵図は、恐らく室町時代の対明貿易で舶載されたものであろう。その勇壮雄大な情景は戦国の武将たちに愛好され、室町末期から江戸初期の狩野派の画家はこれらを模して屏風や襖絵に仕立て、彼らの求めに応じた。元信筆と伝えられる本図の作者をMFAでは「狩野元信派」と紹介している。他にも元信印のある《韃靼人狩猟図》を所蔵しており（ビゲロウ・コレクション 11.6678）、断定を避けたものと思われる。しかしフェノロサがもと大徳寺の襖絵だったと回顧したように、最近の調査で大徳寺興臨院の襖絵だった可能性の高いことが指摘され（辻惟雄他編『MFA日本美術調査図録』）、ほゞ真蹟と言って間違いないようである。

　元信は東山殿と呼ばれた将軍足利義政の近侍として画事を司り狩野派の祖となった正信の嗣子。少年時代から天性の画才を発揮、東山殿没後は将軍義澄・義晴に仕える。青年期の宗元的画風が土佐光信（宮廷絵所預・幕府御用絵師）に認められて光信の娘と結婚、のちに土佐家の後見人として絵所預となり、大和絵と宗元画の調和を図って狩野派の基礎を固めた。

《白狐図》　作品番号 79
円山応挙 (1733-1795) 筆　120.2×70.6 cm　絹本墨画淡彩　MFA:11.4900
　夜霧に包まれ不気味な月光の中、亡霊のように浮かぶ白狐の突きさすような視線は、観る者を驚嘆させずにはおかない。写実を超え、妖狐の霊力を感じさせるこの作品を、フェノロサが応挙の第一級品としたのは当然だった。画面右下の落款「安永己亥仲冬写　応挙」により、安永8年（1879）11月、応挙47歳の作であったことが判る。
　この白狐は信太の森葛の葉の伝説を連想させる。或いは若いころ観た京都嵐松之丞座上演の歌舞伎「芦屋道満大内鑑」の強烈な印象が産んだ作品だったかもしれない。1913年MFA赴任中の岡倉天心はガードナー夫人のために葛の葉伝説を英文戯曲に仕立てた『白狐』を書いた。恐らく美術館で《白狐》を発見したのが機縁だったのであろう。(MFAでは現在、Formerly attributed to Maruyama Okyo とし、応挙作を疑問視している。)

《虎図》　作品番号 80
岸駒（1749-1838）筆　98.9×36.3 cm　絹本墨画淡彩　MFA:11.4698
　フェノロサの蒐集品には岸駒の虎図が数点あり、二曲屏風の虎を岸駒最高作とし本図をそれに次ぐ秀作としてその長所を列挙している。岸駒には虎や孔雀の絵が多い。当時長崎経由で京・大阪の見世物小屋に運ばれたこれら舶載の珍獣が人気を博し、写生に巧みな岸駒の絵を求める顧客の多かったことが推察される。
　岸駒は沈南蘋の画法を学び先輩諸家の長所を折衷して一生面を開いた画家で、とくに師に就くことなく応挙や呉春と比肩する京都画壇の代表者となった。子孫に岸岱・岸礼・岸連山、門人に河村文鳳・横山崋山、望月玉川らを擁する岸派の祖となった。

《鹿を狙う猟師》　作品番号 139
葛飾北斎（1760-1849）筆　42.8×58.8 cm　絹本墨画彩色　MFA:11.4601
　　数えるほどしか残っていない北斎肉筆画の1点。落款の「北斎翁」により北斎晩年作とフェノロサは推定するが、おそらく中年期の制作であろう。フェノロサはまた「油絵のような色彩と独特な筆法」と指摘したが、和漢諸流派の画法に通じた北斎は司馬江漢の銅版画を研究して西洋画の画法をも心得ていた。
　　北斎は19世紀後半ヨーロッパを風靡したジャポニスムの生みの親として特にフランスでは偉大な芸術家として絶大な評価を享けたが、当時の日本の画壇ではそれほどではなく、逆に「画技にのみ走って品格に欠ける、観る者に感動を与えない」と批判する批評家が多かった。狩野派の絵画論に由来するこの主張にフェノロサも公的には同調して1882年の『美術真説』では写実に過ぎると批判し、1884年には「ゴンス氏著『日本の美術』絵画篇批評」では著者の北斎激賞に反論している。しかしこの私的蒐集ノートにはそのような言辞はまったく見られない。逆に当初から北斎にはなみなみならぬ関心を寄せていたようで、帰国後MFAで開催された北斎展（1893年）、再来日して小林文七主催の北斎展（1900年）には詳細な解説文を著している。現在ワシントンのフリーアギャラリー所蔵北斎肉筆画は大部分がフェノロサの手を経たものという。

《雲龍図》双幅　作品番号 151
中林竹洞（1776-1853）147.3×57.7 cm. 147.3×57.5 cm　絹本墨画　MFA:11.4650-4651
　　所翁（南宋の画家陳所翁）は龍図の名手。その《九龍図巻》（MFA蔵 17.1697）は1900年代初期まではまだ日本に在り、最後は早崎稉吉（天心の助手、MFA嘱託）の有であったとする記録がある(斎藤隆三『画題辞典』)。フェノロサはそれを実見したのであろうか、本作を「画面に所翁摸写と記されているが形態はまったく異なり、画法はすべて独創的・・・おそらく竹洞の最優秀作ではないか」と称揚している。
　　竹洞は名古屋出身の画家。のちに京都に出て元明の画蹟を研究し、気韻の高い山水画を描いて京都文人画壇の一翼を担った。竹洞の「竹」は名古屋時代に同地大光院珍蔵の《竹図》（元代の画家李息斎筆）を見て啓発され、画号に用いたという。[※同じく名古屋出身で竹洞より7歳年少の山本梅逸も精妙な花鳥画を描いて京都文人画壇で名を挙げたが、若いころ名古屋大光院で明代画家王元章の《梅図》に感激し、「梅」逸と号して画技の上達を願ったと伝えられている。]

《白衣観音図》　作品番号 152
狩野元信（1476-1559）　157.2×76.4 cm　絹本墨画彩色　MFA:11.4267
　　本図は古来狩野元信筆の伝称があり、MFAでも「伝狩野元信」として断言を避けていたが、最近、山水部分の描法や尊像の表情、細部の手法など改めて検討された結果、十中八九真蹟に間違いないと結論され、「伝」の字が外れている。胡粉を塗った白衣に墨で衣文を描き装身具には金泥などを用いた堂々たる大作である。

この作品には辻惟夫氏と故秋山光和氏の解説がある。(『在外日本の至宝』第3巻、および同別冊『解説資料編』参照)

《双鹿図》 作品番号 164
岸駒 (1749-1838) 筆　167.3×86.6 cm　絹本墨画淡彩　MFA: 11.4701

　フェノロサが「世界の動物画中最優秀作」と讃えたこの作は、来日の1年後、まだ本格的に蒐集を始める以前に入手した逸品だった。この感想は彼の晩年まで変わることが無かった。以下は遺著 "Epochs of Chinese and Japanese Art" に述べられた回想である。

　…岸駒の最高の傑作は、疑いもなく、大幅の絹本に二匹の神鹿を精密に描いた図で、かつては私の秘宝であったが、いまはボストン美術館に収められている。私はこの画を、世界でもっとも優れた動物画の一つだと思っている。そこには、応挙も企てなかった西洋画風の手堅い仕上げと動きの描写がある。構図はきわめて美しく、二匹の頭部を結ぶとS字型を形成する。美しい夏景色が背景の烟霧のなかに輝いている。鹿の毛皮は穏やかな彩色のゆったりした描筆である。この画はルーベンス、ヨルダーンス、パウルス・ポッター、デューラーなどの動物画に匹敵する出来栄えであるといってよい。私はこの画を1879年に、その評価はおろか、岸駒の名も知らない一画商から買い取ったが、1882年以後、毎年上野に開催される美術クラブの展覧会に数回出陳し、天覧に供えるため宮中に差出したこともあり、織物商西村氏はこの図柄を染め出したビロード織の製作を試みている。(森東吾訳『東洋美術史綱』)

MFA 収蔵番号対照表

※S 番号は目録掲載の作品番号。
※画題は MFA 図録等現行の表記に準じた。
※画家名はフェノロサ、ないし同時代の鑑定による。
※寸法は縦×横 cm. 双幅、三幅対の二幅目、三幅目は省略した。

S 番号	画題・画家名・寸法・絹紙着彩の別	MFA 収蔵番号
001	地蔵菩薩図　伝巨勢金岡（鎌倉時代の作か）（即全摸写）87.7×37.3　絹本墨画彩色	11.4080
002	花鳥図（六幅）　尾口雲錦（明治初期）	
003	立葵に鶏図　村田東圃（江戸後期）131.8×44.1　絹本墨画彩色	11.4664
004	山水図　谷文晁（江戸後期）	
005	紅梅に白鷺図　大西圭斎（江戸後期）113.4×44　絹本墨画彩色	11.4793
006	百合鶏図　公紀＝徳川綱方（江戸前期）106.3×40.6　絹本墨画彩色	11.4741
007	岩に鷹図　谷文晁（江戸後期）	
008	琵琶をもつ弁天　狩野常信（江戸中期）	
009	寒山拾得図　望月玉川（江戸後期）132.4×56.2　絹本墨画彩色	11.4712
010	弁天図　土佐光起（江戸前期）118.5×60.8　絹本墨画彩色	11.4565
011	山中滝図　谷文晁（江戸後期）	
012	岩上虎図　岸駒（江戸後期）98.9×36.3　絹本墨画彩色	11.4698
013	樹間の猿　森狙仙（江戸中後期）	
014	寿老人に玄鹿図　秋月等観（室町時代）	
015	雪中野馬図　狩野元信（室町後期）	
016	漁村図　雪舟筆（江戸後期摸写）52.3×80.0　紙本墨画淡彩	11.4139
017	寿老人図　雪舟筆狩野友信模写（明治初期）174.2×86.3　紙本墨画彩色	11.4962
018	五条橋牛若図　浮田一蕙（江戸後期）105.0×34.2	11.4557
019	中国景観図　狩野探幽（江戸初期）	
020	牡丹図　宗琳＝宗紫岡（江戸後期）絹本墨画彩色　108×40.8	11.4672

021	隅田川春景図　狩野友川助信（江戸後期）絹本墨画彩色　62.7×92.7		11.4802
022	鯉魚図　中井藍江（江戸後期）139.3×71.3　絹本墨画淡彩		11.4660
023	狗子図　沈南蘋（江戸中期）79×95.5　絹本墨画彩色		11.4668
024	五大虚空蔵菩薩（江戸時代）97.4×84.1　絹本墨画彩色		11.4541
025	養老の滝真景図　菅原蘭渓（江戸末期）150.3×84.7 絹本墨画淡彩		11.4759
026	李白観瀑（三幅対）狩野探幽（江戸初期）		
027	唐人山荘景観図　狩野探信守道（江戸後期）		
028	邢和璞養蚕山水図（三幅対）狩野探信守道（江戸後期）120×45.6 絹本墨画彩色		11.4254 - 4256
029	寒山拾得（三幅対）狩野探幽（江戸初期）		
030	楼閣山水図（三幅対）　狩野伊川栄信（江戸後期）　119.4×53.3 絹本墨画彩色		11.4212 - 4214
031	三福神図（三幅対）　狩野常信（江戸中期）		
032	雲龍図（三幅対）　狩野探幽（江戸初期）　102.1×42.7　紙本墨画		11.4392 - 4394
033	維摩図（三幅対）狩野探幽（江戸初期）		
034	山水図（三幅対）　狩野晴川（江戸後期）　109.5×40.4　絹本墨画		11.4330 - 4332
035	寿老人鶴亀松竹梅図（三幅対）狩野晴川		
036	寿老人山水図（三幅対）谷文晁（江戸後期）		
037	牡丹に唐獅子図（双幅）狩野常信（江戸中期）130.8×67.7 絹本墨画彩色		11.4418 - 4419
038	龍に仙人図（三幅対）狩野永徳高信（江戸中期）		
039	蜀桟道図　島田元旦（江戸後期）160.4×97.1　絹本墨画彩色		11.4792
040	十羅漢図　画家名不明（江戸～明治前期）182.7×98.6　絹本墨画彩色		11.4646
041	白梅孔雀図　尾口雲錦（明治初期）159.7×98.6　絹本墨画彩色		11.4674
042	竹鹿桜図（双幅）　狩野探幽（江戸初期）143.7×80.4		11.4796・4825
043	韃靼人狩猟図（双幅）狩野元信（江戸初期）164.2×91.2　紙本彩色		11.4265 - 4266
044	猿図　森狙仙（江戸中・後期）		

045	梅の枝に小鳥図　尾口雲錦（明治初期）		
046	月に紅梅図　酒井抱一（江戸後期）		
047	山水図　狩野探幽（江戸初期）		
048	岩に白鷺　不明画家の模写（徽宗皇帝原作）		
049	紅白芙蓉図　狩野常信（江戸中期）95.5×43.9　絹本墨画彩色		11.4420
050	雪松に鷲図　尾口雲錦（明治初期）		
051	鐘馗図　塩川文麟（明治初期）174.2×86.3　絹本墨画彩色		114692
052	西王母図　長山孔寅（江戸後期）128.3×55.1　絹本墨画彩色		11.4740
053	狸図　森一鳳（江戸末・明治初期）107.3×42.1　絹本墨画彩色		11.4724
054	渡船風景図　岸連山（江戸末期）		
055	雲中文殊図　兆殿司＝明兆（室町時代）91.5×35.6　紙本墨画		11.4497
056	海棠に尾長鶏　狩野岑信（江戸前期）		
057	睡狐図　森徹山（江戸後期）103×42　紙本墨画彩色		11.4772
058	鐘馗図　金玉仙（室町時代）122.2×48.7　紙本墨画		11.4228
059	雲龍図　森狙仙（江戸中・後期）104.3×38.2　絹本墨画		11.4155
060	粟鶉図　土佐光起（江戸初期）29.4×41　絹本墨画彩色		11.4558
061	鐘馗騎驢図　雪舟（室町後期）34.5×70.5　紙本墨画		11.4137
062	岩上観音図　可翁（南北朝時代）		
063	七福神図　狩野探信（江戸前期）40.9×83.7　絹本墨画彩色		11.4727
064	雲龍図　田中日華（江戸後期）130.5×52.3　紙本墨画		11.4749
065	維摩図　狩野常信（江戸中期）		
066	岩に鷲図　雪村（室町後期）		
067	岩山に仙人図　呉小仙＝呉偉（明代中期）		
068	花鳥図（雉）沈南蘋（清代18世紀前期）		
069	蓮図　雲渓（室町後期）80.3×40.8 1 0000　紙本墨画彩色		11.4157
070	山景図　円山応挙（江戸後期）		

071	紀伊和歌浦景観図　森一鳳（江戸〜明治初期）	
072	月下双鴉図　別所東渓（江戸後期）117.3×51.2　紙本墨画	11.4773
073	鐘呂伝道図　狩野探幽（江戸初期）模写	
074	魚籃観音図　石垣東山（江戸末〜明治初期）171.2×84.2　絹本墨画彩色	11.4779
075	夕立図　英一蝶（江戸前・中期）49.5×79.5　紙本墨画彩色	11.4218
076	牡丹に竹図　山本梅逸（江戸末期）	
077	岸壁に隼図　狩野探幽（江戸初期）	
078	富士図　鶴沢探山（江戸初期）43.5×84.5　絹本墨画淡彩	11.4407
079	白狐図　円山応挙（江戸後期）120.2×70.6　絹本墨画淡彩	11.4900
080	岩上虎図　岸駒（江戸後期）98.9×36.3　絹本墨画淡彩	11.4698
081	花鳥図（双幅）狩野養川（江戸中期）110.5×46.2　絹本墨画彩色	11.4452‐4453
082	箕面大滝図　石橋李長（江戸後期）145.9×84　絹本墨画淡彩	11.4762
083	松に孔雀図　円山応挙（江戸後期）	
084	雪景山水図　森一鳳（江戸後期）153.1×87.9　絹本墨画淡彩	11.4728
085	観音図　狩野安信（江戸初期）	
086	雨景山水図　狩野養川（江戸中期）102.3×40.6　絹本墨画	11.4455
087	虎母子図　岸駒（江戸後期）	
088	紅鐘馗　森徹山（江戸後期）102.2×34.7　絹本彩色	11.4390
089	岩上虎図　岸駒（江戸後期）	
090	蝦蟇仙人・鉄拐仙人（双幅）狩野周信（江戸前期）	
091	山水図　谷文晁（江戸後期）	
092	雪枝に鷲と鴉　英一蝶（江戸前・中期）	
093	仙人王質図　柴田義董（江戸中期）	
094	東方朔図　中井藍江（江戸後期）101.8×36.2　絹本墨画彩色	11.4659
095	紅白梅に鷹図　中村晩山（江戸〜明治初期）121×45　絹本墨画彩色	11.4666

096	桜に泉　望月業玉泉（江戸～明治初期） ［参考］同画家の類似作にビゲロウ・コレクション 11.8220「桜下鮎図」あり	
097	梅・薔薇図　亀井香雲（明治初期）101.7×36.8　絹本墨画彩色	11.4658
098	岸壁鷲図　尾口雲錦（江戸～明治初期）	
099	山水図　為一＝北斎（江戸末期）	
100	松に鷲図　狩野雅楽之助＝之信（室町末期）	
101	桜に群猿　狙仙（江戸中・後期）	
102	中国山水図　周文（室町時代）	
103	楼閣山水図　遠坂文雍（江戸後期）113.7×32.4　絹本墨画淡彩	11.4790
104	月夜山水図　塩川文麟（江戸～明治初期）100×37.5　絹本墨画	11.4688
105	布袋図　啓書記＝祥啓（室町時代）	
106	羅漢図　土佐光茂（室町時代）	
107	海棠に四十雀　松村景文（江戸後期）	
108	竹に雀　松村景文（江戸後期）	
109	山水図　啓書記＝賢江祥啓（室町後期）39.4×91.5　紙本墨画	11.4127
110	文殊騎獅図　巨勢俊久（南北朝時代）	
111	鳥窠禅師図　顔輝（元代初期）80.3×38　絹本墨画彩色金粉	11.4003
112	釈迦如来像　宅磨爲久（平安末期）92.7×39.3　絹本墨画彩色	11.4093
113	向島三囲稲荷社景観図　高嵩谷（江戸中期）34×52.6　絹本墨画彩色	11.4369
114	雪景山水図（双幅）駒井源琦（江戸中期）84.3×32.5　絹本墨画彩色	11.4770 - 4771
115	山水図（双幅）谷文晁（江戸後期）	
116	寒山拾得図　狩野□□	
117	龍虎図（双幅）　松村呉春（江戸後期）	
118	群猿図　森狙仙（江戸中・後期）	
119	雪景鴨図　万寿＝吉岡茂喬（江戸末期）102.3×47　絹本墨画淡彩	11.4746
120	松に小禽図　狩野元信（桃山～江戸初期）133.4×56.5　絹本墨画	11.4271

121	山水図　岸駒（江戸後期）	
122	山水図　小栗宗湛（室町時代）	
123	早春・秋景図（双幅）塩川文麟（江戸〜明治初期）	
124	福禄寿（三幅対）　狩野探幽（江戸初期）	
125	義経騎馬図　狩洞春義信（江戸前期）113.3×56.3　絹本墨画彩色	11.4183
126	錦鶏図　狩野素川彰信（江戸後期）47.6×66.2　絹本墨画淡彩	11.4356
127	通天橋紅葉図　岡島清曠（江戸・明治初期）46.1×71.6　絹本墨画彩色	11.4765
128	波に鶴図　鶴沢探泉（江戸後期）51.8×69.1　絹本墨画彩色	11.4382
129	梅に鶴図　狩野探雪（江戸初期）84.7×33.7　絹本墨画彩色	11.4328
130	牡丹に唐獅子図（三幅対）狩野晴川（江戸後期）119.1×45.6　絹本墨画彩色	11.4334 - 4336
131	四睡図　狩野清信（江戸初期）31×48.1　絹本墨画	11.4231
132	東方朔図　狩野常川幸信（江戸中期）122.6×49.3　絹本墨画淡彩	11.4465
133	人物画　狩野ユキノブ	
134	柳に白鷺図　狩野洞琳由信（江戸後期）47.3×83.2　絹本墨画	11.4806
135	円中山水図（双幅）周文（室町時代）	
136	流水に菊図　狩野融川寛信（江戸中期）96×28.9　紙本墨画彩色	11.4468
137	栗鼠に粟図　狩野ユーセイ	
138	仙人図　顔輝（元代初期）	
139	鹿を狙う猟師　北斎（江戸末期）42.8×58.8　絹本墨画彩色	11.4601
140	西湖景観図　雲谷等顔（桃山〜江戸初期）42.0×78.4　絹本	11.4509
141	晩冬田園図　河村埼鳳（江戸後期）	
142	花卉図　酒井抱一（江戸後期）	
143	羅漢図　可翁（南北朝時代）	
144	柳に小禽図　山本梅逸（江戸末期）131.3×40.9　絹本墨画彩色	11.4648
145	花鳥、鹿図（双幅）中島来章（江戸〜明治初期）	

146	冨士春景図　鶴沢探鯨（江戸後期）122.1×60.8　絹本墨画淡彩	11.4293
147	布袋図（三幅対）　狩野探幽（江戸初期）	
148	雲龍鐘馗図（三幅対）　狩野探幽（江戸初期）	
149	鷹図（三幅対）　曽我二直庵（江戸初期）	
150	山水人物図（三幅対）　木村永光（桃山～江戸初期）115.8×50.4　紙本墨画	11.4274 - 4276
151	雲龍図（双幅）　中林竹洞（江戸後期）147.3×57.7　絹本墨画	11.4650 - 4651
152	白衣観音図　狩野元信（室町後期）157.2×876.4　絹本墨画彩色	11.4267
153	釈迦図　栄賢（江戸初期）	
154	虎図　岸駒（江戸後期）	
155	豫譲図　横山華山（江戸後期）139.5×88.1　絹本墨画彩色	11.4731
156	山水福禄寿（三幅対）　狩野安信（江戸初期）	
157	孔雀図　西山芳園（江戸後期）146.6×71.2　絹本墨画彩色	11.4722
158	野猿図　森狙仙（江戸（江戸中・後期）	
159	孔雀図　岸駒（江戸後期）	
160	八福神酒宴図　横山崋山（江戸後期）43.8×100.4　絹本墨画彩色	11.4730
161	花鳥図　明代画家	
162	山水図　大原呑舟（江戸末期）121.5×49.3　絹本墨画彩色	11.4695
163	福禄寿　岸駒（江戸後期）	
164	双鹿図　岸駒（江戸後期）167.3×86.6　絹本墨画淡彩	11.4701
165	花鳥図　コヨーシン（明代）	
166	山水図（双幅）　岡本豊彦（江戸後期）109.4×42.2　絹本墨画淡彩	11.4777 - 4778
167	春秋婦女行楽図（双幅）　月岡雪斎（江戸後期）107.4×48　絹本墨画彩色	11.4626 - 4627
168	達磨図（三幅対）　狩野尚信（江戸初期）	
169	李白（三幅対）　狩野探信守政（江戸前期）	

170	杏壇孔子図（三幅対）　狩野探幽（江戸初期）104.3×74.4 絹本墨画淡彩	11.4399 - 4401
171	花鳥図　狩野季頼（室町末期）	
172	扇面仙人図　狩野元信（室町後期）19.4×38.3　紙本墨画	11.4270
173	川景色　久隅守景（江戸前期）	
174	観桜山水図　狩野永納（江戸前期）31.1×46　紙本墨画	11.4429
175	周公図　狩野養川（江戸中期）112×43　絹本墨画彩色	11.4454
176	牡丹図　狩野松栄（室町末期）	
177	社前唐子図　西山芳園（江戸後期）107.8×41.7　絹本墨画彩色	11.4717
178	維摩図　海北友雪（江戸初期）92.6×45.7　紙本墨画	11.4534
179	山水図　藝阿弥（室町後期）29×41.2　紙本墨画	11.4124
180	騎馬人物図　曽我蕭亭（江戸中期）39.5×18.4　紙本墨画	11.4520
181	花鳥図　狩野古永徳（安土桃山時代）	
182	雛鷹図　長柳斎（室町中期）322.3×34.7　紙本墨画淡彩	11.4120
183	滝に鯉図（双幅）　狩野探幽（江戸初期）	
184	観瀑図　西山芳園（江戸後期）114×36　絹本墨画彩色	11.4718
185	楊貴妃に花鳥（三幅対）狩野探幽（江戸初期）38.3×29.9 絹本墨画彩色	11.4395 - 4397
186	松桜図　狩野常信（江戸中期）97×36.4　絹本墨画彩色	11.4417
187	山水図　楊富（室町時代）97×36.4　絹本墨画彩色	11.4159
188	花鳥図　狩野玉樂（室町後期）9.9×27.2　紙本墨画彩色	11.4190
189	山水図　横山華山（江戸後期）	
190	山水図　北斎（江戸末期）	
191	花鳥図　高嵩谷（江戸中期）93.2×34.9　絹本墨画彩色	11.4367
192	羅漢図　兆殿司＝明兆（室町時代）125.4×50.9　絹本墨画彩色	11.4067
193	龍図　狩野山雪（江戸前期）	

194	布袋図　狩野洞白（江戸後期）96.1×40　絹本墨画淡彩	11.4180
195	晩秋微雨図　墨江武禅（江戸中期）33.5×45.8　絹本墨画淡彩	11.4791
196	帰牛図　呉春（江戸後期）103.3×32.6　絹本墨画彩色	11.4716
197	琴高仙人図　海北友松（安土桃山期）	
198	井手玉川図　土佐光起（江戸初期）34.1×83.1　絹本墨画彩色	11.4567
199	武陵桃源図　横山晴暉　江戸後期　101.2×33.7　絹本墨画彩色	11.4764
200	三福神　狩野周信（江戸前期）119.8×49.5　絹本墨画彩色	11.4175
201	大黒図　柴田義董（江戸中期）106.5×28.8　紙本墨画	11.4709
202	八仙図　柴田義董（江戸中期）112.8×53.8　絹本墨画彩色	11.4708
203	花鳥図　小栗宗栗（室町中期）	
204	綬帯鳥図　山田道安（室町時代）	
205	桜樹に女人図　土佐光成（室町時代）104×44.5　絹本墨画彩色	11.4816
206	三聖図　狩野寿石敦信（江戸中期）　115×50　紙本墨画淡彩	11.4171
207	鳥図　一休（室町前期）	
208	炭焼き図　田中日華　江戸末期　99.8×360　絹本墨画淡彩	11.4751
209	中国皇帝図　狩野探幽（江戸初期）	
210	白衣観音図　菊池容斎（江戸〜明治初期）181×57　絹本墨画淡彩	11.4780
211	岩上猿図　渡辺南岳（江戸後期）113.3×27.9　紙本墨画	11.4748
212	三都遊女図　月岡雪鼎（江戸中期）	
213	修紫田舎源氏図　歌川国貞（江戸末期）70×44　絹本墨画彩色	11.4610
214	范蠡と西施　清原雪信（江戸前期）　71.6×32.1　絹本墨画彩色	11.4464
215	蓬莱図　土佐光忠（江戸末期）	
216	運河景観図　岸礼（江戸〜明治初期）	
217	李白観瀑図　狩野孝信（江戸初期）99.5×40.4　紙本墨画淡彩	11.4372
218	雪景山水図　塩川文麟（江戸〜明治初期）	
219	箕面大滝図　久保田桃水（江戸〜明治初期）172×84.3　絹本墨画淡彩	11.4776

220	柳に黄鳥図　宗紫石（江戸中期）114×42.5　絹本墨画彩色	11.4820
221	山水図（双幅）狩野探信守政（江戸初期）106.7×50.8　絹本墨画淡彩	11.4386‐4387
222	女人図（双幅）西川祐信（江戸中期）	
223	山部赤人図　松花堂（江戸初期）97.5×28.2　紙本墨画	11.4518
224	東坡図　足利義持（室町前期）59.5×32　紙本墨画	11.4161
225	蓮に白鷺図　狩野洞雲（江戸初期）101.7×30.4　紙本墨画	11.4238
226	東坡図　久隅守景（江戸前期）	
227	野菊に馬図　曾我蕭白（江戸中期）121.9×54.3　紙本墨画	11.4505
228	山水図（双幅）狩野光信（安土桃山時代）123.2×46.3　紙本墨画淡彩	11.4472‐4473
229	七福神図　土佐光文（江戸〜明治初期）38.7×57.2　絹本墨画彩色	11.4559
230	烏天狗図　大原呑舟（江戸末期）120.6×58.1　紙本墨画彩色	11.4696
231	牡丹図　久隅守景（江戸前期）	
232	東本願寺炎塵之図　横山華渓（江戸末期）47.1×73.5　絹本墨画彩色	11.4735
233	雪景山水図　狩野伊川（江戸中〜後期）125.2×58.1　絹本墨画彩色	11.4215
234	春雨嵐山図　円山応震（江戸中期）40.3×70.4　絹本墨画淡彩	11.4755
235	蓮に白鷺図　狩野休円（江戸中期）96.6×34　絹本墨画	11.4373
236	寿老人に龍（三幅対）　狩野養川（江戸中期）	
237	牡丹に雀図　小田百谷＝海僊（江戸後期）102.4×37.1　絹本墨画彩色	11.4655
238	寿老人に山水（三幅対）　狩野永叔（江戸中期）124.8×53.8 絹本墨画彩色	11.4440‐4442
239	山水図　狩野晴川（江戸後期）	11.4333
240	柳に燕図　狩野周信（江戸前期）	11.4174
241	福禄寿図　狩野常信（江戸中期）	
242	竹雪雀図　狩野岑信（江戸前期）	11.4247
243	遠寺晩鐘・江天暮雪（双幅）狩野玄也（江戸初期）26.5×36 紙本墨画	11.4188‐4189

244	寒山拾得図　可翁（南北朝時代）	
245	山水図（双幅）　長谷川等伯（安土桃山時代）	
246	人物図（双幅）　土岐洞文（戦国時代）	
247	松竹梅（三幅対）　狩野洞春義信（江戸中期）	
248	滝に日輪（三幅対）狩野祐清英信（江戸中期）	11.4411 - 4413
249	群鶴芦雁図（双幅）狩野探牧（江戸後期　114×49.9　絹本墨画彩色	11.4374 - 4375
250	牡丹図（双幅）狩野伊川（江戸後期）112.7×48.5　絹本墨画彩色	11.4210 - 4211
251	花卉図（双幅）狩野□□　墨彩	
252	菊鶉松鶴（三幅対）　土佐光芳（江戸前期）107.3×36.3 絹本墨画彩色	11.4570 - 4572
253	陶淵明図　狩野尚信（江戸初期）	
254	宇治平等院景観図　西山芳園（江戸末期）33×57　絹本墨画彩色	11.4720
255	唐人飴売り図　英一蝶（江戸前期）32.3×71.2　絹本墨画彩色	11.4222
256	布袋図　楊月（室町時代）　41.3×57　紙本墨画	11.4160
257	鷹に小鳥　狩野□□	
258	稲雀図　狩野岑信（江戸前期）　29.5×36.2　絹本墨画淡彩	11.4246
259	旭日松図　木村探原（江戸中期）102×42.9　絹本墨画淡彩	11.4376
260	山水図（双幅）　雲谷等益（江戸初期）104.5×37.2　紙本墨画	11.4528 - 4529
261	屋内女人図　雪信か？	
262	鶴図　狩野勝川（江戸〜明治初期）108.3×43.6　絹本墨画彩色	11.4346
263	福禄寿唐子図　高嵩谷、嵩渓父子（江戸中期）41.7×534.8 絹本墨画彩色	11.4368

Ernest Francisco Fenollosa with his son Kano in ca. 1883.
Photograph formerly possessed by the late Mr. George Manuel Fenollosa and now in the collection of Seiichi Yamaguchi.